Julian Fraillon • John Ainley
Wolfram Schulz • Tim Friedman
Eveline Gebhardt

Preparing for Life in a Digital Age

The IEA International Computer and Information Literacy Study International Report

ICILS
2013
IEA

Springer Open

Julian Fraillon
John Ainley
Wolfram Schulz
Tim Friedman
Eveline Gebhardt
Australian Council for Educational Research (ACER)
Melbourne
Australia

ISBN 978-3-319-14221-0   ISBN 978-3-319-14222-7 (eBook)
DOI 10.1007/978-3-319-14222-7
Springer Cham Heidelberg New York Dordrecht London

Library of Congress Control Number: 2014957709

This work is published jointly with the IEA. A limited print run has been distributed in November 2014 with the following ISBN's: 978-90-79549-26-9 (print), 978-90-79549-27-6 (ebook).

Copyedited by Paula Wagemaker Editorial Services, Oturehua, Central Otago, New Zealand
Design and production by Becky Bliss Design and Production, Wellington, New Zealand

Springer is part of Springer Science+Business Media (www.springer.com)

Foreword

The continuous and increasingly rapid development and implementation of computer and other information technologies over the last decades is a distinct feature of modern societies. In the digital age, information and communications technology (ICT) plays a key role in creating and exchanging knowledge and information around the globe and affects citizens' everyday life in many areas—at school, in the workplace, and in the community. Nowadays, knowledge about, access to, and use of ICT are vital for participating effectively in society in this information age. Acquiring and mastering ICT skills—computer and information literacy (CIL)—has thus become a major component of citizens' education, and many countries have accordingly recognized the importance of education in ICT.

Many countries have made significant investments in equipping schools with ICT, but so far little is known about the effectiveness and use of these technologies. In some countries, students are required to use ICT in learning, and there is a common assumption that students are familiar with using ICT, which is not necessarily true.

The International Computer and Information Literacy Study (ICILS) 2013 sheds some light on students' knowledge and abilities in the key areas of information and technology literacy. The study was carried out by the International Association for the Evaluation of Educational Achievement (IEA), an independent, international cooperative of national research agencies. For over 50 years, IEA has conducted large-scale comparative studies of educational achievement and reported on key aspects of education systems and processes in a number of curriculum areas, including literacy, mathematics, and science, and also civic and citizenship education.

ICILS 2013 is a pioneering study because it is the first international comparative assessment to focus on students' acquisition of CIL in the digital age as well as the ICT learning environment in schools. It was administered to 60,000 students in their eighth year of schooling in over 3,300 schools from 21 participating education systems around the world. Authentic and computer-based, it examined the outcomes of student CIL in and across countries, and it investigated to what extent other factors such as student characteristics and school contexts influence differences in CIL achievement.

ICILS 2013 built on a series of earlier IEA studies focused on ICT in education. The first of these, the Computers in Education Study (COMPED, was conducted in 1989 and 1992 and reported on the educational use of computers in the context of emerging governmental initiatives to implement ICT in schools. It was followed by the Second Information Technology in Education Study (SITES). Carried out in 1998/99, 2001, and 2006, SITES provided updated information on the implementation of computer technology resources in schools and their utilization in the teaching process.

This report on ICILS presents the outcomes of student CIL at the international level and provides information on the contexts in which CIL is taught and learned. It explores the relationship of CIL as a learning outcome to student characteristics and school contexts, and illustrates the national contexts in which CIL education takes place in the participating countries in order to aid understanding of variations in CIL. It explains the measurement of CIL by means of a CIL proficiency scale and presents the international student test results. An analysis of students' use of and engagement with ICT at home and at school is provided, as is information about the roles of schools and teachers in CIL education, and about the extent to which ICT is used in classrooms.

The report also explores the relationship between individual and social aspects of students' backgrounds and CIL.

The rich findings of this international report on ICILS will contribute to a deeper understanding of not only the ways in which students develop CIL but also their learning environment. For policymakers, the ICILS 2013 report contains a wealth of information that will help them gain a better understanding of the contexts and outcomes of ICT-related education programs in their countries and the use of ICT in schools. Researchers will find a wide array of impulses for further analyses into CIL education within and across countries.

The current report will be followed by the international database and technical report to be published in March 2015.

International undertakings of a scale such as ICILS could not be implemented without the dedication, skills, support, and great collaborative effort of a large number of individuals, institutions, and organizations around the world. It is impossible to name all of them individually, but IEA acknowledges the utmost commitment of each and every one of the people involved in making this study possible.

IEA is particularly indebted to the outstanding team of experts at the ICILS 2013 International Study Center, the Australian Council for Educational Research (ACER). On behalf of IEA, I would like to express my sincerest gratitude to ACER's Project Coordinator John Ainley, the Research Director Julian Fraillon, and the Assessment Coordinator Wolfram Schulz who were responsible for designing and implementing the study. They were closely supported by staff of the IEA Secretariat who guided and oversaw the ICILS operations as well as by staff of the IEA Data Processing and Research Center who managed sampling, data management, and preliminary scaling analyses. Their hard work and commitment were imperative for the study's success.

My thanks also go to the Project Advisory Committee (PAC): John Ainley (ACER), Ola Erstad (University of Oslo), Kathleen Scalise (University of Oregon), and Alfons ten Brummelhuis (Kennisnet). I furthermore thank the Joint Management Committee (JMC): John Ainley (ACER), Ralph Carstens (IEA DPC), David Ebbs (IEA Secretariat), Julian Fraillon (ACER), Tim Friedman (ACER), Michael Jung (IEA DPC), Paulína Koršňáková (IEA Secretariat), Sabine Meinck (IEA DPC), and Wolfram Schulz (ACER). I extend my thanks to Eveline Gebhardt (ACER), Jean Dumais (Statistics Canada), and Stephen Birchall (SoNET Systems).

I acknowledge the important role of the IEA Publications and Editorial Committee (PEC) who provided valuable advice for improving this report, and I thank Paula Wagemaker who edited this publication.

ICILS relied heavily on the dedication of the ICILS national research coordinators and their delegates. They not only managed and executed the study at the national level but also provided valuable input into the development of key elements in the study's assessment. Their contribution is highly appreciated.

Finally, I would like to thank the European Commission's Directorate-General for Education and Culture for supporting ICILS 2013 in the form of a grant to participating European countries.

Dirk Hastedt
EXECUTIVE DIRECTOR

Contents

Foreword   *iii*

List of Tables and Figures   *ix*

Executive Summary   **15**

About the study   15

Data   16

Computer and information literacy   17

     The construct   17

     Assessing computer and information literacy   17

     The computer and information literacy scale   18

Variations in student achievement on the CIL scale   20

     Variations across countries   20

     Factors associated with variations in CIL   20

Student use of ICT   21

     Computer use outside school   21

     Use of ICT for school work   22

Teacher and school use of ICT   22

     Teacher use of ICT   22

     School-based ICT provision and use   23

Conclusion   24

Chapter 1: Introduction   **27**

Background   28

Research questions   32

Participating countries, population, and sample design   33

     Population definitions   33

     Sample design   34

The ICILS assessment framework   34

     The computer and information literacy framework   34

     The ICILS contextual framework   35

     The wider community level   38

     The national (system) level   39

     School/classroom level   40

     Home level   41

     Individual level   42

Data collection and ICILS instruments   42

Report context and scope   44

Chapter 2: The Contexts for Education on Computer and Information Literacy   **47**

Introduction   47

Collecting data on contexts for CIL education   47

Characteristics of the education systems in participating ICILS countries   49

Infrastructure and resources for education in CIL   54

Approaches to CIL education in ICILS countries   56

Conclusion   67

Chapter 3: Students' Computer and Information Literacy   **69**
Assessing CIL   69
The CIL described achievement scale   72
Example ICILS test items   76
    The five discrete task items   76
    Example ICILS large-task item   86
Comparison of CIL across countries   94
    Distribution of student achievement scores   94
    CIL relative to the ICT Development Index and national   94
    student–computer ratios
    Pair-wise comparisons of CIL   95
    Achievement across countries with respect to proficiency levels   99
Conclusion   99

Chapter 4: The Influence of Students' Personal and Home Background   **101**
on Computer and Information Literacy
Gender and CIL   102
Home background indicators and CIL   102
    Educational aspirations   102
    Socioeconomic background   104
    Immigrant status and language use   111
    Home ICT resources   113
Influence of combined home background variables on CIL   116
Conclusion   123

Chapter 5: Students' Use of and Engagement with ICT at Home and School   **125**
Introduction   125
ICT at home and school   125
Familiarity with computers   127
    Experience with using computers   127
    Frequency of computer use   128
Student use of computers outside school   132
    Computer-based applications used outside school   132
    Internet use for communication and exchange of information   135
    Computer use for recreation   142
Computer use for and at school   146
    School-related use of computers   146
    Extent of use for particular school-related purposes   146
    Use of computers in subject areas   151
    Learning about computer and information literacy at school   153
Student perceptions of ICT   156
    ICT self-efficacy   156
    Student interest and enjoyment in using computers and computing   161
    Associations between perceptions and achievement   164
Conclusion   164

Chapter 6: School Environments for Teaching and Learning Computer   **167**
and Information Literacy
Introduction   167
Schools' access to ICT resources   168
School policies and practices for using ICT   176
Perceptions of school ICT learning environments   180
Teachers' professional development in using ICT for pedagogical purposes 187
    School perspectives   187
    Teacher perspectives   190
Conclusion   192

Chapter 7: Teaching with and about Information and   **195**
Communication Technologies
Introduction   195
Background   195
Teachers' familiarity with ICT   197
    Experience with and use of computers   197
Teachers' views about ICT   199
    Benefits of ICT in school education   199
    Confidence in using ICT   206
Associations between ICT use and teachers' views   208
Teaching with and about ICT   210
    Prevalence of ICT use   213
Developing computer and information literacy   215
    Factors associated with emphasis on developing CIL 217
The ICT tools teachers were using   221
    Types of tools   221
    Use in learning activities   222
    Use in teaching practices   224
Conclusion   227

Chapter 8: Investigating Variations in Computer and Information Literacy **229**
A model for explaining variation in CIL   229
Influences on variation in CIL   234
    Student-level influences   234
    School-level influences   236
    Student-level and school-level background influences 238
Summary of influences on CIL   240
Conclusion   243

Chapter 9: Conclusions and Discussion   **245**
ICILS guiding questions   246
Student proficiency in using computers   246
    The computer and information literacy (CIL) scale 246
    Student achievement on the CIL scale   250
Students' computer use and CIL   250
    Computer use outside school   251
    Use of ICT for school work   252

Students' perceptions of ICT   252
Teacher, school, and education system characteristics relevant to CIL   253
    General approaches to CIL education   253
    Teachers and CIL   253
    Schools and CIL   254
Results from the multivariate analyses   255
Reflections on policy and practice   255
Future directions for research   258

Appendices   **259**
Appendix A: Samples and participation rates   261
Appendix B: Percentage correct by country for example large task scoring   264
         criteria
Appendix C: Percentiles and standard deviations for computer and   273
         information literacy
Appendix D: The scaling of ICILS questionnaire items   275
Appendix E: Item-by-score maps   277
Appendix F: Effects of indicators of missing school and teacher data   294
Appendix G: Organizations and individuals involved in ICILS   295

References   **299**

List of Tables and Figures

Tables

Table 1.1: Mapping of ICILS context variables to framework grid 37

Table 2.1: Levels of responsibility for school-based education 50

Table 2.2: Characteristics of education systems participating in ICILS: compulsory schooling, years of education by levels, and percentage lower-secondary students in private/public schools 52

Table 2.3: Degree of school autonomy regarding different aspects of school policies 53

Table 2.4: Data on ICT infrastructure and economic characteristics in ICILS countries 55

Table 2.5: Support for ICT at schools by national and/or subnational authorities 57

Table 2.6: References in plans or policies to provision of ICT resources 59

Table 2.7: References in plans or policies to using ICT to support student learning, provide computing in schools, and develop digital resources 60

Table 2.8: ICT-related subjects at different levels of schooling and ICT assessment policies 62

Table 2.9: Support and requirements for developing teachers' capacity to use ICT 65

Table 2.10: Level of support for teacher access to and participation in ICT-based professional development 66

Table 3.1: Summary of ICILS test modules and large tasks 70

Table 3.2: CIL described achievement scale 74

Table 3.3: Example large-task scoring criteria with framework references and overall percent correct 91

Table 3.4: Country averages for CIL, years of schooling, average age, ICT Index, student–computer ratios and percentile graph 96

Table 3.5: Multiple comparisons of average country CIL scores 97

Table 3.6: Percent of students at each proficiency level across countries 98

Table 4.1: Gender differences in CIL 103

Table 4.2: National percentages and CIL score averages for students in categories of expected education 105

Table 4.3: National percentages and CIL score averages for students in categories of parental educational attainment 107

Table 4.4: National percentages and CIL score averages for students in categories of parental occupational status 109

Table 4.5: National percentages and CIL score averages for students in categories of home literacy resources 110

Table 4.6: National percentages and CIL score averages for students with and without immigrant background 112

Table 4.7: National percentages and CIL score averages for students' language use at home 114

Table 4.8: National percentages and CIL score averages for students in categories of computer availability at home 115

Table 4.9:   National percentages and CIL score averages for students in   117
              categories of internet access at home

Table 4.10:   Multiple regression model for students' CIL predicted by personal   120
              and social background variables (unstandardized regression
              coefficients)

Table 4.11:   Multiple regression model for students' CIL predicted by personal   122
              and social background variables (explained variance estimates)

Table 5.1:   National percentages of students' experience with computers   129

Table 5.2:   National percentages of students' computer use at home, school,   131
              and other places at least once a week

Table 5.3:   National percentages of students using computers outside of school   133
              for specific ICT applications at least once a week

Table 5.4:   National averages for students' use of computers for specific ICT   136
              applications overall and by gender

Table 5.5:   National percentages of students using the internet outside of school 138
              for communication and exchange of information at least once a week

Table 5.6:   National averages for students' use of ICT for social communication 140
              overall and by gender

Table 5.7:   National averages for students' use of ICT for exchanging   141
              information overall and by gender

Table 5.8:   National percentages of students using computers for recreation at   143
              least once a week

Table 5.9:   National averages for students' use of computers for recreation   145
              overall and by gender

Table 5.10:   National percentages of students using computers for study   147
              purposes at least once a month

Table 5.11:   National averages for students' use of computers for study purposes 150
              overall and by gender

Table 5.12:   National percentages of students with frequent computer use during   152
              lessons in different learning areas

Table 5.13:   National percentages of students reporting having learned ICT tasks 154
              at school

Table 5.14:   National averages for students' learning of ICT tasks at school overall 155
              and by gender

Table 5.15:   National percentages of student confidence in using computers   157

Table 5.16:   National averages for students' self-efficacy in basic ICT skills   159
              overall and by gender

Table 5.17:   National averages for students' self-efficacy in advanced ICT skills 160
              overall and by gender

Table 5.18:   National percentages of students' agreement with statements about   162
              computers

Table 5.19:   National averages for students' interest and enjoyment in using   163
              computers overall and by gender

Table 5.20:   National values of correlation coefficients for CIL with basic ICT   165
              self-efficacy, advanced ICT self-efficacy, and interest/enjoyment in
              computing

Table 6.1:   National percentages of students at schools with available   169
              internet-related resources for teaching and/or learning

Table 6.2:   National percentages of students at schools with available software   171
              resources for teaching and/or learning

Table 6.3:   National percentages of students at schools with computer resources   172
              for teaching and/or learning

Table 6.4:   National student–computer ratios at schools by school location   174

Table 6.5:   National percentages of students at schools with school computers   175
              at different locations

Table 6.6:   National percentages of students at schools with procedures   177
              regarding different aspects of ICT

Table 6.7:   National percentages of students at schools where medium or high   179
              priority is given to different ways of facilitating ICT use in teaching
              and learning

Table 6.8:   National percentages of teachers who agree with statements   181
              regarding collaborative use of ICT in teaching and learning

Table 6.9:   National averages for teachers collaborating when using ICT overall   182
              and by age group

Table 6.10:   National percentages of students at schools where different   184
              obstacles hinder using ICT in teaching and learning

Table 6.11:   National percentages of teachers who agree with statements about   186
              the use of ICT in their school

Table 6.12:   National averages for teachers' perceptions of ICT resources at their   188
              school overall and by school characteristics

Table 6.13:   National percentages of students at schools where teachers   189
              participate in professional development about ICT for teaching
              and learning

Table 6.14:   National percentages of teachers participating in ICT-related   191
              professional development activities

Table 7.1:   National percentages of teachers' computer experience and use in   198
              different settings (at school teaching, at school for other purposes,
              outside school)

Table 7.2:   National percentages of teachers agreeing with statements about ICT   200
              teaching and learning in schools

Table 7.3:   National averages for teachers with positive views on using ICT in   204
              teaching and learning overall and by age group

Table 7.4:   National averages for teachers with negative views on using ICT in   205
              teaching and learning overall and by age group

Table 7.5:   National percentages of teachers expressing confidence in doing   206
              different computer tasks

Table 7.6:   National averages for teachers' ICT self-efficacy overall and by   209
              age group

Table 7.7:   National mean scale teacher attitude scores for frequent and   211
              infrequent users of ICT when teaching

Table 7.8:   National mean scale teacher environment scores for frequent and   212
              infrequent users of ICT when teaching

Table 7.9:   National percentages of teachers using ICT in teaching and learning   214
              by learning areas

Table 7.10: National percentages of teachers giving strong or some emphasis to   216
             ICT-based capabilities in their students
Table 7.11: Multiple regression analyses of predictors of teacher emphasis on   218
             developing computer and information literacy
Table 7.12: National means for emphasis on developing computer and   220
             information literacy by subject area
Table 7.13: National percentages of teachers using ICT tools for teaching in   222
             most lessons
Table 7.14: National percentages of teachers often using ICT for learning   224
             activities in classrooms
Table 7.15: National percentages of teachers often using ICT for teaching   226
             practices in classrooms

Table 8.1:   Student-level results: ICT-related context factors   235
Table 8.2:   School-level results: ICT-related factors   237
Table 8.3:   Student and school-level results: personal and social background   239
Table 8.4:   Summary of statistically significant effects across countries   240
Table 8.5:   Total and explained variance in computer and information literacy   242

Appendices

Table A.1:   Coverage of ICILS 2013 target population for the student survey   261
Table A.2:   Participation rates and sample sizes for student survey   262
Table A.3:   Participation rates and sample sizes for teacher survey   263

Table B.1:   Percent correct in large task by country for Criterion 1   264
Table B.2:   Percent correct in large task by country for Criterion 2   265
Table B.3:   Percent correct in large task by country for Criterion 3   266
Table B.4:   Percent correct in large task by country for Criterion 4   267
Table B.5:   Percent correct in large task by country for Criterion 5   268
Table B.6:   Percent correct in large task by country for Criterion 6   269
Table B.7:   Percent correct in large task by country for Criterion 7   270
Table B.8:   Percent correct in large task by country for Criterion 8   271
Table B.9:   Percent correct in large task by country for Criterion 9   272

Table C.1:   Percentiles of computer and information literacy   273
Table C.2:   Means and standard deviations for computer and information   274
             literacy

Table F.1:   Effects of indicators of missing school and teaching data   294

Figures

Figure 1.1:   Contexts for CIL learning and learning outcomes   37

Figure 3.1:   Example Item 1 with framework references and overall percent   76
                correct
Figure 3.2:   Example Item 2 with framework references and overall percent   78
                correct
Figure 3.3:   Example Item 3 with framework references and overall percent   80
                correct
Figure 3.4:   Example Item 4 with framework references and overall percent   82
                correct
Figure 3.5:   Example Item 5 with framework references and overall percent   84
                correct
Figure 3.6:   After-School Exercise: large task details   87
Figure 3.7:   After-School Exercise: large task and website resource   88

Figure 9.1:   Example Level 1 task   247
Figure 9.2:   Example Level 2 task   248
Figure 9.3:   Example Level 3 task   248
Figure 9.4:   Example Level 4 task   249

Appendices

Figure D.1:   Example of questionnaire item-by-score map   276

Figure E.1:   Item-by-score map for students' use of specific ICT applications 277
Figure E.2:   Item-by-score map for students' use of ICT for social   278
                communication
Figure E.3:   Item-by-score map for students' use of ICT for exchanging   279
                information
Figure E.4:   Item-by-score map for students' use of ICT for recreation   280
Figure E.5:   Item-by-score map for students' use of ICT for study purposes   281
Figure E.6:   Item-by-score map for students' learning of ICT tasks at school 282
Figure E.7:   Item-by-score map for students' ICT self-efficacy basic skills   283
Figure E.8:   Item-by-score map for students' ICT self-efficacy advanced skills 284
Figure E.9:   Item-by-score map for students' ICT interest and enjoyment   285
Figure E.10:   Item-by-score map for teachers' collaboration in using ICT   286
Figure E.11:   Item-by-score map for teachers' lack of computer resources at   287
                school
Figure E.12:   Item-by-score map for teachers' positive views on using ICT in   288
                teaching and learning
Figure E.13:   Item-by-score map for teachers' negative views on using ICT in   289
                teaching and learning
Figure E.14:   Item-by-score map for teachers' ICT self-efficacy   290
Figure E.15:   Item-by-score map for teachers' use of specific ICT applications 292

Executive Summary

About the study

The International Computer and Information Literacy Study (ICILS) studied the extent to which young people have developed computer and information literacy (CIL) to support their capacity to participate in the digital age. Computer and information literacy is defined as "an individual's ability to use computers to investigate, create, and communicate in order to participate effectively at home, at school, in the workplace, and in society" (Fraillon, Schulz, & Ainley, 2013, p. 17).

ICILS is a response to the increasing use of information and communication technology (ICT) in modern society and the need for citizens to develop relevant skills in order to participate effectively in the digital age. It also addresses the necessity for policymakers and education systems to have a better understanding of the contexts and outcomes of CIL-related education programs in their countries. ICILS is the first crossnational study commissioned by the International Association for the Evaluation of Educational Achievement (IEA) to collect student achievement data on computer.

ICILS used purpose-designed software for the computer-based student assessment and questionnaire. These instruments were administered primarily by way of USB drives attached to school computers. Although the software could have been delivered via internet, the USB delivery ensured a uniform assessment environment for students regardless of the quality of internet connections in participating schools. Data were either uploaded to a server or delivered to the ICILS research center in that country.

ICILS systematically investigated differences among the participating countries in CIL outcomes and how participating countries were providing CIL-related education. The ICILS team also explored differences within and across countries with respect to relationships between CIL education outcomes and student characteristics and school contexts.

ICILS was based around four research questions focused on the following:

1. Variations in CIL within and across countries;

2. Aspects of schools, education systems, and teaching associated with student achievement in CIL;

3. The extent to which students' access to, familiarity with, and self-reported proficiency in using computers is associated with student achievement in CIL; and

4. Aspects of students' personal and social backgrounds associated with CIL.

The publication presenting the ICILS assessment framework (Fraillon et al., 2013) describes the development of these questions. The publication also provides more details relating to the questions and outlines the variables necessary for analyses pertaining to them.

© International Association for the Evaluation of Educational Achievement (IEA) 2014   15
J. Fraillon et al., *Preparing for Life in a Digital Age*, DOI 10.1007/978-3-319-14222-7_1

Data

ICILS gathered data from almost 60,000 Grade 8 (or equivalent) students in more than 3,300 schools from 21 countries or education systems[1] within countries. These student data were augmented by data from almost 35,000 teachers in those schools and by contextual data collected from school ICT-coordinators, school principals, and the ICILS national research centers.

The main ICILS survey took place in the 21 participating countries between February and December 2013. The survey was carried out in countries with a Northern Hemisphere school calendar between February and June 2013 and in those with a Southern Hemisphere school calendar between October and December 2013.

Students completed a computer-based test of CIL that consisted of questions and tasks presented in four 30-minute modules. Each student completed two modules randomly allocated from the set of four so that the total assessment time for each student was one hour.

After completing the two test modules, students answered (again on computer) a 30-minute international student questionnaire. It included questions relating to students' background characteristics, their experience and use of computers and ICT to complete a range of different tasks in school and out of school, and their attitudes toward using computers and ICT.

The three instruments designed to gather information from and about teachers and schools could be completed on computer (over the internet) or on paper. These instruments were:

- *A 30-minute teacher questionnaire:* This asked teachers several basic background questions followed by questions relating to teachers' reported use of ICT in teaching, their attitudes about the use of ICT in teaching, and their participation in professional learning activities relating to pedagogical use of ICT.

- *A 10-minute ICT-coordinator questionnaire:* This asked ICT-coordinators about the resources available in the school to support the use of ICT in teaching and learning. The questionnaire addressed both technological (e.g., infrastructure, hardware, and software) as well as pedagogical support (such as through professional learning).

- *A 10-minute principal questionnaire:* This instrument asked school principals to provide information about school characteristics as well as school approaches to providing CIL-related teaching and incorporating ICT in teaching and learning.

ICILS national research coordinators (NRCs) coordinated information procured from national experts via an online national contexts survey. Experts included education ministry or departmental staff, relevant nongovernmental organizations, specialist organizations concerned with educational technologies, and teacher associations. The information sought concerned the structure of the respective country's education system, plans and policies for using ICT in education, ICT and student learning at lower-secondary level, ICT and teacher development, and ICT-based learning and administrative management systems.

---

1 In the report, we use the terms country and education system interchangeably. Some of the entities that participated were countries and others were education systems that did not cover the whole of a country (e.g., the Canadian provinces of Ontario and Newfoundland and Labrador and the City of Buenos Aries in Argentina).

Computer and information literacy

The construct

The CIL construct was conceptualized in terms of two strands that framed the skills and knowledge addressed by the CIL instruments. Each strand was made up of several aspects, each of which referenced specific content.

Strand 1 of the framework, titled *collecting and managing information*, focuses on the receptive and organizational elements of information processing and management. It incorporates three aspects:

- *Knowing about and understanding computer use:* This refers to a person's declarative and procedural knowledge of the generic characteristics and functions of computers. It focuses on the basic technical knowledge and skills that underpin our use of computers in order to work with information.

- *Accessing and evaluating information:* This refers to the investigative processes that enable a person to find, retrieve, and make judgments about the relevance, integrity, and usefulness of computer-based information.

- *Managing information:* This aspect refers to the capacity of individuals to work with computer-based information. The process includes ability to adopt and adapt information-classification and information-organization schemes in order to arrange and store information so that it can be used or reused efficiently.

Strand 2 of the construct, titled *producing and exchanging information*, focuses on using computers as productive tools for thinking, creating, and communicating. The strand has four aspects:

- *Transforming information:* This refers to a person's ability to use computers to change how information is presented so that it is clearer for specific audiences and purposes.

- *Creating information:* This aspect refers to a person's ability to use computers to design and generate information products for specified purposes and audiences. These original products may be entirely new or they may build on a given set of information in order to generate new understandings.

- *Sharing information:* This aspect refers to a person's understanding of how computers are and can be used as well as his or her ability to use computers to communicate and exchange information with others.

- *Using information safely and securely:* This refers to a person's understanding of the legal and ethical issues of computer-based communication from the perspectives of both the publisher and the consumer of that information.

Assessing computer and information literacy

The student assessment was based on four modules, each of which consisted of a set of questions and tasks based on a realistic theme and following a linear narrative structure. The tasks in the modules comprised a series of small discrete tasks (typically taking less than a minute to complete) followed by a large task that typically took 15 to 20 minutes to complete. Taken together, the modules contained a total of 62 tasks and questions corresponding to 81 score points.

When students began each module, they were presented with an overview of the theme and purpose of the tasks in it. The overview also included a basic description of the content of the large task and what completing it would involve. The narrative of each module typically positioned the smaller discrete tasks as a mix of skill-execution and information-management tasks in preparation for completion of the large task. Students were required to complete the tasks in the allocated sequence and could not return to completed tasks in order to review them.

The four modules were:

- *After School Exercise:* Students set up an online collaborative workspace to share information and then selected and adapted information to create an advertising poster for an after-school exercise program.
- *Band Competition:* Students planned a website, edited an image, and used a simple website builder to create a webpage containing information about a school band competition.
- *Breathing:* Students managed files and collected and evaluated information needed to create a presentation explaining the process of breathing to eight- or nine-year-old students.
- *School Trip:* Students helped plan a school trip using online database tools. The task required students to select and adapt information in order to produce an information sheet about the trip for their peers. Students were told that their information sheet had to include a map that they could create using an online mapping tool.

Each test completed by a student consisted of two of the four modules. There were 12 different possible combinations of module pairs altogether. Each module appeared in six of the combinations—three times as the first and three times as the second module when paired with each of the other three. The module combinations were randomly allocated to students.

This test design made it possible to assess a larger amount of content than could be completed by any individual student and was necessary to ensure broad coverage of the content of the ICILS assessment framework. The design also controlled for the influence of item position on difficulty across the sampled students and provided a variety of contexts for the assessment of CIL.

The computer and information literacy scale

We used the Rasch item response theory (IRT) model to derive the cognitive scale from the data collected from the 62 test questions and tasks corresponding to 81 score points. Most questions and tasks each corresponded to one item. However, raters scored each ICILS large task against a set of criteria (each criterion with its own unique set of scores) relating to the properties of the task. Each large-task assessment criterion was therefore also an item in ICILS.

We set the final reporting scale to a metric that had a mean of 500 (*the ICILS average score*) and a standard deviation of 100 for the equally weighted national samples. We used plausible value methodology with full conditioning to derive summary student achievement statistics.

The ICILS described scale of CIL achievement is based on the content and scaled difficulties of the assessment items. The ICILS research team wrote descriptors for each item. The descriptors designate the CIL knowledge, skills, and understandings demonstrated by a student correctly responding to each item.

Pairing the scaled difficulty of each item with the item descriptors made it possible to order the items from least to most difficult, a process that produced an item map. Analysis of the item map and student achievement data were then used to establish proficiency levels that had a width of 85 scale points.[2] Student scores below 407 scale points indicate CIL proficiency below the lowest level targeted by the assessment instrument.

The scale description comprises syntheses of the common elements of CIL knowledge, skills, and understanding at each proficiency level. It also describes the typical ways in which students working at a level demonstrate their proficiency. Each level of the scale references the characteristics of students' use of computers to access and use information and to communicate with others.

The scale thus reflects a broad range of development, extending from students' application of software commands under direction, through their increasing independence in selecting and using information to communicate with others, and on to their ability to independently and purposefully select information and use a range of software resources in a controlled manner in order to communicate with others. Included in this development is students' knowledge and understanding of issues relating to online safety and to ethical use of electronic information. This understanding encompasses knowledge of information types and security procedures through to demonstrable awareness of the social, ethical, and legal consequences of a broad range of known and unknown users (potentially) accessing electronic information.

The four described levels of the CIL scale were summarized as follows:

- *Level 4 (above 661 scale points):* Students working at Level 4 select the most relevant information to use for communicative purposes. They evaluate usefulness of information based on criteria associated with need and evaluate the reliability of information based on its content and probable origin. These students create information products that demonstrate a consideration of audience and communicative purpose. They also use appropriate software features to restructure and present information in a manner that is consistent with presentation conventions, and they adapt that information to suit the needs of an audience. Students working at Level 4 also demonstrate awareness of problems that can arise with respect to the use of proprietary information on the internet.

- *Level 3 (577 to 661 scale points):* Students working at Level 3 demonstrate the capacity to work independently when using computers as information-gathering and information-management tools. These students select the most appropriate information source to meet a specified purpose, retrieve information from given electronic sources to answer concrete questions, and follow instructions to use conventionally recognized software commands to edit, add content to, and reformat information products. They recognize that the credibility of web-based information can be influenced by the identity, expertise, and motives of the creators of that information.

- *Level 2 (492 to 576 score points):* Students working at Level 2 use computers to complete basic and explicit information-gathering and information-management tasks. They locate explicit information from within given electronic sources. These

---

2   The level width and boundaries were rounded to the nearest whole number. The level width and boundaries to two decimal places are 84.75 and 406.89, 491.63, 576.38 and 661.12.

students make basic edits and add content to existing information products in response to specific instructions. They create simple information products that show consistency of design and adherence to layout conventions. Students working at Level 2 demonstrate awareness of mechanisms for protecting personal information. They also demonstrate awareness of some of the consequences of public access to personal information.

- *Level 1 (407 to 491 score points):* Students working at Level 1 demonstrate a functional working knowledge of computers as tools and a basic understanding of the consequences of computers being accessed by multiple users. They apply conventional software commands to perform basic communication tasks and add simple content to information products. They demonstrate familiarity with the basic layout conventions of electronic documents.

The scale is hierarchical in the sense that CIL proficiency becomes more sophisticated as student achievement progresses up the scale. We can therefore assume that a student located at a particular place on the scale because of his or her achievement score will be able to undertake and successfully accomplish tasks up to that level of achievement.

Variations in student achievement on the CIL scale

Variations across countries

Student CIL varied considerably across ICILS countries. The average national scores on the scale ranged from 361 to 553 scale points, a span that extends from below Level 1 to a standard of proficiency within Level 3. This range was equivalent to almost two standard deviations. However, the distribution of country CIL means was skewed because the means of three countries were significantly below the ICILS 2013 average and the means of 12 other countries were significantly above the ICILS 2013 average. Eighty-one percent of students achieved scores that placed them within CIL Levels 1, 2, and 3. In all but two countries, Turkey and Thailand, the highest percentage of students was in Level 2.

Factors associated with variations in CIL

Higher socioeconomic status was associated with higher CIL proficiency both within and across countries. Female students had higher CIL scale scores in all but two countries. Similarly, students who spoke the language of the CIL assessment (which was also the language of instruction) also performed better on it. Multiple regression techniques showed that the following variables had statistically significant positive associations with CIL in most countries: students' gender (female compared to male), students' expected educational attainment, parental educational attainment, parental occupational status, number of books in the home, and ICT home resources.

Student experience of computer use and their frequency of computer use at home were positively associated with CIL scores in most countries. Student access to a home internet connection and the number of computers students had at home had statistically significant associations with CIL scores in about half of the participating education systems. However, the association between number of home computers and CIL scores disappeared after we had controlled for the effect of socioeconomic background. In addition, student reports of having learned about ICT at school were associated with CIL achievement in eight education systems.

CIL achievement was also positively associated with basic ICT self-efficacy but not with advanced ICT self-efficacy. This finding is consistent with the nature of the CIL assessment construct, which is made up of information literacy and communication skills that are not necessarily related to advanced computer skills such as programming or database management. Even though CIL is computer based, in the sense that students demonstrate CIL in the context of computer use, the CIL construct itself does not emphasize high-level computer-based technical skills. Greater interest in and enjoyment of ICT use was associated with higher CIL scores in nine of the 14 countries that met the ICILS sampling requirements.

We observed statistically significant effects of ICT-related school-level factors on CIL achievement in only a few countries. In several education systems, we recorded evidence of effects on CIL of the school average of students' computer use (at home) and the extent to which students reported learning about ICT-related tasks at school. These findings deserve further analysis in future research. The notion that school learning is an important aspect of developing CIL is a particularly important consideration and therefore worth investigating in greater detail.

Multilevel analyses confirmed that students' experience with computers as well as regular home-based use of computers had significant positive effects on CIL even after we had controlled for the influence of personal and social context. However, ICT resources, particularly the number of computers at home, no longer had effects once we took socioeconomic background into account. A number of the associations between school-level factors and CIL were not significant after we controlled for the effect of the school's socioeconomic context.

Student use of ICT

Almost all ICILS students reported that they were experienced users of computers and had access to them at home and at school. On average across the ICILS countries, more than one third of the Grade 8 students said they had been using computers for seven or more years, with a further 29 percent reporting that they had been using computers for between five and seven years. Ninety-four percent of the students on average crossnationally reported having at least one computer (desktop, laptop, notebook, or tablet device) at home, while 48 percent reported having three or more computers at home. Ninety-two percent of students stated that they had some form of internet connection at home.

Students across the ICILS countries reported using computers more frequently at home than elsewhere. On average, 87 percent said they used a computer at home at least once a week, whereas 54 percent and 13 percent reported this same frequency of computer use at school and at other places respectively.

Computer use outside school

ICILS 2013 data indicated that students were making widespread and frequent use of digital technologies when outside school. Students tended to use the internet for social communication and exchanging information, computers for recreation, and computer utilities for school work and other purposes.

On average across ICILS countries, three quarters of the students said they communicated with others by way of messaging or social networks at least weekly. Just over half said that they used the internet for "searching for information for study or school work" at least once a week, and almost half indicated that they engaged in "posting comments to online profiles or blogs" at least once each week. On average, there was evidence of slightly more frequent use of the internet for social communication and exchanging information among females than among males.

Students were also frequently using computers for recreation. On average across the ICILS countries, 82 percent of students reported "listening to music" on a computer at least once a week, 68 percent reported "watching downloaded or streamed video (e.g., movies, TV shows, or clips)" on a weekly basis, and 62 percent said they used the internet to "get news about things of interest," also on a weekly basis. Just over half of all the ICILS students were "playing games" once a week or more. Overall, males reported slightly higher frequencies of using computers for recreation than did females.

Students also reported using computer utilities (applications) outside school. Generally across the ICILS countries, the most extensive weekly use of computer utilities involved "creating or editing documents" (28% of students). Use of most other utilities was much less frequent. For example, only 18 percent of the students were "using education software designed to help with school study." We found no significant difference between female and male students with respect to using computer utilities outside school.

Use of ICT for school work

Crossnationally, just under half (45%) of the ICILS students, on average, were using computers to "prepare reports or essays" at least once a week. We recorded a similar extent of use for "preparing presentations" (44%). Forty percent of students reported using ICT when working with other students from their own school at least weekly, and 39 percent of students reported using a computer once a week or more to complete worksheets or exercises.

Two school-related uses of computers were reported by less than one fifth of the students. These were "writing about one's own learning," which referred to using a learning log, and "working with other students from other schools." Nineteen percent of students said they used a computer for the first of these tasks; 13 percent said they used a computer for the second.

The subject area in which computers were most frequently being used was, not surprisingly, information technology or computer studies (56%). On average, about one fifth of the students studying (natural) sciences said they used computers in most or all lessons. The same proportion reported using computers in most or all of their human sciences/humanities lessons. In language arts (the test language) and language arts (foreign languages), students were using computers a little less frequently: about one sixth of the students reported computer use in most or all such lessons. Approximately one in seven students studying mathematics reported computer use in most mathematics lessons or almost every lesson. Of the students studying creative arts, just a little more than one in 10 reported computer use in most or all lessons.

Teacher and school use of ICT

Teacher use of ICT

ICILS teachers were making extensive use of ICT in their schools. Across the ICILS countries, three out of every five teachers said they used computers at least once a week when teaching, and four out of five reported using computers on a weekly basis for other work at their schools. Teachers in most countries were experienced users of ICT. Four out of every five of them said they had been using computers for two years or more when teaching.

In general, teachers were confident about their ability to use a variety of computer applications; two thirds of them expressed confidence in their ability to use these for assessing and monitoring student progress. We observed differences, however, among countries in the level of confidence that teachers expressed with regard to using computer technologies. We also noted that younger teachers tended to be more confident ICT users than their older colleagues.

Teachers recognized the positive aspects of using ICT in teaching and learning at school, especially with respect to accessing and managing information. On balance, teachers reported generally positive attitudes toward the use of ICT, although many were aware that ICT use could have some detrimental aspects.

As already indicated, a substantial majority of the ICILS teachers were using ICT in their teaching. This use was greatest among teachers who were confident about their ICT expertise and who were working in school environments where staff collaborated on and planned ICT use, and where there were fewer resource limitations to that use. These were also the conditions that supported the teaching of CIL. These findings suggest that if schools are to develop students' CIL to the greatest extent possible, then teacher expertise in ICT use needs to be augmented (lack of teacher expertise in computing is considered to be a substantial obstacle to ICT use), and ICT use needs to be supported by collaborative environments that incorporate institutional planning.

According to the ICILS teachers, the utilities most frequently used in their respective reference classes were those concerned with wordprocessing, presentations, and computer-based information resources, such as websites, wikis, and encyclopedias. Overall, teachers appeared to be using ICT most frequently for relatively simple tasks and less often for more complex tasks.

School-based ICT provision and use

There were substantial differences across countries in the number of students per available computer in a school. The ICILS 2013 average for this ratio ranged from two (Norway) and three (Australia) through to 22 (Chile) and 26 (Croatia). Turkey had a very high ratio of students per computer (80). Students from countries with greater access to computers in schools tended to have stronger CIL skills.

Computers in schools were most often located in computer laboratories and libraries. However, there were differences among countries as to whether schools had portable class-sets of computers on offer or whether students brought their own computers to class.

ICT-coordinators reported a range of impediments to teaching and learning ICT. In general, the coordinators rated personnel and teaching support issues as more problematic than resource issues. However, there was considerable variation in the types of limitation arising from resource inadequacy.

Teachers and principals provided perspectives on the range of professional development activities relevant to pedagogical use of ICT. According to principals, teachers were most likely to participate in school-provided courses on pedagogical use of ICT, to talk about this type of use when they were within groups of teachers, and to discuss ICT use in education as a regular item during meetings of teaching staff. From the teachers' perspective, the most common professional development activities available included observing other teachers using ICT in their teaching, introductory courses on general applications, and sharing and evaluating digital resources with others via a collaborative workspace.

Conclusion

ICILS has provided a description of the competencies underpinning CIL that incorporates the notions of being able to safely and responsibly access and use digital information as well as produce and develop digital products. ICILS has also provided educational stakeholders with an empirically derived scale and description of CIL learning that they can reference when deliberating about CIL education. This framework and associated measurement scale furthermore provide a basis for understanding variation in CIL at present and for monitoring change in the CIL that results from developments in policy and practice over time.

The CIL construct combines information literacy, critical thinking, technical skills, and communication skills applied across a range of contexts and for a range of purposes. The variations in CIL proficiency show that while some of the young people participating in ICILS were independent and critical users of ICT, there were many who were not. As the volume of computer-based information available to young people continues to increase, so too will the onus on societies to critically evaluate the credibility and value of that information.

Changing technologies (such as social media and mobile technologies) are increasing the ability of young people to communicate with one another and to publish information to a worldwide audience in real time. This facility obliges individuals to consider what is ethically appropriate and to determine how to maximize the communicative efficacy of information products.

ICILS results suggest that the knowledge, skills, and understandings described in the CIL scale can and should be taught. To some extent, this conclusion challenges perspectives of young people as *digital natives* with a self-developed capacity to use digital technology. Even though we can discern within the ICILS findings high levels of access to ICT and high levels of use of these technologies by young people in and (especially) outside school, we need to remain aware of the large variations in CIL proficiency within and across the ICILS countries. Regardless of whether or not we consider young people to be digital natives, we would be naive to expect them to develop CIL in the absence of coherent learning programs.

The ICILS data furthermore showed that emphases relating to CIL outcomes were most frequently being addressed in technology or computer studies classes, the (natural) sciences, and human sciences or humanities. Queries remain, however, about how schools can and should maintain the continuity, completeness, and coherence of their CIL education programs.

Teachers' ICT use was greatest when the teachers were confident about their expertise and were working in school environments that collaborated on and planned ICT use and had few resource limitations hindering that use. These were also the conditions that supported teachers' ability to teach CIL. We therefore suggest that system- and school-level planning should focus on increasing teacher expertise in ICT use. We also consider that schools should endeavor to implement supportive collaborative environments that incorporate institutional planning focused on using ICT and teaching CIL in schools.

ICILS has provided a baseline study for future measurement of CIL and CIL education across countries. A future cycle of ICILS could be developed to support measurement of trends in CIL as well as maintain the study's relevance to innovations in software, hardware, and delivery technologies. Some possibilities for future iterations of ICILS could include internet delivery of the assessment, accommodation of "bring your own device" in schools, adapting a version for use on tablet devices, and incorporating contemporary and relevant software environments, such as multimedia and gaming. The key to the future of such research is to maintain a strong link to the core elements of the construct while accommodating the new contexts in which CIL achievement can be demonstrated.

CHAPTER 1:
Introduction

The International Computer and Information Literacy Study 2013 (ICILS 2013) investigated the ways in which young people develop computer and information literacy (CIL) to support their capacity to participate in the digital age. Computer and information literacy is defined as "an individual's ability to use computers to investigate, create and communicate in order to participate effectively at home, at school, in the workplace and in society" (Fraillon, Schulz, & Ainley, 2013, p. 17).

Computer-based assessments of discipline-specific learning (such as reading, mathematics, and science) have viewed the computer as a tool that students use to express their discipline-specific knowledge, understanding, and skills. In contrast, ICILS aimed to measure students' ability to use computers to gather, manage, and communicate information. The study assessed student CIL achievement through a computer-based assessment administered to students in their eighth year of schooling. It examined differences across countries in student CIL achievement and explored how these differences related to student characteristics and students' use of computer technologies in and out of school. The study also investigated the home, school, and national contexts in which CIL develops.

Within the context of international comparative research, ICILS is the first study to investigate students' acquisition of CIL. It is also the first crossnational study commissioned by the International Association for the Evaluation of Educational Achievement (IEA) to collect student achievement data via computer. It is a response to the increasing use of information and communication technology (ICT) in modern society and the need for citizens to develop relevant skills in order to participate effectively in the digital age. The study furthermore addressed the need for policymakers and education systems to have a better understanding of the contexts and outcomes of CIL-related education programs in their countries.

The ICILS research team systematically investigated differences in CIL outcomes across the participating countries. The team also explored how these countries were providing CIL-related education and looked at differences within and across the countries with respect to associations between CIL-education outcomes and student characteristics and school contexts. In addition, participating countries provided detailed information on the national contexts in which their CIL education takes place. This information included policies, resourcing, curriculum, and assessment.

ICILS researchers gathered data from almost 60,000 Grade 8 (or equivalent) students in more than 3,300 schools from 21 countries or education systems within countries. ICILS used purpose-designed software for the computer-based student assessment (and questionnaire), which was administered primarily using USB drives attached to school computers. These student data were augmented by data from almost 35,000 teachers in those schools and by contextual data collected from school ICT-coordinators, principals, and the ICILS national research centers.

© International Association for the Evaluation of Educational Achievement (IEA) 2014
J. Fraillon et al., *Preparing for Life in a Digital Age*, DOI 10.1007/978-3-319-14222-7_2

Background

Recent decades have witnessed the development and pervasive implementation of computer and other information technologies throughout societies around the world. The use of information technologies is now embedded in societies and in schooling. Information technologies provide the tools for creating, collecting, storing, and using knowledge as well as for communication and collaboration (Kozma, 2003a). The development of these technologies has changed not only the environment in which students develop skills for life but also the basis of many occupations and the ways in which various social transactions take place. Knowing about, understanding, and using information technologies has thus become an important component of life in modern society.

Today, many education systems assess these skills as part of their monitoring of student achievement. Since the late 1980s, this area of education has been a feature of IEA's international comparative research agenda. IEA's Computers in Education Study (COMPED), conducted in two stages in 1989 and 1992 (Pelgrum, Reinen, & Plomp, 1993), focused on computer availability and use in schools. It also estimated the impact of school-based computer use on student achievement. Twenty-one education systems participated in Stage 1, and 12 in Stage 2 of the study (Pelgrum & Plomp, 1991).

In 1998/1999, IEA's Second Information Technology in Education Study (SITES) Module 1 collected data from 27 education systems (Pelgrum & Anderson, 1999). SITES Module 2, a qualitative study based on 174 case studies from 28 countries (Kozma, 2003a) and conducted during 2001/2002, investigated pedagogical innovations that employed information technology. SITES 2006 surveyed the use of ICT by Grade 8 mathematics and science teachers in 22 education systems (Law, Pelgrum, & Plomp, 2008).

The SITES studies also collected information on the resourcing and use of ICT in schools. Module 1 looked at the support on hand for teachers to use ICT in their teaching in schools, Module 2 focused on pedagogical innovations using ICT, and SITES 2006 explored the role of ICT in teaching mathematics and science in Grade 8 classrooms (Kozma, 2003a; Pelgrum & Anderson, 2001).

During the early 2000s, the OECD commissioned a study designed to examine the feasibility of including an ICT literacy assessment as part of its Programme for International Student Assessment (PISA). Although the OECD decided not to include ICT literacy in its suite of PISA assessments, the feasibility study prompted development of a framework for ICT literacy applicable within the crossnational context (Educational Testing Service, 2002). Since then, the OECD has included computer-based assessments of digital reading in its PISA assessments (2009 and 2012), and in 2015 it intends to implement a computer-based assessment of collaborative problem-solving.

The OECD Programme for the International Assessment of Adult Competencies (PIAAC) also includes computer-based assessments of digital reading and problem-solving in technology-rich environments (OECD, 2014a). IEA's ongoing Trends in International Mathematics and Science Study (TIMSS) and Progress in Reading Literacy Study (PIRLS) investigate the role of ICT use in the learning of mathematics, science, and reading (see, for example, Martin, Mullis, Foy, & Stanco, 2012; Mullis, Martin, Foy, & Arora, 2012; Mullis, Martin, Foy, & Drucker, 2012).

These initiatives over the past 25 years illustrate the interest in crossnational assessment of a range of achievement constructs related to the use of ICT not only by school students but also by adults. In addition, there is a general impetus within and across countries to deliver assessment content on computers rather than on paper as previously. The OECD is currently implementing this practice in its PISA assessments.

IEA's PIRLS 2016 will include an electronic reading assessment option (ePIRLS) featuring multi-layered digital texts. An assessment of electronic reading such as ePIRLS focuses on reading constructs that we can regard as "building blocks" enabling development of CIL. Such assessments do not, however, address the richness and depth of the CIL construct. ICILS is unique and groundbreaking within international large-scale assessment research not only because of the nature of the achievement construct being measured but also because of the innovative, authentic, computer-based assessment tasks designed to measure students' CIL.

The importance that ICT-related education and training has for providing citizens with the skills they need to access information and participate in transactions through these technologies is widely recognized worldwide (Kozma, 2008). Evidence of this recognition in recent years can be found in major policy statements, research studies, and other initiatives.

For example, according to the authors of a report on E-learning Nordic, a study that explored the impact of ICT on education in Nordic countries, "ICT is ... an essential cultural technique which can significantly improve the quality of education" (Pedersen et al., 2006, p. 114). In 2007, the United Kingdom's Qualifications and Curriculum Authority positioned ICT as "an essential skill for life and enables learners to participate in a rapidly changing world" (para. 1).

In 2008, under its i2010 strategy, the European Commission reported on 470 digital literacy initiatives in Europe and suggested that digital literacy is "increasingly becoming an essential life competence and the inability to access or use ICT has effectively become a barrier to social integration and personal development" (European Commission, 2008, p. 4). The successor to the i2010 strategy, the Digital Agenda for Europe, included "enhancing digital literacy, inclusion and skills" as one of seven priority areas for action (European Commission, 2013, para 1) and led to the establishment of a conceptual framework for "benchmarking digital Europe" (European Commission, 2009a).

In December 2011, under its Lifelong Learning Programme, the European Commission elucidated the knowledge, skills, and attitudes that people need in order to be deemed digitally competent. The commission had earlier identified digital competence as one of its eight identified key competences in education and argued that this competence goes beyond the use of purely functional ICT skills because it embeds the critical, collaborative, creative use of new technologies for employability and societal inclusion (European Commission, 2006).

As a first step toward developing a digital competence framework, the commission provided an in-depth description of what it perceived to be the various components of digital competence. The description covers 21 subcompetences structured according to five main competences—information management, collaboration, communication and sharing, creation of content, and problem-solving (European Commission Joint Research Center-IPTS, 2013). Each of the 21 subcompetences is briefly defined and accompanied by descriptors of three proficiency levels as well as examples of the requisite knowledge, skills, and attitudes.

European Union (EU) member states were closely involved in the framework's development, and some have already begun implementing it in national contexts. Work is continuing under Erasmus+, an EU program that focuses on formal and informal learning across EU borders. The next version of EUROPASS, another EU initiative that helps Europeans communicate their qualifications and skills across EU member states, will include a set of questions that learners can use to self-assess their digital competency. By the end of 2014, the three proficiency levels will have been extended to eight in order to correspond with the eight levels of the European Qualification Framework (EUROPASS, 2014).

For Ferrari (2012), digital competence is "both a requirement and a right of citizens, if they are to be functional in today's society" (p. 3). She identified from her analysis of existing digital competence frameworks, seven key areas of competence: information management, collaboration, communication and sharing, creation of content and knowledge, ethics and responsibility, evaluation and problem-solving, and technical operations.

In 2011, a European Commission study collected data from over 190,000 students, teachers, and head teachers across 27 EU (and four non-EU) countries in Europe. The study investigated "educational technology in schools: from infrastructure provision to use, confidence and attitudes" (European Commission, 2013, p. 9).

The United States has in place widespread and varied policies designed to encourage the use of ICT in schools (Anderson & Dexter, 2009). In endeavoring to shape their curricula and assessments according to the policy directives, states have generally followed the National Educational Technology Standards established by the International Society for Technology in Education (2007). The US National Education Technology Plan implicitly and explicitly exhorts the development of skills that enable participation in the digital age. Goal 1.1 of the plan stresses that, regardless of the learning domain, "states should continue to consider the integration of 21st-century competencies and expertise, such as critical thinking, complex problem solving, collaboration, multimedia communication, and technological competencies demonstrated by professionals in various disciplines" (Office of Educational Technology, US Department of Education, 2010, p. *xvi*).

In the United States, the start of the 2014/2015 school year marked inclusion of an assessment of technology competency (which has ICT as one of its three areas) in the country's Assessment of Educational Progress (WestEd, 2010). The assessment covers proficiency with computers and software learning tools, networking systems and protocols, hand-held digital devices, and other technologies that enable users to access, create, and communicate information and engage in creative expression. The assessment also identifies five subareas of competence: construction and exchange of ideas and solutions, information research, investigation of problems, acknowledgement of ideas and information, and selection and use of digital tools (Institute of Education Sciences, National Center for Education Statistics, 2012).

Over recent years, a number of countries in Latin America have increased their focus on the use of ICT in classrooms and also introduced one computer to every student in schools (commonly referred to as one-to-one resourcing). Argentina, Brazil, Chile, Peru, and Uruguay are some of the countries that have implemented one-to-one computer policies (see, for example, Ministry of Education of the City of Buenos Aires, 2013;

Ministry of Education of Uruguay, 2013; Severin & Capota, 2011; Severin, Santiago, Ibarrarán, Thompson, & Cueto, 2011).

One-to-one resourcing is also evident in Thailand. In line with its one tablet computer per child program, the government distributed over 800,000 tablet computers to Grade 1 students in 2012. The computers were preloaded with content for the core subjects of science, mathematics, social studies, Thai, and English (UNESCO, 2013).

As early as 1996, Korea established a comprehensive plan for education informatization. The republic has since conducted an ongoing four-phased implementation process: deployment of infrastructure and resources, promotion of ICT use and e-learning, transitioning from e-learning to ubiquitous learning (u-learning), and development of ICT-based creative human resources (Korea Education and Research Information Service, 2013).

Despite increasing international recognition of the importance of ICT-related literacies (Blurton, 1999; Kozma, 2003a), there is considerable variation among (and even within) countries with regard to explicit ICT curricula, resources, and teaching approaches (Educational Testing Service, 2002; Kozma, 2008; OECD, 2005; Sturman & Sizmur, 2011). In addition to questions stemming from the variety of approaches in which ICT curricula are conceptualized and delivered, there are questions about the nature of the role that schools and education systems play in supporting the development of ICT-related literacies among young people.

In some countries, young people claim that they learn more about using computers out of school than they do in school (see, for example, Thomson & De Bortoli, 2007), while adults regard the new generation of young people as "digital natives" (Prensky, 2001) who have developed "sophisticated knowledge of and skills with information technologies" as well as learning styles that differ from those of previous generations (Bennett, Maton, & Kervin, 2008, p. 777).

However, various commentators express concern about the value of labeling the new generation this way. They challenge, in particular, assumptions about the knowledge and skills that these assumed digital natives acquire (see, for example, van den Beemt, 2010). In addition to identifying and discussing the "myths" associated with the notion of digital native, Koutropoulos (2011, p. 531) questions assumptions of homogeneity and pervasiveness, arguing that if we look "at the research … we see that there is no one, monolithic group that we can point to and say that *those are digital natives*. As a matter of fact, the individuals who would fit the stereotype of the digital native appear to be in the minority of the population" (para 36, emphasis original).

Questions are also being raised about the types of ICT use and consequent learning that young people experience, especially when they are away from school. Some scholars query if young people are indeed developing through their ICT use the types of ICT-related knowledge, skills, and understandings that can be of significant value in later life. Crook (2008) characterizes the majority of young people's communicative exchanges as "low bandwidth," where the focus is on role allocation and cooperation rather than on genuine collaboration. Selwyn (2009) similarly challenges suppositions about the quality and value of much of young people's self-directed ICT learning, observing that "if anything young people's use of the internet can be described most accurately as involving the passive consumption of knowledge rather than the active creation of content" (p. 372).

Today, the research community and policymakers continue to grapple with issues revolving around the development of digital literacies in young people. Although there is consistent rhetoric about the value of emergent digital literacies in providing positive life outcomes, just how school education can and should contribute to this process remains unclear. For ICILS, a primary aim has been to bring greater clarity to these matters through the study's systematic investigation of CIL in young people and the ways in which this form of literacy is developed.

Research questions

The research questions underpinning ICILS concern students' acquisition of CIL. The publication elaborating the ICILS assessment framework (Fraillon et al., 2013) describes the development of and provides additional details pertinent to these questions. The publication also outlines the variables that researchers need to consider when conducting analyses of data relevant to the questions.

RQ 1: *What variations exist between countries, and within countries, in student computer and information literacy?*

This research question concerns the distribution of CIL outcomes across participating countries (at the country level) and within these countries. Analyses that address this question focus on the distribution of CIL test data and involve single- and multi-level perspectives.

RQ 2: *What aspects of schools and education systems are related to student achievement in computer and information literacy with respect to the following subquestions?*

(a) *The general approach to computer and information literacy education.*

ICILS collected data at the national level on curriculum and programs as well as at the school level through teacher, ICT-coordinator, and principal questionnaires. Analyses of these data also took into account contextual information about CIL-related learning at the country level as well as more detailed information from schools and classrooms.

(b) *School and teaching practices regarding the use of technologies in computer and information literacy.*

ICILS collected information from schools, teachers, and students in order to ascertain student perceptions of and teacher reports on instructional practices regarding CIL-related teaching and learning processes.

(c) *Teacher attitudes to and proficiency in using computers.*

Teachers reported on their experiences of, attitudes toward, and confidence in using computers. They also reported on their use of computers as tools to support their teaching of content related to their own main subject and with respect to aspects of CIL.

(d) *Access to ICT in schools.*

Students, teachers, ICT-coordinators, and principals reported on their use of and access to ICT in schools.

(e) *Teacher professional development and within-school delivery of computer and information literacy programs.*

Teachers, ICT-coordinators, and principals reported on teachers' access to and use of a range of professional learning opportunities.

RQ 3: *What characteristics of students' levels of access to, familiarity with, and self-reported proficiency in using computers are related to student achievement in computer and information literacy?*

(a) *How do these characteristics differ among and within countries?*

ICILS collected information from students on how long they had been using computers and how often they used computers for a range of recreational and school-related purposes. Information was also sought on student confidence in completing a range of tasks on computer. These data were collected in order to enable descriptions of students' use of computers and were analyzed with respect to their associations with students' CIL.

(b) *To what extent do the strengths of the associations between these characteristics and measured computer and information literacy differ among countries?*

ICILS conducted analyses directed toward determining associations between student access to, familiarity with, and self-reported proficiency in using computers and computer and information literacy within and across countries.

RQ 4: *What aspects of students' personal and social backgrounds (such as gender, socioeconomic background, and language background) are related to computer and information literacy?*

ICILS examined information about student background and home environment in an effort to explain variation in student's CIL. The instrument used to gather this information was the student questionnaire.

Participating countries, population, and sample design

Twenty-one countries[1] participated in ICILS. They were Australia, the City of Buenos Aires (Argentina), Chile, Croatia, the Czech Republic, Denmark, Germany, Hong Kong SAR, Korea, Lithuania, the Netherlands, Norway (Grade 9), Newfoundland and Labrador (Canada), Ontario (Canada), Poland, the Russian Federation, the Slovak Republic, Slovenia, Switzerland, Thailand, and Turkey. Three of these education systems—the City of Buenos Aires (Argentina), Newfoundland and Labrador (Canada), and Ontario (Canada)—took part as benchmarking participants.

Population definitions

The ICILS student population was defined as students in Grade 8 (typically around 14 years of age in most countries), provided that the average age of students in this grade was at least 13.5 at the time of the assessment. If the average age of students in Grade 8 was below 13.5 years, Grade 9 became the target population.

The population for the ICILS teacher survey was defined as all teachers teaching regular school subjects to the students in the target grade at each sampled school. It included only those teachers who were teaching the target grade during the testing period and who had been employed at school since the beginning of the school year. ICILS also administered separate questionnaires to principals and nominated ICT-coordinators in each school.

---

1 Several of the ICILS participants were distinct education systems within countries. We generally use the term "country" in this report for both the countries and the systems within countries that participated in the study.

Sample design

The samples were designed as two-stage cluster samples. During the first stage of sampling, PPS procedures (probability proportional to size as measured by the number of students enrolled in a school) were used to sample schools within each country. The numbers required in the sample to achieve the necessary precision were estimated on the basis of national characteristics. However, as a guide, each country was instructed to plan for a minimum sample size of 150 schools. The sampling of schools constituted the first stage of sampling both students and teachers.

The sample of schools ranged in number between 138 and 318 across countries. Twenty students were then randomly sampled from all students enrolled in the target grade in each sampled school. In schools with fewer than 20 students, all students were invited to participate. Appendix A of this report documents the achieved samples for each country.

Up to 15 teachers were selected at random from all teachers teaching the target grade at each sampled school. In schools with 20 or fewer such teachers, all teachers were invited to participate. In schools with 21 or more such teachers, 15 teachers were sampled at random. Because of the intention that teacher information should not be linked to individual students, all teachers of the target grade were eligible to be sampled regardless of the subjects they taught.

The participation rates required for each country were 85 percent of the selected schools and 85 percent of the selected students within the participating schools, or a weighted overall participation rate of 75 percent. The same criteria were applied to the teacher sample, but the coverage was judged independently of the student sample. In the tables in this report, we use annotations to identify those countries that met these response rates only after the inclusion of replacement schools. Education systems that took part as benchmarking participants also appear in a separate section of the tables in this report. Countries or benchmarking participants that did not meet the response rates, even after replacement, are also reported separately, in this instance below the main section of each table.

The ICILS assessment framework

The assessment framework provided the conceptual underpinning of the ICILS international instrumentation (Fraillon et al., 2013). The assessment framework has two parts:

(1) *The computer and information literacy framework:* This outlines the outcome measures addressed through the student achievement test.

(2) *The contextual framework:* This maps the context factors potentially influencing CIL and explaining variation.

The computer and information literacy framework

The CIL construct has two elements:

(1) *Strand:* This refers to the overarching conceptual category used to frame the skills and knowledge addressed by the CIL instruments.

(2) *Aspect:* This refers to the specific content category within a strand.

Strand 1 of the framework, *collecting and managing information*, focuses on the receptive and organizational elements of information processing and management and consists of the following three aspects:

(a) *Knowing about and understanding computer use* refers to a person's declarative and procedural knowledge of the generic characteristics and functions of computers. It focuses on the basic technical knowledge and skills he or she needs in order to use computers to work with information.

(b) *Accessing and evaluating information* refers to the investigative processes that enable a person to find, retrieve, and make judgments about the relevance, integrity, and usefulness of computer-based information.

(c) *Managing information* refers to individuals' capacity to work with computer-based information. The process includes ability to adopt and adapt information classification and organization schemes in order to arrange and store information so that it can be used or reused efficiently.

Strand 2 of the framework, *producing and exchanging information*, focuses on using computers as productive tools for thinking, creating, and communicating. The strand has four aspects:

(a) *Transforming information* refers to a person's ability to use computers to change how information is presented so that it is clearer for specific audiences and purposes.

(b) *Creating information* refers to a person's ability to use computers to design and generate information products for specified purposes and audiences. These original products may be entirely new or may build upon a given set of information and thereby generate new understandings.

(c) *Sharing information* refers to a person's understanding of how computers are and can be used as well as his or her ability to use computers to communicate and exchange information with others.

(d) *Using information safely and securely* refers to a person's understanding of the legal and ethical issues of computer-based communication from the perspectives of both the generator and the consumer of that information.

A detailed discussion of the contents of each of the strands and aspects of the computer and information literacy framework can be found in the IEA publication detailing the ICILS assessment framework (Fraillon et al., 2013).

The ICILS contextual framework

When studying student outcomes related to CIL, it is important to set these in the context of the different influences on CIL development. Students acquire competence in this area through a variety of activities and experiences at the different levels of their education and through different processes in school and out of school. It is also likely, as Ainley, Enger, and Searle (2009) argue, that students' out-of-school experiences of using ICT influence their learning approaches in school. Contextual variables can also be classified according to their measurement characteristics, namely, factual (e.g., age), attitudinal (e.g., enjoyment of computer use), and behavioral (e.g., frequency of computer use).

Different conceptual frameworks for analyzing educational outcomes frequently point out the multilevel structure inherent in the processes that influence student learning (see, for example, Scheerens, 1990; Scheerens & Bosker, 1997; Schulz, Fraillon, Ainley, Losito, & Kerr, 2008; Travers, Garden, & Rosier, 1989; Travers & Westbury, 1989). The learning of individual students is set in the overlapping contexts of school learning and out-of-school learning, both of which are embedded in the context of the wider community that comprises local, national, supranational, and international contexts. The contextual framework of ICILS therefore distinguishes the following levels:

- *The individual:* This context includes the characteristics of the learner, the processes of learning, and the learner's level of CIL.

- *Home environment:* This context relates to a student's background characteristics, especially in terms of the learning processes associated with family, home, and other immediate out-of-school contexts.

- *Schools and classrooms:* This context encompasses all school-related factors. Given the crosscurricular nature of CIL learning, distinguishing between classroom level and school level is not useful.

- *Wider community:* This level describes the wider context in which CIL learning takes places. It comprises local community contexts (e.g., remoteness and access to internet facilities) as well as characteristics of the education system and country. It also encompasses the global context, a factor widely enhanced by access to the world wide web.

The status of contextual factors within the learning process is also important. Factors can be classified as either antecedents or processes:

- *Antecedents* are exogenous factors that condition the ways in which CIL learning takes place and are therefore not directly influenced by learning-process variables or outcomes. It is important to recognize that antecedent variables are level-specific and may be influenced by antecedents and processes found at higher levels. Variables such as the socioeconomic status of the student's family and the school intake along with home resources fall into this category.

- *Processes* are those factors that directly influence CIL learning. They are constrained by antecedent factors and factors found at higher levels. This category contains variables such as opportunities for CIL learning during class, teacher attitudes toward using ICT for study tasks, and students' use of computers at home.

Both antecedents and processes need to be taken into account when explaining variation in CIL learning outcomes. Whereas antecedent factors shape and constrain the development of CIL, the level of (existing) CIL learning can influence process factors. For example, the level and scope of classroom exercises using ICT generally depend on students' existing CIL-related proficiency.

Figure 1.1 illustrates this basic classification of antecedent and process-related contextual factors and their relationship with CIL outcomes located at the different levels. Examples of variables that have the potential to influence learning processes and outcomes accompany each type of factor at each level. The double arrow in the figure between the process-related factors and outcomes emphasizes the possibility of feedback between learning process and learning outcome. The single-headed arrow between antecedents and processes, in turn, indicates the assumption within the ICILS contextual framework of a unidirectional association at each contextual level.

Figure 1.1: Contexts for CIL learning and learning outcomes

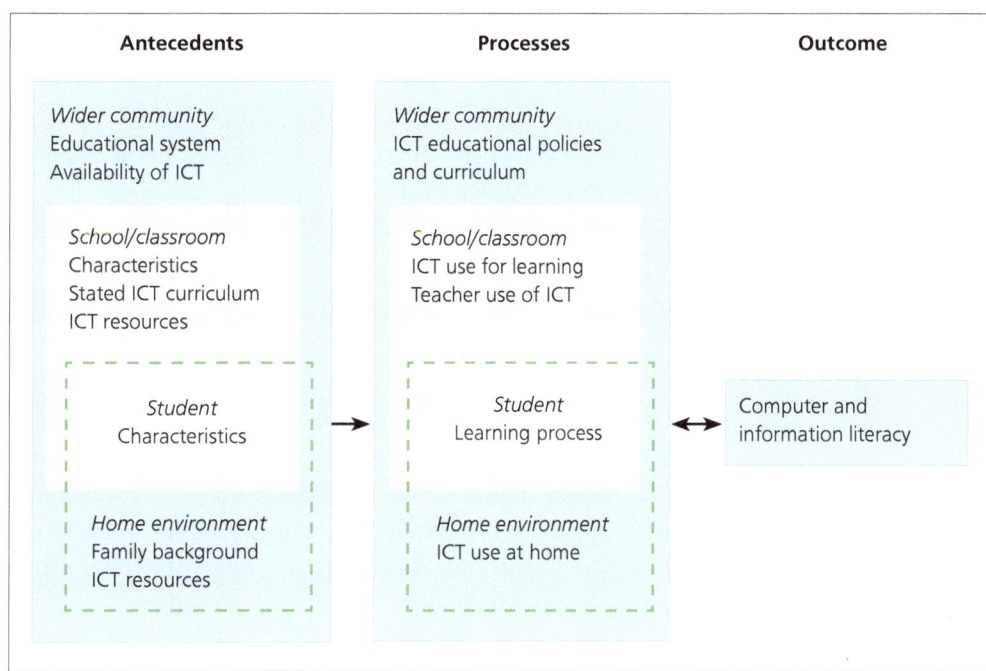

Reference to this general conceptual framework enables us to locate potential contextual factors on a two-by-four grid where antecedents and processes constitute the columns and the four levels the rows. Table 1.1 shows examples in each of these cells of the contextual variables collected by the ICILS instruments. The student questionnaire collected data on contextual factors pertaining to the level of the individual student and his or her home context. The teacher, school principal, and ICT-coordinator questionnaires were designed to locate contextual factors associated with the school/ classroom level, while the national contexts survey and other available sources (e.g., published statistics) were used to gather contextual data at the level of the wider community.

Table 1.1: Mapping of ICILS context variables to framework grid

Level of ...	Antecedents	Processes
Wider community	**NCS & other sources:** Structure of education Accessibilty of ICT	**NCS & other sources:** Role of ICT in curriculum
School/classroom	**PrQ, ICQ, & TQ:** School characteristics ICT resources	**PrQ, ICQ, & TQ:** ICT use in teaching
Student	**StQ:** Gender Age	**StQ:** ICT activities Use of ICT
Home environment	**StQ:** Parent SES ICT resources	**StQ:** Learning about ICT at home

Key: NCS = national contexts survey; PrQ = principal questionnaire; ICQ = ICT-coordinator questionnaire; TQ = teacher questionnaire; StQ = student questionnaire.

The wider community level

Contextual levels and variables

The different levels of this context all have the potential to affect student learning at school or at home. Conceptually, this context has several levels:

- *Local communities*, where remoteness and lack of stable and fast internet connections may affect conditions for ICT use;

- *Regional and national contexts*, where communication infrastructure, educational structures, curricula, and general economic/social factors may be of importance; and

- *Supranational or even international contexts*, where a long-term perspective brings in, for example, factors such as the general advance of ICT globally.

ICILS collected information about the contexts of education systems from published sources as well as through the national contexts survey. Typically, the published sources provided information about antecedent country-context variables while the national contexts survey delivered data on antecedent and process variables at the level of and with respect to the education system. The national contexts survey collected data on, for example, the following:

- Education policy and practice in CIL education (including curriculum approaches to CIL);

- Policies and practices for developing teachers' CIL expertise; and

- Current debates on and reforms to the implementation of digital technology in schools (including approaches to the assessment of CIL and the provision of ICT resources in schools).

Antecedent variables

International comparative research shows relatively strong associations between the general socioeconomic development of countries and student learning outcomes. ICILS therefore selected national and, where appropriate, subnational indicators related to general human development status regularly reported by the United Nations Development Programme (UNDP, 2009). The range of data relating to human development and ICT infrastructure that ICILS collected included measures of mobile phone and broadband connectivity, economic development (such as gross domestic product, income distribution, percentage of public expenditure on education), and ICT development. The latter drew on the ICT Development Index (IDI), which combines 11 indicators into a single measure that can be used as an index of ICT development in 154 countries. Alternatively, each indicator can be used separately.

Data on a range of other wider-community characteristics of the education systems participating in ICILS were also collected. System-level variables related to this aspect include length of schooling, age-grade profiles, educational finance, and structure of school education (e.g., study programs, public/private management), as well as the autonomy of educational providers.

The national (system) level

Process-related variables

The process-related variables on CIL-related education policy collected by the national contexts survey included:

- The definition of and the priority that each country gives to CIL education in its educational policy and provision;
- The name and national or official definition given to CIL education;
- The place of CIL education in educational reforms;
- The main aims and goals of CIL education; and
- The influence of different institutions or groups on decisions relating to these goals and aims.

Because the ICILS contextual framework references policies and practices developed as outcomes of earlier large-scale surveys of ICT in education, ICILS also considered process-related data in these studies' reports and databases. The studies examined included IEA SITES (Plomp, Anderson, Law, & Quale, 2009), the European Commission's Indicators of ICT in Primary and Secondary Education (European Commission, 2009b), and the International Experiences with Technology in Education survey, which covered policies and experiences in 21 countries (Bakia, Murphy, Anderson, & Trinidad, 2011).

The ICILS national contexts survey was used to collect data on:

- The model for including CIL education in the curriculum (i.e., as a separate subject, integrated into different subjects, or crosscurricular);
- The nomenclature for CIL-related curriculum subjects and whether they were compulsory or optional in each program of study; and
- The extent of emphasis in the curriculum on and the amount of instructional time given to CIL education at the target grade.

Another important process-related variable at the system level is the development of teacher expertise in CIL (Charalambos & Glass, 2007; Law et al., 2008). Teacher education programs often provide aspiring teachers with opportunities to develop CIL-related competencies. In ICILS, the national contexts survey and, where appropriate, the teacher, ICT-coordinator, and principal questionnaires were used to collect data on:

- The requirements for becoming a teacher;
- Licensing or certification procedures for teachers;
- The backgrounds of CIL teachers (as a definable class of teacher);
- The extent to which CIL education is part of preservice or initial teacher education;
- The availability of inservice or continuing professional development for CIL education;
- The personnel providing these professional learning activities; and
- The expectations for teachers' ongoing learning about developments in CIL education.

School/classroom level

Any study of students' acquisition of CIL must acknowledge the key role of school and classroom contexts in that acquisition. ICT use is becoming standard practice in education and employment. Helping students gain CIL is therefore an increasingly important part of the work that schools do to prepare young people for participation in modern society.

Factors associated with the school and classroom context were collected through the teacher, school principal, and ICT-coordinator questionnaires. The student questionnaire also included several questions gauging student perceptions about classroom practices related to ICT. Although ICILS did not attempt to investigate the relationship between ICT use in schools or classrooms and achievement in academic learning areas such as language, mathematics, and science, there is suggestion of positive associations in the results of a meta-analysis conducted by Tamin, Bernard, Borokhovski, Abrami, and Schmid (2011).

Antecedent variables

In line with the need to take school characteristics into account when investigating variations in CIL, the questionnaire given to each school principal collected information on student enrolment, teachers, the range of grades, and the location of each participating school. This questionnaire also collected information relating to school management (public or private), including details on who held responsibility for acquiring ICT resources.

The SITES 2006 findings indicated that school principals' views about the pedagogical value of ICT, as well as the ICT-related support teachers had at hand, influenced science teachers' and mathematics teachers' ICT use (Law et al., 2008). Findings also indicated that ICT-related teaching and learning was constrained or facilitated by the school's stated curriculum and its policies with regard to ICT. The ICILS principal questionnaire therefore collected data on the following factors:

- The extent to which the school had policies and procedures relating to ICT use;
- The extent to which the school prioritized ICT acquisition and resourcing;
- The principal's perception of the importance ascribed to ICT use in teaching at the school;
- The school-level expectations for teachers' knowledge of and skills in using ICT; and
- The extent to which teachers were participating in ICT-related professional development.

The ICILS questionnaire for each school's ICT-coordinator included questions on the availability of school-owned computing devices at school, their location within the school, how many students had access to them, which computer operating system the school mainly used, and the number of years the school had been using ICT. The instrument also collected data on the support (in terms of personnel and technology or software resources) the school provided for ICT use in teaching and learning. An additional question measured the coordinator's perceptions of the adequacy of the ICT on hand for learning and teaching at school.

Teachers' backgrounds and experiences have the potential to influence the acquisition of student CIL. Results from SITES 2006 indicated that teachers were more likely to use

ICT in their teaching when they had higher levels of self-confidence in using ICT in general (Law et al., 2008). SITES 2006 also indicated that, in most of the participating countries, ICT was more frequently used in science teaching than in mathematics teaching.

The ICILS teacher questionnaire therefore included questions on the general professional background of teaching staff (such as age, gender, subject taught at school) and on their ICT experience (number of years using ICT for teaching purposes, general use of computers at different locations, participation in ICT-related professional development activities, and perceived self-confidence in using ICT for different tasks). Teachers were also asked to give their views on the positive and negative consequences of using ICT for teaching and learning, and to identify any factors that they thought impeded using ICT for teaching and learning at their school.

Process-related variables

Researchers and commentators have for some time seen ICT in school education as having the potential to influence teaching and learning processes by enabling wider access to a range of resources, allowing greater power to analyze and transform information, and providing enhanced capacities to present information in different forms. However, some scholars have questioned the degree to which the ideal of ICT use in education has been reflected in classroom practice. Burbules (2007), for example, has argued that although e-learning technologies have the potential to bring transformative effects to classrooms, their implementation has been, for various reasons, surprisingly limited (see also Cuban, 2001).

In order to collect data on specific ICT-related teaching practices, the teachers participating in ICILS were asked to consider one of their classes (specified in the questionnaire) and to identify (where applicable) the types of ICT applications used in that class, the type of and extent to which ICT was used as part of teaching practices and for particular learning activities in that class, and the emphasis placed on developing ICT-based student capabilities. The questionnaire also asked teachers to give their perceptions of whether and how ICT was being used as part of collaborative teaching and learning at their school.

Actual student use of ICT in the learning process is another important factor. A segment of the teacher questionnaire therefore asked teachers to report on student involvement in different learning activities involving ICT use. The student questionnaire also asked students to report on how often they used computers at school, their use of computers for different school-related purposes, and the frequency with which they used ICT in their learning of different subjects.

Home level

Antecedent variables

ICILS collected data from students relating to a range of home background factors known from academic literature to relate to student learning outcomes in general and of specific relevance to consideration of CIL-related learning. These factors included:

- Parental (and student) socioeconomic status, measured through parental occupational status (Ganzeboom, de Graaf, & Treiman, 1992);
- Parental educational attainment;

- Home literacy resources;
- Language used at home;
- Whether or not students and their parents had an immigrant background; and
- Student access at home to digital resources, such as computers and other ICT devices.

Process-related variables

Home environment factors that potentially influence the learning process include the use of ICT in the home context and learning through interaction with family members. The student questionnaire therefore included questions about the extent to which students had learned about different aspects of ICT use from family and/or friends and how often they used computers at home in general.

Individual level

Antecedent variables

Antecedent variables at the level of the individual student consist of basic background characteristics that may influence students' CIL-related knowledge and skills. In this category, students provided data on their age, gender, and educational aspirations (i.e., the highest level of education they expected to complete).

Process-related variables

Applying ICT for different purposes on a regular basis has considerable potential to increase knowledge and skills in this area (see, for example, Australian Curriculum, Assessment and Reporting Authority, 2012; Fletcher, Schaffhauser, & Levin, 2012). The ICILS student questionnaire consequently contained questions about the frequency with which students used different ICT applications outside of school. This usage included using the internet for social communication and using ICT for recreational activities.

The student questionnaire also included items designed to measure the extent to which students were confident in completing a range of ICT-related tasks. According to Bandura (1993), students' confidence in their ability to carry out specific tasks in an area (self-efficacy) is strongly associated with their performance as well as their perseverance, emotions, and later study or career choices. Moos and Azevedo (2009) concluded from their review of research on computer self-efficacy that this variable plays an integral role in learning in computer-based learning environments.

The ICILS student questionnaire also collected information on students' enjoyment of using computers to complete tasks and on their ICT self-concept, both of which reflect their perceptions of their ability to cope with a certain learning area (Branden, 1994; Marsh & Shavelson, 1985). Scholars have found associations between both factors and students' effective use of ICT (see, for example, Dede, Ketelhut, Clarke, Nelson, and Bowman, 2005; OECD, 2005; Pekrun, Goetz, Titz, & Perry, 2002).

Data collection and ICILS instruments

The main survey data collection took place in the 21 participating countries between February and December 2013. Countries with a Northern Hemisphere school calendar completed the survey between February and June 2013; those with a Southern Hemisphere school calendar between October and December 2013. ICILS used six instruments to collect data: two for students, one for teachers, one for school ICT-coordinators, one for school principals, and one for staff in the study's national research centers.

The student instruments were delivered using purpose-designed software administered primarily via USB drives attached to school computers. In some cases, sets of notebook computers were provided to schools for the assessment. The software could have been delivered via the internet, but the USB delivery ensured a uniform assessment environment for students regardless of the quality of internet connections in participating schools. After administration of the student instruments, data were either uploaded to a server or delivered on the USB drives to national research centers.

The two student instruments were:

- *The international student test of computer and information literacy:* This consisted of questions and tasks presented in four 30-minute modules. A module was a set of questions and tasks based on a real-life theme and following a linear narrative structure. Each module had a series of small discrete tasks (each of which typically took less than a minute to complete) followed by a large task that typically took 15 to 20 minutes to complete. Each student completed two modules randomly allocated from the set of four. In total, the modules comprised 62 tasks and questions corresponding to 81 score points.

- *A 30-minute international student questionnaire:* This included questions relating to students' background characteristics, their experience of and use of computers and ICT to complete a range of different tasks in school and out of school, and their attitudes toward using computers and other forms of ICT.

The three instruments designed to gather information from and about teachers and schools could be completed on computer (over the internet) or on paper, depending on the availability of resources in schools and countries. These instruments were:

- *A 30-minute teacher questionnaire:* This asked some basic background questions followed by questions relating to teachers' reported use of ICT in teaching, their attitudes about the use of ICT in teaching, and their participation in professional learning activities relating to using ICT in teaching.

- *A 10-minute ICT-coordinator questionnaire:* This asked ICT-coordinators about the resources available in the school to support the use of ICT in teaching and learning. The questionnaire addressed both technological (e.g., infrastructure, hardware, software) as well as pedagogical support (e.g., through professional development learning).

- *A 10-minute principal questionnaire:* Principals provided information about school characteristics and school approaches to providing CIL-related teaching as well as about incorporating ICT in teaching and learning.

ICILS national research coordinators (NRCs) coordinated information procured from national experts in response to an online national contexts survey. This information concerned the structure of the country's education system, the presence and nature of CIL-related education in national curricula, and recent developments in CIL-related education.

The ICILS instruments were developed in three phases:

- Phase 1 encompassed writing the test and questionnaire items. This work was guided by the ICILS assessment framework. Before developing the tasks and items in detail, writers consulted with NRCs in order to reach agreement on module concepts. Instrument development also included extensive consultation with the study's national project coordinators and expert consultants.

- Phase 2 saw the instruments field trialed in all participating countries. Subsequent analysis of the collected data informed judgments about the suitability of the contents of each instrument for inclusion in the ICILS main survey data collection.

- Phase 3 included a final revision of the instruments in light of the field trial results and further feedback from national centers and expert consultants.

Given the importance of ensuring comparability and appropriateness of the measures in this study across the diverse range of participating countries, the ICILS field trial test and questionnaire data underwent a thorough review of crossnational validity.[2]

Report context and scope

This report presents the outcomes of the analyses of data collected across the 21 countries participating in the ICILS main survey in 2013. All data are reported at the international level.

Our aim in this report is to provide overarching international perspectives on the ICILS data relative to the ICILS research questions. Another aim is to provide researchers with observations and questions that may provide the catalyst for further investigation into CIL education within and across countries.

In addition to this current chapter, the report has eight others.

- Chapter 2 describes the national contexts for CIL education in ICILS countries. Here we address common patterns as well as policies, curriculum, resources, and practices in specific countries and groups of countries.

- In Chapter 3, we report on the levels of CIL proficiency across countries. We describe how the ICILS student test was used to measure CIL and present the ICILS scale of CIL proficiency. We also document variance in student achievement scores on the CIL scale across the participating countries.

- Chapter 4 focuses on the associations between aspects of student background and CIL. Also included is the contribution of aspects of student background to variations in CIL achievement.

- In Chapter 5, we draw on student questionnaire data to explore students' use of and engagement with ICT. Throughout the chapter, standardized scale indices are used to report students' use of and attitudes toward using ICT for a range of purposes. Gender-based differences in this regard and in terms of CIL achievement are also reported, and associations between individual and home characteristics with CIL achievement are identified.

- Our focus in Chapter 6 is on the roles of schools in CIL education. The data pertinent to this chapter derive mainly from the teacher, ICT-coordinator, and principal questionnaires. The chapter also describes variation in approaches to providing CIL-related education in schools.

---

2 Examples of the different approaches that were employed to assess measurement equivalence of questionnaire scales can be found in Schulz (2009).

- In Chapter 7, we examine the roles of teachers with respect to CIL education. We also use data from the teacher questionnaire to detail teachers' use of and attitudes toward the use of ICT in their teaching.

- Chapter 8 presents the outcomes of the multivariate and multilevel models that we used to explain variations in CIL within countries.

- Chapter 9 summarizes and discusses the results of ICILS. We also provide in this final chapter a summary of the main findings emerging from ICILS in relation to the research questions and discuss the possible implications of these for policy and practice.

CHAPTER 2:

The Contexts for Education on Computer and Information Literacy

Introduction

The contextual framework for ICILS (Fraillon, Schulz, & Ainley, 2013) emphasizes the importance of establishing students' learning environment when examining outcomes related to computer and information literacy (CIL). The framework distinguishes different levels of influence:

- *Individual*, including the learner's characteristics, learning process, and level of CIL;
- *Home environment*, including student background characteristics associated with family, home, and other proximal out-of-school contexts;
- *School and classroom*, encompassing in-school factors; and
- *Wider community*, encompassing broader contextual factors such as geographical remoteness and access to internet facilities.

In this chapter, we explore the national contexts for CIL education in the 21 ICILS countries. We primarily address Research Question 2 from the ICILS assessment framework: "*What aspects of schools and education systems are related to student achievement in computer and information literacy?*" Most of the emphasis with regard to this question is on its first subquestion concerning countries' "*general approach to computer and information literacy.*"

Our main purpose in this chapter is to describe the similarities and differences in CIL-related contexts across countries in order to provide information that can be used to aid interpretation of variations identified in the data gathered via the student, teacher, and school questionnaires. We begin the chapter by discussing the two data sources we use in it. We then describe the characteristics of the education systems of the participating ICILS countries and consider data relating to the infrastructure of and resources for CIL education. We conclude the chapter with a discussion of the different approaches to CIL education observed across and within the ICILS countries.

Collecting data on contexts for CIL education

In 2009 and 2010, the U.S. Department of Education conducted a study of international experiences with information and communication technology (ICT) in education (U.S. Department of Education, 2011). The study reviewed available data on government initiatives to integrate ICT into teaching and learning and conducted a survey that included interviews with officials of 21 governments[1] across the world. The study also covered such issues as providing infrastructure, improving student learning through the use of ICT, building capacity through ICT, and using ICT to support school improvement. In addition to generating an overview of practice and policy, the study profiled each of the 21 education systems (countries).

---

1 The countries were Australia, Austria, Belgium (Flemish Community), Canada (Alberta), Chile, Denmark, England, Estonia, France, Finland, Hong Kong (SAR, China), Iceland, Israel, Japan, Netherlands, New Zealand, Norway, Portugal, Republic of Korea, Singapore, and Sweden.

© International Association for the Evaluation of Educational Achievement (IEA) 2014
J. Fraillon et al., *Preparing for Life in a Digital Age*, DOI 10.1007/978-3-319-14222-7_3

The study's report pointed to ongoing investment in ICT for education, especially in terms of improved connectivity and student and teacher access to computers. It noted moves to integrate mobile technologies in learning environments and to adopt cloud computing. The report's authors observed that several countries had adopted learning management systems and even online instruction for students.

According to the report, most of the 21 countries regarded the development of teachers' capacities to use ICT in education as a priority. In many countries, there was evidence of teachers being provided with digital resources. Just under half of the countries were using online methods to provide professional development opportunities for teachers. Fewer than half of the countries (8 of the 21) had introduced online delivery of national assessments. The report also noted that the majority of countries (15 of the 21) had established standards for ICT competences among students. Most countries had also articulated in national documents visions "for integrating ICT into primary and secondary education."

As part of a 2011 report on learning and innovation through ICT at schools in Europe, the Eurydice network published a document reporting progress in ICT infrastructure provision across countries (Eurydice, 2011). The network explored how ICT was being used in educational processes and incorporated into curricula. It also looked at ICT's role in the development of innovative teaching methods. The network furthermore found that most European countries had comprehensive national strategies for using ICT in education. However, while these countries referred to the part that ICT can play in assessing competencies, they rarely indicated how such assessment should be implemented in practice. The study also identified within countries a gap between promoting ICT use in teaching and learning in official documents and actually implementing this practice.

A key feature of IEA studies is examination of links between the intended curriculum (what policy requires), the implemented curriculum (what is taught in schools), and the achieved curriculum (what students learn). IEA's Second Information Technology in Education Study (SITES) 2006 gathered information across 22 countries (education systems) on the intended curriculum with respect to ICT use in education (Plomp, Anderson, Law, & Quale, 2009).

The instrument used to collect this information was a questionnaire that asked each country to provide details about its national education system and structure, teacher preparation, change in pedagogical practices in the past five years, and system-wide policies and practice pertaining to ICT use in schools. The survey results identified differences across the countries in how ICT was being used in educational practice. The results also highlighted a lack of centralized policy in many countries for ensuring that teachers and students could actually use ICT-related technologies in their teaching and learning (Anderson & Plomp, 2010).

The main source of information in this chapter came from the data collected by the ICILS national context survey (NCS), which was designed to capture information about the intended curriculum for developing students' CIL capacity. The study by the U.S. Department of Education Office of Technology (2011) and the Second Information Technology in Education Study (SITES) 2006 (Plomp et al., 2009) informed development of the NCS. This work was conducted in consultation with ICILS national research coordinators and other experts. National research centers were asked to coordinate responses to the NCS and, where appropriate, to consult local experts. The latter included education ministry or department of education staff, relevant nongovernmental organizations, specialist organizations concerned with supporting the application of educational technologies, and teacher associations.

The information that the NCS collected was divided into five broad sections:

- Education system;
- Plans and policies for using ICT in education;
- ICT and student learning at lower-secondary level (ISCED 2);
- ICT and teacher development; and
- ICT-based learning and administrative management systems.

Because respondents from the respective participating countries provided much of the NCS data presented in this chapter, the information may not necessarily reflect the content of official published national documentation. Also, because the NCS specified that respondents answer questions in relation to what was occurring during the reference year in which the ICILS main survey took place in participating countries (the 2012/2013 school year for Northern Hemisphere countries, and the 2013 school year for Southern Hemisphere countries), the responses provided in this chapter may not reflect changes in countries that have happened since the time of data collection.

The second type of information used in this chapter focuses on antecedent variables sourced from established international databases. These enabled us to illustrate the relative global standing of each country in terms of economic indices and ICT infrastructure.

Characteristics of the education systems in participating ICILS countries

The first question in the NCS asked respondents to characterize who had responsibility for school-based education in their country and whether this responsibility resided primarily at a national ministry or department of education level, a state or provincial jurisdiction level, or some combination of authorities across levels. Table 2.1 provides a summary of the responses to this question.

Table 2.1 shows substantial variation in the characteristics of education systems at the national level. In a large proportion of these countries, a national ministry of education or other division of central government provides primary direction for planning and implementing educational policy at the school level. Often, aspects of management and administration are carried out at the local level but with the general direction for schools being defined nationally. In several countries, namely Australia, Germany, Switzerland, and the two participating Canadian provinces (Newfoundland and Labrador, and Ontario), the different states or provinces are largely autonomous in setting their own direction for education. This is also the case for Hong Kong SAR, which has autonomy with regard to its education policy. In the third group of education systems (Chile, the City of Buenos Aires, the Czech Republic, Denmark, Lithuania, and the Russian Federation), responsibilities are evenly balanced between national and state and provincial authorities. It is important when reading this report to note these differences across the participating countries' education systems.

Table 2.1: Levels of responsibility for school-based education

Country	Characterization of responsiblity for school education system
Australia	Each of the eight state and territory governments has authority for delivering school education, but must do so on the basis of some national guidance.
Chile	In this decentralized system, national agencies define policies, standards, and regulation, but municipalities and/or private entities administer them.
Croatia	The Croatian Ministry of Science, Education, and Sports is primarily responsible for school education.
Czech Republic	Responsibility for education is distributed across the central government, regions, and communities.
Denmark	The Danish Ministry of Education and the local municipalities share responsibility.
Germany	Each of the 16 federal states has sole responsibility for school education.
Hong Kong SAR	As a special administrative region of China, Hong Kong has total autonomy for delivery of school education.
Korea, Republic of	The national Ministry of Education has primary responsibility for the planning, operation and management of school-based education.
Lithuania	There is a balance in responsibilities between the national level and the state level (municipal council).
Netherlands	Responsibility for school education rests primarily with the National Ministry of Education, Culture, and Science.
Norway	The Ministry of Education and Research shares responsibility for administration and implementation of national educational policy with the National Directorate for Education and local municipalities.
Poland	The Minister of National Education has overall responsibility for setting national standards while local government units (*gmina*) are responsible for administering lower-secondary schools.
Russian Federation	Federal and regional authorities equally share responsibilities for school education.
Slovak Republic	The Ministry of Education, Science, Research, and Sport has primary responsibility for school education.
Slovenia	Responsibility for school education rests primarily with the Ministry of Education, Science, and Sport.
Switzerland	Responsibility for school education rests primarily with the 26 cantons.
Thailand	Responsibility for school education rests primarily with the Ministry of Education, Science, and Sport.
Turkey	The Ministry of National Education has primary responsibility for school education.
Benchmarking participants	
City of Buenos Aires, Argentina	The city of Buenos Aires shares responsibility for school education with the Argentinian National Ministry of Education.
Newfoundland and Labrador, Canada	There is no Canadian ministry or department of education. The province has full responsibility for education.
Ontario, Canada	There is no Canadian ministry or department of education. The province has full responsibility for education.

Note: Data collected from ICILS 2013 national contexts survey.

For those countries with more decentralized systems, the NCS responses, which form the basis for most of the remaining tables in this chapter, are represented as a summary or composite reflection of the national picture. Alternatively, the responses may represent the plans and policies of a particular populous region within the country, such as the North-Rhine-Westphalia state of Germany. Because it is beyond the scope of this report to explore and examine the fine detail of within-country differences in educational policies, interpretation of the country differences presented here needs to take into account the aggregated or selective nature of the NCS responses represented in the tables.

Table 2.2 illustrates the structures of the education systems in the participating countries. In most of the countries (16 out of the 21), the compulsory age for commencing school (not including compulsory pre-primary education) is six. Children in the Russian Federation cannot begin school until they are six and a half years of age. Students from the two Latin American participants (Chile and the City of Buenos Aires) and the Netherlands commence compulsory schooling at age five, whereas students in Lithuania and Poland commence schooling at seven. The number of years of compulsory schooling ranges from eight years in Croatia, up to 13 years in Chile.

Table 2.2 also includes information on the structure of school-based education in each country. The columns show the number of years typically spent at three levels of educational provision, classified according to the International Standard Classification of Education (ISCED) (UNESCO, 2006). ISCED 1 refers to primary education, ISCED 2 to lower-secondary education, and ISCED 3 to upper-secondary education.

Primary education across the 21 countries ranges in duration from between four and seven years, lower-secondary education between two and six years, and upper-secondary education between two and four years. In four countries, lower-secondary education is the second stage of basic education programs (indicated by an asterisk). Table 2.2 does not take into account differences within countries in the number of years of schooling across states and provinces. Nor does it take into account differences according to educational track (e.g., academic, vocational), particularly at the upper-secondary level.

Table 2.2 also shows the percentage of lower-secondary students attending public or government schools and the percentage attending private or other nongovernment schools. Note, however, that the definition of what constitutes a public or private school varies across countries in terms of the proportion of government funding received, school management, and degree of autonomy. In the majority of countries, greater proportions of students at the lower-secondary level attend government schools. Exceptions are the Netherlands and Chile, where the majority of students at this level attend private or other schools, and also the City of Buenos Aires, where the proportions attending the two school types are approximately equal.

The NCS asked the study's national centers to provide information on how much autonomy schools had over the following: school governance, acquisition and purchase of ICT equipment and software, provision of ICT-based inservice opportunities for staff, ICT curriculum planning and delivery, teacher recruitment, student assessment, and technical support for ICT. Table 2.3 summarizes the responses.

Table 2.2: Characteristics of education systems participating in ICILS: compulsory schooling, years of education by levels, and percentage lower-secondary students in private/public schools

Country	School Age		Typical Years of Education at Education Levels			Percentage of Lower-Secondary Students	
	Starting age	Years of compulsory schooling	ISCED 1 (primary)	ISCED 2 (lower secondary)	ISCED 3 (upper secondary)	Public or government schools	Private or other nongovernment schools
Australia	6	11	6	3	3	59	41
Chile	5	13	6	2*	4	42	58
Croatia	6	8	4	4	4	98	2
Czech Republic	6	9	5	4*	4	97	3
Denmark	6	10	7	2	3	80	20
Germany	6	10	4	6	3	98	2
Hong Kong SAR	6	9	6	3	3	81	19
Korea, Republic of	6	9	6	3	3	82	18
Lithuania	7	10	4	6	2	98	2
Netherlands	5	10–12	6	3	1–3	30	70
Norway	6	10	7	3	3	97	3
Poland	7	9	6	3	3	97	3
Russian Federation	6	11	4	5	2	99	1
Slovak Republic	6	10	4	5*	4	93	7
Slovenia	6	9	6	3*	4	100	0
Switzerland	6	9	6	3	3	94	6
Thailand	6	9	6	3	3	87	13
Turkey	6	12	6	2	4	95	5
Benchmarking participants							
City of Buenos Aires, Argentina	5	12	6	3	3	51	49
Newfoundland and Labrador, Canada	6	12	6	3	3	94	6
Ontario, Canada	6	12	6	2	4	95	5

Notes:

*ISCED 2 offered as second stage of combined ISCED 1+2 program.

Data on beginning age and years of compulsory schooling and percentage of students at public or private schools collected through ICILS 2013 national contexts survey.

Table 2.3: Degree of school autonomy regarding different aspects of school policies

Country	School Governance (e.g., School Governing Bodies/ Elected School Boards)	Acquisition/Purchase of ICT Equipment and Software	Provision of Opportunities for Staff to Participate in Inservice Education on Using ICT	ICT Curriculum Planning and Delivery	Teacher Recruitment	Student Assessment	Technical Support for ICT
Australia	◐	◐	●	●	◐	◐	◐
Chile	●	◐	●	◐	◐	●	●
Croatia	◐	●	●	●	●	●	●
Czech Republic	●	◐	●	◐	●	●	●
Denmark	◐	◐	◐	◐	◐	◐	◐
Germany	◐	◐	◐	◐	●	◐	◐
Hong Kong SAR	●	●	●	○	◐	●	●
Korea, Republic of	◐	◐	●	◐	●	●	●
Lithuania	◐	●	●	●	●	◐	●
Netherlands	●	●	●	◐	●	◐	◐
Norway	◐	◐	◐	◐	●	◐	●
Poland	●	●	●	○	●	◐	●
Russian Federation	●	●	●	◐	●	◐	●
Slovak Republic	◐	●	●	◐	●	●	●
Slovenia	◐	●	●	○	●	◐	◐
Switzerland	○	◐	◐	○	○	●	◐
Thailand	◐	◐	●	◐	◐	●	◐
Turkey	○	○	○	○	○	○	○
Benchmarking participants							
City of Buenos Aires, Argentina	◐	○	◐	◐	○	●	○
Newfoundland and Labrador, Canada	◐	◐	●	○	◐	◐	◐
Ontario, Canada	○	◐	◐	◐	◐	◐	◐

● Complete autonomy
◐ Some autonomy
○ No autonomy

Note: Data collected from ICILS 2013 national contexts survey.

In nearly all 21 countries, schools had at least some autonomy for each of these aspects of school management. The high proportion of "some autonomy" indicated in this table most commonly reflects national, state, or provincial policies or recommendations that individual schools have to follow, but within which they have autonomy to decide the most appropriate means of implementing them (e.g., with regard to purchasing equipment and conducting student assessment).

In every country but one, schools had some or complete autonomy over the types and frequency of inservice education on ICT use and student assessment offered to staff. Sixteen of the 21 participating countries indicated that schools had some autonomy with respect to ICT curriculum planning and delivery. In Turkey, where schools have no autonomy for these aspects of school policies, the Ministry of National Education centrally administers all such matters.

Infrastructure and resources for education in CIL

The countries participating in ICILS are diverse in terms of their ICT infrastructure and the ICT resources they have available for their respective populations. Table 2.4 presents data relating to ICT infrastructure (i.e., fixed broadband subscriptions per 100 people and ICT Development Index score[2] and ranking) and economic development (gross domestic product, income Gini coefficient,[3] and the percentage of public expenditure apportioned to education).

The number of fixed broadband subscriptions per 100 people provides an indicator of how widespread internet usage is in a country. Considerable variation with respect to this measure is evident in Table 2.4, with the range extending from 8 subscriptions per 100 people to 40 subscriptions per 100 people. The Netherlands, Switzerland, Korea, Denmark, and Norway each have more than 35 fixed broadband subscriptions per 100 people, whereas Chile, Thailand, and Turkey each have fewer than 15 subscriptions per 100 people.

Large variations can also be seen across countries for the selected economic statistics. Gross domestic product (GDP) per capita (expressed in 2005 international dollars using purchasing power parity rates and divided by the total population during the same period) is relatively higher for Norway, Switzerland, and the Netherlands than for the Russian Federation, Turkey, and Thailand.

Table 2.4 shows that on the basis of the ICT Development Index, the countries participating in ICILS are overall relatively well resourced. Eighteen of the 21 participating countries (or 20 if the two Canadian provinces are considered as one entity for the purpose of the index) had ICT Development Index rankings below 52, thus placing them in the upper third of all countries included in the rankings.

We can see from Table 2.4 that the values of the Gini income coefficient (a measure of the extent of variation in income across households) are relatively low for Denmark, the Czech Republic, and Norway, thus indicating a relatively equal income distribution.

---

2   The ICT Development Index (IDI) is a composite index that incorporates 11 different indicators relating to ICT readiness (infrastructure, access), ICT usage (individuals using the internet), and proxy indicators of ICT skills (adult literacy, secondary and tertiary enrolment). Each country is given a score out of 10 that can be used to provide a benchmarking measure to compare ICT development levels with other countries and within countries over time. Countries are ranked according to their IDI score.

3   The Gini income coefficient is a measure of the deviation of the distribution of income (or consumption) among individuals or households within a country from a perfectly equal distribution. A value of 0 represents absolute equality. A value of 100 represents absolute inequality (see United Nations Development Programme, 2010).

Table 2.4: Data on ICT infrastructure and economic characteristics in ICILS countries

Country	Fixed Broadband Subscriptions per 100 Inhabitants	ICT Development Index Score (and Country Rank)	Gross Domestic Product (GDP) per Capita (2005 PPP $)	Income Gini Coefficient	Public Expenditure on Education (% of GDP)
Australia	24.3	7.90 (11)	34,548	30.3[3]	5.1
Chile	12.3	5.46 (51)	15,272	52.1	4.5
Croatia	20.7	6.31 (38)	16,162	33.7	4.3
Czech Republic	16.4	6.40 (34)	23,967	24.9[3]	4.5
Denmark	38.8	8.35 (4)	32,399	24.8[3]	8.7
Germany	33.7	7.46 (19)	34,437	28.3	4.6
Hong Kong SAR	31.2	7.92 (10)	43,844	53.7[3]	3.6
Korea, Republic of	37.2	8.57 (1)	27,541	31.1[3]	5.0
Lithuania	21.1	5.88 (44)	16,877	37.6	5.7
Netherlands	39.8	8.00 (7)	37,251	30.9[3]	5.9
Norway	36.3	8.13 (6)	46,982	25.8	7.3
Poland	15.6	6.31 (37)	18,087	34.1	5.1
Russian Federation	14.5	6.19 (40)	14,808	40.1	4.1
Slovak Republic	14.7	6.05 (43)	20,757	26.0	4.1
Slovenia	24.3	6.76 (28)	24,967	31.2	5.7
Switzerland	40.1	7.78 (13)	37,979	33.7	5.4
Thailand	6.5	3.54 (95)	7,633	40.0	3.8
Turkey	10.6	4.64 (69)	13,466	39.0	2.9
Benchmarking participants					
City of Buenos Aires, Argentina	10.9[1]	5.36 (53)[1]	15,501[1]	44.5[1]	6.0[1]
Newfoundland and Labrador, Canada	32.5[2]	7.38 (20)[2]	35,716[2]	32.6[2]	4.8[2]
Ontario, Canada	32.5[2]	7.38 (20)[2]	35,716[2]	32.6[2]	4.8[2]

Notes:

Fixed broadband subscriptions, ICT Development Index Score, and country rank data relate to 2012 and were collected from the International Telecommunications Union. Source: http://www.itu.int/en/ITU-D/Statistics/Pages/stat/default.aspx [27/02/14].

Data on gross domestic product per capita, income gini coefficient, and public expenditure on education sourced from the *Human Development Report 2013* unless otherwise stated. Source: http://hdr.undp.org/sites/default/files/reports/14/hdr2013_en_complete.pdf [15/08/14].

Data on gross domestic product per capita relate to 2011.
Data for income Gini coefficients relate to the years 2000—2012.
Data for public expenditure on education relate to the years 2005—2010.
[1] Data relate to Argentina.
[2] Data relate to Canada.
[3] Data sourced from *CIA World Factbook*. Source: https://www.cia.gov/library/publications/the-world-factbook/ [15/08/14].

The relatively high values for Hong Kong SAR, Chile, and the City of Buenos Aires indicate unequal income distributions.

Table 2.4 furthermore includes each country's expenditure on education as a proportion of its GDP. Denmark, which spends almost nine percent of its GDP on education, has the highest proportion. The country with the lowest proportion is Turkey. It spends less than three percent of its GDP on education.

Approaches to CIL education in ICILS countries

In countries worldwide, ICT-related education policies are most likely to be defined at the central administrative level of the education system, with the relevant agencies either taking sole responsibility or working in cooperation with different bodies, including civil society organizations and educational institutions (Eurydice, 2011). The ICILS national context survey asked the national centers to indicate whether their countries had plans or policies from ministries or departments of education specifying support for ICT in education (see Table 2.5).

Only the national centers from the Netherlands, Korea, and Newfoundland and Labrador stated that their systems had no such plans or policies at the national, state, or provincial level. In the Netherlands, however, support is provided through Knowledge Net (*Kennisnet*), which although a nongovernment organization is government funded. While Korea had plans or policies regarding the use of ICT in education, these had been abolished by the time of the ICILS reference year.

All other 18 national centers indicated the presence of plans or policies regarding the use of ICT in education at either the national, state, or provincial level. Fourteen of these countries indicated support at both levels, whereas Switzerland and Ontario (Canada) stated that this support is evident only at the provincial level. In Slovenia and Thailand, support is available only at the national level.

All countries with existing plans and policies for using ICT stated that these include references to improving student learning of specific subject-matter content. Qualitative responses from countries indicated differences in what these references focus on. Some national centers, for example, mentioned ICT-related content within the context of specific subjects such as mathematics, sciences, and humanities; others mentioned crosscurricular themes or capabilities across several subjects.

Nearly all national centers identified the following as important aspects of educational policies and plans: preparing students to use ICT as a learning tool, development of information literacy, and development of ICT-based skills in critical thinking, collaboration, and communication. Between one and three countries indicated that one or more of these aspects are not referenced in educational policies and plans.

There was less support reported for increasing access to online courses of study for the benefit of particular groups of students (e.g., rural students). Only 11 countries said this type of support appears in their plans or policies. Qualitative comments helped explain the reason for the lack of such support in the policies and plans of the other countries. Slovenia, for example, stated that all school students have access to transport to school, and that the distances students needed to travel within the country are relatively small. This type of support is not applicable in the City of Buenos Aires because it is an urban jurisdiction.

Table 2.5: Support for ICT at schools by national and/or subnational authorities

Country	Plans or Policies Supporting the Use of ICT in Education	Inclusion in Plans and Policies of Reference to Aspects of Improving Student Learning				
		Subject-matter content (mathematics, science, etc)	Preparing students for ICT in their future work	Developing information literacy	ICT-based skills in critical thinking, collaboration and communication	Increasing access to online courses of study (e.g., for rural students)
Australia	◀	●	●	●	●	●
Chile	◀	●	○	●	●	●
Croatia	◀	●	●	●	○	○
Czech Republic	◀	●	●	●	●	○
Denmark	◀	●	●	●	●	○
Germany	◀	●	●	●	●	○
Hong Kong SAR	◀	●	●	●	●	●
Korea, Republic of	◇	N/A	N/A	N/A	N/A	N/A
Lithuania	◀	●	●	●	●	●
Netherlands	◇	N/A	N/A	N/A	N/A	N/A
Norway	◀	●	●	●	●	●
Poland	◀	●	●	●	●	○
Russian Federation	◀	●	○	○	○	●
Slovak Republic	◀	●	●	●	●	●
Slovenia	■	●	●	●	●	○
Switzerland	◆	●	●	●	●	○
Thailand	■	●	●	●	●	●
Turkey	◀	●	●	●	●	●
Benchmarking participants						
City of Buenos Aires, Argentina	◀	●	●	●	●	○
Newfoundland and Labrador, Canada	◇	N/A	N/A	N/A	N/A	N/A
Ontario, Canada	◆	●	●	●	●	●

Note: Data collected from ICILS 2013 national contexts survey.

◀ Support at national and state/provincial level ● Reference in plans or policies to using ICT in education
■ Support only at national level ○ No reference in plans or policies to using ICT in education
◆ Support only at state/provincial level
◇ No support at national or state/provincial level

The NCS also asked national centers if plans or policies for using ICT in education referenced seven different items regarding provision, maintenance, accessibility, and support of ICT resources. These data are shown in Table 2.6. Most of these items are referenced in 17 of the 18 countries with national and/or provincial plans. No such references are evident in Norway's plans or policies. In Norway, the local authorities (e.g., counties, municipalities, or schools) are responsible for these resources. Seventeen countries reported provision of computer equipment and other ICT resources, support for teachers when using such equipment, and teacher and student access to digital education resources. Sixteen countries reported internet connectivity, while 14 identified maintenance as well as renewal, updating, and replacement of computer equipment and other ICT resources. Fewer than half of the countries (nine) provided students and teachers with home-based access to school-based digital resources.

Table 2.7 summarizes information from the national centers about the extent to which their countries' plans or policies for using ICT included references to the following: methods of supporting student learning, providing computing in schools, and developing digital resources. With respect to ICT-related methods of supporting student learning, all 18 countries with existing plans and policies said these contained references to inservice teacher education in ICT use. Seventeen countries specified that this provision extended to preservice teacher education. Learning management systems and reporting to parents were referenced in the plans and policies of 11 and 12 countries respectively. Eleven of the 21 countries said there were references to using ICT to provide feedback to students.

Of the countries investing heavily in ICT infrastructure for educational purposes, many have implemented policies directed toward providing each child with access to his or her "own" computer for scholastic purposes. Research in this area suggests a link between this policy and increased academic performance (Bebell, Kay, Suhr, Hernandez, Grimes, & Warschauer, 2010) and that the policy encourages students to be more engaged in their learning, better behaved at school, and more motivated to learn (Sauers & McLeod, 2012).

Table 2.7 includes data showing which countries specify a 1:1 school-based computer–student ratio in their ICT-related education policies and plans. National centers in 11 countries reported this ratio. The information provided by the national centers showed considerable variation in how countries implement this policy, however. Some have implemented it only at a specific level (e.g., in upper-secondary education) or in a specific state or province, whereas others have carried out implementation only on a trial basis in order to evaluate benefit. Variation also exists in the type of computers provided (tablets, notebooks) and the ownership model (i.e., purchased by schools, purchased by students, leased by students, or use of external student-owned computers).

The qualitative responses from the national centers also revealed differences in countries' use and interpretation of the term 1:1 computing. Most countries interpreted 1:1 computing as meaning that every student had access to a computer for all of their studies. However, in Poland, for example, the 1:1 computing policy signifies that each student has access to a computer in a computer laboratory but only for specific instruction in computing and not for other subjects. More than one national center emphasized that despite the country having an official 1:1 computing policy, it had not been implemented in practice.

Table 2.6: References in plans or policies to provision of ICT resources

Country	Inclusion in Plans and Policies of Reference to ICT Resources						
	Provision of computer equipment and other ICT resources	Maintenance of computer equipment and other ICT resources	Renewal, updating, and replacement of computer equipment and other ICT resources	Support for teachers for using computer equipment and other ICT resources in their work	Access to digital educational resources	Internet connectivity	Home access to school-based digital education resources
Australia	●	●	●	●	●	●	●
Chile	●	●	●	●	●	●	○
Croatia	●	○	●	●	●	●	○
Czech Republic	●	●	○	●	●	●	●
Denmark	●	●	●	●	●	●	●
Germany	●	●	●	●	●	○	○
Hong Kong SAR	●	●	●	●	●	●	●
Korea, Republic of	N/A	N/A	N/A	N/A	N/A	N/A	N/A
Lithuania	●	○	○	●	●	●	●
Netherlands	N/A	N/A	N/A	N/A	N/A	N/A	N/A
Norway	○	○	○	○	○	○	○
Poland	●	○	○	●	●	●	○
Russian Federation	●	○	○	●	●	●	○
Slovak Republic	●	●	●	●	●	●	●
Slovenia	●	●	●	●	●	●	●
Switzerland	●	●	●	●	●	●	○
Thailand	●	●	●	●	●	●	○
Turkey	●	●	●	●	●	●	●
Benchmarking participants							
City of Buenos Aires, Argentina	●	●	●	●	●	●	○
Newfoundland and Labrador, Canada	N/A	N/A	N/A	N/A	N/A	N/A	N/A
Ontario, Canada	●	●	●	●	●	●	●

Note: Data collected from ICILS 2013 national contexts survey.

● Reference in plans or policies to using ICT in education   ○ No reference in plans or policies to using ICT in education

Table 2.7: References in plans or policies to using ICT to support student learning, provide computing in schools, and develop digital resources

Country	Inclusion in Plans and Policies of Reference to ICT Resources					Reference to Providing 1:1 Computing in Schools	Formal Support for Development of Digital Resources
	Preservice teacher education in the use of ICT	Inservice teacher education in the use of ICT	The use of learning management systems	Reporting to parents	Providing feedback to students		
Australia	●	●	●	●	●	●	●
Chile	●	●	●	●	●	●	●
Croatia	●	●	○	●	●	○	●
Czech Republic	●	●	○	●	○	●	●
Denmark	●	●	○	●	○	●	●
Germany	●	●	○	○	●	○	●
Hong Kong SAR	○	●	●	●	●	○	●
Korea, Republic of	N/A	N/A	N/A	N/A	N/A	N/A	●
Lithuania	●	●	●	○	○	●	●
Netherlands	N/A	N/A	N/A	N/A	N/A	N/A	●
Norway	●	●	●	●	●	●	●
Poland	●	●	○	○	○	●	●
Russian Federation	●	●	●	●	●	○	●
Slovak Republic	●	●	●	●	●	○	●
Slovenia	●	●	●	●	●	●	●
Switzerland	●	●	○	○	○	○	○
Thailand	●	●	●	○	○	●	●
Turkey	●	●	●	●	●	●	●
Benchmarking participants							
City of Buenos Aires, Argentina	●	●	○	○	○	●	○
Newfoundland and Labrador, Canada	N/A	N/A	N/A	N/A	N/A	N/A	●
Ontario, Canada	●	●	●	●	●	○	●

Note: Data collected from ICILS 2013 national contexts survey.

● Reference in plans or policies to using ICT in education   ○ No reference in plans or policies to using ICT in education

Table 2.7 also presents data generated by a question that asked national centers if their countries' policies and plans specified formal support for the development of digital resources. Responses showed that 19 countries have policies or plans that include this support. Of the two countries that indicated no such support, Switzerland said that while some of its cantons provide it, governmental agencies generally encourage publishers to produce digital resources. In the City of Buenos Aires, educational authorities produce these resources or outsource this work to external agencies. The Eurydice report on learning and innovation through ICT at school (Eurydice, 2011) found that some countries teach ICT as a separate subject largely at the secondary level. In addition, some of these countries, along with a number of other countries, use ICT in a crosscurricular manner, thereby helping students develop various ICT skills during the learning of other subjects as well as aiding students' learning of those subjects. The NCS therefore asked respondents to provide information about the types of ICT-related subjects their countries offer at different stages of school education. Table 2.8 presents a summary of this information.

Nine of the 21 ICILS countries reported having a separate ICT-related subject at the primary level (ISCED 1). Eight of the national centers stated that this subject is compulsory in their countries. One national center (Hong Kong SAR) stated that although this subject is not compulsory, schools are required to meet the mandatory ICT curriculum requirements. Schools can address this mandate either by establishing a separate ICT subject or by integrating ICT into their teaching of existing school subjects.

At the lower-secondary level (ISCED 2), 18 of the 21 national centers said that their countries have an ICT-related subject. This subject is compulsory in 11 of these countries and noncompulsory in the remaining seven. The names given to this subject, also included in Table 2.8, are fairly diverse, although some commonalities are apparent given terms such as "informatics," "computer science," and "technology." Many countries reported considerable within-country variation in this regard, and stated that the name and characteristics of the subject could vary at state, provincial, or even individual school level.

Table 2.8 shows that while 13 of the ICILS countries require assessment of students' ICT capabilities, the assessments are defined at school level. Each of these 13 countries had an ICT-related subject, but the subject was compulsory in only nine. In some of the eight countries where there is no requirement to assess ICT capabilities, such capabilities are assessed as part of broader assessments in other subjects. Eight countries reported having a program designed to monitor ICT competences, with the program established at either the national, state, or provincial level.

Five countries reported having diagnostic assessment; six reported having formative assessment. Eight countries said their ministries or departments of education provide support for conducting summative assessments, and nine indicated that these agencies provide support for digital resources, such as e-portfolios.

Links have been found between teachers' capacity to utilize ICT effectively and increased student engagement with these technologies (European Commission, 2013). Of the 22 education systems that participated in SITES 2006, only seven had ICT-related requirements for teacher certification and only nine had formal requirements for key types of ICT-related professional development (Law, Pelgrum, & Plomp 2008). The

Table 2.8: ICT-related subjects at different levels of schooling and ICT assessment policies

Country	ICT-Related Subjects				Requirement at School Level Regarding Assessment and Monitoring of ICT and Computing Skills of Target Grade Students	ICT Student Assessments Used or Supported by Ministries or Departments of Education				
	ISCED 1 (primary)	ISCED 2 (lower secondary)	ISCED 3 (upper secondary)	Subject name at lower-secondary level		Diagnostic assessments	Formative assessments	Summative assessments	National or state/provincial monitoring programs	Digital work products (e.g., e-portfolio)
Australia	◆[1]	◆[1]	▲[1]	Defined at state/territory or school level	●	●	●	●	●	●
Chile	◆	◆		Technological education	●	○	○	○	●	○
Croatia		◀	◀	Information science	●	○	○	○	○	○
Czech Republic	◆	◆	◆	Defined at school level (e.g., informatics, basics of informatics)	●	○	○	○	●	○
Denmark			◀		○	○	○	○	○	●
Germany		◀	◀	Applied computer science (*informatik*)	○	○	○	○	○	○
Hong Kong SAR	▲[2]	▲[2]	◀	Defined at school level (e.g., information technology, computer studies, computer literacy)	●	●	●	●	○	●
Korea, Republic of		◀	◀	Informatics	○	○	○	●	○	○
Lithuania		◆	◀	Information technologies	●	○	○	●	○	○
Netherlands			◀		○	●	●	●	○	○
Norway			◆		○	●	●	●	●	●
Poland	◆	◆	◆	Computer science	●	○	○	○	●	●
Russian Federation		◆	◆	Informatics and ICT	○	○	○	●	○	○
Slovak Republic	◆	◆	◆	Informatics	●	○	○	○	○	○
Slovenia		◀	◆	Computer studies (word-processing, networks and multimedia)	●	○	○	○	○	●
Switzerland		◀	◆	Defined at canton level (e.g., informatics, *dactylo*, media formation)	○	○	○	○	●	○
Thailand	◆	◆	◆	Information and communication technology (ICT)	●	○	○	○	○	●
Turkey	◆	◆	◀	Information technologies and programming	●	○	○	○	○	○

Table 2.8: ICT-related subjects at different levels of schooling and ICT assessment policies (contd.)

Country	ICT-Related Subjects				Requirement at School Level Regarding Assessment and Monitoring of ICT and Computing Skills of Target Grade Students	ICT Student Assessments Used or Supported by Ministries or Departments of Education				
	ISCED 1 (primary)	ISCED 2 (lower secondary)	ISCED 3 (upper secondary)	Subject name at lower-secondary level		Diagnostic assessments	Formative assessments	Summative assessments	National or state/provincial monitoring programs	Digital work products (e.g., e-portfolio)
Benchmarking participants										
City of Buenos Aires, Argentina	◆	◆		Technology, computer studies/informatics	○	○	○	○	○	○
Newfoundland and Labrador, Canada		◆	◀		●	○	○	○	●	●
Ontario, Canada		◀	◀		●	●	●	●	●	●

Notes:

Data collected from ICILS 2013 national contexts survey.

1 Variation across states/provinces as to whether subject is compulsory/noncompulsory.

2 Schools have autonomy as to whether ICT curriculum requirements are met in ICT subject or integrated into existing subjects.

◆ Compulsory subject

◀ Noncompulsory subject

● Reference in plans or policies on using ICT in education

○ No reference in plans or policies on using ICT in education

2011 Eurydice study on learning and innovation through ICT in European schools reported that teachers were more likely to acquire their ICT teaching skills during their preservice education than in schools (Eurydice, 2011).

The NCS asked national centers to indicate if their countries refer to ability to use ICT in their teacher registration requirements. Centers were also asked if teachers' preservice and inservice education help teachers acquire this ability. In addition to technical capacity to use ICT, the aspects of ability specified included using ICT for pedagogical purposes, using ICT for collaboration and communication, and using ICT for student assessment. The data in Table 2.9 show that most of the ICILS countries help teachers acquire various aspects of ICT proficiency during their preservice and inservice education. The only countries where the above aspects of ICT proficiency are required for teacher registration are Australia and Turkey. In Thailand, knowing how to use ICT for pedagogical purposes is a teacher registration requirement.

Fifteen of the 21 national centers in the participating countries said that national, state, or provincial documentation pertaining to preservice teacher education specifies technical capacity in using ICT. Several of the remaining six centers said that in their countries preservice teacher education institutions can autonomously determine the ICT-related content of their curricula.

Most national centers said their countries provide teacher education (both preservice and inservice) focused on using ICT in pedagogy. Seventeen countries provide this support at the preservice level (with support varying across the different states of Germany), and 18 countries at the inservice level. There is less support for collaboration and communication using ICT and for using ICT for student assessment at the preservice level (12 and 10 countries respectively), but greater support for these two aspects at the inservice level (18 and 15 countries respectively).

The data presented in Table 2.10 show the extent to which ministries or departments of education at the national, state, or provincial level support teacher access to and participation in ICT-based professional development for a range of purposes. All countries, with the exception of the Netherlands, indicated at least some support for three of the five. In the Netherlands, it appears that although professional development activities are available (through *Kennisnet*), they are not explicitly supported.

Improvement of ICT/technical skills and the integration of ICT in teaching and learning activities were the two most common purposes and were reported in 20 out of the 21 countries. According to these data, 19 countries supported improvement of content knowledge, improvement of teaching skills, and integration of ICT in teaching and learning activities. The national centers from 18 countries indicated at least some degree of ministerial or departmental support for development of digital resources. Australia and Turkey accord a large degree of support for each of the five listed purposes of ICT-based professional development. The Chilean, Czech Republic, Slovenian, and Thai national centers indicated a large measure of support for at least some of these purposes. Although, in the Netherlands, teachers can access professional development activities relating to these purposes, there is no documented support at the ministry level for them.

Table 2.9: Support and requirements for developing teachers' capacity to use ICT

Country	Technical Capacity in Using ICT	Using ICT in Pedagogy	Collaboration and Communication in Using ICT	Using ICT for Student Assessment
Australia	● ▲ ■	● ▲ ■	● ▲ ■	● ▲ ■
Chile	● ■	● ■	■	■
Croatia	■	● ■	● ■	■
Czech Republic	● ■	● ■	● ■	● ■
Denmark	■	● ■	■	■
Germany		●		
Hong Kong SAR	● ■	● ■	● ■	● ■
Korea, Republic of	● ■	● ■	■	■
Lithuania	● ■	● ■	■	■
Netherlands	● ■	● ■	● ■	● ■
Norway	●	●	●	●
Poland	● ■	● ■	● ■	● ■
Russian Federation	● ■	● ■	● ■	● ■
Slovak Republic	● ■	● ■	● ■	● ■
Slovenia	● ■	● ■	■	
Switzerland	●			
Thailand	● ■	● ▲ ■	● ■	● ■
Turkey	● ▲ ■	● ▲ ■	● ▲ ■	● ▲ ■
Benchmarking participants				
City of Buenos Aires, Argentina	■	■		
Newfoundland and Labrador, Canada	● ■	● ■	● ■	■
Ontario, Canada	■	■	■	■

Note: Data collected from ICILS 2013 national contexts survey.

● Supported in preservice teacher education

▲ Requirement for registration as a teacher

■ Supported in inservice teacher education or training

Table 2.10: Level of support for teacher access to and participation in ICT-based professional development

Country	To Improve ICT/Technical Skills	To Improve Content Knowledge	To Improve Teaching Skills	To Develop Digital Resources	To Integrate ICT in Teaching and Learning Activities
Australia	●	●	●	●	●
Chile	●	●	●	◐	●
Croatia	◐	◐	◐	◐	◐
Czech Republic	◐	◐	◐	●	●
Denmark	◐	◐	◐	◐	◐
Germany	◐	◐	◐	◐	◐
Hong Kong SAR	◐	◐	◐	◐	◐
Korea, Republic of	◐	◐	◐	◐	◐
Lithuania	◐	◐	◐	◐	◐
Netherlands	○	○	○	○	○
Norway	◐	◐	◐	◐	◐
Poland	◐	◐	◐	◐	◐
Russian Federation	◐	◐	◐	◐	◐
Slovak Republic	◐	◐	◐	◐	◐
Slovenia	◐	○	●	●	●
Switzerland	◐	◐	○	○	◐
Thailand	●	●	●	◐	●
Turkey	●	●	●	●	●
Benchmarking participants					
City of Buenos Aires, Argentina	◐	◐	◐	◐	◐
Newfoundland and Labrador, Canada	◐	◐	◐	◐	◐
Ontario, Canada	◐	◐	◐	◐	◐

Note: Data collected from ICILS 2013 national contexts survey.

● To a large extent
◐ To some extent
○ Not at all

Conclusion

This chapter highlighted differences across countries in terms of the characteristics of their education systems, ICT infrastructure, and approaches to ICT in education (as set down in national policies and plans). In some countries, responsibility for school education is centralized through the national ministry or department of education. In other countries, states or provinces have an equal or greater share of the responsibility. The differences in education systems extend to the number of years students spend at the different school levels, and the relative percentages of public and private schools. In most countries, schools have at least some level of autonomy for decision-making, but less so for aspects such as teacher recruitment.

Antecedent data sourced from international databases show large differences across countries with respect to ICT infrastructure and economic indices. Data from the ICILS national context survey brought to light countries' plans or policies relating to ICT use in education. This information shows that, in most countries, there is support for this use at the national, state, or provincial level. Policies and plans mostly include strategies for improving and supporting student learning via ICT and providing ICT resources.

Differences across countries also exist in relation to inclusion of an ICT-related subject in schools, particularly at the primary and lower-secondary levels of education. The name given to this subject and whether or not it is compulsory varies both across and within countries. Fewer than half of the participating countries reported ministerial or departmental support for using ICT in order to conduct a range of student assessments.

Responses to NCS questions on teacher capacity to use ICT showed this ability is rarely a requirement for teacher registration. However, in most countries support was provided for teacher acquisition of ICT expertise and knowledge during preservice and inservice education. In general, ICILS countries provide teachers with opportunities to access and participate in different areas of ICT-based professional development.

Although this chapter described differences in how countries approach ICT use in education, we can see evidence of a common theme across countries—that of wanting to educate and engage students in ICT use. However, countries differ in terms of the priority they accord this goal and in what they are doing to achieve it.

Overall, the information provided in this chapter should provide readers with an understanding of the contexts in which ICT-related education in the participating ICILS countries plays out. It should also aid interpretation of data pertaining to the student, teacher, and school levels presented in subsequent chapters.

CHAPTER 3:

Students' Computer and Information Literacy

The ICILS *Assessment Framework* defines computer and information literacy (CIL) as an "individual's ability to use computers to investigate, create, and communicate in order to participate effectively at home, at school, in the workplace, and in the community" (Fraillon, Schulz, & Ainley, 2013, p. 18). According to the framework, CIL comprises two strands, each of which is specified in terms of a number of aspects. The strands describe CIL in terms of its two main purposes: receptive (collecting and managing information) and productive (producing and exchanging information). The aspects further articulate CIL in terms of the main processes applied within each strand. These are knowing about and understanding computer use, accessing and evaluating information, managing information, transforming information, creating information, sharing information, and using information safely and securely.

In this chapter, we detail the measurement of CIL in ICILS and discuss student achievement across ICILS countries. We begin the chapter by describing the CIL assessment instrument and the proficiency scale derived from the ICILS test instrument and data. We also describe and discuss the international student test results relating to computer and information literacy.

The content of this chapter relates to ICILS Research Question 1, which focuses on the extent of variation existing among and within countries with respect to student computer and information literacy.

Assessing CIL

Because ICILS is the first international comparative research study to focus on students' acquisition of computer and information literacy, the ICILS assessment instrument is also unique in the field of crossnational assessment. The instrument's design built on existing work in the assessment of digital literacy (Binkley et al., 2012; Dede, 2009) and ICT literacy (Australian Curriculum, Assessment and Reporting Authority, 2012). It also included the following essential features of assessment in this domain:

- Students completing tasks solely on computer;
- The tasks having a real-world crosscurricular focus;
- The tasks combining technical, receptive, productive, and evaluative skills; and
- The tasks referencing safe and ethical use of computer-based information.

In order to ensure standardization of students' test experience and comparability of the resultant data, the ICILS instrument operates in a "walled garden," which means students can explore and create in an authentic environment without the comparability of student data being potentially contaminated by differential exposure to digital resources and information from outside the test environment.

The assessment instrument was developed over a year in consultation with the ICILS national research coordinators (NRCs) and other experts in the field of digital literacy and assessment. Questions and tasks were first created as storyboards, before

© International Association for the Evaluation of Educational Achievement (IEA) 2014
J. Fraillon et al., *Preparing for Life in a Digital Age*, DOI 10.1007/978-3-319-14222-7_4

being authored into the computer-based delivery system. The results of the ICILS field trial, conducted in 2012, were used to inform the content of and refine the final assessment instrument. The ICILS technical report (Fraillon, Schulz, Friedman, Ainley, & Gebhardt, forthcoming) provides more information about the development of the ICILS assessment instrument.

The questions and tasks making up the ICILS test instrument were presented in four modules, each of which took 30 minutes to complete. Each student completed two modules randomly allocated from the set of four. Full details of the ICILS assessment design, including the module rotation sequence and the computer-based test interface, can be found in the ICILS *Assessment Framework* (Fraillon et al., 2013, pp. 36–42).

More specifically, a module is a set of questions and tasks based on an authentic theme and following a linear narrative structure. Each module has a series of smaller discrete tasks,[1] each of which typically takes less than a minute to complete, followed by a large task that typically takes 15 to 20 minutes to complete. The narrative of each module positions the smaller discrete tasks as a mix of skill execution and information management tasks that students need to do in preparation to complete the large task.

When beginning each module, the ICILS students were presented with an overview of the theme and purpose of the tasks in the module as well as a basic description of what the large task would comprise. Students were required to complete the tasks in the allocated sequence and could not return to review completed tasks. Table 3.1 includes a summary of the four ICILS assessment modules and large tasks.

Table 3.1: Summary of ICILS test modules and large tasks

Module	Description and Large Task
After-School Exercise	Students set up an online collaborative workspace to share information and then select and adapt information to create an advertising poster for the after-school exercise program.
Band Competition	Students plan a website, edit an image, and use a simple website builder to create a webpage with information about a school-band competition.
Breathing	Students manage files and evaluate and collect information to create a presentation to explain the process of breathing to eight- or nine-year-old students.
School Trip	Students help plan a school trip using online database tools and select and adapt information to produce an information sheet about the trip for their peers. The information sheet includes a map created using an online mapping tool.

Data collected from the four test modules shown in Table 3.1 were used to measure and describe CIL in this report. In total, the data comprised 81 score points derived from 62 discrete questions and tasks. Just over half of the score points were derived from criteria associated with the four large tasks. Students' responses to these tasks were scored in each country by trained expert scorers. Data were only included where they met or exceeded the IEA technical requirements. The ICILS technical report (Fraillon et al., forthcoming) provides further information on adjudication of the test data.

---

1 These tasks can be described as discrete because, although connected by the common narrative, students completed each one sequentially without explicit reference to the other tasks.

As noted previously, the ICILS assessment framework has two strands, each specified in terms of several aspects. The strands describe CIL in terms of its two main purposes (receptive and productive), while the aspects further articulate CIL in terms of the main (but not exclusive) constituent processes used to address these purposes. We used this structure primarily as an organizational tool to ensure that the full breadth of the CIL construct was included in its description and would thereby make the nature of the construct clear.

The following bulleted list sets out the two strands and corresponding aspects of the CIL framework. Also included are the respective percentages of score points attributed to each strand in total and to each aspect within the strands.

- Strand 1, Collecting and managing information, comprising three aspects, 33 percent:
    - Aspect 1.1: Knowing about and understanding computer use, 13 percent;
    - Aspect 1.2: Accessing and evaluating information, 15 percent;
    - Aspect 1.3: Managing information, 5 percent.

- Strand 2, Producing and exchanging information, comprising four aspects, 67 percent:
    - Aspect 2.1: Transforming information, 17 percent;
    - Aspect 2.2: Creating information, 37 percent;
    - Aspect 2.3: Sharing information, 1 percent;
    - Aspect 2.4: Using information safely and securely, 12 percent.

As stated in the ICILS *Assessment Framework*, "… the test design of ICILS was not planned to assess equal proportions of all aspects of the CIL construct, but rather to ensure some coverage of all aspects as part of an authentic set of assessment activities in context" (Fraillon et al., 2013, p. 43). Approximately twice as many score points relate to Strand 2 as to Strand 1, proportions that correspond to the amount of time the ICILS students were expected to spend on each strand's complement of tasks. The first three aspects of Strand 2 were assessed primarily via the large tasks at the end of each module, with students expected to spend roughly two thirds of their working time on these tasks.

Each test completed by a student consisted of two of the four modules. Altogether, there were 12 different possible combinations of module pairs. Each module appeared in six of the combinations—three times as the first and three times as the second module when paired with each of the other three. The module combinations were randomly allocated to students. This test design made it possible to assess a larger amount of content than could be completed by any individual student and was necessary to ensure a broad coverage of the content of the ICILS assessment framework. This design also controlled for the influence of item position on difficulty across the sampled students and provided a variety of contexts for the assessment of CIL.

We used the Rasch IRT (item response theory) model (Rasch, 1960) to derive the cognitive scale from the data collected from the 62 test questions and tasks. In this report, the term *item* refers to a unit of analysis based on scores associated with student responses to a question or task. Most questions and tasks each corresponded to one item. However, each ICILS large task was scored against a set of criteria (each criterion with its own unique set of scores) relating to the properties of the task. Each large task assessment criterion is therefore also an item in ICILS.

We set the final reporting scale to a metric that had a mean of 500 (the *ICILS average score*) and a standard deviation of 100 for the equally weighted national samples. We used plausible value methodology with full conditioning to derive summary student achievement statistics. This approach enables estimation of the uncertainty inherent in a measurement process (see, in this regard, von Davier, Gonzalez, & Mislevy, 2009). The ICILS technical report provides details on the procedures the study used to scale test items (Fraillon et al., forthcoming).

The CIL described achievement scale

The ICILS described scale of CIL achievement is based on the content and scaled difficulties of the assessment items. As part of the test development process, the ICILS research team wrote descriptors for each item in the assessment instrument. These item descriptors, which also reference the ICILS assessment framework, describe the CIL knowledge, skills, and understandings demonstrated by a student correctly responding to each item.

Pairing the scaled difficulty of each item with the item descriptors made it possible to order the items from least to most difficult, a process that produces an item map. Analysis of the item map and student achievement data were then used to establish proficiency levels that had a width of 85 scale points and level boundaries at 407, 492, 576, and 661 scale points.[2] Student scores below 407 scale points indicate CIL proficiency below the lowest level targeted by the assessment instrument.

The described CIL scale was developed on the basis of a transformation of the original item calibration so that the relative positions of students' scaled scores and the item difficulties would represent a response probability of 0.62. Thus, a student with ability equal to that of the difficulty of a given item on the scale would have a 62 percent chance of answering that item correctly.

The width of the levels was 85 scale points. We can assume that students achieving a score corresponding to the lower boundary of a level correctly answered about 50 percent of items in that level. We can also expect that students with scores within a level (above the lower boundary) correctly answered more than 50 percent of the items in that level. Thus, once we know where a student's proficiency score is located within a given level, we can expect that he or she will have correctly answered at least half of the questions for that level, regardless of the location of his or her score within the level.

The scale description comprises syntheses of the common elements of CIL knowledge, skills, and understanding at each proficiency level. It also describes the typical ways in which students working at a level demonstrate their proficiency. Each level of the scale references the characteristics of students' use of computers to access and use information and to communicate with others. The scale thus reflects a broad range of development, extending from students' application of software commands under direction, through their increasing independence in selecting and using information to communicate with others, and on to their ability to independently and purposefully select information and use a range of software resources in a controlled manner in order to communicate with others. Included in this development is students' knowledge and understanding of issues relating to online safety and ethical use of electronic

---

2   The level boundaries and width have been rounded to the nearest whole number. The level width and boundaries to two
    decimal places are 84.75 and 406.89, 491.63, 576.38 and 661.12.

information. This understanding encompasses knowledge of information types and security procedures through to demonstrable awareness of the social, ethical, and legal consequences of a broad range of known and unknown users (potentially) accessing electronic information.

In summary, the developmental sequence that the CIL scale describes has the following underpinnings: knowledge and understanding of the conventions of electronic information sources and software applications, ability to critically reason out and determine the veracity and usefulness of information from a variety of sources, and the planning and evaluation skills needed to create and refine information products for specified communicative purposes.

The scale is hierarchical in the sense that CIL proficiency becomes more sophisticated as student achievement progresses up the scale. We can therefore assume that a student located at a particular place on the scale because of his or her achievement score will be able to undertake and successfully accomplish tasks up to that level of achievement.

Before constructing the scale, we examined the achievement data in order to determine if the test was measuring more than one aspect of CIL in discernibly different and conceptually coherent ways. Given the distinction in the ICILS assessment framework between Strands 1 and 2, we investigated whether the data were indeed describing and reporting these separately.

We found a latent correlation between student achievement on the two strands of 0.96. We also found that the mean achievement of students across countries varied little when we analyzed the data from Strands 1 and 2 separately. As a consequence, and in the absence of any other dimensionality evident in the data,[3] we concluded that CIL could be reported in a single achievement scale. Although the ICILS assessment framework leaves open the possibility that CIL may comprise more than one measurement dimension, it does "not presuppose an analytic structure with more than one subscale of CIL achievement" (Fraillon et al., 2013, p. 19).

Table 3.2 shows the described CIL scale. The table includes descriptions of the scale's contents and the nature of the progression across the proficiency levels from 1 to 4. A small number of test items had scaled difficulties below Level 1 of the scale. These items represented execution of the most basic skills (such as clicking on a hyperlink) and therefore did not provide sufficient information to warrant description on the scale.

Students working at Level 1 demonstrate familiarity with the basic range of software commands that enable them to access files and complete routine text and layout editing under instruction. They recognize not only some basic conventions used by electronic communications software but also the potential for misuse of computers by unauthorized users.

A key factor differentiating Level 1 achievement from achievement *below* Level 1 is the range of software commands students can use. Students working below Level 1 are unlikely to be able to create digital information products unless they have support and guidance. Key factors differentiating Level 1 achievement from achievement at the higher levels are the breadth of students' familiarity with conventional software commands, the degree to which they can search for and locate information, and their capacity to plan how they will use information when creating information products.

---

3 Further details of the dimensionality analyses are provided in the ICILS technical report (Fraillon et al., forthcoming).

Table 3.2: CIL described achievement scale

Level 2 (from 492 to 576 score points)	
Students working at Level 2 use computers to complete basic and explicit information-gathering and management tasks. They locate explicit information from within given electronic sources. These students make basic edits, and add content to existing information products in response to specific instructions. They create simple information products that show consistency of design and adherence to layout conventions. Students working at Level 2 demonstrate awareness of mechanisms for protecting personal information and some consequences of public access to personal information.	Students working at Level 2, for example: • Add contacts to a collaborative workspace; • Navigate to a URL presented as plain text; • Insert information to a specified cell in a spreadsheet; • Locate explicitly stated simple information within a website with multiple pages; • Differentiate between paid and organic search results returned by a search engine; • Use formatting and location to denote the role of a title in an information sheet; • Use the full page when laying out a poster; • Demonstrate basic control of text layout and color use when creating a presentation; • Use a simple webpage editor to add specified text to a webpage; • Explain a potential problem if a personal email address is publicly available; • Associate the breadth of a character set with the strength of a password.
Level 1 (from 407 to 491 score points)	
Students working at Level 1 demonstrate a functional working knowledge of computers as tools and a basic understanding of the consequences of computers being accessed by multiple users. They apply conventional software commands to perform basic communication tasks and add simple content to information products. They demonstrate familiarity with the basic layout conventions of electronic documents.	Students working at Level 1, for example: • Open a link in a new browser tab; • Use software to crop an image; • Place a title in a prominent position on a webpage; • Create a suitable title for a presentation; • Demonstrate basic control of color when adding content to a simple web document; • Insert an image into a document; • Identify who receives an email by carbon copy (Cc); and • Suggest one or more risks of failing to log out from a user account when using a publicly accessible computer.

Students working at Level 2 can demonstrate basic use of computers as information resources. They are able to locate explicit information in simple digital resources, select and add content to information products, and exercise some control over laying out and formatting text and images in information products. They demonstrate awareness of the need to protect access to some electronic information and of possible consequences of unwanted access to information. A key factor differentiating Level 2 achievement from achievement at the higher levels is the extent to which students can work autonomously and with a critical perspective when accessing information and using it to create information products.

Students working at Level 3 possess sufficient knowledge, skills, and understanding to independently search for and locate information. They also have ability to edit and create information products. They can select relevant information from within electronic resources, and the information products they create exhibit their capacity to control layout and design. Students furthermore demonstrate awareness that the information they access may be biased, inaccurate, or unreliable. The key factors differentiating achievement at Level 3 from Level 4 are the degree of precision with which students

Table 3.2: CIL described achievement scale (contd.)

Level 4 (above 661 scale points)	
Students working at Level 4 select the most relevant information to use for communicative purposes. They evaluate usefulness of information based on criteria associated with need and evaluate the reliability of information based on its content and probable origin. These students create information products that demonstrate a consideration of audience and communicative purpose. They also use appropriate software features to restructure and present information in a manner that is consistent with presentation conventions. They then adapt that information to suit the needs of an audience. Students working at Level 4 demonstrate awareness of problems that can arise regarding the use of proprietary information on the internet.	Students working at Level 4, for example: • Evaluate the reliability of information intended to promote a product on a commercial website; • Select, from a large set of results returned by a search engine, a result that meets specified search criteria; • Select relevant images from electronic sources to represent a three-stage process; • Select from sources and adapt text for a presentation so that it suits a specified audience and purpose; • Demonstrate control of color to support the communicative purpose of a presentation; • Use text layout and formatting features to denote the role of elements in an information poster; • Create a balanced layout of text and images for an information sheet; and • Recognize the difference between legal, technical, and social requirements when using images on a website.
Level 3 (577 to 661 scale points)	
Students working at Level 3 demonstrate the capacity to work independently when using computers as information-gathering and management tools. These students select the most appropriate information source to meet a specified purpose, retrieve information from given electronic sources to answer concrete questions, and follow instructions to use conventionally recognized software commands to edit, add content to, and reformat information products. They recognize that the credibility of web-based information can be influenced by the identity, expertise, and motives of the creators of the information.	Students working at Level 3, for example: • Use generic online mapping software to represent text information as a map route; • Evaluate the reliability of information presented on a crowdsourced website; • Select relevant information according to given criteria to include in a website; • Select an appropriate website navigation structure for given content; • Select and adapt some relevant information from given sources when creating a poster; • Demonstrate control of image layout when creating a poster; • Demonstrate control of color and contrast to support readability of a poster; • Demonstrate control of text layout when creating a presentation; and • Identify that a generic greeting in an email suggests that the sender does not know the recipient.

search for and locate information and the level of control they demonstrate when using layout and formatting features to support the communicative purpose of information products.

Students working at Level 4 execute control and evaluative judgment when searching for information and creating information products. They also demonstrate awareness of audience and purpose when searching for information, selecting information to include in information products, and formatting and laying out the information products they create. Level 4 students additionally demonstrate awareness of the potential for information to be a commercial and malleable commodity. They furthermore have some appreciation of issues relating to using electronically-sourced, third-party intellectual property.

Example ICILS test items

To provide a clearer understanding of the nature of the scale items, we include in this section of the chapter a set of example items. These indicate the types and range of tasks that students were required to complete during the ICILS test. The tasks also provide examples of responses corresponding to the different proficiency levels of the CIL scale. The data for each example item included in the analysis (including calculation of the ICILS average) are drawn only from those countries that met the sample participation, test administration, and coding requirements for that item.

The example items all come from a module called After-School Exercise. This module required students to work on a sequence of discrete tasks associated with planning an after-school exercise program. The students were then asked to create a poster advertising the program. The five discrete tasks immediately below serve as examples of achievement at different levels of the CIL scale. They are followed with a description of the After-School Exercise large task and a discussion of the scoring criteria for the task, with the latter presented within the context of achievement on the CIL scale.

The five discrete task items

Example Item 1 (Figure 3.1), a complex multiple-choice item, required the participating ICILS students to respond by selecting as many check boxes as they thought were appropriate.

Figure 3.1: Example Item 1 with framework references and overall percent correct

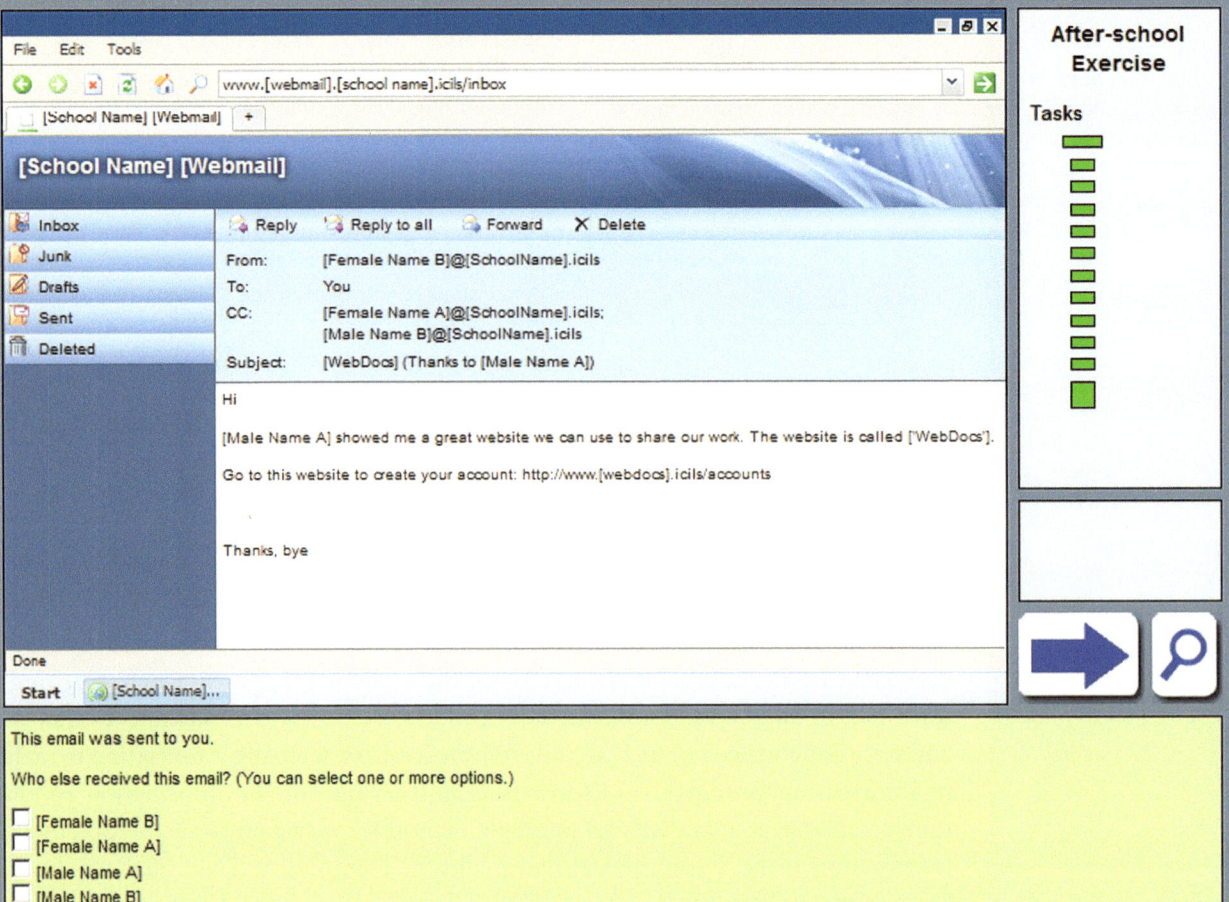

Figure 3.1: Example Item 1 with framework references and overall percent correct (contd.)

CIL Scale Level	CIL Scale Difficulty	ICILS 2013 Average Percent Correct
1	474	66 (0.4)

Item descriptor		
Identifies who received an email by carbon copy		

ICILS assessment framework reference		
2.3	Producing and exchanging information	
	Sharing information	

Country	Percent correct
Australia	80 (1.0)
Chile	62 (1.6)
Croatia	68 (1.5)
Czech Republic	69 (1.3)
Germany[†]	77 (1.6)
Korea, Republic of	57 (1.4)
Lithuania	73 (1.4)
Norway (Grade 9)[1]	85 (1.1)
Poland	71 (1.3)
Russian Federation[2]	74 (1.4)
Slovak Republic	70 (1.3)
Slovenia	69 (1.5)
Thailand[2]	30 (1.9)
Turkey	35 (1.9)
Countries not meeting sample requirements	
Denmark	78 (1.6)
Hong Kong SAR	69 (1.7)
Netherlands	83 (1.4)
Switzerland	80 (2.0)
Benchmarking participants	
Newfoundland and Labrador, Canada	80 (2.1)
Ontario, Canada	79 (1.4)
Benchmarking participant not meeting sample requirements	
City of Buenos Aires, Argentina	62 (2.2)

Notes:

() Standard errors appear in parentheses. Because results are rounded to the nearest whole number, some totals may appear inconsistent.

[†] Met guidelines for sampling participation rates only after replacement schools were included.

[1] National Desired Population does not correspond to International Desired Population.

[2] Country surveyed the same cohort of students but at the beginning of the next school year.

Example Item 1 illustrates achievement at Level 1 on the CIL scale. This item was the first one that students completed in the After-School Exercise module, and it asked them to identify the recipients of an email displaying the "From,"' "To," and "Cc" fields. The item assessed students' familiarity with the conventions used within email information to display the sender and recipients of emails. In particular, it assessed whether students were aware that people listed in the Cc field of an email are also intended recipients of an email. Sixty-six percent of students answered Example Item 1 correctly. The achievement percentages across countries ranged from 30 percent to 85 percent.

Example Item 2 (Figure 3.2) was the second item students completed in the After-School Exercise module. Note that Example Items 1 and 2 use the same email message as stimulus material for students, thus showing how questions are embedded in the narrative theme of each module.

The email message in Example Item 2 told students that they would be working on a collaborative web-based workspace. Regardless of whether students read the text in the body of the email when completing Example Item 1, the tactic of giving them the same email text in the second item was authentic in terms of the narrative theme of the module. This was because students' interaction with the first item (a complex multiple-choice one) meant they did not have to navigate away from the email page when using the internet. This narrative contiguity is a feature of all ICILS assessment modules.

Figure 3.2: Example Item 2 with framework references and overall percent correct

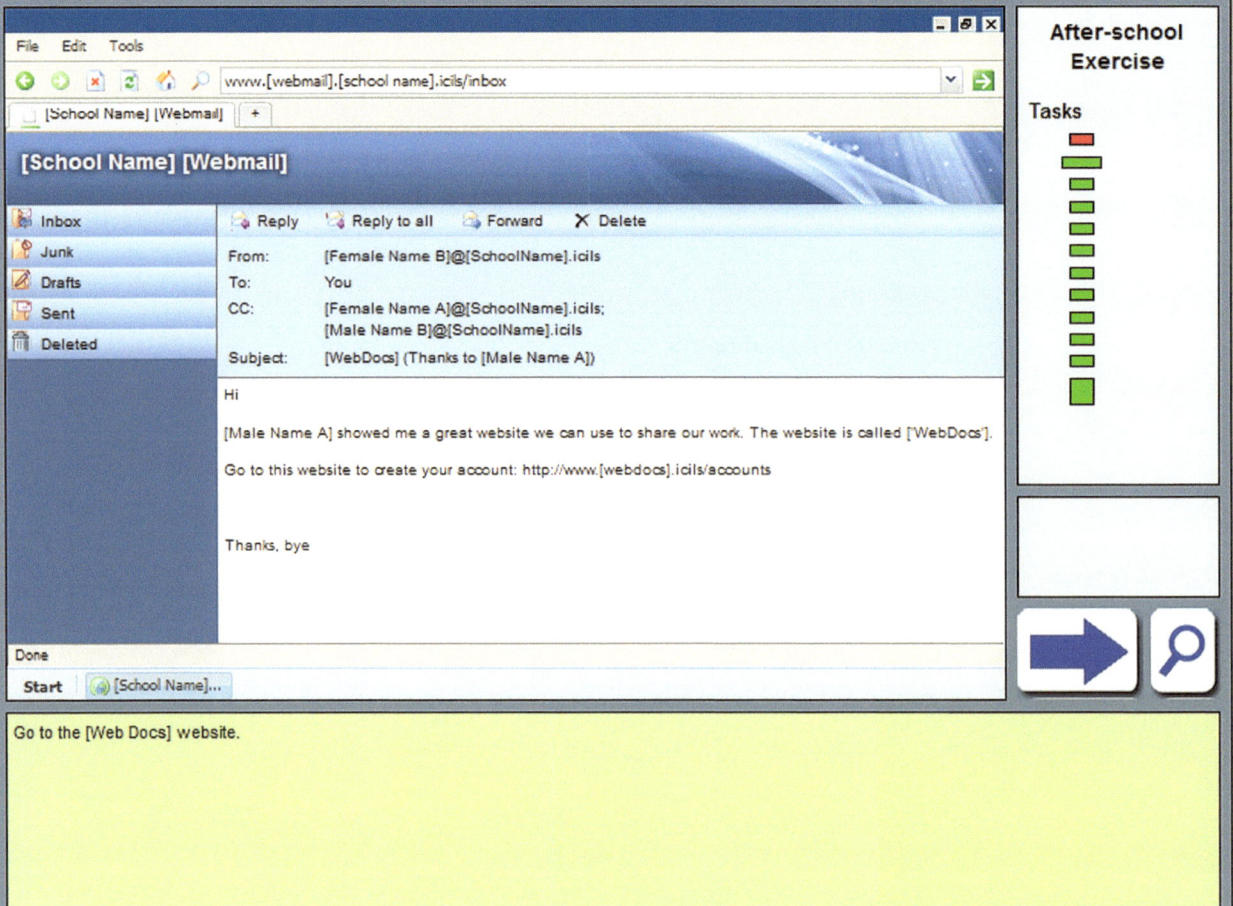

Figure 3.2: Example Item 2 with framework references and overall percent correct (contd.)

CIL Scale Level	CIL Scale Difficulty	ICILS 2013 Average Percent Correct
2	558	49 (0.4)

Item descriptor
Navigate to a URL given as plain text.

ICILS assessment framework reference	
1.1	Collecting and managing information
	Knowing about and understanding computer use

Country	Percent correct
Australia	66 (1.1)
Chile	44 (1.5)
Croatia	45 (1.5)
Czech Republic	54 (1.7)
Germany[†]	50 (1.4)
Korea, Republic of	63 (1.2)
Lithuania	64 (1.8)
Norway (Grade 9)[1]	61 (1.8)
Poland	55 (1.3)
Russian Federation[2]	52 (1.4)
Slovak Republic	42 (1.6)
Slovenia	48 (1.2)
Thailand[2]	21 (1.7)
Turkey	23 (1.6)
Countries not meeting sample requirements	
Denmark	66 (1.9)
Hong Kong SAR	65 (2.1)
Netherlands	61 (1.6)
Switzerland	49 (1.8)
Benchmarking participants	
Newfoundland and Labrador, Canada	58 (2.9)
Ontario, Canada	61 (1.8)
Benchmarking participant not meeting sample requirements	
City of Buenos Aires, Argentina	44 (3.0)

Notes:

() Standard errors appear in parentheses. Because results are rounded to the nearest whole number, some totals may appear inconsistent.

[†] Met guidelines for sampling participation rates only after replacement schools were included.

[1] National Desired Population does not correspond to International Desired Population.

[2] Country surveyed the same cohort of students but at the beginning of the next school year.

Example Item 2 required students to navigate to a URL given as plain text. Ability to do this denoted achievement at Level 2 of the CIL scale. Although the task represents a form of basic navigation, it was made more complex by presenting the URL as plain text rather than as a hyperlink. In order to navigate to the URL, students needed to enter the text in the address bar of the web-browser (by copying and pasting the text from the email or by typing the characters directly into the taskbar) and then to activate the navigation by pressing enter or clicking on the green arrow next to the taskbar. The task required students to know that they needed to enter the URL into the taskbar. They also needed to have the technical skill to enter the text correctly and activate the search. This set of technical knowledge and skills is why the item reflects Level 2 proficiency on the CIL scale.

Scoring of Example Item 2 was completed automatically by the computer-based test-delivery system; all methods of obtaining a correct response were scored as equivalent and correct. Forty-nine percent of students answered Example Item 2 correctly. The percentages correct ranged from 21 to 66 percent across the 21 countries.

Example Item 3 (Figure 3.3) also illustrates achievement at Level 2 on the CIL scale. We include it here to further illustrate the narrative coherence of the CIL modules and also the breadth of skills that are indicative of achievement at Level 2.

Figure 3.3: Example Item 3 with framework references and overall percent correct

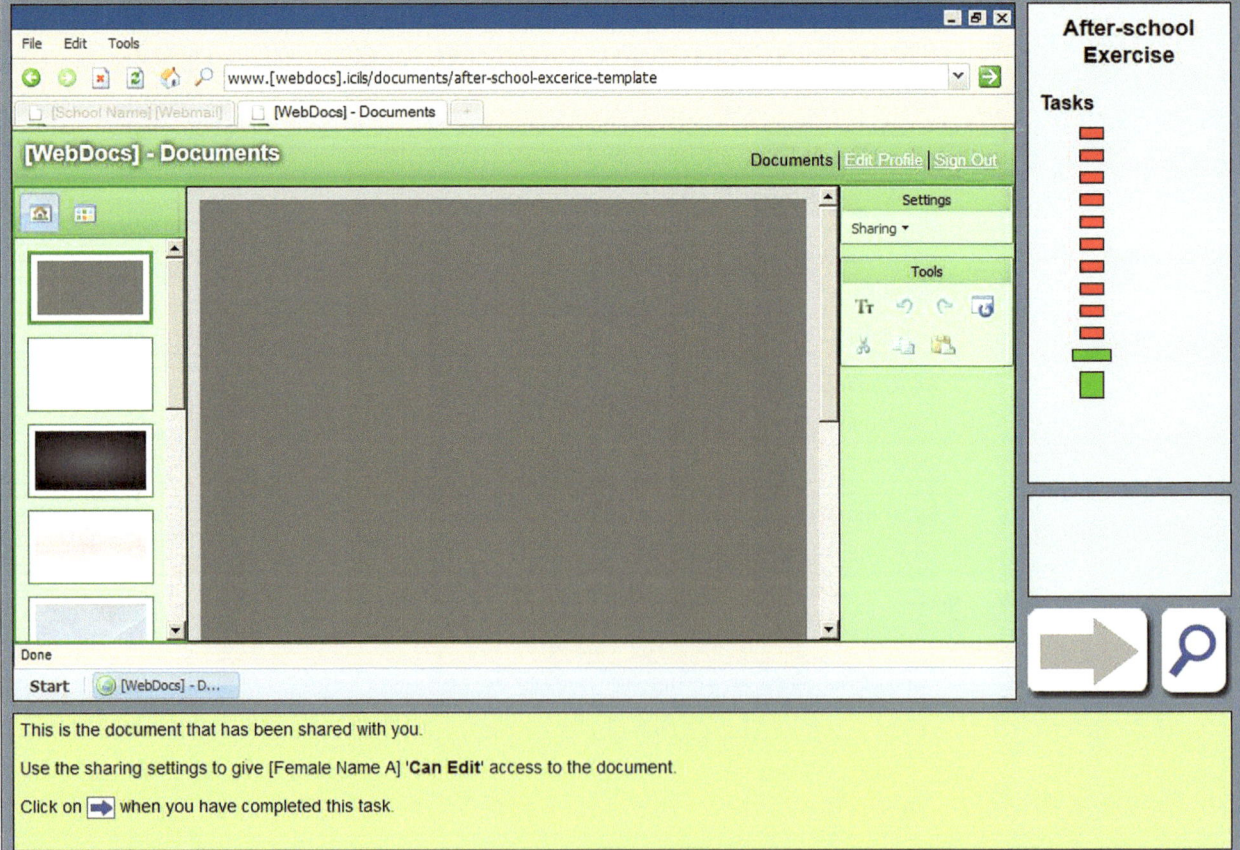

Figure 3.3: Example Item 3 with framework references and overall percent correct (contd.)

CIL Scale Level	CIL Scale Difficulty	ICILS 2013 Average Percent Correct
2	532	54 (0.4)

Item descriptor	
Modify the sharing settings of a collaborative document.	
ICILS assessment framework reference	
1.1	Collecting and managing information
	Knowing about and understanding computer use

Country	Percent correct
Australia	72 (1.1)
Chile	50 (1.5)
Croatia	60 (1.6)
Czech Republic	46 (1.2)
Germany[†]	58 (1.8)
Korea, Republic of	66 (1.2)
Lithuania	49 (1.6)
Norway (Grade 9)[1]	74 (1.2)
Poland	54 (1.4)
Russian Federation[2]	68 (1.5)
Slovak Republic	62 (1.8)
Slovenia	57 (1.8)
Thailand[2]	16 (1.6)
Turkey	30 (1.8)
Countries not meeting sample requirements	
Denmark	72 (1.9)
Hong Kong SAR	50 (2.0)
Netherlands	58 (1.8)
Switzerland	63 (2.2)
Benchmarking participants	
Newfoundland and Labrador, Canada	67 (1.7)
Ontario, Canada	71 (1.9)
Benchmarking participant not meeting sample requirements	
City of Buenos Aires, Argentina	49 (2.8)

Notes:

() Standard errors appear in parentheses. Because results are rounded to the nearest whole number, some totals may appear inconsistent.

[†] Met guidelines for sampling participation rates only after replacement schools were included.

[1] National Desired Population does not correspond to International Desired Population.

[2] Country surveyed the same cohort of students but at the beginning of the next school year.

Example Item 3 was one of the last items leading up to the large task in the After-School Exercise module. Previously, the narrative sequence of the module had required students to navigate to a collaborative workspace website and then complete a set of tasks associated with setting up an account on the site. Now, in order to accomplish the task in Example Item 3, students had to allocate "can edit" rights to another student who was, according to the module narrative, "collaborating" with the student on the task. To complete this nonlinear skills task,[4] students had to navigate within the website to the "settings" menu and then use the options within it to allocate the required user access. The computer-based test-delivery system automatically scored achievement on the task. Fifty-four percent of students answered Example Item 3 correctly. The crossnational percentages ranged from 16 percent to 74 percent.

Example Items 4 and 5 (Figures 3.4 and 3.5) focus on students' familiarity with the characteristics of an email message that suggest it may have come from an untrustworthy source. These two items are set within the part of the module narrative requiring students to create their user accounts on the collaborative workspace. After setting up their accounts, students were presented with the email message and asked to identify which characteristics of it could be evidence that the sender of the email was trying to trick users into sending him or her their password.

Figure 3.4: Example Item 4 with framework references and overall percent correct

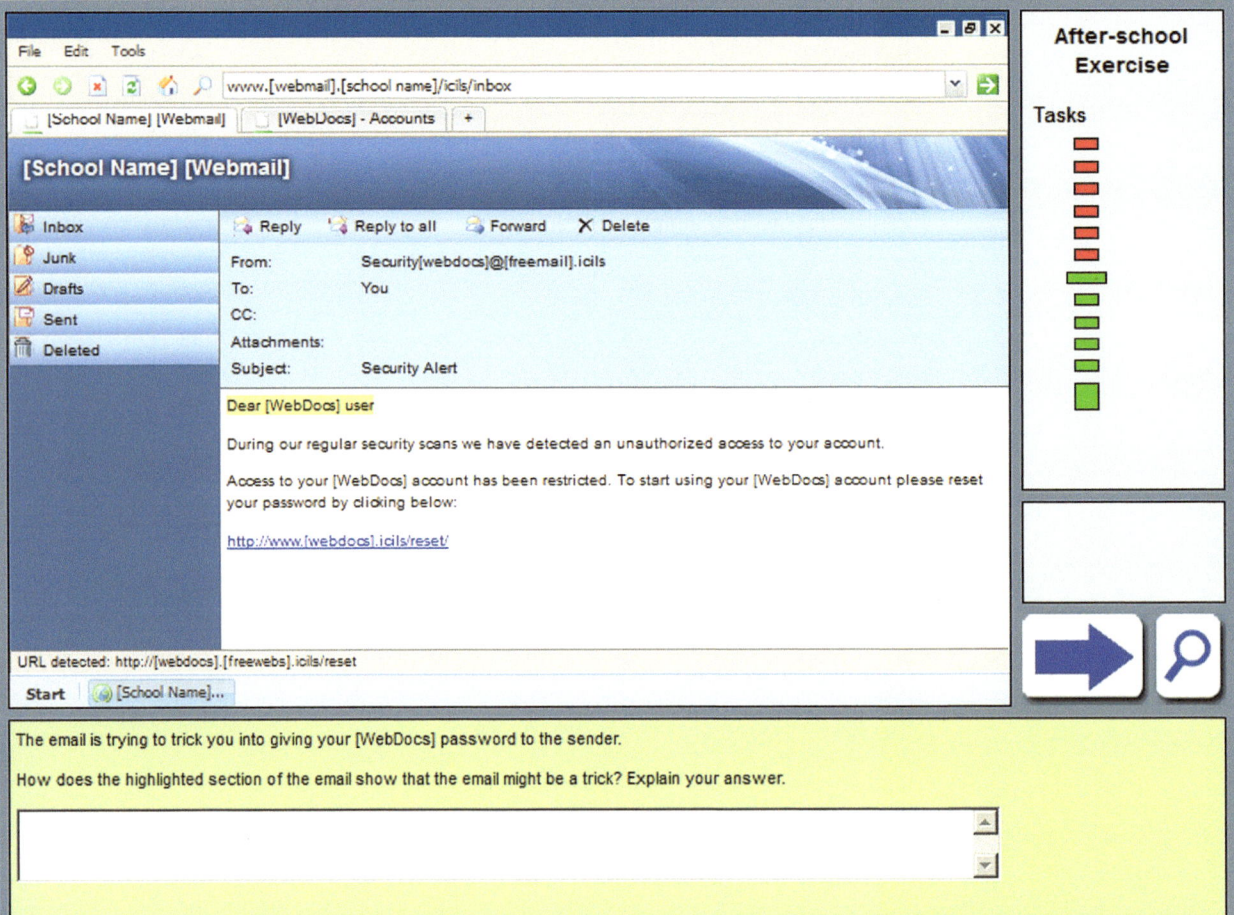

---

4   Nonlinear skills tasks require students to execute a software command (or reach a desired outcome) by executing subcommands in a number of different sequences. Further information about the ICILS task and question types is provided in the *ICILS Assessment Framework* (Fraillon et al., 2013).

Figure 3.4: Example Item 4 with framework references and overall percent correct (contd.)

CIL Scale Level	CIL Scale Difficulty	ICILS 2013 Average Percent Correct
3	646	25 (0.3)

Item descriptor	
Identify that a generic greeting in an email indicates that the sender does not know the recipient.	

ICILS assessment framework reference	
2.4	Producing and exchanging information
	Using information safely and securely

Country	Percent correct
Australia	60 (1.1)
Chile	19 (1.2)
Croatia	14 (1.2)
Czech Republic	21 (1.2)
Germany[†]	28 (1.5)
Korea, Republic of	27 (1.4)
Lithuania	36 (1.5)
Norway (Grade 9)[1]	30 (1.4)
Poland	34 (1.5)
Russian Federation[2]	33 (1.8)
Slovak Republic	23 (1.5)
Slovenia	16 (1.0)
Thailand[2]	7 (0.9)
Turkey	4 (0.7)
Countries not meeting sample requirements	
Denmark	34 (1.9)
Hong Kong SAR	24 (2.2)
Netherlands	42 (1.8)
Switzerland	37 (2.5)
Benchmarking participants	
Newfoundland and Labrador, Canada	56 (2.7)
Ontario, Canada	53 (1.9)
Benchmarking participant not meeting sample requirements	
City of Buenos Aires, Argentina	15 (1.8)

Notes:

() Standard errors appear in parentheses. Because results are rounded to the nearest whole number, some totals may appear inconsistent.

[†] Met guidelines for sampling participation rates only after replacement schools were included.

[1] National Desired Population does not correspond to International Desired Population.

[2] Country surveyed the same cohort of students but at the beginning of the next school year.

Example Item 4 provides one aspect of the developing critical perspective (in this case relating to safety and security) that students working at Level 3 on the CIL scale are able to bring to their access and use of computer-based information. The highlighted email greeting in the item signals that this piece of text forms the focus of the item. Students were asked to explain how the greeting might be evidence that the email sender was trying to trick them. Students who said the greeting was generic (rather than personalized) received credit on this item. Twenty-five percent of students answered the item correctly. The percentages across countries ranged from 4 percent to 60 percent.

The students' written responses to this open response item were sent to scorers in each country by way of an online delivery platform. All scorers had been trained to international standards.[5]

Figure 3.5: Example Item 5 with framework references and overall percent correct

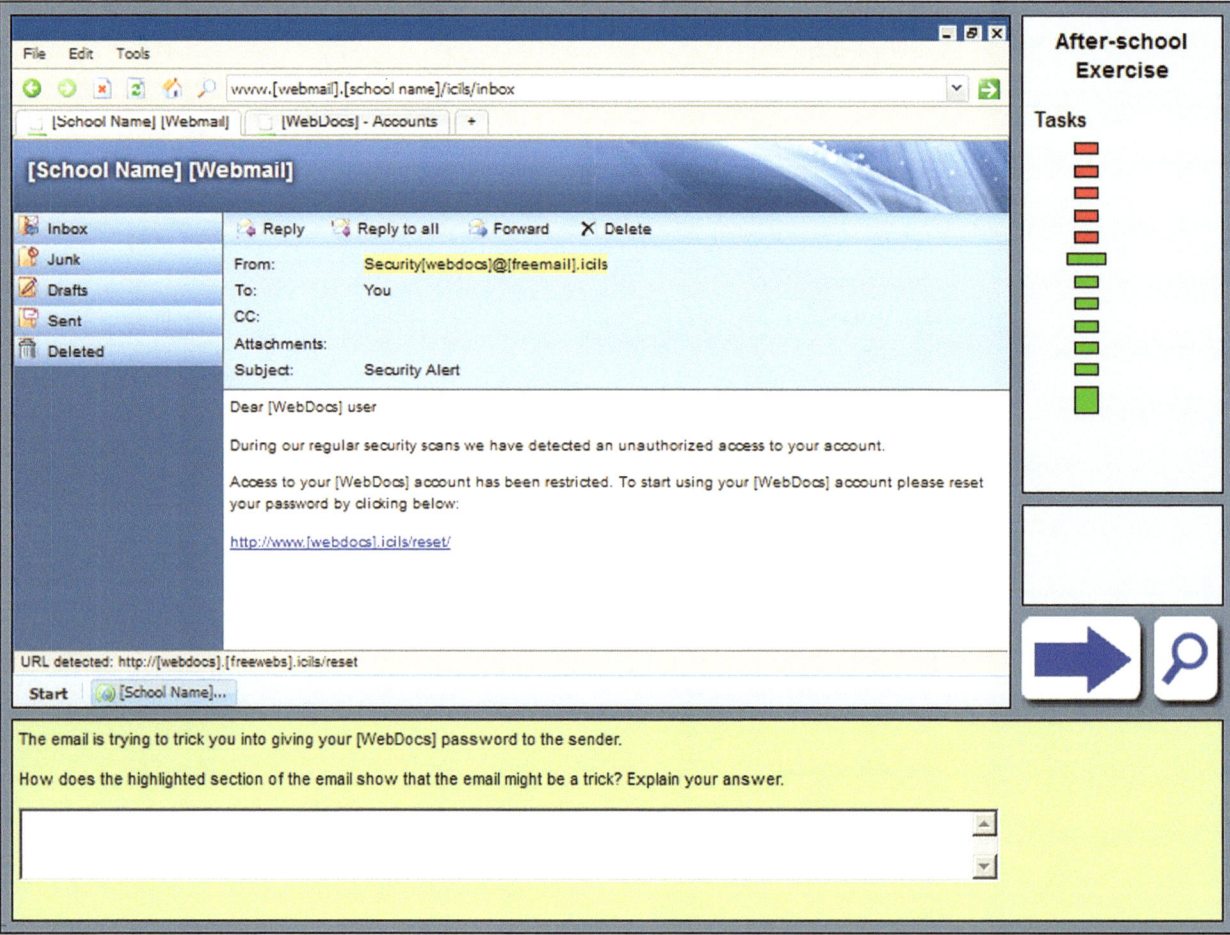

---

5 Twenty percent of student responses to each constructed response item and large task criterion were independently
   scored by two scorers in each country in order to assess the reliability of scoring. The only data included in the analysis
   were those from constructed items with a scoring reliability of at least 75 percent.

Figure 3.5: Example Item 5 with framework references and overall percent correct (contd.)

CIL Scale Level	CIL Scale Difficulty	ICILS 2013 Average Percent Correct
4	707	16 (0.3)

Item descriptor
Identify that a mismatch between a purported sender and their email address may suggest the email is suspicious.

ICILS assessment framework reference	
2.4	Producing and exchanging information
	Using information safely and securely

Country	Percent correct
Australia	19 (1.0)
Chile	17 (1.1)
Croatia	12 (1.1)
Czech Republic	27 (1.3)
Germany[†]	7 (1.0)
Korea, Republic of	21 (1.1)
Lithuania	28 (1.4)
Norway (Grade 9)[1]	25 (1.3)
Poland	14 (0.8)
Russian Federation[2]	15 (1.1)
Slovak Republic	21 (1.2)
Slovenia	13 (1.0)
Thailand[2]	5 (1.0)
Turkey	3 (0.5)
Countries not meeting sample requirements	
Denmark	38 (2.1)
Hong Kong SAR	24 (1.8)
Netherlands	22 (1.4)
Switzerland	16 (1.6)
Benchmarking participants	
Newfoundland and Labrador, Canada	36 (2.7)
Ontario, Canada	36 (1.4)
Benchmarking participant not meeting sample requirements	
City of Buenos Aires, Argentina	16 (2.7)

Notes:

() Standard errors appear in parentheses. Because results are rounded to the nearest whole number, some totals may appear inconsistent.

[†] Met guidelines for sampling participation rates only after replacement schools were included.

[1] National Desired Population does not correspond to International Desired Population.

[2] Country surveyed the same cohort of students but at the beginning of the next school year.

Example Item 5 required students to evaluate a different highlighted aspect of the same email they considered in Example Item 4. In Example Item 5, students' attention was focused on the sender's email address. The team developing the assessment instrument contrived this address to appear as an address registered under a "freemail" account. (National center staff in each country adapted and translated the address to fit the local context.) Note that the root of the address differs from the root of the address the sender provided in the hyperlink presented in the body of the email.

Student responses were scored as correct if they identified the email as a trick either because it originated from a freemail account (and not a company account) or because it did not match the root of the hyperlink they were being asked to click on. Successful completion of the item illustrates achievement at Level 4, the highest level on the CIL scale. It required students to demonstrate sophisticated knowledge and understanding of the conventions of email and web addresses in the context of safe and secure use of information. On average, across ICILS countries, 16 percent of students answered Example Item 5 correctly. The crossnational percentages ranged from 3 to 28 percent.

Example ICILS large-task item

The large task in the After-School Exercise test module required students to create a poster to advertise their selected program. Students were presented with a description of the task details as well as information about how the task would be assessed. This information was followed by a short video designed to familiarize them with the task. The video also highlighted the main features of the software students would need to use to complete the task.

Figure 3.6 shows the task details screen that students saw before beginning the After-School Exercise large task. It also shows the task details and assessment information that students could view at any time during their work on the task.

As evident from Figure 3.6, students were told that they needed to create a poster to advertise an after-school exercise program at their school. They were also told that the poster should make people want to participate in the program. They were then instructed to select an activity they thought would be most suitable for inclusion in the program from a website provided to them within the test environment. The website, Healthy Living, was one they had encountered during their work on the earlier tasks in the module. The upper half of Figure 3.7 shows the large task as presented to students. The bottom half of the figure shows the home page of the Healthy Living website.

Students were also provided with a list of minimum necessary content to include in the poster: a title, information about when the program would take place, what people would do during the program, and what equipment/clothing participants would need. Students were also told that the program should last 30 minutes and be targeted at participants over 12 years of age.

At any time during their work on the large task, students could click on the magnifying glass button to see a summary list of the task's scoring criteria. These related to the suitability of the poster for the target audience, its relevance, the completeness of its information, and the layout of its text and images. The assessment criteria given to the students were a simplified summary of the detailed criteria used by the expert scorers.

Figure 3.6: After-School Exercise: large task details

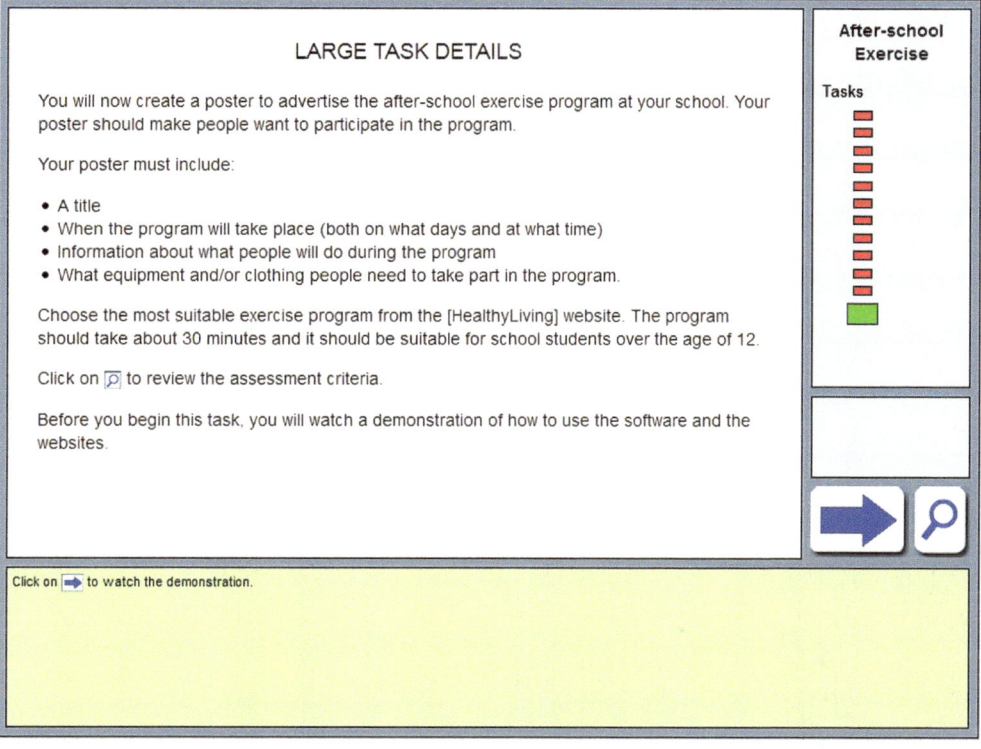

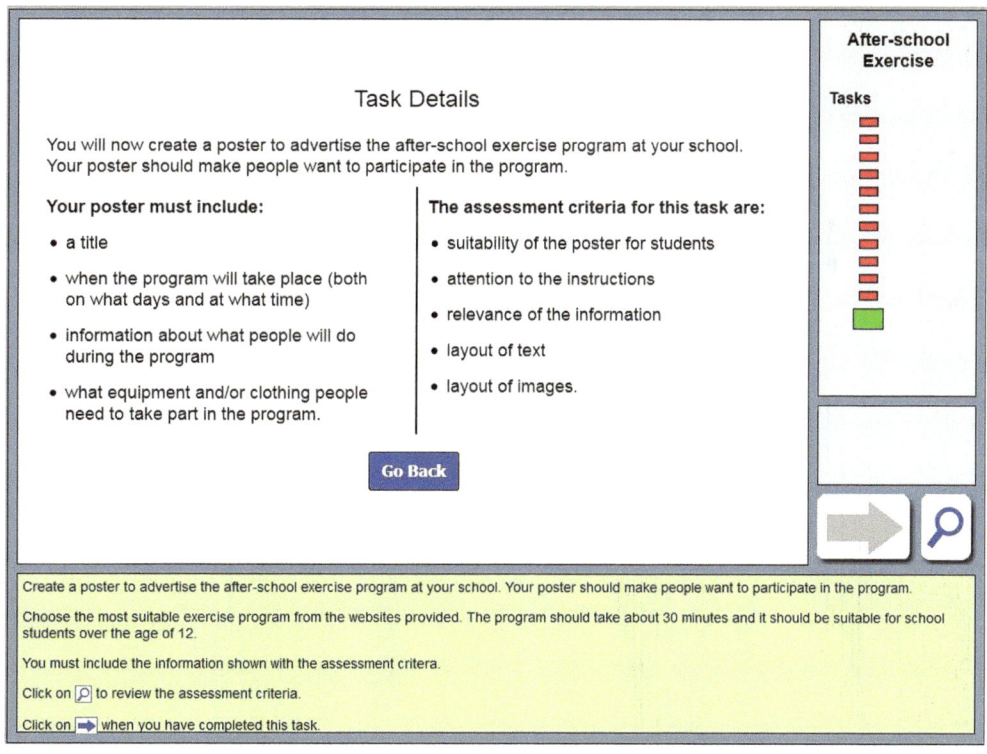

Figure 3.7: After-School Exercise: large task and website resource

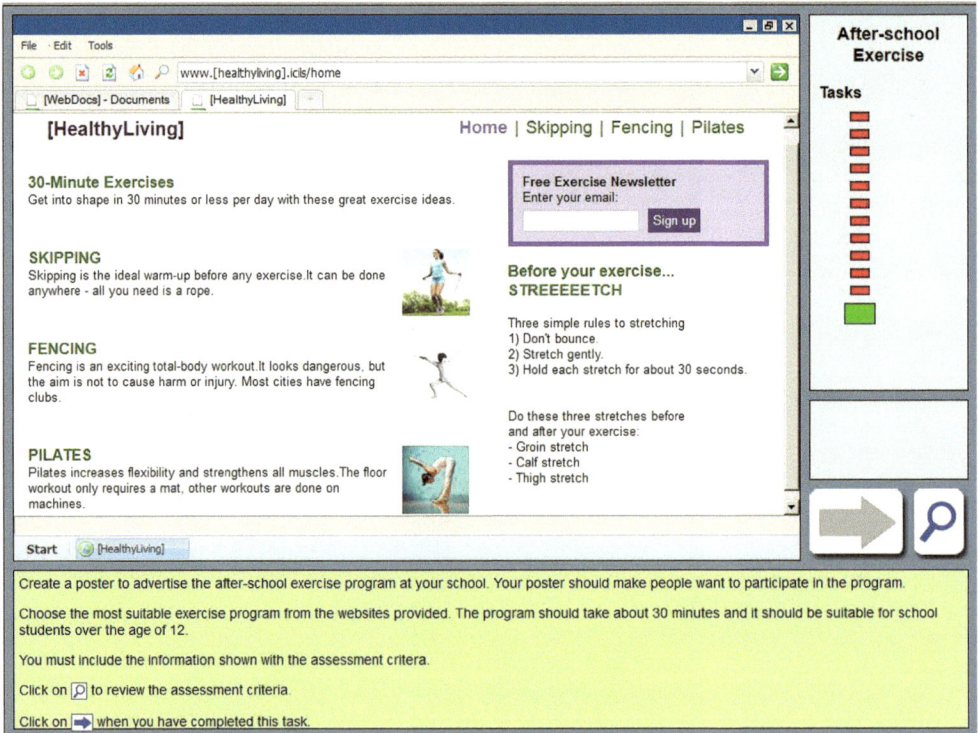

The After-School Exercise large task was presented to students as a blank document on which they could create their poster using the editing software. The software icons and functions matched the conventions of web-based document editors. In addition, all icons in the software included "hover-over" text that brought up the names of the related functions. While these icons were universal across the ICILS test environment, all hover-over labels were translated into the language(s) of administration in each country.

The following software features were available for students to use to create the poster:

- *Add text:* When students clicked on the "Tt" icon, a dialogue box opened that allowed them to add text. The text then appeared in a text box on the poster. Students could also reopen text boxes and edit the contents.
- *Edit text:* The text entry dialogue box included a small range of formatting features—font color, font size, bold, underline, text alignment, and numbered or bulleted lists.
- *General editing:* Students could cut or copy and paste text (such as from the website material), undo and redo images, and revert the poster to its original state (i.e., to start again) by using the icons to the right of the screen. They could also move and resize all text boxes and images by clicking and dragging.
- *Change background:* When students clicked on a background presented on the left of the screen, the poster background changed to match the selection. The task developers deliberately set the default background and text color to gray. This meant that students who used only the default settings could only receive credit for using effective color contrast (such as black on white) if they manipulated the color of at least one of the elements.
- *Insert images:* At the left of the screen, students could toggle between backgrounds (shown in Figure 3.7) and images that they could include in their presentation. Students could insert selected images by clicking and dragging them into the poster. Once inserted in the poster, images could be freely moved and resized.

At the top of the screens shown in Figure 3.7 are clickable website tabs that allowed students to toggle between the poster-making software and the website they had available as an information resource. This website offered information about three forms of 30-minute exercise activities—skipping, Pilates, and fencing. Students could find additional information about each program by clicking on the links within the website. They could also choose any activity (or combination of activities) to be the subject of the poster.

The pages about each activity contained a range of information about it, some of which was relevant within the context of the information poster and some of which was irrelevant. Once students had selected their preferred activity or activities, they needed to filter out the irrelevant information. Students could copy and paste text from the resources into their poster if they wished. They could also insert images shown in the websites into their poster.

When students had completed their poster, they clicked on the "I've finished" button, an action which saved their poster as the "final" version. (The test delivery system also completed periodic automatic saves as a backup while students were working on their tasks.) Students then had the option of exiting the module or returning to their large task to continue editing.

Once students had exited the module, the final version of the poster was saved in preparation for later scoring by trained scorers within each country. These people scored each poster according to a set of 10 criteria (later reduced to nine in the process of data analysis). As was the case for the constructed response items described previously, data were only included in analyses if they met IEA standards for scoring reliability.

The large tasks in the ICILS test modules were all scored using task-specific criteria. In general, these fell into two categories: technical proficiency and information management. Criteria relating to technical proficiency usually related to elements such as text and image formatting and use of color across the tasks.

Assessment of technical proficiency typically included a hierarchy from little or no control at the lower end to the use of the technical features to enhance the communicative impact of the work at the higher end. The criteria thus focused on ability to use the technical features for the purpose of communication rather than on simply an execution of skills. Criteria relating to information management centered on elements such as adapting information to suit audience needs, selecting information relevant to the task (or omitting information irrelevant to it), and structuring the information within the task. Some criteria allowed for *dichotomous* scoring as either 0 (no credit) or 1 (full credit) score points; others allowed for *partial credit* scoring as 0 (no credit), 1 (partial credit), or 2 (full credit) score points.

The manifestation of the assessment criteria across the different tasks depended on the nature of each task. For example, information flow or consistency of formatting to support communication in a presentation with multiple slides requires consideration of the flow within and across the slides. The After-School Exercise large task comprised a single poster. As such, the scoring criteria related to the necessary elements and content of an information poster.

Table 3.3 provides a summary of the scoring criteria used for the After-School Exercise large task. Criteria are presented according to their CIL scale difficulties and levels on the CIL scale as well as their ICILS assessment framework references, relevant score category and maximum score, the percentage of all students achieving each criterion, and the minimum and maximum percentages achieved on each criterion across countries. Full details of the percentages that students in each country achieved on each criterion appear in Appendix B.

The design of the large tasks in the ICILS assessment meant that the tasks could be accessed by students regardless of their level of proficiency. The design also allowed students across this range to demonstrate different levels of achievement against the CIL scale, as evident in the levels shown in the scoring criteria in Table 3.3.

Each of Criteria 2, 5, 8, and 9 takes up a single row in Table 3.3 because each was dichotomous (scored as 0 or 1), with only the description corresponding to a score of one for each criterion included in the table. Each of Criteria 1, 3, 4, 6, and 7 was partial-credit (scored as 0, 1, or 2). Table 3.3 contains a separate row for the descriptions corresponding to a score of one and a score of two for each of these criteria. In most cases, the different creditable levels of quality within the partial-credit criteria correspond to different proficiency levels on the CIL scale. For example, the description of a score of one on Criterion 3 is shown at Level 2 (553 scale points), and the description of a score of two on the same criterion is shown at Level 4 (673 scale points).

Table 3.3: Example large-task scoring criteria with framework references and overall percent correct

Level	CIL Scale Difficulty	Score/Max. Score	ICILS 2013 Average Percent Correct	Max. (%) Min. (%)	Criterion	Descriptor	Assessment Framework Aspect
4	722	2/2	7 (0.2)	33 (1.3) 2 (0.3)	6. Information adaptation	The relevant key points from the resources have been rephrased using student's own words.	2.3. Sharing information
4	673	2/2	15 (0.4)	29 (1.7) 3 (0.5)	3. Text layout and formatting	Formatting tools have been used consistently throughout the poster to show the role of the different text elements.	2.2. Creating information
3	655	2/2	23 (0.3)	79 (1.2) 5 (0.7)	4. Color contrast	There is sufficient contrast to enable all text to be seen and read easily.	2.1. Transforming information
3	643	1/1	26 (0.4)	60 (1.5) 3 (0.6)	8. Persuasiveness	Uses some emotive or persuasive language to make the program appealing to readers.	2.1. Transforming information
3	636	1/2	27 (0.4)	63 (1.4) 6 (0.7)	6. Information adaptation	Some useful information has been copied from the resources and edited to improve ease of comprehension and relevance.	2.3. Sharing information
3	634	2/2	27 (0.3)	53 (1.4) 2 (0.4	7. Information completeness	All required information about the program (when, where, and what equipment is required) has been included in the poster.	1.2. Accessing and evaluating information
3	591	1/1	40 (0.4)	52 (1.5) 11 (1.2)	2. Image layout	One or more images are well aligned with the other elements on the page and appropriately sized.	2.2. Creating information
2	563	1/1	46 (0.4)	61 (1.5) 15 (1.4)	9. Use of full page	Full page has been used when creating poster.	2.1. Transforming information
2	553	1/2	46 (0.6)	73 (1.3) 17 (1.4)	3. Text layout and formatting	Formatting tools have been used to some degree to show the role of the different text elements.	2.2. Creating information
2	548	2/2	48 (0.4)	80 (1.2) 11 (1.2)	1. Title design	A relevant title has been added and formatted to make its role clear.	2.1. Transforming information
2	539	1/2	55 (0.4)	79 (1.2) 7 (0.9)	7. Information completeness	Two of the three required pieces of information about the program (when, where, and what equipment is required) have been included in the poster.	1.2. Accessing and evaluating information
2	492	1/2	67 (0.4)	86 (0.9) 23 (1.8)	1. Title design	A relevant title has been added and placed in a prominent position.	2.2. Creating information
1	472	1/2	68 (0.4)	89 (0.9) 31 (0.2)	4. Color contrast	The text mostly contrasts sufficiently with the background to support reading.	2.2. Creating information
1	417	1/1	80 (0.4)	90 (0.8) 67 (1.5)	5. Color consistency	The poster shows evidence of planning regarding the use of color to denote the role of the text, background, and images in the poster.	2.3. Sharing information

We can see from Table 3.3 that two scoring criteria for the poster corresponded to Level 1 on the CIL scale. These both related to students' use of color and reflected students' familiarity with the basic layout conventions of electronic documents. Overall, 80 percent of students were able to demonstrate some planning in their use of color to denote the role of different components of the poster. Sixty-eight percent of students could ensure that at least some elements of the text in the poster contrasted sufficiently with the background color to aid readability.

Color contrast was a partial credit criterion. The ICILS scoring system automatically scored the relative brightness of the text and background against an adaptation of relevant criteria in the Web Contents Accessibility Guidelines 2.0 (WCAG 2.0). The ICILS technical report provides full details of this process (Fraillon et al., forthcoming).

Human scorers then looked at the automatically generated score for each poster and could either accept or modify the score. Students whose control of color contrast was basic received one score point. Basic color contrast meant that the student used the same text color throughout the poster, used color that did not contrast strongly with the background, or used a range of text colors, with some contrasting well and others contrasting poorly with the background. Students whose posters exhibited sufficient color contrast for all text elements to be read clearly received two score points. These students' achievement aligned with the higher levels of planning control characteristic of Level 3 on the CIL scale.

Four scoring criteria corresponded to Level 2 achievement on the CIL scale. One of these—use of full page—was dichotomous and so appears at Level 2 only. Students were told in the task brief that the quality of the poster's layout was one of the scoring criteria for the task. The other aspect of layout under consideration was whether or not the student used the full space available on the poster. Students who used the full space rather than leaving large sections of it empty received credit on this criterion.

Level 2 achievement on the scale was also exemplified by posters that included two of the three pieces of information that students were instructed to provide, that is, when the program would take place, what people would do during it, and what equipment/ clothing they would need. Posters with some evidence of the use of formatting tools to convey the role of different text elements also exemplified Level 2 achievement. Each of these two categories represented the one-score-point category in the partial credit criteria. The first criterion related to the completeness of information the students provided and the second to students' ability to plan and control their formatting of text elements. Achievement at Level 2 was evidenced by inconsistent or incomplete attempts to meet these criteria.

Students were instructed to include a title in their poster, and this was scored according to its layout and content. The title needed to represent the notion of an exercise program or refer to the activity the student selected in order to be eligible to receive credit. The level of credit on this criterion was then determined according to the layout and formatting of the title. Posters in which the title was situated in a prominent position on the page were credited with a single score point. This level of credit corresponded to 492 CIL scale points, which is on the boundary between Levels 1 and 2 of the scale. Posters in which the title was both in a prominent location and formatted to make its role clear exemplified Level 2 achievement on the scale.

Table 3.3 furthermore shows that, overall, the percentages of students achieving success on the four Level 2 criteria ranged from 46 percent (some control of text formatting and layout and use of full page) to 55 percent (two of the three requisite pieces of information included in the poster). The examples of achievement at Level 2 on the poster are indicative of students who can demonstrate some degree of control in executing procedural skills relating to layout and information.

At Level 3, students' execution of the posters shows greater control and independent planning than at the lower levels. Five categories of criteria indicated Level 3 achievement. Two of these criteria focused on students' ability to include images in their posters and to make their posters persuade readers to participate in the program. The inclusion of at least one image properly laid out in the posters and evidence of some attempt to persuade readers are both indicative of Level 3 achievement.

Also at Level 3 were the consistent use of color in order to denote the meaning of text elements (the full credit category of the partial credit criterion referred to in Level 1), inclusion of all three requisite pieces of information (the full credit category of the partial credit criterion referred to in Level 2), and some adaptation of information taken from the website resources for use in the poster (the partial credit category of a criterion for which full credit is at Level 4).

The use of information in the posters at Level 3 typically showed evidence of independent planning extending beyond completion of the procedural aspects of the task. The posters also included evidence of attempts to fulfill their persuasive purpose. In addition to being relevant, the information included in the posters needed to show evidence of having been adapted to some extent rather than simply copied and pasted into the poster. In essence, Level 3 posters could be positioned as complete products that were largely fit for purpose.

The overall percentages of students achieving at each of the five categories of Level 3 achievement criteria ranged from 23 percent (sufficient contrast to enable all text to be seen and read easily) to 40 percent (one or more images well aligned with the other elements on the page and appropriately sized).

Two categories of scoring criteria on the After-School Exercise large task were evidence of Level 4, the highest level of achievement on the CIL scale. Each category was the highest (worth two score points) within its partial credit criterion. Posters at Level 4 showed a consistent use of formatting of the text elements so that the role of all the elements was clear. This attribute is an example of software features being used to enhance the communicative efficacy of an information product.

Students completing posters at this level were able to go beyond simple application of commands to deliberately and precisely use the software tools so that the text's layout (through such features as bulleted lists, indenting, and paragraph spacing) and format (e.g., different font types, sizes, and features) provided readers with consistent information about the role of the different elements on the poster. Those reading the poster would be immediately clear as to which text represented headings or body information and why the information had been grouped as it had (i.e., to convey different categories of meaning within the poster). In short, these students could use formatting tools in ways that enabled readers to understand the structure of information in the poster and thus gain intended meaning from it.

At Level 4, students could furthermore select *relevant* information about their chosen activity and adapt it, by simplifying or summarizing it, for use in the poster. As noted above, the information presented in the website was discursive, containing detail relevant (e.g., explanation of the activity and equipment) or irrelevant (e.g., the history of the activity) to the explicit purpose of the poster. Although Level 4 might represent an aspiration beyond the capability of most young people in the ICILS target age group, some of the surveyed students did do work commensurate with this level of achievement. Overall, 15 percent of students used the formatting tools sufficiently consistently throughout the poster to show the role of the different text elements. Seven percent of students were able to select the relevant key points from the resources and adapt them to suit the purpose of the poster.

Comparison of CIL across countries

Distribution of student achievement scores

Table 3.4 shows the distribution of student achievement on the CIL test for all countries and benchmarking participants. The length of the bars shows the spread of student scores within each country. The dotted vertical lines indicate the cut-points between proficiency levels. The average country scores on the CIL scale ranged from 361 to 553 scale points, thereby forming a range that spanned a standard of proficiency below Level 1 to a standard of proficiency within Level 3. This range was equivalent to almost two standard deviations. The distribution of country means is skewed. The range in mean scores from Chile to the Czech Republic shown in Table 3.4 is 66 scale points. Two countries, Thailand and Turkey, with respective means of 113 and 126 scale points,[6] sit below Chile. Table 3.4 shows, in effect, a large group of countries with similar mean CIL scale scores, and two countries with substantially lower scores.

Table 3.4 also highlights, through the length of the bars in the graphical part of the table, differences in the within-country student score distributions. The standard deviation of scores ranges from a minimum of 62 scale points in the Czech Republic to 100 scale points in Turkey.[7] The spread appears to be unrelated to the average scale score for each country. Also, the variation in student CIL scores within countries is greater than that between countries, with the median distance between the lowest five percent and the highest five percent of CIL scores being around 258 scale points. Thailand and Turkey have the largest spread of scores, with 316 and 327 respective score points between the lowest five percent and the highest 95 percent of CIL scale scores in those countries.

The differences between the average scores of adjacent countries across the highest achieving 12 countries shown in Table 3.4 are slight. In most cases, the difference is fewer than 10 scale points (one tenth of a standard deviation). Larger differences are evident between Slovenia and Lithuania (16 scale points) and Thailand and Turkey (13 scale points). The average scale score of students in Thailand is, in turn, 113 scale points below the respective average of students in Chile.

CIL relative to the ICT Development Index and national student–computer ratios

Table 3.4 provides information about the average age of students in ICILS countries, the ICT Development Index for those countries,[8] and the student–computer ratio in each country. The ICILS research team considered the ICT Development Index and student–

---

6 In this and subsequent comparisons in this report, the differences reported are differences in the true (unrounded) values that are then rounded to the nearest whole number.

7 The standard deviations of student CIL across countries are shown in Appendix C.

8 The ICT Development Index (IDI) is a composite index that incorporates 11 different indicators relating to ICT readiness (infrastructure, access), ICT usage (individuals using the internet), and proxy indicators of ICT skills (adult literacy, secondary and tertiary enrolment). Each country is given a score out of 10 that can be used to provide a benchmarking measure with which to compare ICT development levels with other countries and within countries over time. Countries are ranked according to their IDI score.

computer ratio as means of ascertaining the *digital divide* across countries. Although this term is a broad-reaching and sometimes contested one, it most commonly refers to the notion of people in societies having varying degrees of opportunity to access and use ICT (see, for example, van Dijk, 2006, p. 223). Where, in this section, we include the ICT Development Index as a means of comparing general access to technology across countries, we also include the student–computer ratio to compare the students' access to computers at school across countries.

The relevant information in Table 3.4 suggests a strong association between a country's average CIL achievement and that country's ICT Development Index score. We recorded, at the country level, a Pearson's correlation coefficient of 0.82, an outcome which suggests that the higher the level of ICT development in a country, the higher the average CIL achievement of its eighth-grade students.

When interpreting this result, it is important to take into account the relatively small number of countries as well as the fact that the two countries with the lowest ICT Development Index scores (Thailand and Turkey) had much lower CIL average scores than all other countries. However, when we removed these two countries from the Pearson calculation, the correlation between average CIL scores and the ICT Development scores remained strong at 0.62.

We also found a strong negative association across countries between the student–computer ratio and a country's average CIL. We recorded a correlation coefficient of -0.70, which suggests that, on average, students had higher levels of CIL in countries with fewer students per computer. This relationship is consistent with the association between the CIL performance and ICT Development Index scores.

However, it is also important, when interpreting this result, to take into account the relatively small number of countries and, in particular, the fact that the country with the lowest CIL average, Turkey, had a much higher ratio of students to computers (80:1) than other ICILS countries had. When we removed Turkey from the calculation, the correlation coefficient between average CIL scores and student–computer ratio dropped to -0.26 (or -0.32 when we included the Canadian provinces).

Pair-wise comparisons of CIL

The information provided in Table 3.5 permits pair-wise comparisons of CIL scale score averages between any two countries. An upwards pointing triangle in a cell indicates that the average CIL scale score in the country at the beginning of the row is statistically significantly higher than the scale score in the comparison country at the top of the column. A downwards pointing triangle in a cell indicates that the average CIL scale score in the country at the beginning of the row is statistically significantly lower than the scale score in the comparison country. The unshaded cells (those without a symbol) indicate that no statistically significant difference was recorded between the CIL scale scores of the two countries. The shaded cells on the diagonal from top left to bottom right of the table are blank because these cells represent comparisons between each country and itself.

Table 3.4: Country averages for CIL, years of schooling, average age, ICT Index, student–computer ratios and percentile graph

Country	Years of Schooling	Average Age	Computer and Information Literacy Score	Average CIL Score	ICT Development Index Score (and Country Rank)	Student–Computer Ratios
Czech Republic	8	14.3		553 (2.1) ▲	6.40 (34)	10 (0.3)
Australia	8	14.0		542 (2.3) ▲	7.90 (11)	3 (0.3)
Poland	8	14.8		537 (2.4) ▲	6.31 (37)	10 (0.5)
Norway (Grade 9)[1]	9	14.8		537 (2.4) ▲	8.13 (6)	2 (0.1)
Korea, Republic of	8	14.2		536 (2.7) ▲	8.57 (1)	20 (2.3)
Germany[†]	8	14.5		523 (2.4) ▲	7.46 (19)	11 (0.8)
Slovak Republic	8	14.3		517 (4.6) ▲	6.05 (43)	9 (0.5)
Russian Federation[2]	8	15.2		516 (2.8) ▲	6.19 (40)	17 (1.0)
Croatia	8	14.6		512 (2.9) ▲	6.31 (38)	26 (0.8)
Slovenia	8	13.8		511 (2.2) ▲	6.76 (28)	15 (0.5)
Lithuania	8	14.7		494 (3.6)	5.88 (44)	13 (0.7)
Chile	8	14.2		487 (3.1) ▼	5.46 (51)	22 (4.7)
Thailand[2]	8	13.9		373 (4.7) ▼	3.54 (95)	14 (0.9)
Turkey	8	14.1		361 (5.0) ▼	4.64 (69)	80 (16.0)
Countries not meeting sample requirements						
Denmark	8	15.1		542 (3.5)	8.35 (4)	4 (0.4)
Hong Kong SAR	8	14.1		509 (7.4)	7.92 (10)	8 (0.8)
Netherlands	8	14.3		535 (4.7)	8.00 (7)	5 (0.8)
Switzerland	8	14.7		526 (4.6)	7.78 (13)	7 (0.6)
Benchmarking participants						
Newfoundland and Labrador, Canada	8	13.8		528 (2.8)	7.38 (20)[3]	6 (0.0)
Ontario, Canada	8	13.8		547 (3.2)	7.38 (20)[3]	6 (0.3)
Benchmarking participant not meeting sample requirements						
City of Buenos Aires, Argentina	8	14.2		450 (8.6)	5.36 (53)[4]	33 (9.4)

Below 1   L1   L2   L3   L4

▲ Achievement significantly higher than ICILS 2013 average   ▼ Achievement significantly lower than ICILS 2013 average

Notes to table on opposite page.

Percentiles of performance
5th   25th   75th   95th
Mean and Confidence Interval (±2SE)

Table 3.5: Multiple comparisons of average country CIL scores

Country	Czech Republic	Australia	Poland	Norway (Grade 9)[1]	Korea, Republic of	Germany[†]	Slovak Republic	Russian Federation[2]	Croatia	Slovenia	Lithuania	Chile	Thailand[2]	Turkey	Ontario, Canada	Newfoundland and Labrador, Canada
Czech Republic		▲	▲	▲	▲	▲	▲	▲	▲	▲	▲	▲	▲	▲		▲
Australia	▼					▲	▲	▲	▲	▲	▲	▲	▲	▲		▲
Poland	▼					▲	▲	▲	▲	▲	▲	▲	▲	▲	▼	▲
Norway (Grade 9)[1]	▼					▲	▲	▲	▲	▲	▲	▲	▲	▲	▼	▲
Korea, Republic of	▼					▲	▲	▲	▲	▲	▲	▲	▲	▲	▼	▲
Germany[†]	▼	▼	▼	▼	▼				▲	▲	▲	▲	▲	▲	▼	
Slovak Republic	▼	▼	▼	▼	▼						▲	▲	▲	▲	▼	▼
Russian Federation[2]	▼	▼	▼	▼	▼						▲	▲	▲	▲	▼	▼
Croatia	▼	▼	▼	▼	▼	▼					▲	▲	▲	▲	▼	▼
Slovenia	▼	▼	▼	▼	▼	▼					▲	▲	▲	▲	▼	▼
Lithuania	▼	▼	▼	▼	▼	▼	▼	▼	▼	▼			▲	▲	▼	▼
Chile	▼	▼	▼	▼	▼	▼	▼	▼	▼	▼			▲	▲	▼	▼
Thailand[2]	▼	▼	▼	▼	▼	▼	▼	▼	▼	▼	▼	▼			▼	▼
Turkey	▼	▼	▼	▼	▼	▼	▼	▼	▼	▼	▼	▼			▼	▼
Benchmarking participants																
Ontario, Canada			▲	▲	▲	▲	▲	▲	▲	▲	▲	▲	▲	▲		▲
Newfoundland and Labrador, Canada	▼	▼	▼	▼	▼		▲	▲	▲	▲	▲	▲	▲	▲	▼	

Notes:

† Met guidelines for sampling participation rates only after replacement schools were included.

1 National Desired Population does not correspond to International Desired Population.

2 Country surveyed the same cohort of students but at the beginning of the next school year.

▲ Average achievement significantly higher than in comparison country

▼ Average achievement significantly lower than in comparison country

☐ Average achievement not statistically significantly different to the comparison country

Table 3.5 also helps us determine whether relatively small differences in average CIL scale scores are statistically significant. The spread of the empty cells around the diagonal shows that the mean of student CIL in most countries was typically not statistically significantly different from the means in the three to five countries with the closest means but significantly different from the means in all other countries. The only exceptions to this pattern can be seen at the extreme ends of the achievement distribution, which, at the lower end, further illustrate the skew of the distribution described previously.

Notes to Table 3.4:

ICT Development Index score and country rank data relate to 2012 and were collected from the International Telecommunications Union. Source: http://www.itu.int/en/ITU-D/Statistics/Pages/stat/default.aspx [27/02/14].

Data on public expenditure on education sourced from the *Human Development Report 2013* unless otherwise stated. Source: http://hdr.undp.org/sites/default/files/reports/14/hdr2013_en_complete.pdf [15/08/14].

() Standard errors appear in parentheses. Because results are rounded to the nearest whole number, some totals may appear inconsistent.

† Met guidelines for sampling participation rates only after replacement schools were included.

1 National Desired Population does not correspond to International Desired Population.

2 Country surveyed the same cohort of students but at the beginning of the next school year.

3 Data relate to all of Canada.

4 Data relate to all of Argentina.

Table 3.6: Percent of students at each proficiency level across countries

Country	Below Level 1 (fewer than 407 score points)	Level 1 (from 407 to 491 score points)	Level 2 (from 492 to 576 score points)	Level 3 (from 577 to 661 score points)	Level 4 (above 661 score points)	Distribution of Students across Levels
Korea, Republic of	9 (0.7)	19 (1.1)	36 (1.6)	30 (1.3)	5 (0.5)	
Australia	5 (0.6)	18 (1.0)	42 (1.1)	30 (1.2)	4 (0.5)	
Poland	6 (0.7)	20 (1.1)	42 (1.3)	29 (1.6)	4 (0.5)	
Czech Republic	2 (0.4)	13 (0.9)	48 (1.2)	34 (1.3)	3 (0.4)	
Norway (Grade 9)[1]	5 (0.7)	19 (1.3)	46 (1.2)	27 (1.3)	3 (0.5)	
Slovak Republic	12 (1.6)	21 (1.0)	40 (1.4)	25 (1.3)	2 (0.4)	
Russian Federation[2]	9 (1.1)	27 (1.6)	41 (1.4)	21 (1.2)	2 (0.3)	
Croatia	11 (1.2)	25 (1.2)	42 (1.5)	21 (1.3)	1 (0.3)	
Germany[†]	7 (0.8)	22 (1.4)	45 (1.5)	24 (1.2)	1 (0.3)	
Lithuania	15 (1.3)	30 (1.5)	39 (1.4)	15 (1.0)	1 (0.3)	
Chile	18 (1.4)	30 (1.7)	40 (1.5)	13 (1.1)	0 (0.2)	
Slovenia	8 (0.7)	28 (1.4)	47 (1.3)	16 (1.1)	0 (0.3)	
Thailand[2]	64 (2.1)	23 (1.4)	11 (1.2)	2 (0.4)	0 (0.1)	
Turkey	67 (1.8)	24 (1.2)	8 (0.9)	1 (0.3)	0 (0.1)	
ICILS 2013 average	17 (0.3)	23 (0.3)	38 (0.4)	21 (0.3)	2 (0.1)	
Countries not meeting sample requirements						
Denmark	4 (0.8)	17 (1.4)	46 (1.7)	30 (1.6)	2 (0.6)	
Hong Kong SAR	15 (2.5)	23 (1.5)	37 (2.0)	23 (1.9)	3 (0.6)	
Netherlands	8 (1.2)	19 (1.6)	41 (2.0)	29 (2.0)	4 (0.7)	
Switzerland	6 (1.4)	24 (1.6)	45 (2.0)	23 (2.0)	2 (0.5)	
Benchmarking participants						
Newfoundland and Labrador, Canada	7 (1.1)	24 (2.1)	40 (2.7)	25 (2.7)	4 (1.3)	
Ontario, Canada	4 (0.7)	18 (1.1)	42 (1.3)	32 (1.4)	5 (0.8)	
Benchmarking participant not meeting sample requirements						
City of Buenos Aires, Argentina	31 (3.6)	34 (2.5)	27 (2.5)	7 (1.6)	0 (0.3)	

Legend: ■ Below Level 1　■ Level 1　■ Level 2　■ Level 3　□ Level 4

Notes:
() Standard errors appear in parentheses. Because results are rounded to the nearest whole number, some totals may appear inconsistent.
† Met guidelines for sampling participation rates only after replacement schools were included.
1 National Desired Population does not correspond to International Desired Population.
2 Country surveyed the same cohort of students but at the beginning of the next school year.

Achievement across countries with respect to proficiency levels

The countries in Table 3.6 appear in descending order according to the percentage of students with scores that positioned them at Level 4 on the CIL scale. The order of countries in Table 3.6 is similar to that in Table 3.4, where the countries are shown in descending order of average score. Smaller differences in the ordering of countries between the two tables are a result of different distributions of students across the levels within the countries that have similar average student CIL scores.

The data in Table 3.6 show that, across all countries, 81 percent of students achieved scores that placed them within CIL Levels 1, 2, and 3. Overall, however, the distribution of student scores across countries sits within Level 2. In all countries except Thailand and Turkey, the highest percentage of students is evident at Level 2. The percentage of students in Level 2 in these countries varies between 48 percent in the Czech Republic and 36 percent in Korea. In Thailand and Turkey, 64 and 67 percent respectively of students are below Level 1. In total, 87 percent of students in Thailand and 91 percent in Turkey were achieving at Level 1 or below.

Although majorities of students in most countries had CIL scores at Level 2, we can see some variation in the distribution of percentages across these countries. In six countries with the highest percentage of students at Level 2—Korea, Australia, Poland, the Czech Republic, Norway (Grade 9), and Ontario—the proportion of students above Level 2 (i.e., at Levels 3 and 4 combined) is higher than the proportion of students below Level 2 (i.e., at Level 1 or below). In the remaining eight countries, that is, those countries with the highest percentage of students in Level 2 (the Slovak Republic, the Russian Federation, Croatia, Germany, Lithuania, Chile, Slovenia, and Newfoundland and Labrador), the number of students above Level 2 is smaller than the number of students below Level 2.

Conclusion

The ICILS assessment, the development of which was based on the ICILS conceptual framework, provided the basis for a set of scores and descriptions of four described levels of CIL proficiency. Those descriptions articulate in concrete form the meaning of the construct *computer and information literacy*. It and related constructs have until now lacked an empirically based interpretation that could underpin measurement and analysis of this form of literacy.

Our comparisons of CIL scores showed considerable variation across the participating ICILS countries. In the five highest-performing countries, 30 percent or more of the student scores could be found at Levels 3 or 4. In contrast, for the two lowest-achieving countries, only one or two percent of students were achieving at Levels 3 or 4. More than 85 percent of the student achievement scores in these two countries were below Level 2. For all other countries, 31 percent of student scores sat, on average, below Level 2.

There was also considerable variation within countries. On average, the achievement scores of 80 percent of students extended across 250 score points or three proficiency levels. The variation within countries was greatest in Turkey, Thailand, and the Slovak Republic and lowest in the Czech Republic, Slovenia, and Denmark.

Across countries, CIL average scores were positively associated with the ICT Development Index, and negatively associated with the ratio of students to computers. ICILS included these indices and their associations with CIL in the hope of inspiring more detailed investigations into the relationship, within and across countries, between access to ICT and CIL.

CHAPTER 4:

The Influence of Students' Personal and Home Background on Computer and Information Literacy

Many studies (among them those by Bradley & Corwyn, 2002; Saha, 1997) show that students' personal and home background influences their acquisition of knowledge as well as other learning outcomes. Among the student background factors found to be statistically significantly associated with educational achievement are gender, parental socioeconomic status, language used at home, ethnicity, and whether or not the student and/or his or her parents have an immigrant background. Research also provides evidence of the particular impact that students' respective socioeconomic backgrounds have on their achievement. This association has been observed across many learning areas (see, for example, Saha, 1997; Sirin, 2005; Woessmann, 2004).

According to more recent research studies, home background factors also influence the learning of information and communication technology (ICT) skills (Ministerial Council for Education, Early Childhood Development and Youth Affairs [MCEECDYA], 2010; Nasah, DaCosta, Kinsell, & Seok, 2010). Evidence from many countries highlights considerable disparities in students' access to digital resources at home. Both researchers and commentators claim that these disparities affect the opportunities students have to develop the capabilities required for living in modern societies (Warschauer & Matuchniak, 2010).

Given this body of research, the ICILS research team deemed inclusion of an additional home factor of particular importance when reviewing the association between home background and communication and information literacy (CIL). That factor was the extent to which students have access to ICT resources in their respective homes.

In this chapter, we investigate ICILS survey data with regard to Research Question 4: *What aspects of students' personal and social background (such as gender, socioeconomic background, and language background) are related to computer and information literacy?* In order to help answer this question, we reviewed potential associations between CIL achievement and gender as well as between CIL and four types of indicators of students' home background.

1. Educational aspirations (expected highest educational attainment);

2. Socioeconomic background (parental occupation, parental education, and number of books at home);

3. Immigrant status and language use; and

4. Home-based IT resources (number of computers or laptops and internet access at home).

After reviewing the bivariate relationships between each of the indicators and the CIL test scores, we report the results of a multivariate regression analysis that we conducted in order to (1) explore the influence of different indicators on CIL after we had controlled for all other indicators, and (2) how much three different types of factor (students' personal background, socioeconomic background, and home ICT resources)

© International Association for the Evaluation of Educational Achievement (IEA) 2014
J. Fraillon et al., *Preparing for Life in a Digital Age*, DOI 10.1007/978-3-319-14222-7_5

contributed to the explanation of variation in CIL. We chose not to include immigrant status and language in the multivariate analysis because many of the ICILS countries had only very small numbers of immigrants or students who spoke languages other than the language of the ICILS assessment at home.

Gender and CIL

Many studies on educational achievement across a broad range of learning areas show differences in achievement between females and males. While crossnational research on reading literacy at most school levels shows larger gender differences in favor of females, males tend to be somewhat more proficient in learning areas such as mathematics and science (Mullis, Martin, Kennedy, & Foy, 2007; OECD, 2010). Results from Australian assessments of ICT literacy in 2008 and 2011 showed significantly higher levels of achievement for females when compared to male students in both Grade 6 and Grade 10 (Australian Curriculum, Assessment and Reporting Authority, 2012; MCEECDYA, 2010).

Table 4.1 shows the average scores of female and male students in each country. The average CIL scale scores of female students were statistically significantly higher than those of male students in all countries except Turkey and Thailand. In these two countries, there was no statistically significant difference between the average scores of female students and male students. The international average score for female students was 509 scale points, and for male students it was 491 scale points—a difference of 18 scale points, equivalent to about one fifth of the ICILS standard deviation.

The magnitude of the statistically significant differences in achievement between female and male students within countries ranged from 12 scale points in the Czech Republic to 38 scale points in Korea.[1] We observed no evidence across most countries of systematic relationships between the magnitude of differences in achievement by geographical location or average scale score.

Home background indicators and CIL

Educational aspirations

Students' aspirations with regard to their education was another variable that ICILS viewed as important when analyzing variation in student CIL. We can reasonably assume that students' home environment, interests, previous study results at school, and sense of their own success at school influence their expectations of undertaking further studies. Various research studies show associations between expectations and achievement in several learning areas (Valentine, DuBois, & Cooper, 2004).

One of the questions in the ICILS student questionnaire asked students to state the level of educational qualification they expected to attain. In order to aid our analysis of students' reponses to this question, we used the International Standard Classification of Education (ISCED: UNESCO, 2006) to define categories for the levels of educational attainment but first asked the study's national research centers to adapt these to local contexts.

---

1 The nonsignificant differences were in Thailand (nine points) and Turkey (two points).

Table 4.1: Gender differences in CIL

Country	Mean Scale Score Males	Mean Scale Score Females	Difference (Females – Males)	Score Point Difference Between Females and Males
Australia	529 (3.3)	554 (2.8)	24 (4.0)	
Chile	474 (3.9)	499 (3.9)	25 (4.8)	
Croatia	505 (3.6)	520 (3.1)	15 (3.5)	
Czech Republic	548 (2.8)	559 (2.0)	12 (2.7)	
Germany[†]	516 (3.2)	532 (2.9)	16 (3.8)	
Korea, Republic of	517 (3.7)	556 (3.1)	38 (4.1)	
Lithuania	486 (3.8)	503 (4.2)	17 (3.4)	
Norway (Grade 9)[1]	525 (3.1)	548 (2.8)	23 (3.5)	
Poland	531 (3.1)	544 (2.9)	13 (3.7)	
Russian Federation[2]	510 (3.4)	523 (2.8)	13 (2.4)	
Slovak Republic	511 (5.1)	524 (4.8)	13 (4.1)	
Slovenia	497 (2.8)	526 (2.8)	29 (3.6)	
Thailand[2]	369 (5.3)	378 (5.7)	9 (5.6)	
Turkey	360 (5.4)	362 (5.2)	2 (3.8)	
ICILS 2013 average	491 (1.0)	509 (1.0)	18 (1.0)	
Countries not meeting sample requirements				
Denmark	534 (4.1)	549 (4.7)	15 (5.4)	
Hong Kong SAR	498 (9.2)	523 (7.5)	25 (8.3)	
Netherlands	525 (5.4)	546 (5.1)	20 (4.9)	
Switzerland	522 (4.6)	529 (5.5)	6 (4.3)	
Benchmarking participants				
Newfoundland and Labrador, Canada	509 (3.7)	544 (4.1)	35 (6.0)	
Ontario, Canada	535 (3.4)	560 (4.0)	25 (3.8)	
Benchmarking participant not meeting sample requirements				
City of Buenos Aires, Argentina	448 (9.7)	453 (8.9)	5 (6.9)	

Chart scale: 0, 25, 50 — Females score higher

■ Gender difference statistically significant at .05 level
□ Gender difference not statistically significant

Notes:
( ) Standard errors appear in parentheses. Because some results are rounded to the nearest whole number, some totals may appear inconsistent.
[†] Met guidelines for sampling participation rates only after replacement schools were included.
[1] National Desired Population does not correspond to International Desired Population.
[2] Country surveyed the same cohort of students but at the beginning of the next school year.

Students were asked whether they expected to complete a tertiary university degree (ISCED Level 5A or 6), a post-secondary nonuniversity degree (ISCED Level 4 or 5B: for example, at a technical college), an upper-secondary degree (ISCED Level 3: general, prevocational, or vocational), a lower-secondary degree (ISCED Level 2), or whether they did not expect to finish lower-secondary schooling. Given the low numbers of students who did not expect to complete lower-secondary education, we combined the last two categories into one (students who did not expect to complete any education beyond lower-secondary).

Table 4.2 shows the percentages in each reporting category, the average CIL score for students in each category, and the overall differences between the highest (university degree) and lowest categories (lower-secondary education or below). On average across the participating countries, about half of the students expected to complete university education, 17 percent expected to attain a post-secondary nonuniversity degree, and 24 percent to obtain an upper-secondary qualification. Eight percent expected to go no further than lower-secondary education. However, large expectation differences were evident across the ICILS education systems (see Table 4.2). For example, while three quarters of Korean students expected to obtain a university degree, only one in five German students expected to do so.

Generally, CIL average scores increased with levels of expected educational attainment. Across participating countries, the difference in CIL scores between students not expecting to have a qualification beyond lower-secondary education and those expecting to complete university was, on average, 89 score points. The range in score points extended from 54 in the benchmarking participant Newfoundland and Labrador (Canada) and 65 in the Czech Republic to 112 in Croatia and 113 in the Slovak Republic. In a few countries, there was no increase in CIL scores from the "expect to complete upper-secondary" category to the "expect to complete post-secondary nonuniversity" category.

Socioeconomic background

Socioeconomic background is a construct regarded as manifest in occupation, education, and wealth (Hauser, 1994). While it is widely regarded internationally as an important correlate of a range of learning outcomes (Sirin, 2005; Woessmann, 2004), there is no scholarly consensus on which measures should be used for capturing family background (Entwistle & Astone, 1994; Hauser, 1994) and no agreed standards for creating composite measures of socioeconomic status (Gottfried, 1985; Mueller & Parcel, 1981). Furthermore, in the context of international studies, there are caveats relating to the validity and crossnational comparability of socioeconomic background measures (Buchmann, 2002). In this chapter, our consideration of the influence of socioeconomic background on CIL focuses on within-country associations between indicators of socioeconomic status and test performance.

In order to gather information on the educational attainment of students' parents, the ICILS student questionnaire asked students to identify their parents' level of attainment on a list of predefined categories. These categories drew on the ISCED definitions and included tertiary university degree (ISCED 5A or 6), post-secondary nonuniversity degree (ISCED 4 or 5B), upper-secondary completion (ISCED 3), lower-secondary completion (ISCED 2), and incomplete lower-secondary education (OECD, 1999; UNESCO, 2006).

Table 4.2: National percentages and CIL score averages for students in categories of expected education

Country	Students Who Expect to Complete:								Difference (University Education - Lower Secondary or Below)*	Score Point Difference Between Lowest and Highest Category
	Lower-secondary education or below		Upper-secondary education		Post-secondary nonuniversity education		Tertiary university education			
	Percentages	Mean CIL score	Percentages	Mean CIL score	Percentages	Mean CIL score	Percentages	Mean CIL score		
Australia	6 (0.4)	463 (7.0)	18 (0.9)	507 (3.7)	16 (0.7)	524 (3.2)	60 (1.2)	566 (2.4)	103 (7.3)	
Chile	0 (0.1)	^	10 (0.8)	422 (6.3)	26 (1.2)	461 (4.9)	63 (1.5)	510 (2.8)	^	
Croatia	2 (0.4)	437 (12.5)	33 (1.3)	472 (3.6)	29 (1.2)	521 (3.2)	36 (1.5)	549 (3.2)	112 (11.9)	
Czech Republic	2 (0.3)	511 (7.8)	40 (1.1)	528 (3.0)	8 (0.5)	557 (4.8)	49 (1.0)	576 (1.8)	65 (7.9)	
Germany†	34 (1.5)	484 (4.4)	41 (1.3)	540 (3.2)	4 (0.5)	526 (7.3)	21 (1.0)	567 (3.4)	83 (5.3)	
Korea, Republic of	4 (0.4)	472 (9.8)	9 (0.7)	489 (7.0)	13 (0.7)	522 (5.2)	74 (1.0)	548 (2.9)	76 (9.8)	
Lithuania	8 (0.7)	429 (6.4)	13 (0.8)	452 (5.7)	31 (1.2)	485 (5.0)	48 (1.3)	525 (3.5)	97 (6.5)	
Norway (Grade 9)[1]	2 (0.4)	481 (12.3)	17 (0.9)	506 (4.9)	16 (0.9)	520 (4.7)	64 (1.2)	552 (2.5)	70 (12.5)	
Poland	3 (0.4)	470 (11.0)	44 (1.1)	505 (3.1)	9 (0.7)	542 (4.9)	44 (1.2)	575 (2.4)	105 (11.2)	
Russian Federation[2]	4 (0.5)	456 (7.1)	9 (0.6)	474 (5.4)	22 (1.1)	491 (5.6)	65 (1.3)	535 (2.5)	79 (6.9)	
Slovak Republic	5 (0.5)	440 (14.7)	41 (1.4)	483 (5.9)	8 (0.6)	536 (7.1)	46 (1.5)	553 (3.7)	113 (14.7)	
Slovenia	4 (0.4)	442 (8.2)	23 (0.8)	478 (3.8)	41 (1.1)	514 (2.6)	32 (1.0)	540 (2.9)	97 (8.1)	
Thailand[2]	11 (0.9)	316 (6.9)	20 (1.4)	330 (6.1)	9 (0.8)	354 (7.7)	60 (1.9)	402 (5.2)	86 (7.9)	
Turkey	19 (1.1)	311 (7.5)	13 (0.8)	334 (7.3)	11 (0.7)	348 (6.5)	57 (1.4)	388 (5.0)	76 (7.8)	
ICILS 2013 average	**8 (0.2)**	**439 (2.6)**	**24 (0.3)**	**466 (1.4)**	**17 (0.2)**	**493 (1.4)**	**51 (0.4)**	**527 (0.9)**	**89 (2.6)**	
Countries not meeting sample requirements										
Denmark	5 (0.7)	498 (8.6)	55 (1.6)	535 (3.4)	11 (0.7)	549 (5.9)	28 (1.5)	568 (4.3)	70 (8.3)	
Hong Kong SAR	14 (1.2)	479 (13.8)	8 (0.8)	454 (10.6)	15 (0.8)	494 (9.9)	63 (1.8)	528 (5.9)	48 (11.1)	
Netherlands	20 (1.5)	474 (6.4)	39 (1.6)	531 (4.3)	15 (1.1)	555 (4.8)	25 (2.2)	584 (5.9)	110 (7.5)	
Switzerland	31 (2.7)	502 (7.5)	45 (2.5)	527 (4.9)	6 (0.8)	541 (9.7)	17 (1.6)	567 (6.2)	65 (8.9)	
Benchmarking participants										
Newfoundland and Labrador, Canada	4 (0.6)	483 (10.0)	6 (0.9)	486 (10.8)	7 (0.8)	484 (12.3)	83 (1.3)	537 (3.1)	54 (10.5)	
Ontario, Canada	3 (0.4)	484 (11.0)	7 (0.6)	505 (8.7)	2 (0.4)	512 (11.2)	88 (0.9)	554 (2.7)	69 (10.7)	
Benchmarking participant not meeting sample requirements										
City of Buenos Aires, Argentina	8 (1.1)	403 (15.4)	19 (1.5)	423 (11.2)	32 (1.5)	469 (7.7)	40 (2.0)	474 (9.7)	71 (14.2)	

Students in highest category score higher than in lowest

■ Difference statistically significant at .05 level

□ Difference not statistically significant

Notes:
* Statistically significant ($p<.05$) coefficients in **bold**.
() Standard errors appear in parentheses. Because some results are rounded to the nearest whole number, some totals may appear inconsistent.
† Met guidelines for sampling participation rates only after replacement schools were included.
[1] National Desired Population does not correspond to International Desired Population.
[2] Country surveyed the same cohort of students but at the beginning of the next school year.
^ Subgroup sample size too small for reporting reliable estimate.

Where students provided data for both their parents, we used the highest ISCED level as the indicator of parental educational attainment. Given the very low percentages of students with parents who had not attained lower-secondary education, we combined the two last categories and referred to the new one as lower-secondary education or below. On average across the ICILS countries, 99 percent of students provided valid parental education data, reflecting the fact that computer-administered questionnaires generally facilitate high response rates.

Table 4.3 records the percentages of students in the categories denoting parental highest educational level, as well as the average CIL scores within each category. It also shows the results from a bivariate regression of CIL on highest parental education (in approximate years of schooling).

Across participating countries, 15 percent of students, on average, had parents who had not completed an educational level higher than lower secondary, 33 percent had at least one parent with an upper-secondary qualification, 17 percent had at least one parent with a post-secondary nonuniversity degree, and 35 percent had at least one parent with a university degree. There was considerable variation across the participating countries. In most countries, the percentages of students with parents whose educational attainment reached no higher than the lower-secondary level were below 10 percent. In Thailand and Turkey, however, the corresponding percentages were 50 percent and 59 percent respectively. In Korea, Norway, Ontario (Canada), and the Russian Federation, more than half of the students reported having at least one parent with a university degree, whereas only a fifth of the students or fewer reported this in Thailand and Turkey. The percentages for parental education in Germany suggest that the ISCED categories may not have adequately captured this country's dual system of vocational and academic qualifications.

In all countries, we observed a pattern wherein CIL scores increased in correspondence with increased parental educational attainment. On average across ICILS countries, we found a difference of 72 CIL score points between students with at least one parent who had a university education and those whose parents had not attained a qualification beyond lower secondary. These score differences ranged from 39 score points in Korea to 132 score points in the Slovak Republic.

The ICILS student questionnaire collected data on parental occupational status through questions that allowed students to give open-ended responses. The students' responses were classified during the analysis process according to the International Standard Classification of Occupations (ISCO-08) framework (International Labour Organization, 2007). Research indicates relatively high consistencies between data on parental occupation collected from students and from parents (Schulz, 2006; Vereecken & Vandegehuchte, 2003).

To generate a continuous measure of occupational status, Ganzeboom, de Graaf, and Treiman (1992) coded the ISCO codes in order to derive their International Socio-economic Index (SEI). The SEI provides a crossnationally comparable framework for organizing occupations in a hierarchical order according to their occupational status. We assigned SEI scores to each parent's occupation and then, for each student with two parents, took the higher of the two SEI scores as the indicator score. For students from single-parent families, the one score served as the indicator.

Table 4.3: National percentages and CIL score averages for students in categories of parental educational attainment

| Country | Students With Parents Whose Highest Attained Educational Level Was: | | | | | | | | Difference (University Education - Lower Secondary or Below)* | Score Point Difference Between Lowest and Highest Category |
| | Lower-secondary education or below | | Upper-secondary education | | Post-secondary nonuniversity education | | Tertiary university education | | | |
	Percentages	Mean CIL score	Percentages	Mean CIL score	Percentages	Mean CIL score	Percentages	Mean CIL score		
Australia	11 (0.7)	506 (5.1)	22 (0.7)	518 (3.5)	22 (0.8)	539 (3.3)	46 (1.0)	564 (2.8)	**58** (5.4)	
Chile	17 (1.0)	436 (5.9)	36 (1.3)	475 (4.1)	25 (1.2)	509 (4.3)	22 (1.4)	525 (3.8)	**90** (6.7)	
Croatia	4 (0.6)	446 (10.5)	56 (1.4)	505 (3.4)	19 (0.8)	522 (4.6)	21 (1.2)	539 (4.2)	**93** (10.9)	
Czech Republic	2 (0.2)	496 (15.4)	63 (1.2)	548 (2.0)	6 (0.5)	553 (5.7)	29 (1.1)	569 (3.4)	**74** (14.5)	
Germany†	40 (1.3)	509 (4.5)	30 (1.3)	534 (3.9)	10 (0.6)	531 (5.6)	20 (1.2)	554 (4.4)	**44** (6.9)	
Korea, Republic of	1 (0.3)	507 (16.2)	31 (1.3)	525 (3.7)	9 (0.6)	519 (6.3)	59 (1.6)	545 (3.1)	**39** (16.0)	
Lithuania	6 (0.6)	451 (8.2)	18 (1.0)	461 (6.6)	36 (1.0)	498 (4.0)	40 (1.3)	514 (3.9)	**63** (8.9)	
Norway (Grade 9)[1]	2 (0.4)	474 (13.3)	12 (0.7)	521 (5.1)	19 (0.9)	537 (4.5)	66 (1.3)	543 (2.4)	**69** (13.1)	
Poland	2 (0.3)	467 (11.5)	56 (1.2)	522 (2.8)	11 (0.7)	548 (5.0)	31 (1.1)	567 (3.4)	**100** (12.2)	
Russian Federation[2]	4 (0.4)	480 (8.5)	9 (0.6)	492 (6.6)	33 (1.1)	504 (4.1)	54 (1.2)	530 (3.2)	**50** (8.3)	
Slovak Republic	2 (0.4)	408 (19.9)	55 (1.4)	509 (4.9)	8 (0.5)	514 (7.9)	35 (1.3)	540 (4.9)	**132** (19.5)	
Slovenia	3 (0.3)	466 (10.1)	30 (1.1)	498 (3.1)	33 (1.0)	515 (3.3)	34 (1.3)	522 (3.5)	**55** (10.8)	
Thailand[2]	50 (1.8)	350 (5.3)	24 (1.0)	366 (6.1)	7 (0.7)	402 (8.3)	18 (1.5)	438 (7.3)	**88** (8.4)	
Turkey	59 (1.7)	342 (5.2)	23 (1.1)	391 (5.6)	6 (0.4)	370 (9.7)	12 (0.9)	401 (9.8)	59 (10.7)	
ICILS 2013 average	15 (0.2)	453 (2.9)	33 (0.3)	490 (1.2)	17 (0.2)	504 (1.5)	35 (0.3)	525 (1.3)	**72** (3.1)	
Countries not meeting sample requirements										
Denmark	7 (0.8)	515 (8.3)	40 (1.5)	535 (3.5)	21 (1.2)	554 (4.1)	33 (1.2)	556 (4.0)	**41** (8.6)	
Hong Kong SAR	19 (1.4)	496 (8.7)	50 (1.3)	511 (6.4)	10 (1.0)	523 (9.2)	21 (1.5)	516 (11.9)	20 (9.3)	
Netherlands	20 (1.1)	508 (6.2)	38 (1.4)	522 (5.6)	22 (1.0)	560 (4.9)	21 (1.7)	565 (6.4)	**57** (8.0)	
Switzerland	26 (1.8)	510 (7.8)	36 (1.6)	526 (4.3)	14 (1.0)	542 (4.6)	24 (1.8)	539 (7.2)	**29** (7.9)	
Benchmarking participants										
Newfoundland and Labrador, Canada	3 (0.6)	496 (13.2)	15 (1.0)	505 (7.2)	35 (1.6)	527 (4.0)	47 (1.6)	539 (4.1)	**43** (12.7)	
Ontario, Canada	2 (0.4)	493 (14.3)	14 (0.8)	535 (5.8)	32 (1.4)	541 (3.1)	52 (1.7)	559 (3.2)	**65** (13.5)	
Benchmarking participant not meeting sample requirements										
City of Buenos Aires, Argentina	21 (2.3)	406 (11.4)	28 (2.1)	435 (7.8)	24 (1.8)	468 (9.8)	28 (2.3)	496 (10.5)	**90** (13.8)	

Students in highest category score higher than in lowest

■ Difference statistically significant at .05 level
□ Difference not statistically significant

Notes:

* Statistically significant (*p*<.05) coefficients in **bold**.
() Standard errors appear in parentheses. Because some results are rounded to the nearest whole number, some totals may appear inconsistent.
† Met guidelines for sampling participation rates only after replacement schools were included.
[1] National Desired Population does not correspond to International Desired Population.
[2] Country surveyed the same cohort of students but at the beginning of the next school year.

The SEI scale is continuous and ranges from 16 to 90 score points. To describe the parental occupation results in terms of broader categories, we divided the SEI scale into three groups based on international cut-off points. These were "low occupational status" (below 40 score points), "medium occupational status" (40 to 59 score points), and "high occupational status" (60 score points or more). On average across the ICILS countries, valid SEI scores were available for 95 percent of the participating students. The Netherlands did not provide data on parental occupation and so were excluded from this analysis.

To assess the influence of parental occupational status on CIL, we estimated bivariate regression models with highest parental occupation as a predictor. We derived the predictor variable by transforming the original SEI scores to a metric in which a value of zero corresponded to the mean and a value of one to the standard deviation for the combined ICILS database of equally weighted national samples meeting sampling requirements.

Table 4.4 shows the percentage of students with parents in each occupational status category as well as the average CIL scores for the students in each of these groups. Across participating ICILS countries, 39 percent (on average) of students reported that their parents were in the lowest occupational status category (SEI below 40), 37 percent identified their parents as being in the middle category (40 to 59), and 24 percent placed their parents in the highest category (SEI 60 and above). However, there were substantial differences in the distribution across countries. In Thailand and Turkey, over 60 percent of the students had parents in the lowest occupational status group; in Korea, Norway, and Ontario (Canada), only about one fifth of the students had parents in this category.

In all participating countries, the average CIL scores were lowest in the occupational status group with SEI scores below 40 and, with the exception of Hong Kong SAR, highest in the group with SEI scores of 60 and above. On average across participating countries, the difference between students in the highest and lowest parental occupation categories was 54 CIL score points, with differences ranging from 26 score points in Korea to 96 score points in Thailand.

To measure home literacy resources as an additional indicator of students' socioeconomic (and cultural) background, the ICILS student questionnaire asked students to report the number of books (broken down into five categories) in their respective homes. Response categories were "0 to 10 books," "11 to 25 books," "26 to 100 books," "101 to 200 books," and "more than 200 books." Given that our exploratory analyses showed only minor CIL score differences between the highest two categories, we combined these into one reporting category labeled "more than 100 books." On average across countries, 99 percent of the ICILS students had valid data for this indicator. Even with the advent of electronic books, and although the average number of printed books in homes appears to have decreased over time, we consider that number of books at home is a valid indicator of home literacy resources because it continues to be consistently correlated with educational achievement.

Table 4.5 shows the percentage of students in each category together with the average CIL score by category. The table also presents the results from our bivariate regression model, developed in order to determine the effect of home literacy resources on CIL.

Table 4.4: National percentages and CIL score averages for students in categories of parental occupational status

Country	Low Occupational Status (SEI below 40)		Medium Occupational Status (SEI 40 to 59)		High Occupational Status (SEI 60 and above)		Difference (Highest - Lowest SEI Category)*	Score Point Difference Between Lowest and Highest Category
	Percentages	Mean CIL score	Percentages	Mean CIL score	Percentages	Mean CIL score		
Australia	25 (1.1)	512 (3.2)	39 (1.1)	544 (2.6)	36 (1.1)	566 (2.7)	54 (3.8)	
Chile	45 (1.3)	464 (4.1)	35 (1.1)	498 (3.3)	20 (1.1)	532 (3.8)	67 (5.1)	
Croatia	43 (1.4)	496 (3.9)	38 (1.0)	521 (2.9)	19 (0.9)	547 (5.2)	51 (5.5)	
Czech Republic	35 (1.2)	533 (3.3)	47 (1.1)	560 (2.0)	18 (0.8)	582 (2.6)	48 (3.0)	
Germany†	35 (1.3)	501 (4.0)	43 (1.2)	537 (3.0)	23 (1.1)	553 (3.5)	52 (5.7)	
Korea, Republic of	18 (1.0)	526 (4.4)	56 (1.1)	535 (3.3)	26 (1.0)	551 (4.1)	26 (6.0)	
Lithuania	33 (1.3)	477 (4.9)	27 (1.0)	500 (4.2)	40 (1.3)	522 (3.5)	45 (5.1)	
Norway (Grade 9)[1]	21 (1.2)	510 (3.9)	41 (1.1)	536 (3.0)	38 (1.2)	558 (2.6)	48 (4.4)	
Poland	50 (1.2)	517 (3.1)	35 (1.1)	550 (2.8)	16 (0.7)	576 (4.2)	59 (5.0)	
Russian Federation[2]	31 (1.0)	495 (4.4)	38 (1.0)	520 (3.7)	32 (0.9)	539 (2.9)	43 (5.1)	
Slovak Republic	41 (1.5)	498 (4.8)	38 (1.0)	534 (3.8)	21 (1.0)	556 (4.7)	58 (5.7)	
Slovenia	39 (1.1)	493 (2.8)	36 (0.9)	519 (2.8)	25 (1.0)	533 (4.0)	39 (4.2)	
Thailand[2]	61 (1.7)	349 (4.6)	27 (1.2)	399 (7.7)	13 (1.1)	445 (7.6)	96 (9.1)	
Turkey	69 (1.6)	355 (4.3)	20 (1.1)	391 (6.6)	11 (1.0)	424 (9.0)	69 (9.3)	
ICILS 2013 average	39 (0.3)	481 (1.1)	37 (0.3)	510 (1.1)	24 (0.3)	535 (1.3)	54 (1.5)	
Countries not meeting sample requirements								
Denmark	26 (1.3)	523 (4.5)	38 (1.0)	547 (3.0)	37 (1.5)	563 (3.8)	40 (5.2)	
Hong Kong SAR	37 (1.9)	517 (6.7)	26 (1.3)	535 (7.2)	37 (1.9)	532 (6.8)	15 (6.9)	
Netherlands	N/A	N/A	N/A	N/A	N/A	N/A	N/A	
Switzerland	29 (2.0)	506 (8.1)	34 (1.4)	530 (4.3)	37 (1.9)	541 (4.3)	35 (7.8)	
Benchmarking participants								
Newfoundland and Labrador, Canada	28 (1.4)	509 (4.1)	40 (2.1)	532 (4.6)	32 (1.8)	552 (6.5)	42 (7.7)	
Ontario, Canada	22 (1.6)	526 (4.7)	34 (1.2)	550 (3.1)	44 (1.8)	564 (3.1)	38 (5.2)	
Benchmarking participant not meeting sample requirements								
City of Buenos Aires, Argentina	41 (3.7)	421 (7.6)	30 (1.8)	470 (8.7)	29 (3.3)	505 (9.7)	84 (11.5)	

Students in highest category score higher than in lowest

■ Difference statistically significant at .05 level
□ Difference not statistically significant

Notes:
* Statistically significant (p<.05) coefficients in **bold**.
() Standard errors appear in parentheses. Because some results are rounded to the nearest whole number, some totals may appear inconsistent.
† Met guidelines for sampling participation rates only after replacement schools were included.
1 National Desired Population does not correspond to International Desired Population.
2 Country surveyed the same cohort of students but at the beginning of the next school year.

Table 4.5: National percentages and CIL score averages for students in categories of home literacy resources

Country	Home Literacy Category 1 (0 to 10 books)		Home Literacy Category 2 (11 to 25 books)		Home Literacy Category 3 (26 to 100 books)		Home Literacy Category 4 (more than 100 books)		Difference (Highest - Lowest Home Literacy Category)*	Score Point Difference Between Lowest and Highest Category
	Percentages	Mean CIL score	Percentages	Mean CIL score	Percentages	Mean CIL score	Percentages	Mean CIL score		
Australia	9 (0.5)	482 (5.3)	13 (0.7)	510 (4.5)	31 (0.9)	539 (3.2)	47 (1.1)	565 (2.2)	83 (5.5)	
Chile	20 (0.9)	455 (5.8)	33 (1.1)	474 (3.8)	30 (0.8)	506 (3.4)	17 (0.9)	520 (5.3)	65 (6.8)	
Croatia	13 (0.9)	468 (5.4)	30 (1.1)	498 (3.8)	35 (1.1)	525 (3.2)	23 (1.0)	539 (3.7)	71 (5.9)	
Czech Republic	7 (0.6)	513 (8.2)	17 (0.8)	530 (3.6)	37 (0.9)	553 (2.2)	39 (1.1)	572 (2.2)	59 (8.0)	
Germany†	7 (0.8)	462 (6.6)	15 (1.0)	490 (4.9)	30 (1.0)	522 (3.3)	48 (1.6)	550 (2.7)	88 (7.5)	
Korea, Republic of	7 (0.5)	470 (6.5)	6 (0.5)	512 (9.0)	21 (0.8)	531 (3.9)	66 (1.0)	547 (2.7)	77 (6.6)	
Lithuania	13 (0.8)	456 (6.9)	26 (1.1)	476 (4.0)	34 (1.0)	505 (4.2)	27 (1.1)	519 (4.8)	63 (6.4)	
Norway (Grade 9)†	7 (0.7)	496 (5.9)	13 (0.7)	515 (5.6)	31 (1.1)	528 (2.7)	50 (1.3)	554 (2.9)	58 (5.9)	
Poland	5 (0.5)	494 (7.2)	22 (0.9)	509 (3.4)	33 (1.0)	531 (3.4)	40 (1.1)	564 (3.1)	69 (7.5)	
Russian Federation²	6 (0.4)	478 (7.2)	22 (1.0)	494 (5.3)	38 (0.9)	516 (3.0)	34 (1.1)	537 (2.9)	59 (7.3)	
Slovak Republic	11 (1.1)	432 (11.0)	24 (1.1)	495 (5.5)	36 (1.2)	533 (3.9)	29 (1.3)	552 (4.4)	119 (11.0)	
Slovenia	9 (0.7)	471 (6.1)	21 (1.0)	494 (3.9)	38 (1.1)	514 (2.8)	32 (0.9)	529 (3.3)	59 (6.8)	
Thailand²	19 (0.9)	352 (6.9)	47 (1.3)	363 (5.0)	24 (1.1)	394 (5.7)	10 (0.7)	415 (9.7)	63 (9.9)	
Turkey	20 (1.3)	316 (7.5)	34 (1.0)	352 (4.7)	28 (1.1)	379 (5.4)	18 (1.1)	405 (7.8)	90 (10.6)	
ICILS 2013 average	11 (0.2)	453 (1.9)	23 (0.3)	479 (1.3)	32 (0.3)	505 (1.0)	34 (0.3)	526 (1.2)	73 (2.1)	
Countries not meeting sample requirements										
Denmark	8 (0.7)	508 (7.0)	17 (0.9)	522 (5.1)	35 (1.4)	540 (3.6)	40 (2.0)	563 (3.6)	55 (7.1)	
Hong Kong SAR	14 (1.3)	474 (9.1)	23 (1.2)	504 (9.3)	33 (1.1)	519 (5.5)	30 (1.8)	525 (7.1)	51 (7.9)	
Netherlands	17 (1.1)	483 (6.9)	21 (1.0)	529 (4.7)	32 (1.2)	544 (4.8)	31 (1.6)	559 (6.3)	76 (8.1)	
Switzerland	11 (1.8)	485 (7.6)	19 (1.6)	516 (6.7)	30 (1.7)	530 (4.7)	40 (1.9)	539 (5.3)	54 (7.0)	
Benchmarking participants										
Newfoundland and Labrador, Canada	9 (0.8)	476 (10.4)	14 (1.3)	499 (7.6)	33 (1.5)	530 (4.7)	44 (1.6)	549 (5.1)	72 (11.6)	
Ontario, Canada	6 (0.6)	499 (8.4)	15 (0.9)	524 (4.8)	30 (1.2)	544 (3.3)	49 (1.6)	565 (3.0)	65 (8.4)	
City of Buenos Aires, Argentina	13 (1.4)	391 (14.7)	27 (2.2)	432 (9.7)	27 (1.7)	462 (9.4)	33 (3.0)	487 (8.0)	96 (15.6)	

Students in highest category score higher than in lowest

■ Difference statistically significant at .05 level
□ Difference not statistically significant

Notes:
* Statistically significant (p<.05) coefficients in **bold**.
() Standard errors appear in parentheses. Because some results are rounded to the nearest whole number, some totals may appear inconsistent.
† Met guidelines for sampling participation rates only after replacement schools were included.
1 National Desired Population does not correspond to International Desired Population.
2 Country surveyed the same cohort of students but at the beginning of the next school year.

Across countries, the average percentages for books in the home were 11 percent for 10 or fewer books, 23 percent for between 11 and 25 books, and 32 percent for between 26 and 100 books. An average of 34 percent of students reported more than 100 books at home. There was again a high level of variation across countries. In Chile, Thailand, and Turkey, about every fifth student had fewer than 10 books in his or her home. Less than 20 percent of the students in these countries were living in homes with more than 100 books. In contrast, in Australia, Germany, Norway, Korea, and Ontario (Canada), almost half or more of the ICILS students reported having 100 or more books in their homes.

Students from homes with the higher numbers of books tended to have higher CIL scores. Across the ICILS countries, the difference between students reporting more than 100 books at home and those reporting 10 or fewer was, on average, 73 CIL score points. The differences ranged from 58 score points in Norway and 59 in the Czech Republic, the Russian Federation, and Slovenia to 119 in the Slovak Republic.

Immigrant status and language use

Many studies provide evidence of the influence of students' cultural and language background on their educational performance (see, for example, Elley, 1992; Kao, 2004; Kao & Thompson, 2003; Stanat & Christensen, 2006; Mullis et al., 2007). Students from immigrant families, especially those families recently arrived in a country, often lack proficiency in the language of instruction and may be unfamiliar with the norms of the dominant culture. Ethnic minorities also tend to have a lower socioeconomic status, which in turn is often negatively associated with learning and engagement. A number of studies indicate that when socioeconomic background is controlled for, immigrant status and language provide unique predictors of students' literacy achievement (Lehmann, 1996).

As a means of measuring these aspects of student background, the ICILS student questionnaire asked students about their own and their parents' countries of birth. The questionnaire also asked students to specify which language was spoken most frequently at home.

We created an index of students' immigrant status based on the information students provided about their country of birth and their parents' respective country of birth. We then recoded these data into categories that specified whether students had a solely immigrant background (both of the parents in two-parent households or the one parent in single-parent households born in another country)[2] or without a solely immigrant background (at least one parent born in the country of the test).[3] Nearly all students across nearly all participating countries provided valid responses to these questions.

Table 4.6 shows the percentages of students in the two immigrant background categories as well as the average CIL score in each category. The table also records the differences in average CIL scores between the two categories of students. Note that within each country, average CIL scores (and subsequently score point differences) are not reported for categories that have 30 students or less.

Variations across countries were large. While, in the majority of countries, more than 90 percent of the students did not have an immigrant background, in Australia,

---

2 This category is referred to as with an immigrant background.
3 This category is referred to as without an immigrant background.

Table 4.6: National percentages and CIL score averages for students with and without immigrant background

Country	Students With Immigrant Background		Students Without Immigrant Background		Difference (Without Immigrant Background - with Immigrant Background)*	Score Point Difference Between Categories
	Percentages	Mean CIL score	Percentages	Mean CIL score		
Australia	25 (1.7)	547 (5.1)	75 (1.7)	541 (2.3)	-6 (5.4)	
Chile	2 (0.3)	478 (13.5)	98 (0.3)	488 (3.1)	10 (13.5)	
Croatia	13 (0.9)	504 (4.9)	87 (0.9)	514 (3.0)	10 (4.6)	
Czech Republic	3 (0.4)	551 (9.7)	97 (0.4)	554 (2.1)	2 (10.0)	
Germany†	20 (1.5)	498 (4.6)	80 (1.5)	534 (2.7)	36 (6.1)	
Korea, Republic of	0 (0.1)	^	100 (0.1)	537 (2.6)	^	
Lithuania	2 (0.3)	462 (15.4)	98 (0.3)	497 (3.4)	35 (15.3)	
Norway (Grade 9)[1]	13 (1.2)	498 (6.2)	87 (1.2)	543 (2.3)	46 (6.0)	
Poland	0 (0.1)	^	100 (0.1)	538 (2.4)	^	
Russian Federation[2]	5 (0.6)	521 (6.8)	95 (0.6)	516 (2.8)	-5 (6.9)	
Slovak Republic	1 (0.3)	428 (27.5)	99 (0.3)	520 (4.3)	92 (26.9)	
Slovenia	10 (1.2)	474 (5.9)	90 (1.2)	515 (2.2)	41 (6.1)	
Thailand[2]	3 (0.4)	313 (14.8)	97 (0.4)	376 (4.7)	63 (14.7)	
Turkey	2 (0.2)	339 (16.7)	98 (0.2)	366 (4.5)	27 (16.3)	
ICILS 2013 average	7 (0.2)	468 (3.7)	93 (0.2)	503 (0.8)	29 (3.7)	
Countries not meeting sample requirements						
Denmark	9 (1.5)	499 (7.1)	91 (1.5)	549 (2.8)	49 (7.2)	
Hong Kong SAR	37 (1.4)	518 (6.7)	63 (1.4)	508 (8.1)	-10 (5.4)	
Netherlands	11 (1.7)	498 (11.8)	89 (1.7)	541 (4.6)	42 (11.8)	
Switzerland	29 (3.0)	510 (8.6)	71 (3.0)	533 (3.7)	23 (7.8)	
Benchmarking participants						
Newfoundland and Labrador, Canada	2 (0.7)	^	98 (0.7)	530 (2.7)	^	
Ontario, Canada	32 (2.1)	557 (5.3)	68 (2.1)	545 (3.0)	-12 (5.8)	
Benchmarking participant not meeting sample requirements						
City of Buenos Aires, Argentina	32 (2.1)	410 (9.7)	68 (2.1)	465 (7.7)	56 (10.0)	

Chart legend (Score Point Difference Between Categories): Students with immigrant background score higher / Students without immigrant background score higher

■ Difference statistically significant at .05 level
□ Difference not statistically significant

Notes:
* Statistically significant (*p*<.05) coefficients in **bold**.
( ) Standard errors appear in parentheses. Because some results are rounded to the nearest whole number, some totals may appear inconsistent.
† Met guidelines for sampling participation rates only after replacement schools were included.
[1] National Desired Population does not correspond to International Desired Population.
[2] Country surveyed the same cohort of students but at the beginning of the next school year.
^ Subgroup sample size too small for reporting reliable estimate.

Croatia, Germany, Hong Kong SAR, the Netherlands, Norway, Ontario (Canada), and Switzerland, the proportions of students with an immigrant background were 10 percent or more.

In the countries other than those with very small numbers of students with immigrant backgrounds (Korea, Poland, and Newfoundland and Labrador), students without immigrant backgrounds tended to have higher CIL average scores than those with an immigrant background. On average across the participating countries, the difference between students with immigrant backgrounds and those without was 29 CIL score points, with the differences ranging from 10 score points in Croatia to 92 in the Slovak Republic. We found statistically significant effects in only seven of the 14 participating countries that met sampling requirements.

To investigate the influence of language use at home on CIL, we distinguished between students who reported using the test language at home and those who said they spoke a different language at home. Across countries, 99 percent of the students provided valid responses to this question. Table 4.7 shows the percentages and the average CIL scores for each category as well as the results of our bivariate regression of test scores on the language indicator variable.

In most participating countries, majorities of students indicated speaking the test language at home. In Australia, Germany, Lithuania, Norway, Hong Kong SAR, Switzerland, and Ontario (Canada), one tenth or more of the students reported speaking a language other than the test language at home. Across countries, CIL scores tended to be higher among students speaking the test language at home; the average difference was 31 score points. For eight of the 14 participating countries meeting sampling requirements, we recorded statistically significant differences between students speaking the test language and those speaking other languages at home. The statistically significant positive differences ranged from 25 score points in Croatia to 73 in the Slovak Republic.

Home ICT resources

To review the influence of IT resources at home on CIL, we chose two indicators. One was the number of computers at home; the other was the type of internet access available to students and their families.

Students were asked to report separately the number of desktop computers and the number of portable computers (notebooks, netbooks, and tablets) at home. We divided the sum of the two variables into the following categories: "no computers," "one computer," "two computers," and "three or more computers." On average across participating countries, 99 percent of the students provided data on the numbers of computers at home.

Table 4.8 shows the percentage in each reporting category along with the respective CIL score average and the results from an analysis that involved regressing the CIL scores on the indicator variable reflecting number of computers. Across countries, the average percentage of students who said there was no computer at home was only six percent. However, on average across countries, 48 percent of students had three or more computers at home, 24 percent had two computers at home, and 21 percent had one computer.

Table 4.7: National percentages and CIL score averages for students' language use at home

Country	Test Language Not Spoken At Home		Test Language Spoken At Home		Difference (Test Language Spoken - Other Language Spoken)*	Score Point Difference Between Categories
	Percentages	Mean CIL score	Percentages	Mean CIL score		
Australia	11 (1.0)	534 (6.9)	89 (1.0)	543 (2.2)	8 (6.8)	
Chile	1 (0.3)	508 (16.4)	99 (0.3)	487 (3.1)	-21 (16.2)	
Croatia	3 (0.4)	488 (11.9)	97 (0.4)	513 (3.0)	25 (12.5)	
Czech Republic	3 (0.4)	541 (8.4)	97 (0.4)	554 (2.1)	13 (8.6)	
Germany†	14 (1.3)	488 (7.7)	86 (1.3)	532 (3.0)	44 (9.6)	
Korea, Republic of	1 (0.2)	^	99 (0.2)	537 (2.7)	^	
Lithuania	11 (1.0)	462 (8.8)	89 (1.0)	499 (3.7)	38 (8.9)	
Norway (Grade 9)[1]	10 (0.8)	500 (6.4)	90 (0.8)	541 (2.4)	41 (6.6)	
Poland	3 (0.7)	525 (12.1)	97 (0.7)	538 (2.4)	13 (12.3)	
Russian Federation[2]	6 (1.4)	491 (14.0)	94 (1.4)	518 (2.6)	27 (13.7)	
Slovak Republic	5 (0.8)	449 (18.2)	95 (0.8)	522 (4.2)	73 (17.6)	
Slovenia	9 (1.0)	467 (6.3)	91 (1.0)	515 (2.1)	48 (6.5)	
Thailand[2]	4 (0.8)	336 (13.3)	96 (0.8)	375 (4.6)	39 (13.3)	
Turkey	6 (0.9)	304 (14.8)	94 (0.9)	365 (4.7)	61 (15.1)	
ICILS 2013 average	6 (0.2)	469 (3.3)	94 (0.2)	503 (0.9)	31 (3.3)	
Countries not meeting sample requirements						
Denmark	6 (1.0)	500 (8.2)	94 (1.0)	546 (3.0)	46 (8.1)	
Hong Kong SAR	11 (1.2)	486 (12.8)	89 (1.2)	512 (7.3)	26 (10.6)	
Netherlands	8 (1.1)	501 (14.6)	92 (1.1)	539 (4.7)	38 (14.6)	
Switzerland	23 (2.4)	513 (7.2)	77 (2.4)	530 (4.5)	17 (6.6)	
Benchmarking participants						
Newfoundland and Labrador, Canada	2 (0.6)	^	98 (0.6)	529 (2.9)	^	
Ontario, Canada	17 (1.3)	544 (6.1)	83 (1.3)	549 (3.0)	5 (5.7)	
Benchmarking participant not meeting sample requirements						
City of Buenos Aires, Argentina	17 (1.3)	400 (15.4)	83 (1.3)	455 (8.3)	55 (13.8)	

Chart legend (Score Point Difference Between Categories): Students speaking other language score higher | Students speaking test language score higher

■ Difference statistically significant at .05 level
□ Difference not statistically significant

Notes:
* Statistically significant (*p*<.05) coefficients in **bold**.
( ) Standard errors appear in parentheses. Because some results are rounded to the nearest whole number, some totals may appear inconsistent.
† Met guidelines for sampling participation rates only after replacement schools were included.
[1] National Desired Population does not correspond to International Desired Population.
[2] Country surveyed the same cohort of students but at the beginning of the next school year.
^ Subgroup sample size too small for reporting reliable estimate.

Table 4.8: National percentages and CIL score averages for students in categories of computer availability at home

Country	No computers		One Computer		Two Computers		Three or More Computers		Difference (Three or more Computers — No Computers)*	Score Point Difference Between Lowest and Highest Category
	Percentages	Mean CIL score	Percentages	Mean CIL score	Percentages	Mean CIL score	Percentages	Mean CIL score		
Australia	1 (0.2)	440 (14.8)	4 (0.4)	487 (9.0)	10 (0.6)	523 (4.4)	85 (0.8)	548 (2.2)	108 (15.0)	
Chile	7 (0.6)	405 (10.1)	24 (1.2)	475 (4.0)	24 (0.9)	486 (4.3)	45 (1.3)	506 (3.5)	101 (10.1)	
Croatia	2 (0.3)	414 (14.0)	29 (0.9)	497 (3.6)	31 (1.1)	517 (3.6)	38 (1.1)	526 (3.4)	112 (14.0)	
Czech Republic	1 (0.2)	511 (17.7)	13 (0.8)	537 (4.3)	26 (1.0)	548 (3.0)	60 (1.3)	561 (2.2)	49 (17.4)	
Germany†	2 (0.5)	^	10 (1.0)	507 (7.3)	22 (1.0)	520 (4.0)	66 (1.4)	533 (2.5)	^	
Korea, Republic of	2 (0.2)	474 (16.1)	33 (1.0)	527 (3.7)	33 (1.0)	539 (3.8)	32 (1.0)	546 (3.4)	72 (15.0)	
Lithuania	4 (0.5)	411 (11.2)	30 (1.1)	487 (4.2)	33 (1.0)	503 (4.7)	32 (0.9)	505 (4.4)	95 (11.9)	
Norway (Grade 9)[1]	1 (0.2)	^	1 (0.3)	514 (21.4)	6 (0.5)	535 (5.8)	92 (0.7)	538 (2.5)	^	
Poland	1 (0.2)	464 (21.3)	24 (1.2)	517 (3.9)	31 (1.0)	533 (3.6)	44 (1.3)	554 (3.0)	90 (20.7)	
Russian Federation[2]	4 (0.5)	446 (8.9)	25 (1.1)	500 (5.3)	31 (0.8)	519 (3.5)	40 (1.2)	532 (3.8)	86 (9.7)	
Slovak Republic	3 (0.5)	406 (14.5)	18 (0.8)	499 (5.9)	27 (1.0)	516 (6.0)	52 (1.3)	532 (5.0)	126 (14.8)	
Slovenia	1 (0.2)	448 (11.0)	13 (0.8)	500 (3.9)	28 (1.0)	506 (3.3)	58 (1.3)	517 (2.3)	69 (11.1)	
Thailand[2]	28 (1.6)	316 (6.0)	31 (1.3)	374 (5.3)	19 (0.8)	385 (6.3)	23 (1.2)	431 (6.0)	115 (8.2)	
Turkey	31 (1.6)	308 (8.2)	39 (1.3)	374 (4.1)	19 (1.1)	392 (5.2)	11 (1.0)	409 (10.0)	101 (11.2)	
ICILS 2013 average	6 (0.2)	420 (3.9)	21 (0.3)	485 (2.0)	24 (0.2)	502 (1.2)	48 (0.3)	517 (1.2)	94 (4.0)	
Countries not meeting sample requirements										
Denmark	1 (0.2)	^	1 (0.2)	^	4 (0.5)	539 (7.7)	94 (0.7)	544 (3.1)	^	
Hong Kong SAR	2 (0.4)	422 (20.6)	19 (1.1)	501 (8.2)	24 (1.0)	505 (7.9)	55 (1.6)	518 (8.1)	95 (20.1)	
Netherlands	2 (0.4)	444 (17.8)	4 (0.4)	505 (11.2)	10 (0.8)	519 (9.8)	85 (1.0)	540 (4.4)	97 (17.0)	
Switzerland	1 (0.3)	503 (15.0)	6 (0.7)	513 (10.3)	18 (1.4)	511 (7.0)	75 (1.6)	531 (4.3)	28 (14.0)	
Benchmarking participants										
Newfoundland and Labrador, Canada	2 (0.4)	432 (26.3)	5 (0.8)	480 (12.2)	9 (0.9)	505 (8.7)	84 (1.4)	535 (3.0)	103 (26.4)	
Ontario, Canada	2 (0.4)	474 (17.4)	5 (0.5)	521 (9.2)	11 (0.7)	541 (5.9)	82 (1.0)	552 (2.7)	77 (16.9)	
Benchmarking participant not meeting sample requirements										
City of Buenos Aires, Argentina	8 (1.9)	395 (19.2)	9 (0.8)	415 (13.2)	21 (1.6)	450 (10.2)	63 (2.5)	463 (8.5)	68 (17.7)	

Students in highest category score higher than in lowest

■ Difference statistically significant at .05 level
☐ Difference not statistically significant

Notes:
* Statistically significant (*p*<.05) coefficients in **bold**.
( ) Standard errors appear in parentheses. Because some results are rounded to the nearest whole number, some totals may appear inconsistent.
† Met guidelines for sampling participation rates only after replacement schools were included.
[1] National Desired Population does not correspond to International Desired Population.
[2] Country surveyed the same cohort of students but at the beginning of the next school year.
^ Subgroup sample size too small for reporting reliable estimate.

As we expected, these percentages varied among countries. Although, in most countries, only very small percentages (below 5%) reported not having any computers at home, this was the case for every third student in Thailand and Turkey. Large majorities in Australia and Norway (85% and 92% respectively) as well as the two Canadian provinces of Ontario and Newfoundland and Labrador (82% and 84% respectively) said they had three or more computers at home. Only one in 10 Turkish students had this level of computer resourcing at home.

Students with more computers at home tended to have higher CIL scores. On average across countries, the difference in score points between students reporting three or more computers and those who indicated no computers at home was 94 points. This difference ranged from 49 points in the Czech Republic to 126 points in the Slovak Republic. In three countries (Germany, Norway, and Denmark), no comparisons could be reported because of the very small number of students in the no computers at home category.

The ICILS student questionnaire also asked students about the type of internet access they had at home. The question had five response categories: "no internet," "dial-up connection," "broadband," "connection through a mobile phone network," and "have internet at home but do not know what type of connection." Given that a number of students were not able to provide information on the type of internet access at home, only students with and without access were distinguished for the analysis in this report. The percentages of students who provided data on internet access at home averaged 99 percent across countries.

As Table 4.9 illustrates, internet access at students' homes varied across countries. While, in most countries, no more than five percent of students reported not having any access to the internet, larger proportions were recorded as having no internet access in Chile (10%), Turkey (37%), and Thailand (43%).

Across countries, students with no internet access at home had lower CIL average scores than those who reported having this access at home. On average, students without internet access scored 72 points lower on CIL than those who reported having internet access. Statistically significant differences ranged from 38 score points in the Czech Republic to 120 in the Slovak Republic. In a number of countries (Germany, Norway, Denmark, Hong Kong SAR, the Netherlands, Switzerland, and Newfoundland and Labrador), the subgroup of students who said they had no internet access at home was too small to permit valid reporting of CIL average scores and comparison with the other group.

Influence of combined home background variables on CIL

To analyze the combined effects of the home background variables, including gender, on CIL, we used the following three blocks of predictor variables in a multiple regression model:

- Immigrant background and language use;
- Socioeconomic background (parental occupation, parental educational attainment, and home literacy resources); and
- ICT resources at home.

Table 4.9: National percentages and CIL score averages for students in categories of internet access at home

| Country | Students Without Internet Access At Home | | Students With Internet Access At Home | | Difference (With Internet Access - Without Internet Access)* | Score Point Difference Between Categories |
	Percentages	Mean CIL score	Percentages	Mean CIL score		
Australia	2 (0.2)	449 (12.1)	98 (0.2)	544 (2.1)	95 (11.9)	
Chile	10 (0.8)	444 (6.9)	90 (0.8)	492 (3.1)	48 (6.9)	
Croatia	3 (0.4)	444 (11.7)	97 (0.4)	515 (2.9)	71 (12.1)	
Czech Republic	2 (0.3)	516 (10.3)	98 (0.3)	554 (2.1)	38 (10.3)	
Germany[†]	1 (0.3)	^	99 (0.3)	527 (2.3)	^	
Korea, Republic of	2 (0.3)	444 (14.5)	98 (0.3)	538 (2.6)	94 (14.5)	
Lithuania	3 (0.4)	419 (12.5)	97 (0.4)	497 (3.6)	78 (12.7)	
Norway (Grade 9)[1]	0 (0.1)	^	100 (0.1)	538 (2.4)	^	
Poland	3 (0.3)	462 (10.9)	97 (0.3)	540 (2.3)	78 (10.7)	
Russian Federation[2]	3 (0.4)	440 (10.5)	97 (0.4)	518 (2.8)	79 (10.6)	
Slovak Republic	3 (0.4)	402 (12.6)	97 (0.4)	522 (4.3)	120 (11.5)	
Slovenia	1 (0.2)	463 (12.4)	99 (0.2)	512 (2.2)	49 (12.9)	
Thailand[2]	43 (1.5)	339 (5.5)	57 (1.5)	400 (5.4)	61 (6.7)	
Turkey	37 (1.6)	326 (6.4)	63 (1.6)	384 (4.6)	58 (6.4)	
ICILS 2013 average	8 (0.2)	429 (3.1)	92 (0.2)	506 (0.9)	72 (3.1)	
Countries not meeting sample requirements						
Denmark	0 (0.1)	^	100 (0.1)	544 (3.1)	^	
Hong Kong SAR	1 (0.2)	^	99 (0.2)	511 (7.4)	^	
Netherlands	0 (0.1)	^	100 (0.1)	536 (4.6)	^	
Switzerland	0 (0.1)	^	100 (0.1)	526 (4.5)	^	
Benchmarking participants						
Newfoundland and Labrador, Canada	1 (0.5)	^	99 (0.5)	529 (2.8)	^	
Ontario, Canada	2 (0.4)	485 (16.7)	98 (0.4)	549 (2.8)	64 (16.1)	
Benchmarking participant not meeting sample requirements						
City of Buenos Aires, Argentina	2 (0.4)	391 (16.7)	98 (0.4)	457 (8.2)	66 (15.4)	

Students with internet access score higher

■ Difference statistically significant at .05 level
□ Difference not statistically significant

Notes:
* Statistically significant (*p*<.05) coefficients in **bold**.
() Standard errors appear in parentheses. Because some results are rounded to the nearest whole number, some totals may appear inconsistent.
[†] Met guidelines for sampling participation rates only after replacement schools were included.
[1] National Desired Population does not correspond to International Desired Population.
[2] Country surveyed the same cohort of students but at the beginning of the next school year.
^ Subgroup sample size too small for reporting reliable estimate.

In the previous section, we documented the associations between these variables and CIL that we observed when we compared CIL scores across the reporting categories. In this section, we present the findings of our regression analysis. This analysis allowed us to study the net effects of each indicator variable after controlling for all other variables. We coded the predictor variables as follows:

- *Gender:* Female students were assigned a code of one; male students were assigned a code of zero. The regression coefficients indicate the difference in CIL score points between males and females after we had controlled for the effects of all other variables.

- *Expected educational attainment:* The categorical nature of the variable and our observation that the association with CIL was not linear in all countries led to the development of three dummy indicator variables: "expected lower-secondary education or below," "expected post-secondary nonuniversity education," and "expected university education." We assigned a value of one for each variable if the student was in that category and a value of zero if they were not in that category (i.e., the remaining students). The category "expected upper-secondary education" was the reference group. Those students were assigned a value of zero for all three dummy variables. The regression coefficients indicate the difference in CIL score points between the respective category and students who anticipated that upper-secondary education would be their highest level of attainment (the reference group). [4]

- *Parental educational attainment:* As with students' expected education, three dummy variables indicated the highest level of parental educational attainment: "both parents with lower-secondary education or below," "at least one parent with post-secondary nonuniversity education," and "at least one parent with university education." For each dummy variable, we assigned a value of one if parental education was in the category and a value of zero to all other students (i.e., those not in the category). Parental education at the upper-secondary level was chosen as the reference group. The students in this group received a value of zero for all three dummy indicators. The regression coefficients indicate the net difference in CIL score points between the respective category and students whose parents had upper-secondary education as their highest level of attainment (the reference group).

- *Parental occupational status:* Occupational status (SEI) scores were standardized to have a mean of zero and a standard deviation of one across equally weighted ICILS countries. The regression coefficients indicate increases in CIL corresponding to an increase in SEI scores of one standard deviation.

- *Home literacy resources:* Because the increase in CIL score points across the four reporting categories was approximately linear (among and within countries), the indicator variable had four categories, with a value of zero assigned to students with "0–10 books at home," a value of one to those with "11–25 books at home," two to those with "26–100 books," and three to those with "100 or more books." The regression coefficients indicate the increase in CIL points from one home literacy category to the next higher category.

- *Computer resources at home:* The "number of computers at home" categories ranged from "no computers" (assigned a value of zero) to "three computers or more"

---

4 Another way of expressing this is that we did not include, with respect to expected educational attainment, "upper-secondary education" in the model as a dummy variable. It therefore became the reference category for the dummy variables of the other categories. We applied an analogous procedure for parental education.

(assigned a value of three). The regression coefficients indicate the increase in CIL points from one category to the next.

- *Internet access at home:* Students who reported having internet access at home were coded as one and those with no internet access were coded as zero. The regression coefficients indicate the net difference in CIL score points between students with and without internet access.

Students with missing data for any of the predictor variables were excluded from the regression analysis. Across the participating countries, about 93 percent of students with valid data for all variables were included in the regression model. Data from the Netherlands could not be included in the analysis because it did not provide data on parental occupational status.

Some indicator variables reflected results from very small subgroups (fewer than 30 students) in a number of countries. This was the case for expected lower-secondary education in Chile and also in a number of countries for internet access at home. In these cases, we included the variables in the analyses but did not report the corresponding regression coefficients in the tables because we considered these insufficiently reliable.

Table 4.10 shows the results from the multiple regression analysis. The table sets out, for each predictor, the unstandardized regression coefficients for each national dataset and the ICILS (international) averages along with their respective standard errors.

After controlling for other personal and social background variables, we found that being female had a positive and statistically significant effect in seven of the 14 participating countries meeting sampling requirements as well as in the two Canadian benchmarking participants (Newfoundland and Labrador and Ontario). On average, the effect recorded was 10 score points. The largest regression coefficient was found amongst Korean students (33 score points).

Statistically significant associations between students' expected educational attainment (which ICILS considers to be a measure of educational aspiration) and CIL emerged across all participating countries. After controlling for all other predictor variables, we found that expectation of completing a university degree compared to expectation of no more than an upper-secondary education had an effect of (on average) 43 score points across countries. Expectation of completing a post-secondary nonuniversity qualification had (on average) a positive effect equivalent to 20 score points. Expectation of an education that went no further than lower-secondary school had a negative effect of -20 score points.

Having controlled for all other indicators, we noted that highest parental educational attainment had statistically significant positive effects on CIL in Australia, Chile, the Czech Republic, Lithuania, Poland, the Slovak Republic, Slovenia, Thailand, and Turkey. On average, having parents whose level of attainment was lower-secondary education or below had a negative effect of -12 score points (when compared to the reference category; that is, parental educational attainment at the level of upper-secondary only).

In three countries (the Czech Republic, Slovenia, and Turkey), having at least one parent with a university degree had statistically significant negative effects on CIL. When interpreting this result, we need to be mindful that these results refer to net effects after controlling for the effects of other indicators that may be associated with

Table 4.10: Multiple regression model for students' CIL predicted by personal and social background variables (unstandardized regression coefficients)

| | Student characteristics | | | | Socioeconomic background | | | | | ICT home resources | |
| | Gender | Expected education | | | Parental education | | | Highest parental occupation | Home literacy | Number of computers at home | Home internet connection |
Country	(0=male, 1=female)	Lower-secondary education or below	Post-secondary nonuniversity education	Tertiary university education	Lower-secondary education or below	Post-secondary nonuniversity education	Tertiary university education	(Per standard deviation of SEI scores)	(Per category)	(Per category)	(0=no internet, 1=internet)
Australia	14 (2.9)	-31 (6.0)	9 (3.5)	37 (3.7)	-2 (4.9)	8 (3.8)	11 (3.8)	9 (1.5)	16 (1.6)	11 (2.8)	30 (11.4)
Chile	19 (3.8)	^	27 (6.6)	56 (5.7)	-21 (4.8)	13 (5.0)	13 (6.3)	11 (2.2)	10 (1.9)	6 (2.2)	17 (6.6)
Croatia	6 (3.0)	-17 (10.7)	37 (4.3)	60 (3.7)	-15 (10.5)	-2 (4.9)	-12 (6.3)	8 (2.1)	9 (1.8)	7 (2.0)	35 (11.6)
Czech Republic	4 (2.4)	-8 (8.4)	20 (4.7)	36 (3.2)	-31 (17.2)	-7 (5.1)	-8 (3.9)	12 (1.6)	11 (1.6)	4 (1.8)	6 (10.1)
Germany†	11 (3.7)	-39 (4.9)	-8 (7.7)	22 (4.0)	1 (5.5)	-1 (7.0)	-6 (4.4)	5 (2.4)	19 (2.4)	6 (3.2)	^
Korea, Republic of	33 (3.8)	-17 (9.6)	24 (8.0)	37 (6.7)	12 (12.5)	-9 (7.2)	3 (4.1)	8 (2.2)	14 (2.2)	4 (1.7)	52 (13.4)
Lithuania	3 (3.5)	-12 (8.9)	29 (6.4)	57 (6.2)	2 (9.9)	12 (5.4)	5 (6.7)	9 (2.1)	9 (2.1)	2 (1.9)	50 (12.5)
Norway (Grade 9)[1]	19 (3.5)	-17 (12.7)	10 (6.1)	30 (5.0)	-24 (13.9)	8 (5.9)	-8 (5.1)	15 (1.9)	12 (1.6)	3 (4.3)	^
Poland	3 (3.3)	-39 (10.5)	28 (4.9)	50 (3.8)	-25 (11.8)	6 (5.3)	5 (3.9)	8 (2.6)	10 (1.8)	4 (2.3)	36 (10.4)
Russian Federation[2]	3 (2.6)	-12 (8.3)	17 (6.3)	48 (5.0)	6 (7.9)	2 (5.4)	3 (6.6)	9 (1.9)	9 (2.0)	8 (2.4)	41 (11.2)
Slovak Republic	4 (3.6)	-11 (9.9)	37 (5.2)	47 (4.3)	-36 (16.4)	-17 (6.5)	-7 (4.4)	10 (2.5)	18 (2.5)	4 (2.2)	74 (10.2)
Slovenia	22 (3.4)	-29 (9.7)	27 (4.1)	46 (4.8)	-16 (9.9)	0 (4.6)	-12 (5.3)	10 (2.1)	10 (1.6)	3 (1.7)	26 (9.6)
Thailand[2]	0 (4.4)	-14 (6.4)	15 (9.0)	42 (6.4)	6 (6.4)	15 (8.1)	25 (8.0)	15 (2.5)	3 (2.3)	17 (2.2)	18 (5.3)
Turkey	-4 (3.8)	-19 (7.5)	11 (8.4)	33 (7.1)	-22 (4.9)	-30 (9.5)	-25 (8.8)	12 (2.9)	12 (2.4)	14 (2.6)	22 (5.2)
ICILS 2013 average	10 (0.9)	-20 (2.5)	20 (1.7)	43 (1.4)	-12 (2.8)	0 (1.6)	-1 (1.5)	10 (0.6)	12 (0.5)	7 (0.7)	34 (2.9)
Countries not meeting sample requirements											
Denmark	13 (3.8)	-23 (7.9)	10 (6.1)	22 (4.4)	-8 (8.4)	8 (4.4)	1 (4.4)	9 (2.0)	10 (1.8)	4 (7.2)	^
Hong Kong SAR	13 (6.1)	33 (15.4)	35 (13.6)	60 (12.0)	-1 (6.4)	4 (7.1)	1 (6.3)	2 (3.2)	8 (2.7)	7 (2.8)	^
Switzerland	7 (4.9)	-21 (7.6)	9 (10.6)	35 (7.2)	2 (7.4)	7 (5.4)	-3 (8.3)	4 (3.4)	10 (2.2)	8 (3.6)	^
Benchmarking participants											
Newfoundland and Labrador, Canada	29 (5.7)	-10 (17.3)	0 (14.2)	27 (10.5)	13 (14.5)	6 (7.6)	5 (8.6)	10 (3.2)	18 (3.3)	17 (3.8)	^
Ontario, Canada	21 (3.7)	-16 (14.2)	8 (15.6)	34 (7.6)	-16 (13.3)	-4 (5.8)	2 (6.4)	10 (2.4)	13 (1.8)	5 (2.5)	24 (12.6)
Benchmarking participant not meeting sample requirements											
City of Buenos Aires, Argentina	3 (8.2)	-12 (17.2)	34 (11.1)	29 (10.9)	-21 (11.5)	3 (8.4)	19 (10.5)	14 (3.8)	13 (4.0)	13 (5.0)	15 (16.1)

Notes:
* Statistically significant (p<.05) coefficients in **bold**.
() Standard errors appear in parentheses. Because some results are rounded to the nearest whole number, some totals may appear inconsistent.
† Met guidelines for sampling participation rates only after replacement schools were included.

[1] National Desired Population does not correspond to International Desired Population.
[2] Country surveyed the same cohort of students but at the beginning of the next school year.
^ Subgroup sample size too small for reporting reliable estimate.

both parental education and CIL.[5] This caveat is also relevant to interpretation of the results of other regression analyses reported in the following paragraphs.

In all participating countries, parental occupational status had statistically significant positive effects on CIL net of other background indicators. On average, an increase of 10 CIL points was associated with an increase of one standard deviation of SEI scores, with the differences ranging from five points in Germany to 15 points in Norway and Thailand. In all participating countries and benchmarking participants meeting sample participation requirements, except Thailand, home literacy resources had positive net effects on CIL.

Across the ICILS countries, an increase in one home literacy category was associated with an increase of 12 CIL score points. The largest effects were recorded for Germany (19 score points) as well as the Slovak Republic and the Canadian province of Newfoundland and Labrador (18 score points apiece).

In eight of the 14 ICILS countries that met sampling requirements and also in the two Canadian provinces (Newfoundland and Labrador and Ontario), availability of computers at home had statistically significant net effects on CIL. Across countries, each additional computer was associated with an increase of seven CIL score points, with the largest effects recorded for Thailand (17 score points), Turkey (14 score points), and the benchmarking participant Newfoundland and Labrador (17 score points). Internet access at home had a positive effect equivalent to 34 score points across the ICILS countries. Statistically significant positive net effects were recorded in most countries. The largest effects were found in the Slovak Republic (74 score points), Korea (52 score points), and Lithuania (50 score points).

Within a multiple regression model, the combined effect of more than one predictor or block of predictors can explain variance in the criterion variable. This facility makes it possible to estimate how much of the explained variance is attributable uniquely to each of the predictors or blocks of predictors, and how much of this variance is explained by these predictors or blocks of predictors in combination. We carried out this estimation by comparing the variance explanation of three additional regression models (each time leaving out one of the three blocks of predictors) with a model that had all predictors in combination.[6]

Table 4.11 indicates how much variance was explained by the model as well as the relative contribution of the subsets of indicators. The table shows the explained variances (R^2*100) and their standard errors. The graph at the right side of the table depicts the size of the explained variance and the proportions of common variance as well as the variance uniquely attributable to each of the three predictor blocks.

The multiple regression model explained, on average, 22 percent of the variance in CIL scores. The range extended from 14 percent in Korea to 29 percent in Thailand. Across and within most countries, the largest part of the explained variance could be uniquely attributed to indicators of students' personal background (on average 7% of the total variance in CIL) while socioeconomic indicators uniquely explained about four percent of the variance in CIL. Only a relatively small proportion of the variance was due to a unique contribution from ICT resources (on average less than 1%).

---

5 A description of unadjusted effects can be found in the discussion pertaining to Tables 7.1 to 7.9 in Chapter 7.

6 The differences between each of the comparison models with the full model provide an estimate of the unique variance attributable to each block of variables. The difference between the sum of block variances and the explained variance by all predictors provides an estimate of the common variance attributable to more than one block of variables.

Table 4.11: Multiple regression model for students' CIL predicted by personal and social background variables (explained variance estimates)

Country	Percentage of Explained Variance	Proportion of Unique Variance Explained by Each Predictor Block and of the Variance Explained by More Than One Predictor Block
Australia	26 (1.7)	
Chile	26 (2.3)	
Croatia	21 (1.8)	
Czech Republic	21 (1.7)	
Germany[†]	25 (2.1)	
Korea, Republic of	14 (1.6)	
Lithuania	20 (1.7)	
Norway (Grade 9)[1]	18 (1.5)	
Poland	26 (1.8)	
Russian Federation[2]	17 (1.9)	
Slovak Republic	26 (2.5)	
Slovenia	21 (1.9)	
Thailand[2]	29 (2.8)	
Turkey	23 (2.5)	
ICILS 2013 average	22 (0.5)	
Countries not meeting sample requirements		
Denmark	14 (1.9)	
Hong Kong SAR	9 (1.7)	
Switzerland	14 (2.6)	
Benchmarking participants		
Newfoundland and Labrador, Canada	18 (2.9)	
Ontario, Canada	15 (2.2)	
Benchmarking participant not meeting sample requirements		
City of Buenos Aires, Argentina	24 (4.1)	

Notes:

() Standard errors appear in parentheses. Because some results are rounded to the nearest whole number, some totals may appear inconsistent.

† Met guidelines for sampling participation rates only after replacement schools were included.

[1] National Desired Population does not correspond to International Desired Population.

[2] Country surveyed the same cohort of students but at the beginning of the next school year.

■ Variance uniquely explained by student characteristics

■ Variance uniquely explained by parental occupation, parental education, and number of books

▫ Variance uniquely explained by IT home resources

□ Variance explained by all factors

There was also a substantial proportion of variance due to more than one factor (9% of the total variation in CIL across countries). In Thailand, in particular, the model explained 29 percent of the variation in CIL, with more than half of this explained variance due to more than one predictor block. This finding is plausible given that many indicators are likely to be associated with one another. For example, ICT resources are likely to be more often found in households with higher socioeconomic status, and parents' educational attainment is likely to influence students' expected educational attainment.

Conclusion

In this chapter, we reviewed the associations between students' personal and social background factors and CIL. Because of the likelihood that development of CIL is influenced not only by students' individual characteristics and their respective socioeconomic background but also by the extent of access students have to computers and the internet, we included ICT resources in students' homes in our analyses.

We found that personal characteristics such as gender and expected educational attainment as well as socioeconomic indicators consistently explained a considerable amount of the variance in CIL test scores. Both gender and students' educational aspirations were associated with higher levels of CIL. Among the socioeconomic indicators, parental occupational status and home literacy resources in particular were positively associated with CIL across the participating countries.

We also found that availability of home ICT resources had a positive effect on CIL in many countries. In particular, home access to the internet appeared to be associated with the higher CIL scores among students. The results of our multiple regression analysis, which enabled us to review the net effects on CIL as well as the unique variance contributions of different predictor blocks, suggest that ICT resources may also reflect (in part) the socioeconomic status of students' homes. Another observation is that in some highly developed countries, home ICT resources have only minor effects probably because students in almost all households in these countries have computers and internet access.

When we combined all home background variables into a multivariate analysis model, the variables that emerged as the most consistent predictors were expected university education, parental occupational status, and home literacy resources as well as the availability of internet access. The model explained about a fifth of the variation in CIL on average. However, in some countries, this proportion was more than one quarter.

These findings suggest that while personal and social background does not predict large proportions of the variance at the individual level, it is nonetheless important to take these factors into account when explaining variation in CIL. In Chapter 8, we review a wider range of potential predictors of CIL variation. There we use hierarchical linear modeling to explore the extent to which factors at both the individual (including personal and social background indicators) and the school level explained student performance on the ICILS assessment of computer and information literacy.

CHAPTER 5:

Students' Use of and Engagement with ICT at Home and School

Introduction

As part of the ICILS 2013 survey, Grade 8 students in the 21 participating ICILS countries completed a questionnaire concerning their use of information and communication technology (ICT) at home and at school, their experience of using ICT, and their access to ICT resources. Students answered this computer-based questionnaire after completing the ICILS assessment of computer and information literacy (CIL).

More specifically, the ICILS student questionnaire included questions relating to students' background characteristics, their experience and use of computers and ICT to complete a range of different tasks in school and out of school, and their attitudes toward the use of computers and ICT. The introduction to the questionnaire advised students that a computer could refer to a desktop computer, a notebook or laptop computer, a netbook computer, or a tablet device such as an iPad. The responses from this questionnaire thus provided information about aspects of Grade 8 students' familiarity with ICT[1] and their perceptions of using ICT at school and at home.

Our focus in this chapter is mainly on Research Question 3: *What characteristics of students' levels of access to, familiarity with, and self-reported proficiency in using computers are related to student achievement in computer and information literacy?* When reporting the information presented in this chapter, we provide detailed results for each country (typically percentages) pertaining to particular questionnaire items. We use scale scores based on sets of items to provide a more parsimonious picture of differences across countries as well as differences between subgroups such as females and males.

Following the engagement taxonomy proposed by Fredericks, Blumenfeld, and Paris (2004), we use the term "engagement" to encompass behavioral engagement (i.e., how students use ICT and how often they use it) and emotional engagement (students' perceptions of, attitudes toward, and feelings about ICT).

ICT at home and school

The last 30 or so years have seen rapid growth in the availability and use of ICT. Use of this technology has thus become ubiquitous in a relatively short period of time. Today, ICT permeates many occupations and homes throughout the world. Computer and internet access varies across countries, however, and also within countries. At the level of the home, this variation is typically associated with household income. Meta-analyses (Li & Ma, 2010; Tamin, Bernard, Borokhovski, Abrami, & Schmid, 2011) suggest positive associations between ICT use and student achievement in different subject areas.

The Trends in International Mathematics and Science Study (TIMSS), conducted by the International Association for the Evaluation of Educational Achievement (IEA) in 2011, reported that, on average, more than half (53%) of the Grade 8 students participating

---

1 In Norway, Grade 9 students completed the questionnaire.

© International Association for the Evaluation of Educational Achievement (IEA) 2014
J. Fraillon et al., *Preparing for Life in a Digital Age*, DOI 10.1007/978-3-319-14222-7_6

in the study had their own room and an internet connection at home (Mullis, Martin, Foy, & Arora, 2012, p. 184).[2] In some countries, this figure was higher than 80 percent (Australia, England, Finland, New Zealand, Norway, Slovenia, and Sweden as well as the Canadian provinces of Alberta, Ontario, and Quebec).

The survey of ICT familiarity conducted in 2012 as part of the OECD's Programme for International Student Assessment (PISA) showed that across the 34 participating OECD countries 93 percent of 15-year-old students had a computer at home that they could use for school work (OECD, 2013, p. 184). In 2000, the corresponding figure was 77 percent. Other PISA 2012 data showed that, on average across the participating countries, 93 percent of 15-year-old students had access to the internet at home (OECD, 2013, p. 184).

Evidence of widespread and growing use of digital technologies in schools for teaching and learning also exists. One example is a report from the United States Department of Education that documented the policies and practices 22 countries had adopted in order to encourage educational application of ICT (Bakia, Murphy, Anderson, & Trinidad, 2011).

TIMSS 2011 likewise reported high levels of access to computers for teaching and learning in schools (Mullis et al., 2012, p. 244). Forty percent of the Grade 8 students (one of the two TIMSS target grades) were in schools that had, on average, one computer for every one to two students, 28 percent were in schools with one computer for every three to five students, and 28 percent were in schools with one computer for six or more students. Only four percent of the Grade 8 students were attending schools with no provision for computers for instruction. The countries with the highest levels of computer availability (70% of students in schools with one computer for every one or two students) included Australia, England, Georgia, Hungary, Macedonia, New Zealand, Norway, and Slovenia.

Growth in student use of ICT at home and school has been accompanied by a growing interest in how these technologies are being used. IEA's Second International Technology in Education Study (SITES, Module 2), a major qualitative study of innovative pedagogical practices involving ICT use, conducted between 2000 and 2002, considered 174 case studies from across 28 countries (Kozma, 2003b). The case studies focused primarily on innovative ICT use, covered primary (one third of the cases) and secondary schooling (two thirds of the cases), and encompassed a range of subjects and crosscurricular topics.

SITES 2006 explored the use of ICT by Grade 8 science and mathematics teachers in 22 countries (Law, Pelgrum, & Plomp, 2008). The report of that study highlighted the importance of system and school factors in supporting teachers' pedagogical use of ICT. The report also documented the more extensive use of ICT by science teachers than mathematics teachers and the wide variation in the pedagogical use of ICT across education systems.

A survey of ICT in school education commissioned by the European Commission and reported on in 2013 included a survey of students at ISCED 2 (Grade 8) and ISCED 3 (Grade 11). Eighty percent of the Grade 8 students and 90 percent of the Grade 11 students said they had been using computers for more than four years. Students

---

2 These two items (own room and internet connection) cannot be separated in the reported data.

reported undertaking ICT-based activities more frequently at home than at school. However, considerable crossnational differences existed in the frequency with which students participated in ICT-based activities.

Students in the European Commission study rarely reported using, during lessons, applications (e.g., data-logging tools and computer simulations) that the commission research team considered particularly well suited to ICT use. One third of the students said they used digital textbooks and multimedia resources on at least a weekly basis. Students furthermore considered teacher-centered activities to be more extensive than student-centered activities. The report provided evidence of a positive association between amount of student-centered learning and frequency of ICT use for classroom activities.

The European Commission survey also identified three groups of ICT-based activities at home that the report authors termed "fun" (e.g., streaming or downloading multimedia, music, movies, videos), "learning" (e.g., online news, information searching, and learning programs), and "games." Apparently missing from the classification, however, were activities involving the use of computer utilities (software applications) for school-related document preparation.

The report's authors indicated that students were more confident in their "digital competences when they [had] high access to/use of ICT at home and at school" (European Commission, 2013, p. 15). Confident students also tended to be positive about the impact of ICT on their work and leisure. The authors furthermore reported evidence showing that pedagogical use of ICT is not simply associated with more abundant ICT resourcing. They observed that despite enhanced resourcing in the several years before the study, school use of ICT had not increased since 2006. This context enabled the study's authors to draw attention to the lack of ICT policies in schools.

In this chapter, we extend the body of information about student engagement with ICT by referencing data from the representative samples of Grade 8 students across 21 countries who participated in the study. We examine the extent to which, and the ways in which, these students were using ICT at home and at school. We also look at their perceptions of using ICT in these two environments.

Familiarity with computers

Our focus with regard to familiarity with computers is on students' ICT experience (in terms of the number of years students said they had been using computers) and the frequency with which (according to the students) they were using computers at home, school, and other places.

Experience with using computers

Table 5.1 records the length of time that students had been using computers. It also sets out the association between computer experience and students' CIL. Students reported their experience via five question response categories ("less than one year," "at least one year but less than three years," "at least three years but less than five years," "at least five years but less than seven years," and "seven or more years"). We transformed these categories into values reflecting approximate years of experience (0, 2, 4, 6, and 8) to obtain estimates of average years of experience. We then used these in a regression analysis so that we could review the association between this variable and CIL.

As is evident in Table 5.1, on average across the ICILS countries, more than one third (36%) of Grade 8 students reported having used computers for seven or more years. A further 29 percent had been using computers for between five and seven years. Fourteen percent said they had been using computers for under three years. Only five percent (or one in 20) of the surveyed students said they had been using computers for less than one year. Crossnationally, the estimated average length of time that students had been using computers was about six years.

Grade 8 students' experience with computers varied across the ICILS countries. If we take the percentage of students with five years or more experience of using computers as an indication of an "experienced computer user," we can see from Table 5.1 that many of the countries that met IEA sampling requirements had 69 percent or more of their students in this group. These countries included Poland (85%), the Canadian provinces of Ontario and Newfoundland and Labrador (both 83%), Norway (79%), Australia (78%), Slovenia (76%), Croatia (76%), the Czech Republic (75%), the Slovak Republic (71%), Lithuania (70%), and Korea (69%). In the next, much smaller group of countries, where about half the students had five or more years' experience of using computers, we find the Russian Federation (60% of students in this category) and Germany (49% of students). In the remaining two countries, Turkey and Thailand, the respective percentages of students reporting five or more years' experience of using computers were 38 and 34 percent.

We used a bivariate regression to investigate the relationship between students' computer experience (in approximate years) and CIL achievement. The results of this regression appear in the final two columns of Table 5.1. Statistically significant positive associations between computer experience and test performance emerged in all but one country (Germany). On average across countries, one year of computer experience was associated with an increase of nine CIL score points, and the model explained six percent of the variation in CIL. In Thailand and Turkey, computer experience accounted for 10 percent or more of the variance in student CIL achievement. Between one quarter and one fifth of the students in these two countries said they had been using computers for less than one year, an outcome perhaps of limited ICT resources. However, the relationship between experience of computer use and CIL achievement appeared to be similar in most countries.

Frequency of computer use

Students can use computers at home, school, and other places (such as a library or internet cafe). Table 5.2 records the percentages of Grade 8 students who reported using computers at least once a week at each of these places.[3] We chose to adopt the category of "at least once per week" as a summary indicator, not only because we could apply it uniformly to the various out-of-school computer-based activities reported in this chapter but also because it allowed us to generate reasonable distributions across those varied activities. We also used "at least once per month" as a summary indicator for school-based computer activities.[4]

---

3 The full range of response categories was "never," "less than once a month," "at least once a month but not every week," "at least once a week but not every day," and "every day." Because the relationship between frequency of use and CIL was weaker than the relationship between computer experience and CIL, Table 5.2 does not show it.

4 The full range of response categories for school-based computer activities was "never," "less than once a month," "at least once a month but not every week," and "at least once a week."

Table 5.1: National percentages of students' experience with computers

Country	Length of Time Using Computers					Average Length of Time Using Computers (Years)	Effect of Computer Experience on CIL Score	
	Less than one year	At least one year but fewer than three years	At least three years but fewer than five years	At least five years but fewer than seven years	Seven or more years		Difference in score points per year of experience	Variance explained
Australia	1 (0.2)	5 (0.4)	15 (0.6)	28 (0.8)	50 (1.1)	6 (0.0)	**10** (0.7)	6 (0.9)
Chile	8 (0.8)	14 (0.7)	25 (1.0)	25 (0.9)	28 (1.1)	5 (0.1)	**9** (0.9)	7 (1.5)
Croatia	2 (0.3)	4 (0.3)	19 (0.7)	33 (0.7)	43 (0.9)	6 (0.0)	**11** (0.8)	7 (1.0)
Czech Republic	1 (0.2)	4 (0.4)	20 (0.8)	37 (1.1)	38 (1.1)	6 (0.0)	**4** (0.7)	2 (0.5)
Germany†	2 (0.3)	14 (1.0)	35 (1.3)	30 (1.2)	19 (1.1)	5 (0.1)	2 (1.3)	0 (0.3)
Korea, Republic of	5 (0.4)	11 (0.7)	15 (0.8)	25 (0.9)	44 (1.1)	6 (0.1)	**10** (0.7)	7 (1.0)
Lithuania	3 (0.4)	7 (0.6)	20 (1.0)	29 (1.0)	41 (1.2)	6 (0.1)	**11** (1.0)	9 (1.3)
Norway (Grade 9)[1]	0 (0.1)	3 (0.3)	17 (0.8)	35 (0.9)	44 (1.0)	6 (0.0)	**6** (0.9)	2 (0.6)
Poland	1 (0.2)	3 (0.4)	11 (0.7)	31 (1.0)	53 (1.0)	7 (0.0)	**12** (1.2)	7 (1.4)
Russian Federation[2]	4 (0.4)	11 (0.6)	25 (0.7)	28 (0.8)	32 (0.9)	6 (0.1)	**9** (1.0)	7 (1.5)
Slovak Republic	3 (0.4)	7 (0.7)	20 (0.9)	34 (1.1)	37 (1.2)	6 (0.1)	**12** (1.7)	7 (1.9)
Slovenia	1 (0.2)	4 (0.5)	19 (0.9)	37 (0.8)	39 (1.2)	6 (0.1)	2 (0.7)	0 (0.2)
Thailand[2]	23 (1.3)	24 (1.1)	19 (1.0)	16 (1.1)	18 (0.8)	4 (0.1)	**12** (1.1)	12 (1.9)
Turkey	22 (1.2)	19 (1.0)	22 (0.8)	18 (0.8)	20 (1.0)	4 (0.1)	**15** (1.0)	18 (1.9)
ICILS 2013 average	5 (0.2)	9 (0.2)	20 (0.2)	29 (0.3)	36 (0.3)	6 (0.0)	**9** (0.3)	6 (0.3)
Countries not meeting sample requirements								
Denmark	1 (0.2)	4 (0.5)	17 (1.1)	29 (1.2)	49 (1.6)	6 (0.1)	**4** (1.0)	1 (0.5)
Hong Kong SAR	2 (0.4)	7 (0.7)	19 (0.9)	27 (1.0)	45 (1.4)	6 (0.1)	**6** (1.2)	2 (0.8)
Netherlands	1 (0.2)	3 (0.4)	14 (0.7)	31 (1.1)	52 (1.3)	7 (0.0)	**6** (1.5)	1 (0.7)
Switzerland	1 (0.4)	13 (1.2)	31 (1.4)	36 (1.6)	20 (1.6)	5 (0.1)	**4** (1.4)	1 (0.8)
Benchmarking participants								
Newfoundland and Labrador, Canada	1 (0.4)	3 (0.6)	12 (1.2)	27 (1.3)	56 (1.4)	7 (0.1)	**9** (1.8)	4 (1.7)
Ontario, Canada	1 (0.2)	3 (0.4)	12 (0.7)	25 (1.0)	58 (1.1)	7 (0.0)	**7** (1.1)	3 (0.8)
Benchmarking participant not meeting sample requirements								
City of Buenos Aires, Argentina	5 (1.0)	11 (1.2)	19 (1.4)	27 (2.1)	37 (1.7)	6 (0.1)	**12** (1.8)	10 (2.5)

Notes:
* Statistically significant (*p*<.05) coefficients in **bold**.
() Standard errors appear in parentheses. Because some results are rounded to the nearest whole number, some totals may appear inconsistent.
† Met guidelines for sampling participation rates only after replacement schools were included.
[1] National Desired Population does not correspond to International Desired Population.
[2] Country surveyed the same cohort of students but at the beginning of the next school year.

The data showed that, on average across countries, the percentages of frequent computer usage were higher for home use (87%) than school use (54%) and considerably higher than for use at other places (13%). In Croatia, the Czech Republic, Lithuania, Norway, Poland, the Russian Federation, the Slovak Republic, and Slovenia, the percentages of students who reported using their computers at home at least once a week were significantly higher than the ICILS 2013 average.[5] Notably high percentages of students were also using computers at home at least once a week in the Canadian provinces of Newfoundland and Labrador and Ontario. The percentages of weekly home users of computers were significantly below the ICILS 2013 average in Chile, Korea, Thailand, and Turkey. The percentages of weekly home users in Germany and Australia were the same as the ICILS 2013 average.[6]

Although more than half of the ICILS students reported using a computer at school at least once a week (the ICILS 2013 average was 54%), there were notable differences among countries. The use of computers at school at least once each week was more than 10 percentage points higher than the ICILS 2013 average in Australia, Poland, the Slovak Republic, the Russian Federation, and Thailand. The percentage of students using school computers at least once a week was also significantly higher than average (but by no more than 10 percentage points) in Croatia and the Czech Republic. The percentage of students reporting at least weekly use of computers at school was more than 10 percentage points lower than the ICILS average in Chile, Germany, Korea, Slovenia, and Turkey.[7]

The data in Table 5.2 also indicate the relative extent of weekly home and school use of computers. Slovenia stands out as a country where the extent of weekly home use was far greater than school use (96% compared to 26%). In Germany, Korea, and Switzerland, the extent of weekly home computer use was substantially greater (with a difference of more than 50 percentage points) than the extent of weekly school use. In Chile, Norway, Lithuania, the Czech Republic, and Croatia, the extent of weekly home computer use was greater than the extent of weekly school computer use by between 31 and 46 percentage points. The Canadian provinces of Newfoundland and Labrador and Ontario were also in this group. In Turkey, the Russian Federation, Denmark, the Slovak Republic, and Poland, the difference between home and school use ranged from only 17 to 27 percentage points. In Australia, the proportions of students using computers at home and at school were almost similar (87% and 81%). Thailand was the only country where more students reported using computers at least weekly at school (66%) than at home (59%).

In most countries, the frequency with which students were using computers at places other than the home or school was small. Fewer than 10 percent of students in most countries reported using computers beyond the home or school on a weekly basis. In Thailand (31%), Korea (30%), Turkey (23%), and the Russian Federation (18%), students' computer use in places other than at home or at school was significantly above the ICILS 2013 average.

---

5 The ICILS 2013 average is the average across those participating countries that met the sampling requirements, with each country given an equal weight.

6 More than half of the Grade 8 students said they used a computer every day (the ICILS 2013 average was 54%).

7 Only six percent of students across the participating countries said they used a computer at school every day. In Australia, one third of students (33%) reported this frequency, as did one tenth (11%) of the students in the Canadian province of Ontario. Denmark (33%) and the Netherlands (13%) also had a similar apparently high level of daily school-based computer use.

Table 5.2: National percentages of students' computer use at home, school, and other places at least once a week

Country	Percent of Students Using a Computer at Least Once a Week							
	At home			At school			At other places (e.g., local library, internet cafe)	
Australia	87	(0.7)		81	(1.3)	▲	9	(0.5)	▽
Chile	81	(1.0)	▽	35	(2.1)	▼	8	(0.5)	▽
Croatia	95	(0.5)	△	61	(1.6)	△	7	(0.6)	▽
Czech Republic	96	(0.4)	△	60	(2.2)	△	7	(0.5)	▽
Germany[†]	88	(0.8)		31	(2.5)	▼	5	(0.5)	▽
Korea, Republic of	71	(1.2)	▼	18	(2.1)	▼	30	(1.3)	▲
Lithuania	95	(0.5)	△	55	(2.5)		9	(0.6)	▽
Norway (Grade 9)[1]	96	(0.4)	△	52	(2.4)		7	(0.5)	▽
Poland	96	(0.4)	△	79	(2.1)	▲	5	(0.5)	▽
Russian Federation[2]	94	(0.6)	△	73	(1.3)	▲	18	(0.9)	△
Slovak Republic	95	(0.5)	△	77	(2.1)	▲	12	(0.7)	
Slovenia	96	(0.5)	△	26	(1.2)	▼	7	(0.5)	▽
Thailand[2]	59	(1.5)	▼	66	(1.8)	▲	31	(1.5)	▲
Turkey	62	(1.6)	▼	35	(2.7)	▼	23	(1.0)	▲
ICILS 2013 average	87	(0.2)		54	(0.5)		13	(0.2)	

Countries not meeting sample requirements								
Denmark	95	(0.4)		76	(2.1)		8	(0.7)	
Hong Kong SAR	88	(1.0)		57	(2.0)		8	(0.7)	
Netherlands	95	(0.6)		63	(2.6)		5	(0.7)	
Switzerland	86	(1.2)		34	(3.1)		6	(0.8)	

Benchmarking participants								
Newfoundland and Labrador, Canada	91	(1.1)		54	(1.7)		11	(1.1)	
Ontario, Canada	91	(0.7)		60	(2.2)		11	(0.7)	

Benchmarking participant not meeting sample requirements								
City of Buenos Aires, Argentina	89	(1.1)		57	(3.3)		13	(1.2)	

▲ More than 10 percentage points above ICILS 2013 average
△ Significantly above ICILS 2013 average
▽ Significantly below ICILS 2013 average
▼ More than 10 percentage points below ICILS 2013 average

Notes:
() Standard errors appear in parentheses. Because some results are rounded to the nearest whole number, some totals may appear inconsistent.
[†] Met guidelines for sampling participation rates only after replacement schools were included.
[1] National Desired Population does not correspond to International Desired Population.
[2] Country surveyed the same cohort of students but at the beginning of the next school year.

Student use of computers outside school

The preceding section of this chapter indicated that in most of the ICILS countries a larger percentage of students reported using computers at least once per week outside school than at school. In this section, we take a closer look at aspects of students' ICT use outside school. We consider the frequency of computer use outside of school for specified applications and the frequency of internet use for specified purposes.

Computer-based applications used outside school

We asked students about the frequency with which they used computer-based work-oriented applications (computer utilities) outside school. The response categories were "never," "less than once a month," "at least once a month but not every week," "at least once a week but not every day," and "every day." Students were asked to indicate the frequency with which they used work-oriented computer applications for the following purposes:

- Creating or editing documents;
- Using a spreadsheet to do calculations, store data, or plot graphs;
- Creating a simple "slideshow" presentation;
- Creating a multimedia presentation;
- Using education software designed to help with school study;
- Writing computer programs, macros, or scripts; and
- Using drawing, painting, or graphics software.

Table 5.3 records the percentages of students who said they used work-oriented computer applications for these seven purposes at least once a week. On average across the ICILS countries, 28 percent of students reported using computer technology to "create or edit documents" at least once a week. Of the seven activities, this was the one most extensively done on a weekly basis across the countries.

In Australia (48%), the Russian Federation (44%), and Thailand (39%), the percentages were significantly above the international average, by more than 10 percentage points.[8] In Chile (33%), Thailand (32%), Norway (31%), and Poland (31%), the percentages for creating and editing documents at least weekly were significantly higher than the ICILS 2013 average but by fewer than 10 percentage points. The percentages were significantly below the ICILS 2013 average for the Czech Republic (25%), the Slovak Republic (25%), Croatia (20%), and Slovenia (19%). In Lithuania (16%), Germany (15%), and Korea (13%), the percentages were significantly below the ICILS 2013 average by more than 10 percentage points.

On average, 18 percent of students across the participating countries reported using "education software designed to help with school study (e.g., mathematics or reading software)" at least once a week. The largest percentages of students who were weekly users of this type of software were recorded for the Russian Federation (42%) and Turkey (29%). These percentages were significantly above the ICILS 2013 average by more than 10 percentage points. The percentages in Australia (28%), Lithuania (28%), and Poland (22%) were also above the ICILS 2013 average. The percentages in Germany

---

8 When describing the extent of participation on a weekly basis, we identify those countries that differed significantly from the ICILS 2013 average and those that differed by an amount that was significant and greater than 10 percentage points. We sometimes use the term "notable" to characterize this latter group.

Table 5.3: National percentages of students using computers outside of school for specific ICT applications at least once a week

Country	Creating or Editing Documents (e.g., to Write Stories or Assignments)		Using a Spreadsheet to Do Calculations, Store Data, or Plot Graphs (e.g., Using [Microsoft EXCEL®])		Creating a Simple "Slideshow" Presentation (e.g., Using [Microsoft PowerPoint®])		Creating a Multimedia Presentation (With Sound, Pictures, Video)		Using Education Software Designed to Help With School Study (e.g., Mathematics or Reading Software)		Writing Computer Programs, Macros, or Scripts (e.g., Using [Logo, Basic, or HTML])		Using Drawing, Painting, or Graphics Software	
Australia	48 (1.3)	▲	9 (0.5)	▽	20 (1.0)	◁	15 (0.6)		28 (1.2)	◁	14 (0.7)	◁	19 (0.7)	
Chile	33 (1.3)	◁	11 (0.6)		27 (1.3)	▲	22 (0.9)	◁	11 (0.8)	▽	9 (0.7)		15 (0.8)	▽
Croatia	20 (0.9)	▽	7 (0.5)	▽	14 (0.8)	▽	12 (0.8)	▽	9 (0.6)	▽	7 (0.6)	▽	13 (0.7)	▽
Czech Republic	25 (1.4)	▽	8 (0.7)	▽	14 (1.0)	▽	13 (0.6)	▽	8 (0.7)	▲	6 (0.5)	▽	20 (0.8)	◁
Germany†	15 (1.0)	▼	7 (0.6)	▽	6 (0.8)	▼	8 (0.6)	▽	7 (0.7)	▲	7 (0.6)	▽	11 (0.8)	▽
Korea, Republic of	13 (0.8)	▼	5 (0.4)	▽	5 (0.5)	▼	7 (0.5)	▽	11 (0.6)	▽	5 (0.5)	▽	8 (0.5)	▼
Lithuania	16 (0.9)	▽	20 (1.2)	◁	19 (1.1)		27 (1.0)	▲	28 (1.1)	◁	11 (0.6)		19 (1.0)	
Norway (Grade 9)[1]	31 (1.6)	◁	4 (0.5)	▽	11 (1.1)	▽	9 (0.7)	▽	12 (0.7)	▽	7 (0.5)	▽	12 (0.7)	▽
Poland	31 (1.0)	◁	10 (0.8)		9 (0.7)	▽	12 (0.7)	▽	22 (1.0)	◁	9 (0.7)		23 (1.0)	◁
Russian Federation[2]	44 (1.4)	▲	18 (1.0)	◁	29 (1.5)	▲	19 (0.9)	◁	42 (1.0)	◁	15 (0.6)	◁	31 (1.0)	▲
Slovak Republic	25 (0.9)	▽	14 (0.9)	◁	22 (1.2)	◁	18 (0.8)	◁	14 (0.8)	▽	11 (0.6)		18 (0.9)	
Slovenia	19 (0.9)	▽	11 (0.7)		14 (1.0)	▽	15 (0.9)		15 (0.8)	▽	10 (0.7)		16 (0.8)	▽
Thailand[2]	32 (1.2)	◁	15 (1.0)	◁	19 (1.2)		20 (1.1)	◁	20 (1.1)		12 (0.9)	◁	27 (1.0)	◁
Turkey	39 (1.0)	▲	19 (0.9)	◁	25 (1.2)	◁	21 (0.9)	◁	29 (1.3)	▼	17 (0.9)	◁	25 (1.1)	◁
ICILS 2013 average	28 (0.3)		11 (0.2)		17 (0.3)		15 (0.2)		18 (0.2)		10 (0.2)		18 (0.2)	
Countries not meeting sample requirements														
Denmark	52 (1.8)		18 (1.4)		11 (1.2)		12 (0.8)		17 (1.0)		9 (0.7)		13 (0.9)	
Hong Kong SAR	26 (1.6)		11 (0.7)		10 (0.8)		13 (0.8)		15 (1.0)		8 (0.5)		12 (0.7)	
Netherlands	32 (1.6)		7 (0.7)		9 (0.9)		10 (0.9)		24 (1.4)		9 (0.7)		11 (0.9)	
Switzerland	17 (1.2)		6 (0.9)		5 (0.8)		7 (0.9)		11 (1.0)		6 (1.0)		10 (1.0)	
Benchmarking participants														
Newfoundland and Labrador, Canada	18 (1.2)		5 (0.6)		8 (1.1)		9 (0.9)		14 (1.1)		8 (0.9)		16 (1.0)	
Ontario, Canada	35 (1.7)		7 (0.6)		10 (0.9)		11 (0.7)		17 (0.8)		12 (0.8)		17 (1.1)	
Benchmarking participant not meeting sample requirements														
City of Buenos Aires, Argentina	31 (2.3)		13 (1.2)		14 (1.4)		23 (1.3)		17 (1.5)		9 (1.1)		22 (1.5)	

▲ More than 10 percentage points above ICILS 2013 average

△ Significantly above ICILS 2013 average

▽ Significantly below ICILS 2013 average

▼ More than 10 percentage points below ICILS 2013 average

Notes:

() Standard errors errors appear in parentheses. Because some results are rounded to the nearest whole number, some totals may appear inconsistent.

† Met guidelines for sampling participation rates only after replacement schools were included.

[1] National Desired Population does not correspond to International Desired Population.

[2] Country surveyed the same cohort of students but at the beginning of the next school year.

(7%) and the Czech Republic (7%) were significantly, and by more than 10 percentage points, below the ICILS 2013 average. The percentages in Croatia (9%), Chile (11%), Korea (11%), Norway (12%), the Slovak Republic (14%), and Slovenia (15%) were also significantly below the ICILS 2013 average.

On average across ICILS countries, 18 percent of students reported using "drawing, painting, or graphics software" at least once a week outside of school. The proportion of Russian Federation students reporting this usage was, at 31 percent, more than 10 percentage points above the ICILS 2013 average. Other countries that were also significantly above the ICILS 2013 average were Thailand (27%), Turkey (25%), Poland (23%), and the Czech Republic (20%). The eight percent of Korean students reporting use of this application were below the ICILS 2013 average by more than 10 percentage points. Other countries that were also significantly below the ICILS 2013 average were Germany (11%), Norway (12%), Croatia (13%), Chile (15%), and Slovenia (16%).

On average across the ICILS countries, 17 percent of students said they "created a simple 'slideshow' presentation" at least weekly outside of school. The percentages in the Russian Federation (29%) and Chile (27%) were more than 10 percentage points above the ICILS 2013 average. In Turkey (25%), the Slovak Republic (22%), and Australia (20%), the percentages were also significantly higher than the ICILS 2013 average. For Korea (5%) and Germany (6%), the percentages were 10 percentage points or more below the ICILS 2013 average. In addition, the percentages in Poland (9%), Norway (11%), Croatia (14%), the Czech Republic (14%), and Slovenia (14%) were also significantly lower than the ICILS 2013 average.

An application similar to but more complex than developing a slideshow was "creating a multimedia presentation (with sound, pictures, video)." On average across the ICILS countries, 15 percent of students reported carrying out this activity at least once a week. In Lithuania, 27 percent of students said they used this application at least once a week. This figure was more than 10 percentage points above the ICILS 2013 average. The percentages in Chile (22%), Turkey (21%), Thailand (20%), the Russian Federation (19%), and the Slovak Republic (18%) were also significantly higher than the ICILS 2013 average. Countries where the percentages were significantly below the ICILS 2013 average were the Czech Republic (13%), Croatia (12%), and Poland (12%).

Crossnationally, 11 percent of students (the ICILS 2013 average) reported "using a spreadsheet to do calculations, store data, or plot graphs" at least once a week. The percentages were significantly higher than the average across ICILS countries in Lithuania (20%), Turkey (19%), the Russian Federation (18%), Thailand (15%), and the Slovak Republic (14%). In Norway (4%), Korea (5%), Germany (7%), Croatia (7%), the Czech Republic (8%), and Australia (9%), these percentages were significantly lower than the ICILS 2013 average.

Only 10 percent of students (on average across ICILS countries) reported engaging at least once a week in "writing computer programs, macros, or scripts (e.g., using Logo, Basic, or HTML)." National percentages ranged from five percent in Korea to 17 percent in Turkey.

The scale derived from the seven items reflecting use of different applications had an average reliability of 0.80 (Cronbach's alpha) across the ICILS countries. We used the Rasch partial credit model to construct this scale and standardized its item response theory (IRT) scores to have an ICILS 2013 average score of 50 points and a standard deviation of 10 points.[9] The higher scores on the scale indicate higher frequencies of using these applications.

Table 5.4 shows the national average scores on the *students' use of computer applications scale* overall and within gender groups. We recorded significantly more frequent use of these applications in the Russian Federation, Australia, Lithuania, Chile, Poland, the Slovak Republic, Slovenia, Thailand, and Turkey. They were less extensively used in Korea, Germany, Croatia, the Czech Republic, Norway, and the Canadian province of Newfoundland and Labrador.

On average across ICILS countries, no statistically significant differences could be discerned between females and males in out-of-school use of the seven applications. In some countries, small but statistically significant differences were apparent. In Turkey, the Czech Republic, Poland, and the Slovak Republic, male students were slightly more likely than female students to use these applications on a frequent basis. However, in Australia, Chile, Korea, and the Russian Federation, female students were more likely than males to report using these applications on a frequent basis.

Internet use for communication and exchange of information

Several publications have not only documented students' extensive use of ICT for communication and accessing information but also looked at the implications of this use for education (see, for example, Ainley, Enger, & Searle, 2009). The ICILS student questionnaire asked students to identify the frequency with which they were using the internet for a variety of communication and information-exchange activities outside of school. The response categories were "never," "less than once a month," "at least once a month but not every week," "at least once a week but not every day," and "every day."

The 10 activities that the questionnaire required the students to respond to were the following:

- Searching for information for study or school work;
- Accessing wikis or online encyclopedias for study or school work;
- Communicating with others using messaging or social networks (e.g., instant messaging or [status updates]);
- Posting comments to online profiles or blogs;
- Asking questions on forums or [question and answer] websites;
- Answering other people's questions on forums or websites;
- Writing posts for your [the student's] own blog;
- Uploading images or video to an [online profile] or [online community] (e.g., Facebook or YouTube);
- Using voice chat (e.g., Skype) to chat with friends or family online; and
- Building or editing a webpage.

---

9 This metric was used for most questionnaire-based scales in ICILS. Setting the international standard deviation to 10 points was deemed appropriate given the limited numbers of items used for deriving questionnaire scales. (The achievement scale was based on many more items, so an international metric with a standard deviation of 100 was chosen.)

Table 5.4: National averages for students' use of computers for specific ICT applications overall and by gender

Country	Students' Use of Computers for Specific ICT Applications				Score Distribution by Gender
	All students	Females	Males	Differences (males - females)*	
Australia	52 (0.2) △	53 (0.2)	52 (0.3)	-1 (0.4)	
Chile	51 (0.2) △	51 (0.2)	50 (0.4)	-1 (0.4)	
Croatia	47 (0.2) ▽	47 (0.3)	48 (0.3)	1 (0.4)	
Czech Republic	49 (0.2) ▽	49 (0.3)	50 (0.3)	1 (0.3)	
Germany†	46 (0.3) ▶	46 (0.4)	46 (0.4)	0 (0.4)	
Korea, Republic of	45 (0.3) ▶	45 (0.3)	44 (0.4)	-1 (0.5)	
Lithuania	52 (0.3) △	52 (0.3)	51 (0.4)	-1 (0.4)	
Norway (Grade 9)[1]	49 (0.2) ▽	49 (0.3)	49 (0.3)	0 (0.4)	
Poland	51 (0.2) △	50 (0.3)	51 (0.3)	1 (0.4)	
Russian Federation[2]	54 (0.3) ◀	54 (0.3)	53 (0.4)	-1 (0.3)	
Slovak Republic	51 (0.2) △	50 (0.3)	52 (0.3)	1 (0.4)	
Slovenia	51 (0.2) △	51 (0.3)	51 (0.4)	1 (0.5)	
Thailand[2]	51 (0.3) △	51 (0.3)	51 (0.4)	-1 (0.4)	
Turkey	51 (0.3) △	50 (0.4)	53 (0.4)	3 (0.5)	
ICILS 2013 average	50 (0.1)	50 (0.1)	50 (0.1)	0 (0.1)	
Countries not meeting sample requirements					
Denmark	52 (0.3)	52 (0.3)	52 (0.3)	1 (0.4)	
Hong Kong SAR	48 (0.4)	48 (0.6)	48 (0.5)	0 (0.6)	
Netherlands	49 (0.3)	49 (0.3)	50 (0.4)	1 (0.4)	
Switzerland	47 (0.3)	47 (0.3)	47 (0.5)	1 (0.5)	
Benchmarking participants					
Newfoundland and Labrador, Canada	48 (0.3)	48 (0.4)	48 (0.5)	-1 (0.6)	
Ontario, Canada	50 (0.3)	50 (0.3)	50 (0.4)	0 (0.5)	
Benchmarking participant not meeting sample requirements					
City of Buenos Aires, Argentina	48 (0.5)	48 (0.5)	47 (0.8)	-1 (0.9)	

▲ More than three score points above ICILS 2013 average
△ Significantly above ICILS 2013 average
▽ Significantly below ICILS 2013 average
▶ More than three score points below ICILS 2013 average

■ Female average score +/– confidence interval
■ Male average score +/– confidence interval

On average, students with a score in the range indicated by this color have more than a 50% probability of reporting use of computers for specific ICT applications:

Less than once a week
Once a week or more frequently

Notes:
* Statistically significant (*p*<.05) coefficients in **bold**.
() Standard errors appear in parentheses. Because some results are rounded to the nearest whole number, some totals may appear inconsistent.
† Met guidelines for sampling participation rates only after replacement schools were included.
[1] National Desired Population does not correspond to International Desired Population.
[2] Country surveyed the same cohort of students but at the beginning of the next school year.

Table 5.5 records the national percentages of students who reported doing each of these activities at least once a week. Across the ICILS countries, one activity stood out from the others in terms of weekly use, namely "communicating with others using messaging or social networks." The crossnational average for this activity was 75 percent. Student percentages in several countries exceeded the ICILS 2013 average by more than 10 such points. They were Norway (89%), Poland (88%), the Slovak Republic (87%), and the Czech Republic (86%). Those countries where the respective percentage was more than 10 percentage points below the ICILS 2013 average were Korea (42%), Thailand (49%), and Turkey (56%).

On average across the ICILS countries, just over half of the students (52%) said they used internet for "searching for information for study or school work" at least once a week. The countries where the average percentages exceeded the ICILS 2013 average by 10 or more percentage points included Poland (74%), the Russian Federation (72%), Australia (65%), and Turkey (63%). The countries with percentages 10 or more points below the ICILS 2013 average included Korea (30%), Slovenia (38%), Germany (38%), and the Slovak Republic (42%).

Crossnationally, about half of the students (49%), on average, indicated that they engaged in "posting comments to online profiles or blogs" at least once a week. This percentage was 10 points or more above the ICILS 2013 average in the Russian Federation (69%) and Poland (63%), and was 10 percentage points or more below this average in Thailand (30%), Korea (35%), and Turkey (38%).

Across all ICILS countries, an average of 48 percent of students indicated that they used internet for "voice chat in order to chat with friends or family online." The highest percentages of students reporting they did this at least once a week were recorded in Lithuania (64%), Slovenia (62%), the Czech Republic (61%), the Slovak Republic (60%), and the Russian Federation (58%). The lowest national percentages were found in Korea (26%), Turkey (31%), Thailand (35%), and Australia (36%).

On average across ICILS countries, 43 percent of students indicated using internet at least once a week for "accessing wikis or online encyclopedias for study or school work." The highest national percentages of students reporting at least weekly use of this activity were in the Russian Federation (63%) and Poland (63%); the lowest percentages were in Korea (23%), Newfoundland and Labrador (25%), and Germany (30%).

Thirty-eight percent of students on average across all countries said they "uploaded images or video to an online profile or community" such as Facebook or YouTube at least once a week. The highest national percentages were found in the Russian Federation (54%) and Croatia (49%), while the lowest percentages were observed in Norway (22%) and Korea (23%).

On average across the ICILS countries, only small percentages of students reported using the four remaining activities at least once a week. These activities were:

- Answering other people's questions on forums or websites (ICILS 2013 average: 24%);
- Asking questions on forums or [question and answer] websites (ICILS 2013 average: 22%);
- Writing posts for your own blog (ICILS 2013 average: 21%); and
- Building or editing a webpage (ICILS 2013 average: 11%).

Table 5.5: National percentages of students using the internet outside of school for communication and exchange of information at least once a week

Country	Searching for Information for Study or School Work	Accessing Wikis or Online Encyclopedia for Study or School Work	Communicating With Others Using Messaging or Social Networks (e.g., Instant Messaging or [Status Updates])	Posting Comments to Online Profiles or Blogs	Asking Questions on Forums or [Question and Answer] Websites	Answering Other People's Questions on Forums or Websites	Writing Posts for Your Own Blog	Uploading Images or Video to an [Online Profile] or [Online Community] (e.g., Facebook or YouTube)	Using Voice Chat (e.g., Skype) to Chat with Friends or Family Online	Building or Editing a Webpage
Australia	65 (1.4) ▲	50 (1.3) △	80 (0.8) △	48 (0.8)	17 (0.8) ▽	13 (0.5) ▼	22 (0.7)	36 (0.9) ▽	36 (1.0) ▼	8 (0.5) ▽
Chile	49 (1.4) ▽	40 (1.4) ▽	72 (1.1) ▽	48 (1.3)	24 (1.2)	20 (0.9) ▽	24 (1.0) △	47 (1.1) △	42 (1.3) ▽	10 (0.7)
Croatia	44 (1.2) ▽	39 (1.0) ▽	85 (0.8) △	56 (1.0) △	18 (0.7) ▽	19 (0.9) ▽	17 (0.9) ▽	49 (1.1) ▲	49 (1.2)	8 (0.6) ▽
Czech Republic	48 (1.3) ▽	50 (1.3) △	86 (0.8) ▲	47 (1.1)	14 (0.7) ▽	23 (0.9)	16 (0.8) ▽	39 (1.0)	61 (1.3) ▲	10 (0.7)
Germany†	38 (1.1) ▼	30 (1.1) ▼	80 (0.9) △	46 (1.1) ▽	13 (0.8) ▽	11 (0.8) ▼	12 (0.7) ▽	30 (1.3) ▽	48 (1.6)	6 (0.6) ▽
Korea, Republic of	30 (1.1) ▼	23 (0.9) ▼	42 (1.1) ▼	35 (1.1) ▼	18 (0.8) ▽	16 (0.7) ▽	11 (0.6) ▽	23 (0.9) ▼	26 (0.9) ▼	5 (0.4) ▽
Lithuania	62 (1.2) △	45 (1.1)	85 (0.9) △	54 (1.0) △	32 (1.1) △	37 (1.0) ▲	24 (0.9) △	32 (1.1) ▽	64 (1.2) ▲	13 (0.9)
Norway (Grade 9)[1]	55 (1.6) △	47 (1.6) △	89 (0.7) ▲	46 (1.1) ▽	11 (0.7) ▼	11 (0.7) ▼	7 (0.6) ▼	22 (0.9) ▼	48 (1.1)	7 (0.6) ▽
Poland	74 (1.0) ▲	63 (1.0) ▲	88 (0.7) ▲	63 (0.9) ▲	30 (1.1) △	33 (1.2) △	11 (0.8) ▽	37 (0.9)	52 (1.2) △	10 (0.7)
Russian Federation[2]	72 (1.1) ▲	63 (1.0) ▲	85 (0.7) △	69 (0.9) ▲	34 (1.0) ▲	36 (1.0) ▲	34 (0.9) ▲	54 (1.2) ▲	58 (1.2) ▲	22 (0.9) ▲
Slovak Republic	42 (1.2) ▽	39 (1.1) ▽	87 (0.9) ▲	53 (1.0) △	21 (0.9)	29 (0.9) △	24 (1.0) △	47 (1.2) △	60 (1.1) ▲	14 (0.7) △
Slovenia	38 (1.0) ▼	37 (0.9) ▽	73 (0.9) ▽	49 (1.2)	21 (1.0)	24 (1.1)	32 (1.4) ▲	30 (1.2) ▽	62 (1.2) ▲	14 (0.8) △
Thailand[2]	51 (1.4)	33 (1.3) ▽	49 (1.5) ▼	30 (1.5) ▼	34 (1.4) ▲	36 (1.6) ▲	34 (1.3) ▲	43 (1.2) △	35 (1.4) ▼	15 (1.0) △
Turkey	63 (1.3) ▲	40 (1.3) ▽	56 (1.6) ▼	38 (1.4) ▼	27 (1.0) △	26 (1.0)	27 (1.1) △	45 (1.4) △	31 (1.1) ▼	18 (0.8) △
ICILS 2013 average	52 (0.3)	43 (0.3)	75 (0.3)	49 (0.3)	22 (0.3)	24 (0.3)	21 (0.2)	38 (0.3)	48 (0.3)	11 (0.2)
Countries not meeting sample requirements										
Denmark	65 (1.8)	48 (1.6)	90 (0.8)	42 (1.8)	12 (1.0)	11 (1.0)	8 (0.7)	28 (1.2)	50 (1.6)	5 (0.5)
Hong Kong SAR	37 (2.1)	33 (1.7)	60 (1.6)	36 (1.3)	23 (1.0)	30 (0.9)	13 (0.8)	33 (1.1)	39 (1.3)	9 (0.8)
Netherlands	50 (1.6)	30 (1.5)	80 (1.2)	36 (1.1)	9 (0.7)	11 (0.8)	17 (1.0)	42 (1.2)	54 (1.2)	9 (0.7)
Switzerland	33 (1.8)	31 (1.5)	77 (1.3)	45 (1.7)	12 (1.2)	8 (0.8)	16 (1.3)	31 (1.8)	50 (2.0)	7 (0.8)
Benchmarking participants										
Newfoundland and Labrador, Canada	39 (1.4)	25 (1.4)	75 (2.0)	54 (1.5)	13 (0.9)	10 (1.1)	29 (1.4)	41 (1.3)	41 (2.0)	10 (1.0)
Ontario, Canada	56 (1.7)	41 (1.8)	79 (0.9)	55 (1.2)	19 (1.1)	13 (1.0)	25 (1.3)	40 (1.1)	41 (1.2)	10 (0.8)
Benchmarking participant not meeting sample requirements										
City of Buenos Aires, Argentina	58 (1.9)	48 (2.2)	74 (1.7)	51 (2.0)	24 (1.5)	22 (1.7)	30 (2.2)	54 (2.0)	45 (1.8)	13 (1.3)

Notes:
() Standard errors appear in parentheses. Because some results are rounded to the nearest whole number, some totals may appear inconsistent.
† Met guidelines for sampling participation rates only after replacement schools were included.
[1] National Desired Population does not correspond to International Desired Population.
[2] Country surveyed the same cohort of students but at the beginning of the next school year.

▲ More than 10 percentage points above ICILS 2013 average
△ Significantly above ICILS 2013 average
▽ Significantly below ICILS 2013 average
▼ More than 10 percentage points below ICILS 2013 average

Four items reflecting internet use for social communication[10] provided the basis for deriving a scale that had a satisfactory reliability (i.e., a Cronbach's alpha of 0.74 on average across the participating countries). We used the Rasch partial credit model to construct the scale and standardized the IRT scores to have an ICILS 2013 average score of 50 points and a standard deviation of 10 points. The higher scores on the scale indicate higher frequencies of engaging in ICT use for social communication.

Table 5.6 shows the national average scores on the *students' ICT use for social communication scale* overall and within gender groups. The students who made the most use of internet as a means of social communication were those in the Russian Federation. They, along with students in the Slovak Republic, Poland, Lithuania, the Czech Republic, and Croatia, were significantly more likely than their peers internationally to use internet for social communication. This usage was lowest in Korea, Turkey, and Thailand (more than three score points below the ICILS 2013 average), and significantly so. Usage was also significantly lower than the international average in Germany and Australia. In Chile, Norway, and Slovenia, using internet for social communication was not significantly different from the ICILS 2013 average. The average scores for the Canadian provinces of Ontario and Newfoundland and Labrador also appeared to be similar to the ICILS 2013 average.

The data presented evidence that females were using the internet for social communication slightly more often (on average) than males. We recorded statistically significant gender differences in favor of female students in Chile, Australia, Korea, and Lithuania as well as in the two Canadian provinces of Newfoundland and Labrador and Ontario. On average, females scored two or more scale score points higher than males in these countries. The only country where male students' scores on the social communication scale were significantly higher than the females' was Turkey.

Four items reflecting *internet use for exchanging information*[11] provided the basis for deriving a scale that had a satisfactory reliability of 0.75 (Cronbach's alpha) on average across the ICILS countries. The Rasch partial credit model was again used to construct the scale, and we standardized the IRT scores to have an ICILS 2013 average score of 50 points and a standard deviation of 10 points. The higher scale scores indicate higher frequencies of using ICT for exchanging information.

Table 5.7 records the national average scale score overall and within gender groups. The results indicate that using internet for information exchange was highest in the Russian Federation and Thailand (three or more points above the ICILS 2013 average) and also significantly higher than the ICILS 2013 average in Lithuania, Slovenia, the Slovak Republic, and Turkey. National averages were lowest in Germany and Norway and also significantly lower than the ICILS 2013 average in Australia, Croatia, the Czech Republic, and Korea. In Chile and Poland, the national averages did not differ significantly from the ICILS 2013 average. The Canadian provinces of Ontario and Newfoundland and Labrador both recorded national average scale scores of 49.

---

10 The four items were "communicating with others using messaging or social networks (e.g., instant messaging or [status updates])," "posting comments to online profiles or blogs," "uploading images or video to an [online profile] or [online community] (e.g., Facebook or YouTube)," and "using voice chat (e.g., Skype) to chat with friends or family online."

11 The four items were "asking questions on forums or [question and answer] websites," "answering other people's questions on forums or websites," "writing posts for your own blog," and "building or editing a webpage."

Table 5.6: National averages for students' use of ICT for social communication overall and by gender

Country	Students' Use of the Internet for Social Communication				Score Distribution by Gender
	All students	Females	Males	Differences (males - females)*	
Australia	49 (0.2) ▽	50 (0.2)	49 (0.3)	-2 (0.4)	
Chile	50 (0.3)	52 (0.4)	49 (0.3)	-3 (0.4)	
Croatia	52 (0.3) △	52 (0.3)	52 (0.3)	0 (0.4)	
Czech Republic	52 (0.2) △	52 (0.3)	51 (0.3)	-1 (0.4)	
Germany†	49 (0.2) ▽	50 (0.3)	49 (0.3)	-1 (0.4)	
Korea, Republic of	44 (0.2) ▶	45 (0.3)	43 (0.3)	-2 (0.4)	
Lithuania	52 (0.2) △	52 (0.3)	51 (0.3)	-2 (0.4)	
Norway (Grade 9)[1]	50 (0.2)	50 (0.2)	50 (0.2)	0 (0.3)	
Poland	52 (0.2) △	52 (0.2)	51 (0.3)	-1 (0.4)	
Russian Federation[2]	54 (0.3) ◀	55 (0.3)	53 (0.4)	-1 (0.4)	
Slovak Republic	53 (0.2) △	53 (0.3)	52 (0.3)	-1 (0.5)	
Slovenia	50 (0.2)	51 (0.3)	50 (0.3)	0 (0.4)	
Thailand[2]	46 (0.4) ▶	47 (0.5)	45 (0.4)	-1 (0.5)	
Turkey	46 (0.4) ▶	45 (0.5)	48 (0.4)	2 (0.5)	
ICILS 2013 average	50 (0.1)	50 (0.1)	50 (0.1)	-1 (0.1)	
Countries not meeting sample requirements					
Denmark	50 (0.2)	50 (0.3)	50 (0.3)	0 (0.3)	
Hong Kong SAR	48 (0.3)	48 (0.5)	47 (0.3)	-1 (0.7)	
Netherlands	50 (0.3)	51 (0.4)	49 (0.3)	-2 (0.4)	
Switzerland	49 (0.4)	50 (0.5)	49 (0.5)	0 (0.6)	
Benchmarking participants					
Newfoundland and Labrador, Canada	51 (0.3)	53 (0.5)	48 (0.5)	-5 (0.8)	
Ontario, Canada	50 (0.3)	52 (0.4)	49 (0.3)	-3 (0.5)	
Benchmarking participant not meeting sample requirements					
City of Buenos Aires, Argentina	51 (0.3)	52 (0.4)	50 (0.5)	-2 (0.7)	

Notes:

* Statistically significant (*p*<.05) coefficients in **bold**.

( ) Standard errors appear in parentheses. Because some results are rounded to the nearest whole number, some totals may appear inconsistent.

† Met guidelines for sampling participation rates only after replacement schools were included.

[1] National Desired Population does not correspond to International Desired Population.

[2] Country surveyed the same cohort of students but at the beginning of the next school year.

▲ More than three score points above ICILS 2013 average
△ Significantly above ICILS 2013 average
▽ Significantly below ICILS 2013 average
▶ More than three score points below ICILS 2013 average

■ Female average score +/− confidence interval
■ Male average score +/− confidence interval

On average, students with a score in the range indicated by this color have more than a 50% probability of reporting use of ICT for social communication:

Less than once a week

Once a week or more frequently

Table 5.7: National averages for students' use of ICT for exchanging information overall and by gender

Country	Students' Use of the Internet for Exchanging Information				Score Distribution by Gender
	All students	Females	Males	Differences (males - females)*	
Australia	48 (0.2) ▽	48 (0.2)	47 (0.2)	-1 (0.3)	
Chile	50 (0.3)	51 (0.3)	49 (0.3)	-1 (0.4)	
Croatia	48 (0.2) ▽	47 (0.3)	50 (0.3)	3 (0.4)	
Czech Republic	49 (0.2) ▽	48 (0.3)	49 (0.3)	2 (0.4)	
Germany†	46 (0.2) ▶	45 (0.3)	46 (0.3)	1 (0.4)	
Korea, Republic of	49 (0.1) ▽	49 (0.2)	49 (0.2)	0 (0.3)	
Lithuania	53 (0.2) ◁	52 (0.3)	53 (0.4)	1 (0.5)	
Norway (Grade 9)[1]	46 (0.2) ▶	45 (0.2)	46 (0.3)	1 (0.3)	
Poland	50 (0.2)	51 (0.3)	50 (0.3)	-1 (0.4)	
Russian Federation[2]	54 (0.2) ◀	55 (0.3)	54 (0.3)	-1 (0.3)	
Slovak Republic	51 (0.2) ◁	50 (0.3)	52 (0.3)	1 (0.5)	
Slovenia	52 (0.3) ◁	51 (0.3)	52 (0.3)	1 (0.4)	
Thailand[2]	54 (0.3) ◀	54 (0.4)	54 (0.4)	-1 (0.5)	
Turkey	52 (0.3) ◁	50 (0.4)	53 (0.4)	4 (0.5)	
ICILS 2013 average	50 (0.1)	50 (0.1)	50 (0.1)	1 (0.1)	
Countries not meeting sample requirements					
Denmark	45 (0.2)	44 (0.3)	45 (0.3)	1 (0.4)	
Hong Kong SAR	50 (0.2)	50 (0.3)	51 (0.4)	1 (0.6)	
Netherlands	46 (0.3)	45 (0.4)	46 (0.4)	1 (0.5)	
Switzerland	46 (0.4)	46 (0.5)	47 (0.5)	1 (0.6)	
Benchmarking participants					
Newfoundland and Labrador, Canada	49 (0.3)	50 (0.4)	48 (0.4)	-2 (0.6)	
Ontario, Canada	49 (0.3)	49 (0.4)	48 (0.4)	-1 (0.4)	
Benchmarking participant not meeting sample requirements					
City of Buenos Aires, Argentina	50 (0.5)	50 (0.6)	50 (0.7)	1 (0.7)	

Legend (Score Distribution by Gender):
■ Female average score +/− confidence interval
■ Male average score +/− confidence interval

On average, students with a score in the range indicated by this color have more than a 50% probability of reporting use of ICT for exchanging information:

Less than once a week
Once a week or more frequently

▲ More than three score points above ICILS 2013 average
△ Significantly above ICILS 2013 average
▽ Significantly below ICILS 2013 average
▼ More than three score points below ICILS 2013 average

Notes:
* Statistically significant (p<.05) coefficients in **bold**.
( ) Standard errors appear in parentheses. Because some results are rounded to the nearest whole number, some totals may appear inconsistent.
† Met guidelines for sampling participation rates only after replacement schools were included.
1 National Desired Population does not correspond to International Desired Population.
2 Country surveyed the same cohort of students but at the beginning of the next school year.

On average internationally, males seemed to be using the internet for information exchange slightly more frequently than females were. In Turkey, Croatia, and the Czech Republic, male students' scores were two or more score points higher than females'. However, in the Russian Federation, Australia, and Chile, females scored significantly higher than males.

Computer use for recreation

Students frequently use ICT for recreation, with these leisuretime pursuits including playing games (Tobias, Fletcher, Yun Dai, & Wind, 2011) and listening to music. The ICILS student questionnaire asked students to use the following response options to indicate how often they used computers for specified recreational purposes: "never," "less than once a month," "at least once a month but not every week," "at least once a week but not every day," and "every day." The recreational activities listed for this question were:

• Accessing the internet to find out about places to go or activities to do;

• Reading reviews on the internet of things you might want to buy;

• Playing games;

• Listening to music;

• Watching downloaded or streamed video (e.g., movies, TV shows or clips); and

• Using the internet to get news about things of interest.

Table 5.8 records the national percentages of students who reported doing each of these activities at least once a week.

Across the ICILS countries, "listening to music" stood out as a very common activity. On average, 82 percent of students reported using ICT at least once a week to listen to music. Percentages exceeded the ICILS 2013 average by a statistically significant amount in Norway (91%), Croatia (90%), the Czech Republic (90%), Poland (90%), the Russian Federation (89%), the Slovak Republic (88%), and Slovenia (86%). These percentages were lowest in Korea (63%) and Turkey (67%). The percentages were significantly lower than the ICILS 2013 average not only in these two countries but also in Thailand (74%), Germany (78%), and Australia (80%).

Using computers to "watch downloaded or streamed video (e.g., movies, TV shows or clips)" was also a common activity. On average across the ICILS countries, about two thirds of students engaged in this activity on a weekly basis (68%). In two countries, the respective percentages were significantly greater than the ICILS 2013 average by more than 10 percentage points. They were the Russian Federation (83%) and the Czech Republic (78%). Other countries where the percentages were significantly greater than the ICILS 2013 average were Poland (78%), Norway (75%), the Slovak Republic (74%), Chile (73%), and Slovenia (73%). We recorded significantly less extensive engagement in this activity in a number of other countries, however. In Turkey (52%), Germany (54%), Korea (54%), and Thailand (56%), participation was more than 10 percentage points lower than the ICILS 2013 average. The percentage was also significantly lower than the ICILS 2013 average in Australia (65%).

Crossnationally, 62 percent of students, on average, said they used the internet on a weekly basis to "get news about things of interest." In the Russian Federation (79%) and Poland (75%), the national percentages of students engaging in this activity on at least a weekly basis were more than 10 percentage points higher than the ICILS 2013

Table 5.8: National percentages of students using computers for recreation at least once a week

Country	Accessing the Internet to Find Out About Places to Go or Activities to Do	Reading Reviews on the Internet of Things You Might Want to Buy	Playing Games	Listening to Music	Watching Downloaded or Streamed Video (e.g., Movies, TV Shows, or Clips)	Using the Internet to Get News About Things I Am Interested In
Australia	31 (0.8) △	34 (1.1) △	55 (1.2)	80 (0.7) ▽	65 (1.1) ▽	51 (1.1) ▼
Chile	25 (1.0) ▽	24 (1.0) ▽	51 (1.2) ▽	80 (1.0)	73 (1.1) △	47 (1.3) ▼
Croatia	30 (0.9) △	34 (1.0) △	63 (1.1) △	90 (0.7) △	68 (0.9)	70 (1.0) △
Czech Republic	29 (1.0)	33 (1.0)	65 (1.0) △	90 (0.5) △	78 (0.8) ▲	64 (0.9) △
Germany†	11 (0.9) ▼	18 (0.9) ▼	48 (1.2) ▽	78 (1.0) ▽	54 (1.2) ▼	62 (1.2)
Korea, Republic of	25 (0.9) ▽	30 (1.0)	56 (1.3)	63 (1.0) ▼	54 (1.1) ▼	57 (1.1) ▽
Lithuania	21 (0.9) ▽	28 (1.0) ▽	56 (1.0)	81 (0.9)	66 (1.0)	66 (1.1) △
Norway (Grade 9)[1]	18 (0.9) ▼	37 (1.1) △	47 (1.0) ▽	91 (0.7) △	75 (0.9) △	67 (1.1) △
Poland	33 (1.1) △	43 (1.1) ▲	56 (1.2)	90 (0.7) △	78 (0.9) △	75 (0.8) ▲
Russian Federation[2]	44 (0.9) ▲	43 (0.9) ▲	60 (0.9) △	89 (0.6) △	83 (0.8) ▲	79 (0.8) ▲
Slovak Republic	35 (1.0) △	38 (1.0) △	61 (1.0) △	88 (1.0) △	74 (1.1) △	69 (1.1) △
Slovenia	26 (0.9) ▽	21 (0.8) ▼	54 (1.3)	86 (0.7) △	73 (0.9) △	60 (1.0)
Thailand[2]	32 (1.2) △	21 (1.1) ▽	61 (1.5) △	74 (1.1) ▽	56 (1.4) ▼	45 (1.2) ▼
Turkey	36 (1.2) △	32 (1.1) ▽	52 (1.4) ▽	67 (1.4) ▼	52 (1.4) ▼	52 (1.3) ▽
ICILS 2013 average	28 (0.3)	31 (0.3)	56 (0.3)	82 (0.2)	68 (0.3)	62 (0.3)
Countries not meeting sample requirements						
Denmark	18 (0.9)	32 (1.4)	54 (1.3)	92 (0.8)	68 (1.3)	68 (1.2)
Hong Kong SAR	29 (1.0)	30 (1.0)	58 (1.3)	72 (1.0)	64 (1.1)	68 (1.4)
Netherlands	11 (0.7)	21 (0.8)	52 (1.0)	84 (1.0)	65 (1.2)	49 (1.5)
Switzerland	13 (1.0)	14 (1.0)	41 (1.7)	76 (1.9)	58 (1.5)	56 (1.7)
Benchmarking participants						
Newfoundland and Labrador, Canada	25 (1.3)	33 (1.8)	55 (1.9)	80 (1.7)	66 (1.5)	53 (1.7)
Ontario, Canada	30 (1.2)	33 (1.4)	57 (1.4)	80 (1.2)	67 (1.1)	54 (1.4)
Benchmarking participant not meeting sample requirements						
City of Buenos Aires, Argentina	32 (1.6)	30 (2.0)	59 (2.0)	84 (1.1)	73 (1.7)	51 (1.7)

▲ More than 10 percentage points above ICILS 2013 average
△ Significantly above ICILS 2013 average
▽ Significantly below ICILS 2013 average
▼ More than 10 percentage points below ICILS 2013 average

Notes:
() Standard errors appear in parentheses. Because some results are rounded to the nearest whole number, some totals may appear inconsistent.
† Met guidelines for sampling participation rates only after replacement schools were included.
[1] National Desired Population does not correspond to International Desired Population.
[2] Country surveyed the same cohort of students but at the beginning of the next school year.

average. In the Slovak Republic (69%), Croatia (70%), Norway (67%), Lithuania (66%), and the Czech Republic (64%), the percentages of students participating at least once a week were also significantly greater than the ICILS 2013 average. In Thailand (45%), Chile (47%), and Australia (51%), the percentages of weekly student participation in this activity were more than 10 percentage points lower than the ICILS 2013 average. Percentages were also significantly lower than the international average in Turkey (52%) and Korea (57%). Percentages were likewise low in Newfoundland and Labrador (53%) and Ontario (54%).

A little over half of the ICILS students said they used computers to "play games" on at least a weekly basis (ICILS 2013 average: 56%). The national percentages of students using computers in this way and with this degree of frequency were significantly higher than the ICILS 2013 average in the Czech Republic (65%), Croatia (63%), the Slovak Republic (61%), Thailand (61%), and the Russian Federation (60%). The percentages were significantly lower than the ICILS average in Norway (47%), Germany (48%), Chile (51%), and Turkey (52%).

According to the relevant data, relatively few students were participating frequently (on a weekly basis) in the remaining two activities: "reading reviews on the internet of things to buy" and "accessing internet to find out about places to go or activities to do." The ICILS 2013 average for the first of these two activities was 31 percent. Prevalence was notably higher in Poland and the Russian Federation (43%) and notably lower in Germany (18%) and Slovenia (21%). The ICILS average for the second activity (28%) was exceeded to a considerable extent in the Russian Federation (44%). However, it was well above the national averages in Germany (11%) and Norway (18%).

Five of six items reflecting *use of computer technology for recreational purposes*[12] provided the basis for deriving a scale that had a satisfactory reliability of 0.76 (Cronbach's alpha) on average across the ICILS countries. The scale was constructed using the Rasch partial credit model, and its IRT scores were standardized to an ICILS 2013 average score of 50 points and a standard deviation of 10 points. The higher scores on the scale indicate higher frequencies of using computer technology for recreational purposes.

Table 5.9 shows the national average scale scores overall and within gender groups. As evident in the table, the students most frequently using computer technology for recreational purposes were those in the Russian Federation and Poland (by more than three score points above the ICILS 2013 average). The national average scores of the students in the Slovak Republic, Croatia, the Czech Republic, and Norway were also all significantly higher than the ICILS 2013 average. Compared to their peers in all other ICILS countries, German students were the most infrequent users of computers for recreational purposes. The national averages for these students and for the students in Thailand, Turkey, Chile, Korea, and Lithuania were significantly below the ICILS 2013 average.

Overall, there was only a small, albeit statistically significant, gender difference in the extent of recreational use of computers. The difference, which favored males, was less than half of a scale point (equal to one 20th of an international standard deviation).

---

12 The five items were "accessing the internet to find out about places to go or activities to do," "reading reviews on the internet of things you [the student] might want to buy," "listening to music," "watching downloaded or streamed video (e.g., movies, TV shows or clips)," and "using the internet to get news about things I am interested in."

Table 5.9: National averages for students' use of computers for recreation overall and by gender

Country	Students' Use of the Internet for Recreation				Score Distribution by Gender
	All students	Females	Males	Differences (males - females)*	
Australia	50 (0.2)	50 (0.2)	50 (0.3)	0 (0.4)	
Chile	48 (0.2) ▽	49 (0.3)	48 (0.4)	-1 (0.4)	
Croatia	52 (0.2) △	51 (0.2)	52 (0.4)	1 (0.4)	
Czech Republic	51 (0.2) △	51 (0.2)	52 (0.3)	1 (0.3)	
Germany†	47 (0.2) ▶	46 (0.2)	47 (0.2)	1 (0.3)	
Korea, Republic of	48 (0.2) ▽	48 (0.3)	47 (0.3)	-1 (0.4)	
Lithuania	49 (0.2) ▽	49 (0.3)	48 (0.3)	-1 (0.4)	
Norway (Grade 9)[1]	51 (0.2) △	50 (0.3)	52 (0.2)	1 (0.3)	
Poland	53 (0.2) ◀	52 (0.3)	54 (0.3)	1 (0.5)	
Russian Federation[2]	55 (0.3) ◀	54 (0.3)	55 (0.4)	1 (0.4)	
Slovak Republic	52 (0.2) △	52 (0.3)	52 (0.3)	0 (0.4)	
Slovenia	50 (0.2)	49 (0.1)	50 (0.3)	1 (0.3)	
Thailand[2]	47 (0.3) ▽	48 (0.4)	47 (0.3)	-1 (0.4)	
Turkey	48 (0.4) ▽	47 (0.5)	48 (0.4)	1 (0.5)	
ICILS 2013 average	50 (0.1)	50 (0.1)	50 (0.1)	0 (0.1)	
Countries not meeting sample requirements					
Denmark	50 (0.2)	49 (0.3)	51 (0.3)	2 (0.4)	
Hong Kong SAR	50 (0.3)	50 (0.5)	49 (0.4)	-1 (0.7)	
Netherlands	47 (0.2)	47 (0.3)	48 (0.3)	1 (0.4)	
Switzerland	46 (0.3)	46 (0.3)	47 (0.4)	1 (0.4)	
Benchmarking participants					
Newfoundland and Labrador, Canada	50 (0.4)	50 (0.5)	49 (0.5)	-1 (0.7)	
Ontario, Canada	50 (0.3)	49 (0.4)	50 (0.4)	1 (0.5)	
Benchmarking participant not meeting sample requirements					
City of Buenos Aires, Argentina	50 (0.3)	50 (0.5)	50 (0.5)	-1 (0.7)	

Legend (Score Distribution by Gender):
- ▮ Female average score +/− confidence interval
- ▮ Male average score +/− confidence interval

On average, students with a score in the range indicated by this color have more than a 50% probability of responding to the statements about students' use for recreation with:
- Disagreement to positive, agreement to negative statements
- Agreement to positive, disagreement to negative items

Notes:
* Statistically significant (p<.05) coefficients in **bold**.

() Standard errors appear in parentheses. Because some results are rounded to the nearest whole number, some totals may appear inconsistent.

▲ More than three score points above ICILS 2013 average
△ Significantly above ICILS 2013 average
▽ Significantly below ICILS 2013 average
▼ More than three score points below ICILS 2013 average

† Met guidelines for sampling participation rates only after replacement schools were included.

1 National Desired Population does not correspond to International Desired Population.
2 Country surveyed the same cohort of students but at the beginning of the next school year.

In Turkey, Slovenia, Germany, Poland, and the Czech Republic, the differences in favor of males were statistically significant. We also observed smaller but still statistically significant differences in Chile, Korea, and Thailand. However, in these countries, it was the female students who reported somewhat more frequent recreational use of computers.

Computer use for and at school

The ICILS student questionnaire asked students about a number of aspects of computer use for school work and in their schools. Specifically, it asked them about school-related purposes of computer use, the subject areas in which they used computers, and aspects of learning how to use computers and the internet.

School-related use of computers

The relevant question in this regard asked students to report how often they used computers for specified school-related purposes (listed below). The response categories were "never," "less than once a month," "at least once a month but not every week," and "at least once a week."[13]

- Preparing reports or essays;
- Preparing presentations;
- Working with other students from your [the student's] own school;
- Working with other students from other schools;
- Completing worksheets or exercises;
- Organizing your time and work;
- Writing about your learning; and
- Completing tests.

Extent of use for particular school-related purposes

Table 5.10 records the national percentages of students who reported doing each of these activities at least once a month. For four of the activities, the crossnational average percentages of students doing them at least weekly were 39 percent or higher. These activities included preparing reports or essays, preparing presentations, working with other students from the student's own school, and completing worksheets or exercises.

Just under half of all students across the ICILS countries reported using computers for "preparing reports or essays" at least once a month; the ICILS 2013 average percentage was 45 percent. Frequency of use was highest in Australia (70%), the Russian Federation (68%), Ontario (67%), Norway (61%), and Thailand (60%). The two other countries where this level of use was also significantly higher than the ICILS 2013 average were Chile (54%) and the Slovak Republic (52%). In Newfoundland and Labrador, 55 percent of students said they used computers for preparing reports or essays at least once per month. This frequency of use was lowest in Korea (21%), Croatia (24%), Slovenia (26%), and Lithuania (28%). Other countries where this level of use was also significantly lower than the ICILS 2013 average were Turkey (40%), the Czech Republic (41%), and Germany (42%). The percentage for Poland did not differ significantly from the ICILS 2013 average.

---

13 The range of response categories differed from the range used for out-of-school uses, and the summary category was at least once per month rather than at least once per week. These differences reflect the lower frequency of in-school use than out-of-school use.

Table 5.10: National percentages of students using computers for study purposes at least once a month

Country	Preparing Reports or Essays	Preparing Presentations	Working with Other Students from Your Own School	Working with Other Students from Other Schools	Completing [Worksheets] or Exercises	Organizing Your Time and Work	Writing about Your Learning	Completing Tests
Australia	70 (1.0) ◄	68 (1.1) ◄	56 (1.2) ◄	11 (0.6) ▷	64 (1.3) ◄	45 (1.2) ◄	22 (0.9) △	44 (1.1) ◄
Chile	54 (1.5) △	61 (1.4) ◄	55 (1.3) ◄	12 (0.8)	54 (1.2) ◄	31 (1.0)	21 (1.0)	30 (1.1) ▷
Croatia	24 (1.0) ▶	41 (1.4) ▷	33 (0.8) ▷	7 (0.6) ▷	20 (0.9) ▶	20 (0.8) ▷	10 (0.5) ▷	22 (0.9) ▶
Czech Republic	41 (1.4) ▷	37 (1.6) ▷	35 (1.1) ▷	11 (0.7) ▷	36 (1.3) ▷	25 (0.9) ▷	17 (1.0)	26 (1.0) ▷
Germany†	42 (1.3) ▷	32 (1.2) ▶	29 (1.2) ▶	9 (0.7) ▷	23 (1.0) ▶	12 (0.9) ▶	5 (0.6) ▶	12 (0.9) ▶
Korea, Republic of	21 (1.0) ▶	23 (1.1) ▶	16 (0.8) ▶	11 (0.7) ▷	20 (0.8) ▶	17 (0.8) ▶	16 (0.7) ▷	17 (0.8) ▶
Lithuania	28 (1.4) ▶	30 (1.3) ▶	33 (1.2) ▷	14 (0.9)	19 (1.1) ▶	25 (1.2) ▷	14 (0.9) ▷	29 (1.3) ▷
Norway (Grade 9)[1]	61 (1.4) ◄	64 (1.6) ◄	58 (1.6) ◄	13 (0.8)	53 (1.3) ◄	30 (1.0)	9 (0.7) ▶	34 (1.6)
Poland	43 (1.1)	31 (1.2) ▶	32 (1.1) ▷	9 (0.6) ▷	28 (0.9) ▶	44 (1.0) ◄	16 (0.8) ▷	24 (0.9) ▷
Russian Federation[2]	68 (1.5) ◄	50 (1.7) △	40 (1.2)	15 (0.7) △	62 (1.0) ◄	40 (1.0) △	29 (0.7) ◄	52 (1.2) ◄
Slovak Republic	52 (1.5) △	51 (1.3) △	41 (1.2)	14 (0.7)	35 (1.2) ▷	27 (0.9) ▷	13 (0.7) ▷	30 (1.4)
Slovenia	26 (1.0) ▶	40 (1.3) ▷	32 (1.2) ▷	15 (0.9) △	30 (1.0) ▷	23 (0.9) ▷	11 (0.6) ▷	27 (1.0) ▷
Thailand[2]	60 (1.4) ◄	51 (1.4) ◄	61 (1.4) ◄	23 (1.1) ◄	59 (1.5) ◄	38 (1.2) △	36 (1.2) ◄	55 (1.3) ◄
Turkey	40 (1.2) ▷	44 (1.4)	42 (1.3)	19 (0.9) △	45 (1.4) △	48 (1.2) ◄	50 (1.1) ◄	60 (1.3) ◄
ICILS 2013 average	45 (0.3)	44 (0.4)	40 (0.3)	13 (0.2)	39 (0.3)	30 (0.3)	19 (0.2)	33 (0.3)
Countries not meeting sample requirements								
Denmark	84 (1.3)	69 (1.6)	69 (1.5)	9 (0.8)	56 (1.6)	36 (1.6)	28 (1.5)	44 (1.9)
Hong Kong SAR	43 (1.7)	36 (1.4)	44 (1.8)	19 (1.2)	51 (1.3)	25 (1.4)	17 (1.1)	27 (1.3)
Netherlands	48 (1.8)	36 (1.8)	52 (2.1)	9 (0.9)	54 (1.9)	26 (1.5)	12 (1.1)	33 (1.6)
Switzerland	30 (1.8)	30 (2.2)	29 (1.5)	8 (0.8)	24 (1.3)	14 (1.2)	6 (0.9)	15 (1.4)
Benchmarking participants								
Newfoundland and Labrador, Canada	55 (2.2)	50 (2.3)	41 (1.4)	10 (1.1)	37 (1.9)	25 (1.3)	19 (1.2)	19 (1.6)
Ontario, Canada	67 (1.6)	59 (1.6)	53 (1.5)	12 (0.7)	42 (1.4)	35 (1.2)	20 (1.0)	24 (1.2)
Benchmarking participant not meeting sample requirements								
City of Buenos Aires, Argentina	44 (2.3)	40 (2.5)	49 (2.2)	15 (1.5)	56 (2.7)	27 (2.1)	21 (1.7)	33 (2.2)

◄ More than 10 percentage points above ICILS 2013 average
△ Significantly above ICILS 2013 average
▷ Significantly below ICILS 2013 average
▶ More than 10 percentage points below ICILS 2013 average

Notes:
() Standard errors appear in parentheses. Because some results are rounded to the nearest whole number, some totals may appear inconsistent.
† Met guidelines for sampling participation rates only after replacement schools were included.
[1] National Desired Population does not correspond to International Desired Population.
[2] Country surveyed the same cohort of students but at the beginning of the next school year.

A similar extent of use (i.e., on a monthly or more frequent basis) was evident for "preparing presentations." The ICILS 2013 average percentage of students reporting at least monthly participation in this activity was 44 percent. The extent of at least monthly involvement in this activity was highest in Australia (68%), Norway (64%), Chile (61%), and Ontario (59%). Other countries where the extent of use was also significantly greater than the ICILS 2013 average were the Slovak Republic (51%), Thailand (51%), and the Russian Federation (50%). In Newfoundland and Labrador, 50 percent of students said they used computers to prepare presentations at least once a month. The national percentages were lowest in Korea (23%), Lithuania (30%), Poland (31%), and Germany (32%). The other countries with national averages significantly lower than the ICILS 2013 average were the Czech Republic (37%), Slovenia (40%), and Croatia (41%). The figure for Turkey (44%) did not differ significantly from the ICILS 2013 average.

For students, using computers when working with other students from their own school is a different type of school-related use of ICT. The ICILS 2013 average for undertaking this activity at least monthly was 40 percent. National percentages were highest in Thailand (61%), Norway (58%), Australia (56%), Chile (55%), and Ontario (53%). They were lowest in Korea (16%) and Germany (29%). National percentages were also significantly lower than the ICILS 2013 average in Poland (32%), Slovenia (32%), Croatia (33%), Lithuania (33%), and the Czech Republic (35%). There was no discernible difference between the national percentages and the international average in the Russian Federation, Slovak Republic, and Turkey. In Newfoundland and Labrador, 41 percent of students were using computers to work with other students from their school at least once a month.

Table 5.10 shows how often the ICILS students were using computers to complete computer-based worksheets or exercises. The ICILS 2013 average for monthly use of the practice was 39 percent. The countries with the highest national percentages were Australia (64%), the Russian Federation (62%), Chile (54%), and Norway (53%). The average national percentage was also significantly higher than the ICILS 2013 average in Turkey (45%). Use of computer-based worksheets and exercises was lowest (and significantly so) in Lithuania (19%), Croatia (20%), Germany (23%), Korea (20%), and Poland (28%). Percentages were also significantly lower than the international average in Slovenia (30%) and the Slovak Republic (35%). In the Canadian provinces of Ontario and Newfoundland and Labrador, 42 and 37 percent of students respectively reported using computers for completing worksheets on a monthly basis. Both percentages were close to the ICILS 2013 average.

On average across the ICILS countries, about one third of students reported using computers to complete tests at least once each month. The highest percentages were found in Turkey (60%), Thailand (55%), the Russian Federation (52%), and Australia (44%); the lowest were evident in Germany (12%), Korea (17%), and Croatia (22%). We also recorded relatively low percentages for Ontario (24%) and Newfoundland and Labrador (19%). These percentages and those for Poland (24%), the Czech Republic (26%), Slovenia (27%), Lithuania (29%), and Chile (30%) were all significantly lower than the ICILS 2013 average. The percentages in Norway and the Slovak Republic did not differ significantly from the international average.

Another question for the students focused on how often they used computers for organizing their time and work. The intent behind this question was to obtain information about computer applications such as "moodles" and the explicit use of learning management systems. The highest national percentages for using computers for this purpose on an at least monthly basis were observed in Turkey (48%), Australia (45%), and Poland (44%). These percentages and the national percentages for the Russian Federation (40%) and Thailand (38%) were all significantly higher than the ICILS 2013 average of 30 percent. The countries with the lowest national percentages were Germany (12%) and Korea (17%). A further group of countries where frequency of use was significantly lower than the ICILS 2013 average included Croatia (20%), Slovenia (23%), the Czech Republic (25%), Lithuania (25%), and the Slovak Republic (27%). The national percentages for Chile and Norway did not differ significantly from the ICILS 2013 average. In Ontario and Newfoundland and Labrador, 35 and 25 percent of students respectively were using computers on at least a monthly basis to organize their time and work.

No more than one fifth of students on average across the ICILS countries said they used school computers for the two remaining activities on the "school-related purposes" list. The first of these two activities, "writing about one's own learning," referred to using a learning log. The ICILS 2013 average percentage for this activity was 19 percent. The crossnational average for the second activity, "working with other students from other schools," was 13 percent, a figure that corresponds to about one student in eight doing this activity on a monthly basis.

We constructed a scale (derived from the eight activities considered in this section of the chapter) that measured the extent of using *computers for school-related purposes*. The Rasch partial credit model was again used to construct the scale, and we standardized the IRT scores to have an ICILS 2013 average score of 50 points and a standard deviation of 10 points. The scale reliability (Cronbach's alpha) was 0.83 on average across the ICILS countries. The higher scores on this scale indicate higher frequencies of using computers for school-related purposes.

Table 5.11 presents the national scale score averages. The extent to which computers were being used for school-related purposes was highest in Thailand, Australia, and the Russian Federation. The national averages for these countries were three or more scale score points higher than the ICILS 2013 average. The use of computers for school-related purposes was also significantly higher than the international average in Turkey, Norway, and Chile. Computer use for school-related purposes was lowest, by three or more points below the average, in Croatia, Germany, and Korea. These three countries, along with the Czech Republic, Lithuania, Poland, and Slovenia, all had national averages significantly lower than the international one. The average scale score for Ontario was 52 points. For Newfoundland and Labrador, it was 49 points.

In about half of the participating countries, female students were more likely than males to be using computers for school-related purposes. This difference was significant in the Russian Federation by two scale score points. We also recorded small but still statistically significant differences in Australia, Croatia, the Czech Republic, Germany, the Slovak Republic, Slovenia, Thailand, and Newfoundland and Labrador. None of the countries recorded a significant difference in favor of males.

Table 5.11: National averages for students' use of computers for study purposes overall and by gender

Country	Students' Use of Computers for Study Purposes				Score Distribution by Gender
	All students	Females	Males	Differences (males - females)*	
Australia	54 (0.3) ◄	55 (0.3)	54 (0.4)	-1 (0.4)	
Chile	52 (0.2) △	52 (0.2)	52 (0.3)	-1 (0.3)	
Croatia	46 (0.2) ►	47 (0.2)	45 (0.2)	-1 (0.3)	
Czech Republic	48 (0.3) ▽	49 (0.3)	48 (0.3)	-1 (0.3)	
Germany†	46 (0.2) ►	47 (0.2)	46 (0.3)	-1 (0.4)	
Korea, Republic of	44 (0.3) ►	44 (0.4)	44 (0.4)	-1 (0.5)	
Lithuania	47 (0.3) ▽	47 (0.3)	47 (0.5)	0 (0.4)	
Norway (Grade 9)[1]	53 (0.2) △	53 (0.3)	53 (0.3)	0 (0.2)	
Poland	49 (0.2) ▽	49 (0.2)	49 (0.3)	0 (0.3)	
Russian Federation[2]	54 (0.3) ◄	54 (0.2)	53 (0.4)	-2 (0.3)	
Slovak Republic	50 (0.2) ▽	51 (0.3)	50 (0.3)	-1 (0.3)	
Slovenia	49 (0.2) ▽	49 (0.2)	48 (0.3)	-1 (0.3)	
Thailand[2]	55 (0.2) ◄	56 (0.3)	54 (0.3)	-1 (0.4)	
Turkey	53 (0.3) △	53 (0.4)	53 (0.4)	0 (0.5)	
ICILS 2013 average	50 (0.1)	50 (0.1)	50 (0.1)	-1 (0.1)	
Countries not meeting sample requirements					
Denmark	55 (0.3)	55 (0.3)	54 (0.3)	-1 (0.3)	
Hong Kong SAR	50 (0.4)	51 (0.6)	50 (0.5)	-1 (0.5)	
Netherlands	50 (0.4)	50 (0.4)	51 (0.5)	1 (0.5)	
Switzerland	46 (0.4)	46 (0.5)	46 (0.5)	0 (0.6)	
Benchmarking participants					
Newfoundland and Labrador, Canada	49 (0.3)	51 (0.5)	48 (0.5)	-2 (0.7)	
Ontario, Canada	52 (0.3)	52 (0.3)	52 (0.3)	0 (0.4)	
Benchmarking participant not meeting sample requirements					
City of Buenos Aires, Argentina	50 (0.6)	50 (0.5)	50 (0.9)	-1 (0.7)	

■ Female average score +/− confidence interval
■ Male average score +/− confidence interval

On average, students with a score in the range indicated by this color have more than a 50% probability of responding to the statements about students' ICT use for study purposes with:

Disagreement to positive, agreement to negative statements
Agreement to positive, disagreement to negative items

Notes:
* Statistically significant (*p*<.05) coefficients in **bold**.
() Standard errors appear in parentheses. Because some results are rounded to the nearest whole number, some totals may appear inconsistent.
† Met guidelines for sampling participation rates only after replacement schools were included.
[1] National Desired Population does not correspond to International Desired Population.
[2] Country surveyed the same cohort of students but at the beginning of the next school year.

◄ More than three score points above ICILS 2013 average
△ Significantly above ICILS 2013 average
▽ Significantly below ICILS 2013 average
► More than three score points below ICILS 2013 average

Use of computers in subject areas

When answering the question on how often they used computers during lessons in designated subjects or subject areas, students had at hand five response options: "never," "in some lessons," "in most lessons," "in every or almost every lesson," and "I don't study this subject/these subjects." Student responses in the last category were treated as missing responses. The list of subjects or subject areas that students had to consider was based on a list developed for the OECD Teaching and Learning International Study (TALIS) (OECD, 2014b).

- Language arts: test language;
- Language arts: foreign or other national languages;
- Mathematics;
- Sciences (general science and/or physics, chemistry, biology, geology, Earth sciences);
- Human sciences or humanities (history, geography, civics, law, economics, etc.);
- Creative arts (visual arts, music, dance, drama, etc.);
- Information technology, computer studies, or similar; and
- Other (practical or vocational subjects, morals/ethics, physical education, home economics, personal and social development).

Table 5.12 records the national percentages of students who indicated that they used computers in "most lessons" or in "every or almost every" lesson. The ICILS 2013 average percentages recorded for each subject area provide an overall indication of the extent to which students were using computers in the specified subject areas. The figures for each country also provide profiles of computer use in classrooms across the participating ICILS countries.

The subject area in which computers were being most frequently used was information technology or computer studies (56% on average). National percentages were highest in the Slovak Republic (82%), Poland (81%), and Croatia (70%) and lowest in Chile (22%), Korea (33%), Turkey (34%), and Germany (44%). The national percentage in Australia did not differ significantly from the ICILS 2013 average.

On average, internationally, in both the (natural) sciences and human sciences or humanities, about one fifth of students said that they used computers in most or all lessons. The ICILS 2013 averages were 21 percent and 20 percent respectively. The countries where we recorded the highest percentages for computer use in science classes were Thailand (45%), Turkey (34%), and Australia (34%). Our lowest recordings were for Germany (7%) and Norway (9%). The national percentages for computer use in humanities or human sciences classes were highest in Australia (42%) and Thailand (37%) and lowest in Germany (8%) and Poland (8%).

In language arts (the test language) and language arts (foreign languages), the ICILS 2013 averages were 16 percent and 17 percent respectively. These averages correspond to about one in six students using computers in most lessons for these subject areas. Computer use for language arts in the test language was highest in Thailand (36%), Australia (34%), and Turkey (32%) and lowest in Germany (4%) and Croatia (5%). For language arts (foreign languages), computer usage was highest in Thailand (39%) and Korea (37%) and lowest in Germany (3%) and Croatia (5%).

Table 5.12: National percentages of students with frequent computer use during lessons in different learning areas

Country	[Language Arts: Test Language]	[Language Arts: Foreign or Other National Languages]	Mathematics	Sciences (General Science and/or Physics, Chemistry, Biology, Geology, Earth Sciences)	Human Sciences/Humanities (History, Geography, Civics, Law, Economics, etc.)	Creative Arts (Visual Arts, Music, Dance, Drama, etc.)	[Information Technology, Computer Studies, or Similar]	Other (Practical or Vocational Subjects, Moral/Ethics, Physical Education, Home Economics, Personal and Social Development)
Australia	34 (1.8) ◄	24 (1.9) △	23 (1.8) △	34 (1.8) ◄	42 (1.7) ◄	14 (0.9) △	58 (1.8)	14 (0.8) △
Chile	9 (0.9) ▽	9 (0.7) ▽	11 (1.2) ▽	13 (1.1) ▽	12 (1.1) ▽	11 (1.3)	22 (2.0) ▶	8 (0.7) ▽
Croatia	5 (0.5) ▶	5 (0.5) ▶	6 (0.7) ▽	11 (0.8) ▶	12 (0.9) ▽	5 (0.4) ▽	70 (1.6) ◄	4 (0.4) ▽
Czech Republic	6 (0.7) ▽	10 (0.7) ▽	7 (0.7) ▽	13 (1.0) ▽	13 (1.0) ▽	5 (0.7) ▽	52 (1.8) ▽	6 (0.6) ▽
Germany†	4 (0.4) ▶	3 (0.4) ▶	4 (0.4) ▶	7 (0.7) ▶	8 (0.8) ▶	3 (0.4) ▽	44 (3.1) ▶	4 (0.5) ▽
Korea, Republic of	25 (1.2) △	37 (1.2) ◄	15 (1.0)	30 (1.2) △	22 (1.2)	18 (0.8) △	33 (1.7) ▶	19 (0.9) △
Lithuania	11 (0.7) ▽	14 (0.9) ▽	13 (0.9)	21 (1.0)	21 (1.3)	8 (0.9) ▽	65 (1.5) △	9 (0.7) ▽
Norway (Grade 9)[1]	16 (1.4)	12 (0.9) ▽	3 (0.5) ▶	9 (1.0) ▶	14 (1.1) ▽	7 (0.9) ▽		6 (0.7) ▽
Poland	6 (0.7) ▽	8 (0.8) ▽	9 (0.8) ▽	11 (1.0) ▽	8 (0.6) ▶	7 (0.8) ▽	81 (1.3) ◄	7 (0.7) ▽
Russian Federation[2]	15 (1.1)	20 (1.1) △	16 (0.9) △	21 (0.9)	22 (1.0)	14 (1.0) △	62 (1.1) △	9 (0.5) ▽
Slovak Republic	10 (0.8) ▽	16 (1.4)	11 (1.0) ▽	17 (1.3) ▽	18 (1.2)	10 (1.1)	82 (1.7) ◄	11 (1.0)
Slovenia	11 (0.9) ▽	18 (1.0)	13 (1.0)	27 (1.5) △	29 (1.2) △	12 (1.0)	73 (1.4) ▽	9 (0.7) ▽
Thailand[2]	36 (1.3) ◄	39 (1.3) ◄	37 (1.2) ◄	45 (1.3) ◄	37 (1.1) ◄	23 (1.1) ◄	51 (1.4) ▽	29 (1.1) ◄
Turkey	32 (1.4) ◄	23 (1.1) △	29 (1.4) ◄	34 (1.4) ◄	29 (1.4) △	15 (0.8) △	34 (1.7) ▶	20 (1.0) △
ICILS 2013 average	16 (0.3)	17 (0.3)	14 (0.3)	21 (0.3)	20 (0.3)	11 (0.2)	56 (0.4)	11 (0.2)
Countries not meeting sample requirements								
Denmark	44 (2.5)	34 (2.4)	30 (2.6)	33 (2.5)	44 (2.3)	4 (0.6)	29 (2.3)	8 (1.0)
Hong Kong SAR	12 (1.1)	13 (1.2)	9 (1.2)	15 (1.1)	15 (1.4)	11 (1.1)	81 (1.6)	8 (1.0)
Netherlands	13 (1.8)	13 (1.5)	3 (0.7)	10 (1.6)	14 (1.7)	10 (1.4)	9 (1.0)	26 (3.3)
Switzerland	6 (0.9)	9 (1.8)	6 (1.1)	7 (1.0)	7 (1.1)	6 (1.1)	40 (2.7)	6 (0.9)
Benchmarking participants								
Newfoundland and Labrador, Canada	21 (1.5)	15 (1.2)	13 (1.1)	19 (1.3)	23 (1.5)	9 (1.0)	58 (1.5)	9 (1.1)
Ontario, Canada	31 (1.5)	15 (1.2)	16 (1.1)	28 (1.6)	28 (1.7)	11 (0.8)	38 (1.7)	10 (0.9)
Benchmarking participant not meeting sample requirements								
City of Buenos Aires, Argentina	11 (1.5)	12 (1.9)	12 (2.1)	13 (2.7)	12 (2.6)	6 (0.9)	49 (2.9)	10 (1.1)

Notes:
* Percentages reflect students who selected "in most lessons" or "in every or almost every lesson"
() Standard errors appear in parentheses. Because some results are rounded to the nearest whole number, some totals may appear inconsistent.
† Met guidelines for sampling participation rates only after replacement schools were included.
[1] National Desired Population does not correspond to International Desired Population.
[2] Country surveyed the same cohort of students but at the beginning of the next school year.

◄ More than 10 percentage points above ICILS 2013 average
△ Significantly above ICILS 2013 average
▽ Significantly below ICILS 2013 average
▶ More than 10 percentage points below ICILS 2013 average

In mathematics, the ICILS 2013 average was 14 percent, which corresponds to about one in seven students reporting computer use in most lessons or almost every lesson in this subject area. National percentages were highest in Thailand (37%) and Turkey (29%) and lowest in Norway (3%) and Germany (4%).

The ICILS 2013 average for creative arts was 11 percent, which corresponds to just a little more than one student in 10 reporting computer use in most lessons or almost every lesson. Thailand recorded the highest national percentage of computer use in class for this subject area (23%).

Learning about computer and information literacy at school

The student questionnaire asked students to indicate whether they had learned ("yes" or "no") how to do various ICT tasks at school. The tasks were:

- Providing references to internet sources;
- Accessing information with a computer;
- Presenting information for a given audience or purpose with a computer;
- Working out whether to trust information from the internet;
- Deciding what information is relevant to include in school work;
- Organizing information obtained from internet sources;
- Deciding where to look for information about an unfamiliar topic; and
- Looking for different types of digital information on a topic.

Results based on the percentages recording a response of "yes" are shown in Table 5.13. While an answer of "no" signals students who said they did not learn that skill at school, we acknowledge that students may have learned it at other places (e.g., at home or from peers). The data indicate some smaller variations across the various tasks, ranging from 33 percent for "looking for different types of digital information on a topic" and 30 percent for "working out whether to trust information from the internet" to 15 percent for "accessing information with a computer." The remaining ICILS 2013 average percentages ranged from 24 to 28 percent. Overall, the results suggest that students learn about ICT through school, and that school is more important for learning the "information literacy" aspects of ICT than for learning the operational aspects of ICT.

In order to explore differences among countries relating to students' reported learning of ICT tasks, we derived a scale based on student responses to the eight aspects of ICT learning shown above. The scale, which we constructed using the Rasch partial credit model, measured the extent to which students attributed their *learning about ICT to schools*. We standardized the scale's IRT scores to have an ICILS 2013 average of 50 points and a standard deviation of 10 points. We found the scale to have a reliability of 0.81 (Cronbach's alpha) on average across ICILS countries. The higher scores on the scale indicate greater attribution to school-based ICT learning. Table 5.14 presents the results of our analysis based on this scale.

As evident from Table 5.14, the differences between females and males in the extent to which they attributed their ICT learning to school instruction were very small, no more than half a scale point in favor of females. However, in Chile and the Czech Republic, female students scored significantly higher (by two scale score points) than males. Germany was the only country where the gender difference favored males.

Table 5.13: National percentages of students reporting having learned ICT tasks at school

Country	Providing References to Internet Sources	Accessing Information with a Computer	Using a Computer to Present Information for a Given Audience or Purpose	Working out Whether to Trust Information from the Internet	Deciding What Information is Relevant to Include in School Work	Organizing Information Obtained from Internet Sources	Deciding Where to Look for Information About an Unfamiliar Topic	Looking for Different Types of Digital Information on a Topic
Australia	87 (0.9) ◀	96 (0.4) ◀	92 (0.6) ◀	82 (0.8) ◀	91 (0.5) ◀	83 (0.8) ◀	77 (0.9) △	74 (1.0) △
Chile	73 (1.3)	86 (1.0)	76 (1.0)	68 (1.0) ▽	79 (1.0) △	80 (1.1) △	75 (1.1) △	78 (1.1) ◀
Croatia	45 (1.2) ▶	85 (0.8)	70 (1.1) ▽	78 (0.8) △	77 (0.9) △	74 (0.9)	78 (0.9) △	68 (1.1)
Czech Republic	70 (1.3) ▽	78 (1.2) ▽	80 (1.1) △	59 (1.3) ▶	76 (1.0)	67 (1.1) ▽	73 (1.1)	66 (1.1)
Germany†	78 (1.2) △	83 (1.0) ▽	75 (1.5)	45 (1.5) ▶	54 (1.3) ▶	71 (1.3)	60 (1.1) ▶	52 (1.4) ▶
Korea, Republic of	70 (1.0) ▽	74 (1.0) ▶	60 (1.1) ▶	60 (1.0) ▽	60 (1.1) ▶	67 (1.1) ▽	59 (1.0) ▶	54 (1.1) ▶
Lithuania	75 (1.2)	89 (0.7) △	78 (1.0)	71 (1.5)	75 (1.1)	77 (1.1) △	73 (1.1)	70 (1.2) △
Norway (Grade 9)[1]	85 (0.9) ◀	86 (0.8)	88 (0.9) ◀	79 (1.2) △	82 (0.9) △	71 (1.0)	72 (0.9)	71 (1.0) △
Poland	72 (1.0)	80 (0.8) ▽	76 (1.1)	70 (1.1)	70 (1.1) ▽	72 (1.0)	69 (1.1) ▽	75 (1.0) △
Russian Federation[2]	72 (1.3)	90 (0.7) △	73 (1.0) ▽	70 (1.4)	75 (1.0)	69 (1.0) ▽	74 (0.9) △	74 (1.1) △
Slovak Republic	67 (1.6) ▽	84 (0.9)	76 (1.1)	59 (1.8) ▶	71 (1.1) ▽	63 (1.5) ▽	71 (1.2)	68 (1.2)
Slovenia	81 (1.2) △	83 (1.1)	71 (1.0) ▽	73 (1.0)	75 (1.0)	68 (1.1) ▽	73 (1.0)	58 (1.1) ▽
Thailand[2]	91 (0.7) ◀	94 (0.7) △	84 (1.1) △	84 (1.0) ◀	81 (1.1) △	83 (1.0) ◀	75 (1.2) △	71 (1.3) △
Turkey	60 (1.2) ▶	88 (0.9) △	69 (1.2) ▽	79 (1.2) △	80 (1.0) △	74 (1.3)	73 (1.2)	64 (1.2) ▽
ICILS 2013 average	73 (0.3)	85 (0.2)	76 (0.3)	70 (0.3)	75 (0.3)	73 (0.3)	72 (0.3)	67 (0.3)
Countries not meeting sample requirements								
Denmark	86 (1.1)	90 (0.8)	86 (0.9)	77 (1.4)	86 (0.7)	67 (1.1)	75 (1.0)	79 (1.1)
Hong Kong SAR	72 (1.4)	81 (1.4)	66 (1.9)	53 (1.4)	70 (1.7)	74 (1.4)	71 (1.8)	64 (1.8)
Netherlands	65 (1.4)	76 (1.3)	79 (1.2)	58 (1.7)	59 (1.4)	53 (1.4)	61 (1.1)	65 (1.2)
Switzerland	72 (1.7)	84 (1.9)	71 (2.1)	49 (1.9)	59 (1.7)	63 (1.5)	67 (1.5)	66 (1.8)
Benchmarking participants								
Newfoundland and Labrador, Canada	83 (0.9)	91 (0.8)	87 (0.9)	73 (1.6)	81 (1.2)	80 (1.2)	77 (1.6)	71 (1.8)
Ontario, Canada	84 (1.1)	94 (0.7)	89 (0.9)	80 (1.2)	87 (0.7)	82 (0.9)	78 (1.1)	71 (1.3)
Benchmarking participant not meeting sample requirements								
City of Buenos Aires, Argentina	69 (2.1)	81 (1.9)	64 (1.8)	62 (2.4)	72 (2.2)	72 (2.0)	66 (1.8)	67 (1.8)

◀ More than 10 percentage points above ICILS 2013 average
△ Significantly above ICILS 2013 average
▽ Significantly below ICILS 2013 average
▶ More than 10 percentage points below ICILS 2013 average

Notes:
() Standard errors appear in parentheses. Because some results are rounded to the nearest whole number, some totals may appear inconsistent.
† Met guidelines for sampling participation rates only after replacement schools were included.
1 National Desired Population does not correspond to International Desired Population.
2 Country surveyed the same cohort of students but at the beginning of the next school year.

Table 5.14: National averages for students' learning of ICT tasks at school overall and by gender

Country	Students' Learning of ICT Tasks at School				Score Distribution by Gender
	All students	Females	Males	Differences (males - females)*	
Australia	54 (0.2) ◀	54 (0.2)	54 (0.2)	0 (0.2)	
Chile	51 (0.3) △	52 (0.4)	50 (0.4)	-2 (0.5)	
Croatia	49 (0.2) ▽	49 (0.3)	49 (0.3)	0 (0.4)	
Czech Republic	49 (0.3) ▽	50 (0.4)	48 (0.4)	-2 (0.4)	
Germany†	47 (0.3) ▶	46 (0.3)	47 (0.4)	1 (0.4)	
Korea, Republic of	46 (0.3) ▶	46 (0.4)	47 (0.4)	1 (0.5)	
Lithuania	51 (0.3) △	51 (0.3)	50 (0.4)	-1 (0.4)	
Norway (Grade 9)[1]	52 (0.3) △	52 (0.3)	52 (0.4)	0 (0.4)	
Poland	50 (0.3)	50 (0.4)	49 (0.3)	-1 (0.5)	
Russian Federation[2]	50 (0.3)	51 (0.3)	50 (0.3)	-1 (0.4)	
Slovak Republic	49 (0.3) ▽	48 (0.4)	49 (0.4)	0 (0.4)	
Slovenia	50 (0.3)	50 (0.3)	49 (0.4)	-1 (0.4)	
Thailand[2]	53 (0.3) △	53 (0.3)	53 (0.3)	-1 (0.3)	
Turkey	50 (0.3)	50 (0.4)	50 (0.4)	0 (0.4)	
ICILS 2013 average	50 (0.1)	50 (0.1)	50 (0.1)	**0 (0.1)**	
Countries not meeting sample requirements					
Denmark	52 (0.2)	52 (0.3)	52 (0.3)	0 (0.4)	
Hong Kong SAR	48 (0.5)	49 (0.5)	47 (0.5)	-2 (0.5)	
Netherlands	47 (0.3)	47 (0.4)	47 (0.4)	0 (0.5)	
Switzerland	47 (0.4)	46 (0.4)	48 (0.5)	2 (0.4)	
Benchmarking participants					
Newfoundland and Labrador, Canada	52 (0.2)	53 (0.4)	52 (0.4)	-1 (0.8)	
Ontario, Canada	53 (0.3)	53 (0.3)	53 (0.4)	0 (0.3)	
Benchmarking participant not meeting sample requirements					
City of Buenos Aires, Argentina	48 (0.5)	49 (0.5)	48 (0.7)	-1 (0.6)	

■ Female average score +/− confidence interval
■ Male average score +/− confidence interval

On average, students with a score in the range indicated by this color have more than a 50% probability of responding to having learned ICT tasks at school with:

No
Yes

Notes:

* Statistically significant (*p*<.05) coefficients in **bold**.

( ) Standard errors appear in parentheses. Because some results are rounded to the nearest whole number, some totals may appear inconsistent.

† Met guidelines for sampling participation rates only after replacement schools were included.

[1] National Desired Population does not correspond to International Desired Population.

[2] Country surveyed the same cohort of students but at the beginning of the next school year.

▲ More than three score points above ICILS 2013 average
△ Significantly above ICILS 2013 average
▽ Significantly below ICILS 2013 average
▼ More than three score points below ICILS 2013 average

We can also see from Table 5.14 some crossnational differences in regard to the extent to which students attributed their ICT learning to schools. In Australia, this attribution was notably stronger, by four scale score points, than the ICILS 2013 average. Significantly stronger attribution to schools can also be observed in Thailand, Norway, Chile, and Lithuania. In Germany and Korea, the attributions were notably weaker than the ICILS 2013 average (by three and four scale score points respectively). Attributions were also significantly weaker than the international average attribution in Croatia, the Czech Republic, and the Slovak Republic. In four countries—Poland, the Russian Federation, Slovenia, and Turkey—the measure of attribution did not differ significantly from the ICILS average. In the two Canadian provinces, Ontario and Newfoundland and Labrador, attribution to school-based learning about ICT was relatively strong.

Student perceptions of ICT

The ICILS student questionnaire also gathered information about two student perceptions of ICT. The first concerned students' confidence in using computers (ICT self-efficacy). The other related to students' interest and enjoyment in using ICT.

ICT self-efficacy

When responding to the ICILS student questionnaire, students indicated how well they thought they could do each of 13 computer-based tasks. The response categories were "I know how to do this," "I could work out how to do this," and "I do not think I could do this." For the purposes of analyses at the item level, we collapsed the second and third categories and gave the first category a score of one and the second a score of zero.

The tasks that the questionnaire listed were (in order of increasing difficulty):

• Search for and find information you need on the internet;

• Search for and find a file on your computer;

• Create or edit documents (e.g., assignments for school);

• Upload text, images, or video to an online profile;

• Edit digital photographs or other graphic images;

• Create a multimedia presentation (with sound, pictures, or video);

• Change the settings on your computer to improve the way it operates or to fix problems;

• Use a spreadsheet to do calculations, store data, or plot a graph;

• Use software to find and get rid of viruses;

• Build or edit a webpage;

• Set up a computer network;

• Create a database; and

• Create a computer program or macro.

Table 5.15 records the percentages, both as ICILS 2013 averages and for each country, of students who indicated that they knew how to do each task. The percentages, which reflect how difficult students perceived each task to be, ranged from 21 percent ("create a computer program or macro") to 89 percent ("search for and find information you need on the internet").

Table 5.15: National percentages of student confidence in using computers

Country	Search for and Find a File on Your Computer	Use Software to Find and Get Rid of Viruses	Edit Digital Photographs or Other Graphic Images	Create a Database (e.g., Using [Microsoft Access®])	Create or Edit Documents (e.g., Assignments for School)	Search For and Find Information You Need on the Internet	Build or Edit a Webpage	Change the Settings on Your Computer to Improve the Way It Operates or to Fix Problems	Use a Spreadsheet to Do Calculations, Store Data, or Plot a Graph	Create a Computer Program or Macro (e.g., in [Basic, Visual Basic])	Set up a Computer Network	Create a Multimedia Presentation (with Sound, Pictures, or Video)	Upload Text, Images, or Video to an Online Profile
Australia	91 (0.6) △	32 (0.9) ▶	69 (0.7) ▽	24 (0.9) ▽	90 (0.6) △	94 (0.5) △	31 (1.0) ▽	59 (0.8)	50 (1.1) ▽	17 (0.7) ▽	27 (0.8) ▽	73 (0.8) △	83 (0.7) △
Chile	94 (0.6) △	50 (1.3) △	84 (0.8) ◀	37 (1.2) △	88 (0.8) △	94 (0.6) △	42 (1.1) △	59 (1.2)	56 (1.3)	27 (1.0) △	46 (1.4) ◀	75 (1.1) ◀	84 (1.0) △
Croatia	93 (0.6) △	45 (1.0) ▽	83 (1.0) ◀	48 (1.4) ◀	82 (0.8)	93 (0.7) △	47 (1.3) △	70 (1.0) ◀	54 (1.1)	27 (1.2) △	44 (1.1) △	77 (1.0) ◀	84 (1.0) △
Czech Republic	93 (0.5) △	43 (1.0) ▽	76 (0.8) △	19 (0.9) ▶	87 (0.7) △	95 (0.5) △	41 (1.0) △	59 (1.2)	47 (1.6) ▽	15 (1.0) ▽	20 (1.0) ▶	66 (1.2)	79 (0.8)
Germany†	86 (0.8)	45 (1.2) ▽	77 (1.2) △	18 (1.1) ▶	84 (0.9) △	91 (0.7) △	29 (1.0) ▽	55 (1.4)	49 (1.4) ▽	17 (1.1) ▽	30 (1.0) ▽	59 (1.4) ▽	80 (1.1) △
Korea, Republic of	87 (0.7) △	55 (1.0) △	61 (1.1) ▶	25 (0.9) ▽	80 (0.8) △	87 (0.7) ▽	37 (0.8)	38 (1.0) ▶	35 (1.0) ▶	16 (0.8) ▽	56 (1.0) △	52 (1.1) ◀	73 (1.0) ▽
Lithuania	91 (0.7) △	60 (1.1) ◀	79 (1.0) △	30 (1.1)	75 (1.0) ▽	90 (0.8)	36 (1.0) ▽	56 (1.0)	76 (1.0) ◀	23 (1.2)	23 (1.0)	53 (1.2) ◀	77 (1.1)
Norway (Grade 9)[1]	92 (0.6) △	44 (0.9) ▽	75 (1.0)	17 (0.8) ▶	91 (0.6) ◀	95 (0.4) △	37 (1.2)	64 (1.1) △	62 (1.2) △	16 (0.9) ▽	30 (1.0) ▽	66 (1.1)	79 (1.0) △
Poland	95 (0.4) △	51 (1.0) △	83 (0.9) △	33 (1.5) △	90 (0.8) △	96 (0.4) △	39 (1.2)	58 (0.9)	67 (1.3) ◀	15 (0.7) ▽	21 (1.0) ▶	81 (1.0) ◀	86 (0.9) △
Russian Federation[2]	90 (0.6) △	66 (0.8) ◀	78 (0.9) △	29 (1.2)	80 (0.9)	91 (0.6) △	44 (0.9) △	66 (0.9) △	46 (1.4) ▽	21 (0.9)	45 (1.2) △	70 (1.1) △	86 (0.6) △
Slovak Republic	95 (0.6) △	54 (1.1) △	79 (0.9) △	16 (0.9) ▶	79 (1.0)	92 (0.8) △	46 (1.2) △	67 (1.2) ◀	62 (1.2) △	21 (1.0)	48 (1.2) ◀	70 (1.1) △	82 (1.0) △
Slovenia	95 (0.4) △	45 (1.1) ▽	85 (0.7) ◀	44 (1.3) ◀	91 (0.7) ◀	95 (0.4) △	39 (1.1)	61 (1.1) △	67 (1.2) ◀	28 (1.2) △	46 (1.1) ◀	73 (0.8) △	85 (0.7) △
Thailand[2]	52 (1.2) ▶	31 (1.3) ▶	37 (1.2) ▶	32 (1.2)	50 (1.1) ▶	56 (1.4) ▶	27 (1.0) ▶	34 (1.1) ▶	34 (1.1) ▶	22 (0.9)	23 (0.9) ▶	33 (1.1) ▶	45 (1.5) ▶
Turkey	69 (1.2) ▶	43 (1.3) ▽	61 (1.2) ▶	42 (1.2) ◀	62 (1.3) ▶	71 (1.0) ▶	41 (1.1) △	54 (1.4) ▽	52 (1.3)	33 (1.1) ◀	38 (1.1) △	51 (1.2) ▶	60 (1.3) ▶
ICILS 2013 average	87 (0.2)	47 (0.3)	73 (0.3)	30 (0.3)	81 (0.2)	89 (0.2)	38 (0.3)	57 (0.3)	54 (0.3)	21 (0.3)	35 (0.3)	64 (0.3)	77 (0.3)
Countries not meeting sample requirements													
Denmark	92 (0.6)	40 (1.0)	68 (1.0)	16 (1.0)	93 (0.7)	96 (0.5)	32 (1.2)	65 (1.1)	69 (1.9)	14 (1.0)	42 (1.3)	71 (1.3)	84 (0.9)
Hong Kong SAR	79 (1.4)	53 (1.2)	65 (1.3)	37 (1.4)	75 (1.5)	79 (1.5)	42 (1.2)	59 (1.4)	64 (1.5)	28 (1.3)	29 (1.3)	66 (1.5)	72 (1.5)
Netherlands	94 (0.7)	45 (1.2)	82 (1.1)	29 (1.1)	90 (1.0)	93 (0.8)	45 (1.2)	59 (1.2)	38 (1.2)	22 (1.3)	32 (1.3)	70 (1.3)	82 (1.1)
Switzerland	87 (1.2)	36 (1.1)	73 (1.8)	21 (1.3)	84 (1.3)	90 (1.2)	25 (1.5)	56 (1.4)	48 (1.6)	20 (1.6)	25 (1.3)	58 (1.8)	74 (1.7)
Benchmarking participants													
Newfoundland and Labrador, Canada	88 (1.2)	41 (1.4)	71 (2.1)	30 (1.4)	84 (1.4)	91 (0.9)	41 (2.0)	65 (1.4)	35 (1.4)	26 (1.4)	39 (1.4)	70 (1.7)	84 (1.2)
Ontario, Canada	88 (0.8)	36 (1.2)	70 (1.2)	29 (1.1)	86 (0.9)	93 (0.6)	34 (1.2)	63 (1.1)	45 (1.2)	21 (0.9)	35 (1.1)	74 (1.2)	85 (0.8)
Benchmarking participant not meeting sample requirements													
City of Buenos Aires, Argentina	91 (0.9)	44 (1.7)	77 (1.8)	24 (1.5)	82 (1.9)	90 (1.7)	35 (1.9)	55 (1.9)	48 (2.2)	23 (2.2)	37 (2.2)	71 (2.1)	83 (1.7)

▲	More than 10 percentage points above ICILS 2013 average
△	Significantly above ICILS 2013 average
▽	Significantly below ICILS 2013 average
▼	More than 10 percentage points below ICILS 2013 average

Notes:

() Standard errors appear in parentheses. Because some results are rounded to the nearest whole number, some totals may appear inconsistent.

† Met guidelines for sampling participation rates only after replacement schools were included.

1 National Desired Population does not correspond to International Desired Population.

2 Country surveyed the same cohort of students but at the beginning of the next school year.

We formed two scales based on these items in order to explore across-country differences in students' ICT self-efficacy. One of those scales (based on six items) focused on basic ICT skills.[14] It had a reliability (coefficient alpha) of 0.76. The other (based on seven items) was concerned with advanced ICT skills.[15] It had a reliability (coefficient alpha) of 0.80. We used the Rasch partial credit model to construct the scales and standardized the IRT scores to have an ICILS 2013 average score of 50 points and a standard deviation of 10 points. The higher scores on the scales indicate higher levels of self-efficacy.

Table 5.16 presents the national average scores on the *basic ICT skills self-efficacy scale*. These data show differences across countries and gender. In both Poland and Slovenia, the level of self-efficacy was notably higher than the ICILS 2013 average (by four and three scale points respectively in the two countries). The average scale scores for Australia, Chile, Croatia, the Czech Republic, Norway, the Russian Federation, Ontario, Newfoundland and Labrador, and the Slovak Republic were also significantly higher than the ICILS 2013 average (typically by one or two scale score points). Scores in Thailand and Turkey were notably lower than the ICILS 2013 average (by 11 and six points respectively), while those in Korea and Lithuania were significantly lower than the ICILS 2013 average (by about one point).

Statistically significant gender differences in basic ICT self-efficacy favoring females emerged in Chile, Korea, and Newfoundland and Labrador. On average, the females' scores were two scale points higher than the males'. The only country (among the ICILS countries that met sampling requirements) where males scored higher was Norway.

Table 5.17 records the average scale scores on the *advanced ICT self-efficacy scale*. These data show larger gender differences than the gender differences observed on the basic scale. On average, males' scores on the advanced scale were higher than the females' average scores, with the difference as much as five scale points in some countries. Differences between males and females within countries were as large as six or seven scale points. There was no country where females scored higher than males; the smallest difference (of two scale score points) was recorded in Thailand.

Crossnational differences were also apparent on the advanced ICT self-efficacy scale. In Chile, Croatia, Korea, Lithuania, the Russian Federation, and Slovenia, the national average scale scores were significantly higher than the ICILS 2013 average. In Australia, the Czech Republic, Germany, Norway, Poland, Ontario, and Newfoundland and Labrador, the mean scores were significantly lower than the ICILS 2013 average. The average national score for Thailand was notably lower than the ICILS 2013 average.

---

14 The following items were used to derive this scale: "search for and find a file on your computer," "edit digital photographs or other graphic images," "create or edit documents (e.g., assignments for school)," "search for and find information you need on the internet," "create a multimedia presentation (with sound, pictures, or video)," and "upload text, images, or video to an online profile."

15 The following items were used to derive this scale: "use software to find and get rid of viruses," "create a database (e.g., using [Microsoft access ®])," "build or edit a webpage," "change the settings on your computer to improve the way it operates or to fix problems," "use a spreadsheet to do calculations, store data, or plot a graph," "create a computer program or macro (e.g., in [Basic, Visual Basic])," and "set up a computer network."

Table 5.16: National averages for students' self-efficacy in basic ICT skills overall and by gender

Country	Students' Self-Efficacy in Basic ICT Skills				Score Distribution by Gender
	All students	Females	Males	Differences (males - females)*	
Australia	52 (0.2) △	52 (0.2)	51 (0.2)	-1 (0.3)	
Chile	53 (0.2) △	54 (0.3)	52 (0.3)	-2 (0.3)	
Croatia	52 (0.3) △	53 (0.3)	52 (0.3)	-1 (0.3)	
Czech Republic	51 (0.2) △	51 (0.2)	51 (0.2)	0 (0.3)	
Germany†	50 (0.3)	49 (0.4)	50 (0.3)	1 (0.5)	
Korea, Republic of	49 (0.2) ▽	50 (0.3)	48 (0.3)	-2 (0.3)	
Lithuania	49 (0.2) ▽	49 (0.3)	49 (0.3)	0 (0.4)	
Norway (Grade 9)[1]	51 (0.2) △	51 (0.2)	52 (0.3)	1 (0.3)	
Poland	54 (0.2) ◀	54 (0.3)	54 (0.2)	0 (0.3)	
Russian Federation[2]	51 (0.2) △	52 (0.2)	51 (0.3)	-1 (0.3)	
Slovak Republic	51 (0.3) △	51 (0.4)	51 (0.3)	-1 (0.5)	
Slovenia	53 (0.2) ◀	54 (0.3)	53 (0.3)	-1 (0.4)	
Thailand[2]	39 (0.3) ▶	40 (0.4)	39 (0.4)	-1 (0.4)	
Turkey	44 (0.4) ▶	44 (0.5)	44 (0.4)	0 (0.6)	
ICILS 2013 average	50 (0.1)	50 (0.1)	50 (0.1)	-1 (0.1)	
Countries not meeting sample requirements					
Denmark	52 (0.2)	51 (0.3)	52 (0.3)	1 (0.3)	
Hong Kong SAR	48 (0.5)	49 (0.5)	48 (0.6)	-1 (0.7)	
Netherlands	52 (0.3)	52 (0.4)	52 (0.4)	1 (0.4)	
Switzerland	49 (0.4)	48 (0.4)	50 (0.6)	2 (0.7)	
Benchmarking participants					
Newfoundland and Labrador, Canada	51 (0.3)	52 (0.5)	50 (0.5)	-2 (0.6)	
Ontario, Canada	52 (0.2)	52 (0.3)	51 (0.3)	0 (0.4)	
Benchmarking participant not meeting sample requirements					
City of Buenos Aires, Argentina	51 (0.5)	52 (0.6)	50 (0.6)	-2 (0.6)	

▲ More than three score points above ICILS 2013 average
△ Significantly above ICILS 2013 average
▽ Significantly below ICILS 2013 average
▶ More than three score points below ICILS 2013 average

■ Female average score +/− confidence interval
■ Male average score +/− confidence interval

On average, students with a score in the range indicated by this color have more than a 50% probability of responding to the statements about students' self-efficacy in basic ICT skills with:
  Disagreement to positive, agreement to negative statements
  Agreement to positive, disagreement to negative items

Notes:
* Statistically significant (*p*<.05) coefficients in **bold**.
() Standard errors appear in parentheses. Because some results are rounded to the nearest whole number, some totals may appear inconsistent.
† Met guidelines for sampling participation rates only after replacement schools were included.
[1] National Desired Population does not correspond to International Desired Population.
[2] Country surveyed the same cohort of students but at the beginning of the next school year.

Table 5.17: National averages for students' self-efficacy in advanced ICT skills overall and by gender

160

Country	All students			Females		Males		Differences (males - females)*	
Australia	48	(0.2)	▽	46	(0.2)	50	(0.3)	4	(0.3)
Chile	52	(0.3)	△	51	(0.4)	53	(0.3)	3	(0.4)
Croatia	53	(0.2)	△	50	(0.3)	55	(0.3)	4	(0.4)
Czech Republic	48	(0.2)	▽	45	(0.3)	51	(0.3)	6	(0.4)
Germany[†]	48	(0.3)	▽	44	(0.4)	51	(0.3)	7	(0.5)
Korea, Republic of	52	(0.2)	△	50	(0.2)	53	(0.2)	3	(0.3)
Lithuania	51	(0.2)	△	48	(0.3)	53	(0.3)	5	(0.4)
Norway (Grade 9)[1]	49	(0.2)	▽	46	(0.3)	52	(0.3)	6	(0.4)
Poland	49	(0.2)	▽	46	(0.3)	52	(0.3)	6	(0.4)
Russian Federation[2]	52	(0.2)	△	50	(0.3)	54	(0.3)	4	(0.3)
Slovak Republic	50	(0.3)		47	(0.4)	54	(0.3)	6	(0.5)
Slovenia	52	(0.3)	△	49	(0.3)	54	(0.4)	5	(0.4)
Thailand[2]	47	(0.3)	▼	46	(0.4)	48	(0.4)	2	(0.4)
Turkey	50	(0.4)		48	(0.4)	52	(0.4)	4	(0.5)
ICILS 2013 average	50	(0.1)		48	(0.1)	52	(0.1)	5	(0.1)
Countries not meeting sample requirements									
Denmark	49	(0.2)		45	(0.3)	53	(0.3)	7	(0.4)
Hong Kong SAR	51	(0.3)		50	(0.4)	52	(0.5)	3	(0.6)
Netherlands	49	(0.3)		45	(0.3)	52	(0.4)	7	(0.5)
Switzerland	47	(0.4)		44	(0.5)	50	(0.5)	5	(0.5)
Benchmarking participants									
Newfoundland and Labrador, Canada	49	(0.3)		48	(0.5)	51	(0.5)	3	(0.8)
Ontario, Canada	49	(0.3)		47	(0.3)	51	(0.4)	4	(0.5)
Benchmarking participant not meeting sample requirements									
City of Buenos Aires, Argentina	49	(0.4)		48	(0.6)	50	(0.6)	2	(0.8)

Notes:
* Statistically significant (p<.05) coefficients in **bold**.
() Standard errors appear in parentheses. Because some results are rounded to the nearest whole number, some totals may appear inconsistent.
[†] Met guidelines for sampling participation rates only after replacement schools were included.
[1] National Desired Population does not correspond to International Desired Population.
[2] Country surveyed the same cohort of students but at the beginning of the next school year.

▲ More than three score points above ICILS 2013 average
△ Significantly above ICILS 2013 average
▽ Significantly below ICILS 2013 average
▼ More than three score points below ICILS 2013 average

■ Female average score +/− confidence interval
■ Male average score +/− confidence interval

On average, students with a score in the range indicated by this color have more than a 50% probability of responding to the statements about students' self-efficacy in advanced ICT skills with:
Disagreement to positive, agreement to negative statements
Agreement to positive, disagreement to negative items

PREPARING FOR LIFE IN A DIGITAL AGE

Student interest and enjoyment in using computers and computing

Students were asked to record their level of agreement with the following statements (each denoting interest and enjoyment[16] in using computers and doing computing) on a four-point Likert scale ("strongly agree," "agree," "disagree," and "strongly disagree"):

- It is very important to me to work with a computer;
- I think using a computer is fun;
- It is more fun to do my work using a computer than without a computer;
- I use a computer because I am very interested in the technology;
- I like learning how to do new things using a computer;
- I often look for new ways to do things using a computer;
- I enjoy using the internet to find out information.

Table 5.18 records the percentages of agreement (a combination of the categories "strongly agree" and "agree") with each item. The table shows the generally high level of agreement with these statements. These "high-level" percentages ranged from 63 percent ("I use a computer because I am very interested in the technology") to 92 percent ("I enjoy using the internet to find out information").

Table 5.19 records the scale scores for the *interest and enjoyment in computing scale*. This seven-item scale, constructed using the Rasch partial credit model and with IRT scores standardized to an ICILS 2013 average score of 50 points and a standard deviation of 10 points, had reliabilities (coefficient alpha) that ranged across countries from 0.74 to 0.87.

In all countries, males expressed greater interest and enjoyment in computing than females did. The difference between gender groups was, on average, four scale points. In some countries (Germany and the Czech Republic[17]), the difference was as large as six scale points. The difference was statistically significant in all countries.

There were some notable crossnational differences with respect to interest and enjoyment in computing. In Chile and Croatia, attitudes were notably more favorable than the ICILS 2013 average, by five and three scale score points respectively. In Poland and Turkey, attitudes were significantly more favorable than the international average, by one and two scale points respectively. In Korea, the scale score was notably lower than the ICILS 2013 average (by four points). In Australia, the Czech Republic, Germany, Norway, the Russian Federation, and the Slovak Republic, the respective national averages were significantly lower than the ICILS 2013 average (by one or two scale points). The average scale scores for Ontario (51 points) and Newfoundland and Labrador (53 points) also suggested relatively high levels of interest and enjoyment among students in those education systems.

---

16 When analyzing these data, we were unable to identify the separate dimensions of "interest" and "enjoyment." The questionnaire also included four ICT self-concept items not analyzed in this report: "learning how to use a new computer program is very easy for me," "I have always been good at working with computers," "I know more about computers than most people of my age," and "I am able to give advice to others when they have problems with computers."

17 There were also large gender differences in Denmark (eight points) and Switzerland (seven points).

Table 5.18: National percentages of students' agreement with statements about computers

Country	It is Very Important to Me to Work With a Computer		I Think Using a Computer is Fun		It Is More Fun to Do My Work Using a Computer than without a Computer		I Use a Computer Because I Am Very Interested in the Technology		I Like Learning How to Do New Things Using a Computer		I Often Look for New Ways to Do Things Using a Computer		I Enjoy Using the Internet to Find out Information	
Australia	88 (0.6)		93 (0.5)	◁	85 (0.6)	◁	65 (0.9)	◁	91 (0.5)		75 (0.8)	▽	93 (0.5)	
Chile	95 (0.6)	◁	97 (0.4)	◁	92 (0.6)	◁	85 (1.0)	◀	98 (0.3)	◁	87 (0.8)	◁	93 (0.6)	
Croatia	95 (0.5)	◁	97 (0.3)	◁	85 (0.7)	◁	73 (0.9)	◁	92 (0.6)		82 (0.8)	◁	95 (0.5)	◁
Czech Republic	93 (0.5)	◁	94 (0.4)	◁	81 (0.9)		57 (1.1)	▽	92 (0.5)		81 (0.7)	◁	94 (0.4)	◁
Germany†	89 (0.7)		96 (0.4)	◁	80 (1.0)	▽	51 (1.2)	▶	89 (0.8)	▽	63 (1.1)	▶	89 (0.7)	▽
Korea, Republic of	79 (0.9)	▶	88 (0.6)	▷	76 (0.9)	▷	42 (1.3)	▶	86 (0.8)	▷	67 (0.9)	▶	88 (0.7)	▷
Lithuania	89 (0.6)		90 (0.6)		81 (0.9)		57 (1.2)	▷	90 (0.6)		77 (1.0)		90 (0.7)	▽
Norway (Grade 9)[1]	84 (0.9)	▷	96 (0.4)	◁	89 (0.7)	◁	52 (1.1)	▶	90 (0.6)	▷	76 (0.9)		96 (0.4)	◁
Poland	92 (0.6)	◁	97 (0.4)	◁	86 (0.9)	◁	62 (1.1)		88 (0.8)	▷	77 (1.0)		96 (0.4)	◁
Russian Federation[2]	86 (0.6)	▷	58 (1.1)	▶	79 (0.9)	▷	52 (0.9)	▶	93 (0.4)	◁	77 (0.8)		96 (0.3)	◁
Slovak Republic	90 (0.8)		92 (0.7)		80 (0.9)	▷	52 (1.2)	▶	90 (0.9)		76 (0.9)	▽	91 (0.8)	
Slovenia	90 (0.7)		96 (0.5)	◁	83 (1.0)		66 (1.0)	◁	91 (0.5)		78 (0.9)		84 (1.0)	▷
Thailand[2]	94 (0.6)	◁	88 (0.9)	▷	82 (1.2)		86 (0.8)	◀	96 (0.5)	◁	87 (0.9)	◁	94 (0.7)	◁
Turkey	87 (0.8)	▷	90 (0.7)		76 (1.0)	▷	79 (1.1)	◀	94 (0.6)	◁	83 (0.9)	◁	90 (0.8)	▽
ICILS 2013 average	89 (0.2)		91 (0.2)		83 (0.2)		63 (0.3)		91 (0.2)		78 (0.2)		92 (0.2)	
Countries not meeting sample requirements														
Denmark	93 (0.6)		97 (0.4)		89 (0.8)		48 (1.2)		91 (0.7)		63 (1.3)		98 (0.4)	
Hong Kong SAR	92 (0.7)		92 (1.0)		77 (1.0)		69 (1.3)		86 (1.1)		80 (1.1)		93 (0.8)	
Netherlands	92 (0.8)		95 (0.6)		82 (1.0)		41 (1.5)		86 (1.0)		57 (1.3)		71 (1.2)	
Switzerland	85 (1.4)		91 (1.0)		76 (1.4)		49 (1.8)		83 (0.8)		65 (2.0)		89 (1.1)	
Benchmarking participants														
Newfoundland and Labrador, Canada	91 (1.0)		95 (0.6)		88 (1.0)		76 (1.5)		93 (0.8)		79 (1.6)		93 (0.9)	
Ontario, Canada	90 (0.8)		96 (0.4)		85 (0.8)		72 (1.3)		93 (0.7)		77 (1.1)		93 (0.6)	
Benchmarking participant not meeting sample requirements														
City of Buenos Aires, Argentina	95 (0.8)		95 (0.7)		82 (1.6)		76 (1.9)		95 (0.9)		77 (1.4)		86 (1.1)	

▲ More than 10 percentage points above ICILS 2013 average
◁ Significantly above ICILS 2013 average
▽ Significantly below ICILS 2013 average
▶ More than 10 percentage points below ICILS 2013 average

Notes:
() Standard errors appear in parentheses. Because some results are rounded to the nearest whole number, some totals may appear inconsistent.
† Met guidelines for sampling participation rates only after replacement schools were included.
[1] National Desired Population does not correspond to International Desired Population.
[2] Country surveyed the same cohort of students but at the beginning of the next school year.

Table 5.19: National averages for students' interest and enjoyment in using computers overall and by gender

Country	Students' Interest and Enjoyment in Using Computers				Score Distribution by Gender
	All students	Females	Males	Differences (males - females)*	
Australia	49 (0.2) ▷	47 (0.3)	52 (0.3)	5 (0.4)	
Chile	56 (0.3) ◀	55 (0.3)	56 (0.4)	1 (0.4)	
Croatia	53 (0.2) ◀	51 (0.2)	56 (0.3)	5 (0.3)	
Czech Republic	50 (0.2)	47 (0.3)	53 (0.3)	6 (0.4)	
Germany†	48 (0.2) ▷	45 (0.3)	51 (0.3)	6 (0.4)	
Korea, Republic of	46 (0.3) ▶	43 (0.3)	48 (0.3)	5 (0.4)	
Lithuania	49 (0.2) ▷	47 (0.3)	51 (0.3)	4 (0.4)	
Norway (Grade 9)[1]	50 (0.2)	47 (0.2)	52 (0.3)	5 (0.3)	
Poland	51 (0.2) △	49 (0.3)	53 (0.3)	4 (0.4)	
Russian Federation[2]	48 (0.2) ▷	46 (0.2)	49 (0.2)	3 (0.3)	
Slovak Republic	48 (0.3) ▷	46 (0.3)	50 (0.4)	4 (0.5)	
Slovenia	50 (0.2)	47 (0.2)	53 (0.4)	5 (0.4)	
Thailand[2]	50 (0.3)	50 (0.3)	50 (0.4)	0 (0.4)	
Turkey	52 (0.3) △	51 (0.4)	53 (0.4)	2 (0.5)	
ICILS 2013 average	50 (0.1)	48 (0.1)	52 (0.1)	4 (0.1)	
Countries not meeting sample requirements					
Denmark	50 (0.3)	46 (0.3)	53 (0.4)	7 (0.4)	
Hong Kong SAR	50 (0.4)	48 (0.3)	52 (0.6)	4 (0.6)	
Netherlands	46 (0.3)	44 (0.3)	49 (0.4)	5 (0.5)	
Switzerland	47 (0.4)	43 (0.4)	51 (0.5)	8 (0.6)	
Benchmarking participants					
Newfoundland and Labrador, Canada	53 (0.3)	51 (0.4)	54 (0.4)	3 (0.6)	
Ontario, Canada	51 (0.3)	49 (0.4)	54 (0.4)	5 (0.5)	
Benchmarking participant not meeting sample requirements					
City of Buenos Aires, Argentina	51 (0.4)	50 (0.4)	52 (0.6)	2 (0.8)	

Legend (Score Distribution by Gender):
■ Female average score +/− confidence interval
■ Male average score +/− confidence interval

On average, students with a score in the range indicated by this color have more than a 50% probability of responding to the statements about students' interest and enjoyment in using ICT with:
Disagreement to positive, agreement to negative items
Agreement to positive, disagreement to negative items

Notes:
* Statistically significant (*p*<.05) coefficients in **bold**.
( ) Standard errors appear in parentheses. Because some results are rounded to the nearest whole number, some totals may appear inconsistent.
† Met guidelines for sampling participation rates only after replacement schools were included.
[1] National Desired Population does not correspond to International Desired Population.
[2] Country surveyed the same cohort of students but at the beginning of the next school year.

▲ More than three score points above ICILS 2013 average
△ Significantly above ICILS 2013 average
▽ Significantly below ICILS 2013 average
▼ More than three score points below ICILS 2013 average

Associations between perceptions and achievement

In order to review the association of students' CIL with ICT self-efficacy beliefs and with ICT interest and enjoyment, we computed correlation coefficients for each ICILS country. These coefficients are shown in Table 5.20, with the statistically significant ones presented in bold. We recorded positive and statistically significant correlations between basic ICT self-efficacy and CIL scores at both the international level and in every country. The ICILS 2013 average correlation coefficient was 0.32, and the values for countries that met sampling requirements ranged from 0.20 in Germany to 0.42 in Korea. In Ontario, the correlation coefficient was 0.31; in Newfoundland and Labrador, it was 0.25.

The association between advanced ICT self-efficacy and CIL was much weaker. The ICILS 2013 average for the correlation coefficient was 0.04, while the coefficients for the participating countries were statistically significant only in Turkey (0.20), Korea (0.13), Croatia (0.12), Lithuania (0.07), the Russian Federation (0.05), and the Slovak Republic (0.06). A small but statistically significant positive association was evident in Ontario (0.07), and statistically significant but small negative correlation coefficients were evident in Norway (-0.07) and in Newfoundland and Labrador (-0.10).

The patterns for the two scales suggest that while basic ICT self-efficacy is quite strongly associated with CIL, the same cannot be said of the relationship between advanced ICT self-efficacy and CIL. In fact, the associations with respect to the latter were weak to the point of being almost nonexistent. When interpreting this difference, we need to remember that the CIL achievement construct combines two sets of skills: fundamental technical skills and the skills associated with information literacy and communication. As such, we need not expect students with higher levels of advanced ICT self-efficacy (encompassing advanced ICT tasks) to have higher levels of CIL proficiency. In contrast, however, it is reasonable to expect that students with higher levels of basic ICT self-efficacy will have higher CIL achievement scores because the skills described in the basic self-efficacy questions are similar to those required for demonstration of CIL proficiency.

Interest and enjoyment was also weakly and inconsistently associated with CIL. The ICILS 2013 average for this coefficient was 0.07. The coefficient was statistically significant in 10 of the 14 countries that met sampling requirements: Turkey (0.25), Thailand (0.23), Australia (0.11), the Slovak Republic (0.11), Korea (0.11), Lithuania (0.08), Chile (0.06), Norway (0.06), Croatia (0.05), and Poland (0.05). We recorded a statistically significant negative correlation coefficient in the Russian Federation (-0.07). The coefficient for Ontario was 0.09.

Conclusion

The ICILS 2013 data considered in this chapter show that in most of the participating countries Grade 8 students had been using computers and other forms of ICT for a considerable period of time, typically for five years or more. The ICILS students also presented as frequent users of ICT, with that use occurring more often at home than at school. They reported using ICT for study, communication, information exchange, and recreation. Many of the ICILS students were clearly managing to learn and live in this digital age.

Table 5.20: National values of correlation coefficients for CIL with basic ICT self-efficacy, advanced ICT self-efficacy, and interest/enjoyment in computing

Country	Basic ICT Self-Efficacy*		Advanced ICT Self-Efficacy*		Interest - Enjoyment in ICT*	
Australia	0.36	(0.02)	0.04	(0.02)	0.11	(0.02)
Chile	0.36	(0.02)	0.00	(0.02)	0.06	(0.03)
Croatia	0.34	(0.02)	0.12	(0.02)	0.05	(0.02)
Czech Republic	0.22	(0.02)	0.01	(0.02)	-0.02	(0.03)
Germany[†]	0.20	(0.02)	-0.03	(0.02)	0.00	(0.03)
Korea, Republic of	0.42	(0.02)	0.13	(0.02)	0.11	(0.02)
Lithuania	0.38	(0.02)	0.07	(0.02)	0.08	(0.03)
Norway (Grade 9)[1]	0.24	(0.02)	-0.07	(0.03)	0.06	(0.03)
Poland	0.33	(0.02)	0.05	(0.02)	0.05	(0.02)
Russian Federation[2]	0.28	(0.02)	0.01	(0.02)	-0.07	(0.02)
Slovak Republic	0.37	(0.02)	0.06	(0.03)	0.11	(0.03)
Slovenia	0.28	(0.02)	-0.03	(0.03)	0.05	(0.03)
Thailand[2]	0.29	(0.02)	0.00	(0.03)	0.23	(0.03)
Turkey	0.37	(0.03)	0.21	(0.03)	0.25	(0.03)
ICILS 2013 average	0.32	(0.01)	0.04	(0.01)	0.08	(0.01)
Countries not meeting sample requirements						
Denmark	0.20	(0.03)	-0.12	(0.02)	-0.01	(0.03)
Hong Kong SAR	0.40	(0.03)	0.09	(0.03)	0.12	(0.05)
Netherlands	0.28	(0.03)	-0.08	(0.03)	0.01	(0.03)
Switzerland	0.20	(0.03)	-0.02	(0.04)	0.05	(0.04)
Benchmarking participants						
Newfoundland and Labrador, Canada	0.25	(0.04)	-0.08	(0.04)	0.07	(0.02)
Ontario, Canada	0.31	(0.03)	-0.10	(0.03)	0.09	(0.06)
Benchmarking participant not meeting sample requirements						
City of Buenos Aires, Argentina	0.26	(0.04)	0.07	(0.04)	-0.03	(0.04)

Notes:
* Statistically significant (p < 0.05) coefficients in **bold**.
() Standard errors appear in parentheses. Because some results are rounded to the nearest whole number, some totals may appear inconsistent.
[†] Met guidelines for sampling participation rates only after replacement schools were included.
[1] National Desired Population does not correspond to International Desired Population.
[2] Country surveyed the same cohort of students but at the beginning of the next school year.

The difference between the percentages of females and males using computers at home at least once a week was small (78% compared to 82%), and almost nonexistent with respect to using computers at school at least once a month. On average across ICILS countries, we found no statistically significant differences between females and males in terms of out-of-school use of common computer applications. However, females were making greater use than males of computers for school-related purposes, albeit by a small but significant amount. Females were also slightly more likely than males to attribute their ICT learning to school instruction.

We also found evidence that females were making slightly more frequent use than males of the internet for social communication. However, males were slightly more likely than females to frequently use the internet for information exchange. Similarly, there was greater prevalence of recreational use of computers among males than females. Our conclusion is that although there are differences between males and females in the way they use information and communication technology, these differences are small.

At school, students were using computer technology across most subject areas as well as in the specialist subject area of information technology or computer studies. Beyond this specialist subject area, the most frequent use of computer technology was in the (natural) sciences and in the human sciences and humanities. Use was least frequent in the creative arts.

The Grade 8 ICILS students also indicated that they were confident in their capacity to use basic ICT applications but a little less confident about using more advanced ICT functions. Females recorded slightly higher scores than males (the difference was about one tenth of a standard deviation) on the basic ICT self-efficacy scale (encompassing common ICT applications). However, much larger differences (of about half of a standard deviation) in favor of males were evident with regard to the advanced ICT self-efficacy scale (encompassing multimedia and technical aspects).

Students generally expressed high levels of interest and enjoyment in using computer technology. Males expressed relatively higher levels of interest and enjoyment than females (the difference was about two fifths of a standard deviation). There were also notable differences across countries in average levels of interest and enjoyment in computing.

Student confidence in their basic ICT skills was moderately highly associated with measured computer and information literacy (CIL) achievement. Confidence in using advanced ICT skills was not associated to any appreciable extent with CIL achievement. Interest and enjoyment in using ICT was only weakly associated with CIL achievement, overall, and the association was inconsistent across countries. This finding is consistent with findings from cross-sectional surveys in other areas of learning.

CHAPTER 6:

School Environments for Teaching and Learning Computer and Information Literacy

Introduction

Using information and communication technology (ICT) for teaching and learning has become an increasingly common practice in educational settings, especially given that ability to use ICT is a requisite skill in today's digital age (Ananiadou & Claro, 2009; European Commission, 2013). Research suggests that schools must have certain conditions in place if they are to support effective pedagogical use of ICT in their classrooms. These conditions include not only sufficient ICT infrastructure and a positive and collaborative atmosphere where teachers receive training in how to best use ICT but also a minimum or preferably none of the obstacles that can limit teachers' ability to use ICT in their teaching (Law, Pelgrum, & Plomp, 2008).

Several surveys have reported crossnational comparisons of the ICT-related resources available in schools for teaching and learning purposes. The Second Information Technology in Education Study (SITES-M1), conducted by the International Association for the Evaluation of Educational Achievement (IEA), noted a large increase in the uptake of ICT in schools in comparison to earlier such data. However, the study also identified large differences in infrastructure across countries (Pelgrum & Anderson, 2001). A follow-up study found a similar rate of increase in infrastructure development and crosscountry discrepancies (Law et al., 2008). Neither study, however, found an association between schools' ICT resources and the proportions of teachers at these schools using ICT for teaching and learning activities.

A recent study, funded by the European Commission, on the state of ICT use in European schools noted the increase in ICT-capabilities of schools but stated urgency in remedying the fact that some of these countries were lagging behind others in this regard (European Commission, 2013). The study also found no relationships between high levels of ICT provision in schools and teachers' confidence in, use of, and attitudes toward using ICT. Despite these findings, teachers considered insufficient ICT equipment to be an obstacle to effective use of ICT in teaching and learning activities. They also highlighted a lack of technical and pedagogical support as a major obstacle to their use of ICT in classroom teaching. The study's authors concluded that providing teachers with support and appropriate pedagogical development is as important as ensuring ICT provision and support (European Commission, 2013, p. 156).

Our focus in this chapter is on describing the school contexts for CIL learning based on data from the ICILS teacher, ICT-coordinator, and principal questionnaires. The data that we present here pertain to three considerations set down in ICILS Research Question 2: *What aspects of schools and education systems are related to student achievement in computer and information literacy with respect to (b) school and teaching practices regarding the use of technologies in computer and information literacy, (d) access*

© International Association for the Evaluation of Educational Achievement (IEA) 2014
J. Fraillon et al., *Preparing for Life in a Digital Age,* DOI 10.1007/978-3-319-14222-7_7

*to ICT in schools, and (e) teacher professional development and within-school delivery of
computer and information literacy programs?"*

We begin the chapter by reporting on the types of ICT resources evident in the
schools that participated in ICILS. We then explore the different policies and practices
identified across the ICILS countries and discuss the survey respondents' perceptions of
school ICT learning environments. In the final section of the chapter, we describe the
ICT-related professional development activities undertaken by teachers, as reported by
principals and teachers.

Schools' access to ICT resources

Previous comparative crossnational surveys show that the provision of ICT resources
in schools varies widely across countries (see, for example, Anderson & Ainley, 2010;
Pelgrum & Doornekamp, 2009). The ICILS research team therefore considered
collecting data on the following to be an important facet of the study: the availability of
computing devices at school, the location of these devices within the school, students'
access to them, and schools' connectivity to internet.

The ICT-coordinator questionnaire included a question about the availability of
technology resources for teaching and/or learning. Table 6.1 shows the percentages of
Grade 8 students (Grade 8 being the ICILS target grade) at schools where, according
to the ICT-coordinators, each of the technology resources listed was available in their
respective schools. We established these student percentages by using the sampling
weights of the students in each sampled school. These allowed us to estimate the
proportion of students in each country enrolled at schools providing each of the
featured resources.

According to these results, almost every student (99% on average) participating in ICILS
was studying at a school with access to the World Wide Web. The national averages
ranged from 96 percent to 100 percent across the 14 countries that met sampling
requirements. Crossnationally, large majorities of the Grade 8 students also had access
to computer-based information resources. On average, these resources were available to
96 percent of students. In many countries, 100 percent of students had this access. The
lowest national percentage was found in Turkey, with 71 percent.

Eighty-seven percent of students across ICILS countries were at schools that provided
access to an education site or network maintained by an education system. National
percentages were highest in Korea (99%), Ontario (99%), Australia (97%), Croatia
(97%), and Newfoundland and Labrador (97%), and lowest in Germany (50%). Eighty-
four percent of students were attending schools that made interactive digital learning
resources available. The national average percentages ranged from 44 percent in Turkey
to 98 percent in Australia and the Slovak Republic and 99 percent in Norway.

Most students were studying at schools that had email accounts for teachers (83%
on average across countries). The lowest national percentages were evident in Turkey
(65%), Chile (67%), and Germany (67%). The highest percentages indicated universal
or almost universal such provision. These percentages were observed in Australia and
the Canadian province of Newfoundland and Labrador, both 100 percent, as well as
Croatia, Norway, and Ontario, all 99 percent. The average percentage for students at
schools where the students themselves had email accounts was 59 percent. The lowest
national percentages were evident in Turkey (28%), Germany (29%), Chile (34%), and
the Czech Republic (42%). These results show considerable variation across countries
with regard to email accounts for teachers and, in particular, for their students.

Table 6.1: National percentages of students at schools with available internet-related resources for teaching and/or learning

Country	Computer-Based Information Resources (e.g., Websites, Wikis, Encyclopedias)	Interactive Digital Learning Resources (e.g., Learning Objects)	Access to the World Wide Web	Access to an Education Site or Network Maintained by an Education System	Email Accounts for Teachers	Email Accounts for Students
Australia	100 (0.0) △	98 (0.6) ◄	100 (0.0) △	97 (1.2) △	100 (0.0) ◄	96 (1.4) ◄
Chile	94 (1.8)	94 (2.1) △	97 (1.5)	68 (4.4) ►	67 (4.2) ►	34 (4.6) ►
Croatia	100 (0.0) △	84 (3.2)	100 (0.0) △	97 (1.3) ◄	99 (0.8) ◄	95 (1.9) ◄
Czech Republic	100 (0.0) △	94 (2.4) ◄	100 (0.0) △	78 (3.4) ▽	90 (2.4) △	42 (4.1) ►
Germany†	99 (0.7) △	75 (3.8) ▽	98 (1.2)	50 (4.9) ►	67 (4.4) ►	29 (4.0) ►
Korea, Republic of	99 (0.7) △	67 (4.0) ►	97 (0.8)	99 (0.0) ◄	80 (3.3)	62 (4.0)
Lithuania	99 (1.0)	91 (2.3) △	99 (0.9)	95 (1.9) △	87 (2.8)	76 (3.6) ◄
Norway (Grade 9)[1]	100 (0.0) △	99 (0.8) ◄	100 (0.0)	96 (2.0) △	99 (0.8) ◄	49 (5.1)
Poland	100 (0.0) △	78 (4.0)	100 (0.0) △	82 (3.6)	79 (3.7)	61 (4.3)
Russian Federation[2]	98 (1.1)	90 (2.0) △	100 (0.5) △	95 (1.5) △	87 (1.8) △	60 (3.6)
Slovak Republic	99 (0.9) △	98 (1.1) ◄	99 (0.4)	96 (1.8) △	79 (3.5)	66 (3.6)
Slovenia	98 (1.5)	90 (2.5) △	100 (0.0) △	95 (2.1) △	91 (2.6) △	65 (4.1)
Thailand[2]	93 (2.4)	75 (4.2) ▽	97 (2.0)	94 (2.1) △	75 (3.6) ▽	59 (4.7)
Turkey	71 (3.9) ►	44 (3.9) ►	96 (1.7)	77 (3.9) ▽	65 (4.4) ►	28 (4.2) ►
ICILS 2013 average	96 (0.4)	84 (0.8)	99 (0.3)	87 (0.7)	83 (0.8)	59 (1.0)
Countries not meeting sample requirements						
Denmark	99 (1.0)	98 (1.6)	100 (0.0)	97 (1.7)	98 (1.6)	94 (2.0)
Hong Kong SAR	99 (0.8)	91 (3.1)	100 (0.0)	97 (1.7)	98 (1.1)	89 (3.5)
Netherlands	100 (0.0)	100 (0.0)	100 (0.0)	100 (0.0)	100 (0.0)	72 (6.6)
Switzerland	100 (0.0)	84 (4.9)	100 (0.0)	77 (6.7)	97 (2.4)	48 (7.6)
Benchmarking participants						
Newfoundland and Labrador, Canada	100 (0.0)	96 (0.2)	100 (0.0)	97 (0.1)	100 (0.0)	42 (0.3)
Ontario, Canada	99 (1.0)	90 (3.5)	100 (0.0)	99 (1.0)	99 (0.0)	58 (4.9)
Benchmarking participant not meeting sample requirements						
City of Buenos Aires, Argentina	89 (6.9)	72 (8.3)	87 (7.4)	61 (10.4)	62 (8.1)	33 (10.2)

◄ More than 10 percentage points above ICILS 2013 average
△ Significantly above ICILS 2013 average
▽ Significantly below ICILS 2013 average
► More than 10 percentage points below ICILS 2013 average

Notes:

() Standard errors appear in parentheses. Because some results are rounded to the nearest whole number, some totals may appear inconsistent.

† Met guidelines for sampling participation rates only after replacement schools were included.

[1] National Desired Population does not correspond to International Desired Population.

[2] Country surveyed the same cohort of students but at the beginning of the next school year.

The ICILS ICT-coordinator questionnaire also collected data on the availability of software resources for teaching and/or learning. Table 6.2 records the national percentages of students studying at schools where the specified learning resources were reported by the ICT-coordinator as available. Almost all students (99% on average) across the ICILS countries were studying at schools where presentation software (e.g., Microsoft PowerPoint ®) was available. We observed similar results for the availability of wordprocessing, database, and spreadsheet software (98%). In many countries, all ICT-coordinators said these resources were present in their schools. The lowest percentage recorded was for Turkey (88%).

Large majorities of students were at schools that had the following software available:

- Communication (91% on average, with national percentages ranging from 62% in Germany to 100% in Croatia);

- Tutorial or practice programs (88% on average, with national percentages ranging from 49% in Turkey to 98% in the Czech Republic);

- Multimedia production tools (80% on average, with national percentages ranging from 46% in Turkey to 99% in Australia);

- Data-logging and monitoring tools, such as devices that automatically record data such as temperature over time (54% on average, with national percentages ranging from 15% in the Czech Republic to 86% in Lithuania); and

- Simulation and modeling software (41% on average, with national percentages ranging from 9% in Turkey to 85% in Australia).

As with the internet-related resources, we observed marked differences across countries with respect to these software resources.

ICILS also asked the ICT-coordinators to provide information about the availability of the different computer resources for teaching and/or learning in their schools. Table 6.3 records the national percentages of students enrolled at schools that had each of the different computer resources available. Across all ICILS countries, majorities of students (on average 94%, with national percentages ranging from 84% in Lithuania to 100% in Australia) were studying at schools with access to a local area network (LAN). On average, about two thirds (65%) of students were enrolled at schools with space on a school network for students to store their work. The national percentages ranged from 24 percent in Turkey to 98 percent in Australia.

On average across the ICILS countries, fewer than half (46%) of the students were at schools with internet-based applications for collaborative work (with national percentages ranging from 14% in Germany to 82% in Newfoundland and Labrador), and 37 percent were at schools with a school intranet that provided applications and workspaces for students. The range in national percentages for a school intranet extended from 11 percent in Turkey to 83 percent in Australia. Learning management systems were available at the schools of about one third of students on average. Again, the national percentages ranged widely—from two percent in Turkey to 95 percent in Norway.

We also observed considerable differences with regard to the provision of tablet devices to students. On average, only about every fifth student was enrolled at a school that provided tablet devices. The national percentages ranged from three, four, and six percent respectively in Croatia, Turkey, and the Czech Republic as well as Germany to

Table 6.2: National percentages of students at schools with available software resources for teaching and/or learning

Country	Tutorial Software or [Practice Programs]	Digital Learning Games	Wordprocessing, Databases, Spreadsheets (e.g., [Microsoft© Office Suite])	Multimedia Production Tools (e.g., Media Capture and Editing, Web Production)	Data-Logging and Monitoring Tools	Simulations and Modeling Software	Presentation Software (e.g. [Microsoft PowerPoint ®], [Keynote ®])	Communication Software (e.g., Email, Chat, Blogs, Other Social Media)	Graphing or Drawing Software
Australia	92 (2.2)	95 (1.7) ▲	100 (0.0) △	99 (0.3) ▲	85 (2.4) ▲	85 (2.8) ▲	100 (0.0) △	98 (1.0) △	99 (0.6) ▲
Chile	90 (2.3)	77 (3.6)	98 (1.1)	60 (4.2) ▼	59 (4.4)	24 (3.7) ▼	97 (1.4)	86 (3.0)	49 (4.6) ▼
Croatia	85 (3.1)	80 (2.9)	100 (0.0) △	74 (3.3)	56 (3.7)	16 (2.7) ▼	99 (0.6)	100 (0.0) △	70 (4.2) ▼
Czech Republic	98 (1.5) △	72 (3.0)	100 (0.0) △	75 (3.6)	15 (3.1) ▼	15 (2.6) ▼	100 (0.0) △	94 (2.3)	96 (1.6) △
Germany†	87 (3.2)	62 (4.2) ▼	100 (0.0) △	71 (3.7) ▽	57 (4.7)	41 (4.3)	100 (0.0) △	62 (5.0) ▼	96 (1.3) △
Korea, Republic of	88 (2.5)	78 (3.5)	98 (1.1)	87 (3.0) △	56 (4.4)	38 (4.0)	99 (0.9)	94 (1.9)	89 (2.6)
Lithuania	97 (1.2) △	93 (1.7) ▲	99 (0.5)	85 (3.2)	86 (3.3) ▲	54 (4.4) ▲	100 (0.5)	95 (2.1)	98 (0.9) ▲
Norway (Grade 9)[1]	95 (1.8) △	93 (2.6) ▲	100 (0.0) △	89 (3.0) △	34 (3.4) ▼	56 (4.4) ▲	100 (0.0) △	91 (2.6)	97 (1.7) △
Poland	89 (2.9)	83 (3.3) △	99 (0.5)	92 (2.0) ▲	42 (4.4) ▼	53 (3.9) ▲	99 (0.7)	98 (1.5) △	91 (2.4)
Russian Federation[2]	93 (1.7) △	72 (3.2)	100 (0.0) △	78 (2.6)	65 (3.3) ▲	48 (3.2) △	100 (0.0) △	93 (1.4)	96 (1.7) △
Slovak Republic	96 (1.7) △	89 (2.6) ▲	100 (0.0) △	75 (3.6)	58 (4.3)	33 (4.6)	100 (0.0) △	98 (1.0) △	98 (1.2) ▲
Slovenia	97 (1.7) △	93 (2.1) ▲	100 (0.0) △	98 (1.1) ▲	45 (3.7) ▽	50 (3.9) △	100 (0.0) △	99 (0.6) △	97 (1.6) △
Thailand[2]	74 (3.8) ▼	51 (4.5)	95 (1.8)	88 (2.9) △	58 (4.7)	46 (5.0)	98 (1.5)	99 (0.9) △	98 (1.0) ▲
Turkey	49 (4.9) ▼	28 (3.8) ▼	88 (2.9) ▼	46 (4.4) ▼	40 (4.6) ▼	9 (2.4) ▼	98 (1.4)	73 (3.9) ▼	48 (4.4) ▼
ICILS 2013 average	88 (0.7)	76 (0.8)	98 (0.3)	80 (0.8)	54 (1.1)	41 (1.0)	99 (0.2)	91 (0.6)	87 (0.7)
Countries not meeting sample requirements									
Denmark	95 (2.1)	94 (3.1)	100 (0.0)	96 (2.1)	60 (5.8)	48 (5.2)	100 (0.0)	98 (1.5)	87 (3.5)
Hong Kong SAR	91 (3.5)	65 (4.9)	100 (0.0)	100 (0.0)	83 (4.1)	63 (5.3)	100 (0.0)	94 (2.8)	98 (1.4)
Netherlands	100 (0.0)	85 (5.0)	100 (0.0)	78 (5.9)	90 (3.7)	79 (5.2)	100 (0.0)	97 (2.1)	86 (4.7)
Switzerland	98 (1.5)	68 (6.7)	100 (0.0)	89 (3.2)	52 (6.8)	30 (6.8)	100 (0.0)	74 (6.9)	99 (0.4)
Benchmarking participants									
Newfoundland and Labrador, Canada	80 (0.2)	97 (0.1)	100 (0.0)	93 (0.1)	63 (0.3)	64 (0.3)	100 (0.0)	86 (0.2)	93 (0.1)
Ontario, Canada	88 (3.5)	96 (1.8)	99 (1.2)	89 (3.1)	73 (4.6)	67 (5.3)	99 (0.8)	97 (1.7)	94 (2.8)
Benchmarking participant not meeting sample requirements									
City of Buenos Aires, Argentina	83 (6.2)	60 (7.6)	100 (0.0)	81 (7.9)	45 (8.9)	39 (9.7)	91 (5.1)	94 (5.9)	81 (7.1)

▲ More than 10 percentage points above ICILS 2013 average
△ Significantly above ICILS 2013 average
▽ Significantly below ICILS 2013 average
▼ More than 10 percentage points below ICILS 2013 average

Notes:

() Standard errors appear in parentheses. Because some results are rounded to the nearest whole number, some totals may appear inconsistent.

† Met guidelines for sampling participation rates only after replacement schools were included.

[1] National Desired Population does not correspond to International Desired Population.

[2] Country surveyed the same cohort of students but at the beginning of the next school year.

Table 6.3: National percentages of students at schools with computer resources for teaching and/or learning

Country	Access to a Local Area Network (LAN) in the School		Tablet Devices (e.g., [iPad] and Similar)		Space on a School Network for Students to Store their Work		A School Intranet with Applications and Workspaces for Students to Use (e.g., [Moodle])		Internet-Based Applications for Collaborative Work (e.g., [Google Docs®])		A Learning Management System (e.g., [WebCT®])	
Australia	100 (0.1)	△	64 (3.7)	◄	98 (0.9)	◄	83 (2.5)	◄	67 (3.1)	◄	77 (2.8)	◄
Chile	97 (1.3)		14 (3.4)		44 (4.0)	►	19 (3.5)	►	49 (4.3)		11 (2.9)	►
Croatia	95 (1.9)		3 (1.3)	►	54 (3.7)	►	16 (3.4)	►	40 (3.8)		22 (2.5)	►
Czech Republic	94 (2.1)		6 (2.0)	►	87 (3.3)	◄	30 (3.4)		33 (3.9)	►	17 (2.9)	►
Germany†	99 (0.8)	△	6 (2.8)	►	94 (1.9)	◄	54 (3.9)	◄	14 (2.7)	►	8 (2.2)	►
Korea, Republic of	93 (2.3)		48 (3.7)	◄	39 (4.1)	◄	69 (3.8)	◄	62 (4.1)	◄	94 (2.0)	◄
Lithuania	84 (3.2)	►	13 (3.2)		54 (4.4)	►	24 (4.0)	►	60 (4.3)	◄	27 (4.1)	
Norway (Grade 9)[1]	89 (3.0)		12 (2.5)	▽	89 (3.1)	◄	35 (4.6)		42 (4.6)		95 (1.8)	◄
Poland	96 (1.8)		9 (2.8)	▽	77 (3.8)	◄	25 (3.8)	►	26 (4.0)	►	6 (2.1)	►
Russian Federation[2]	89 (2.3)	▽	11 (2.3)	▽	72 (3.0)	△	25 (3.3)	►	39 (3.0)	▽	51 (4.1)	◄
Slovak Republic	87 (3.2)	▽	15 (3.3)		63 (4.2)		13 (2.6)	►	57 (4.2)	◄	24 (3.8)	►
Slovenia	98 (0.7)	△	11 (2.8)	▽	66 (3.6)		73 (3.7)	◄	78 (2.9)	◄	6 (1.7)	►
Thailand[2]	99 (0.7)	△	47 (4.8)	◄	50 (5.3)	►	40 (4.4)		51 (4.6)		46 (4.4)	◄
Turkey	99 (0.9)	△	4 (1.8)	►	24 (4.0)	►	11 (2.6)	►	27 (4.1)	►	2 (1.2)	►
ICILS 2013 average	94 (0.5)		19 (0.8)		65 (1.0)		37 (1.0)		46 (1.0)		35 (0.8)	
Countries not meeting sample requirements												
Denmark	98 (0.2)		45 (5.5)		96 (2.1)		97 (0.7)		74 (5.1)		90 (3.1)	
Hong Kong SAR	99 (0.7)		36 (5.4)		95 (2.3)		90 (3.3)		52 (5.6)		65 (5.3)	
Netherlands	98 (1.6)		35 (6.6)		90 (4.1)		92 (2.7)		60 (6.6)		70 (6.8)	
Switzerland	97 (2.8)		27 (8.0)		100 (0.3)		49 (7.1)		36 (8.1)		12 (4.8)	
Benchmarking participants												
Newfoundland and Labrador, Canada	95 (0.2)		77 (0.2)		94 (0.2)		44 (0.3)		82 (0.2)		38 (0.3)	
Ontario, Canada	97 (1.5)		64 (4.5)		96 (2.1)		70 (5.2)		79 (4.1)		46 (5.6)	
Benchmarking participant not meeting sample requirements												
City of Buenos Aires, Argentina	84 (7.9)		16 (8.2)		64 (10.0)		61 (9.8)		63 (10.5)		9 (5.0)	

Notes:

() Standard errors appear in parentheses. Because some results are rounded to the nearest whole number, some totals may appear inconsistent.

† Met guidelines for sampling participation rates only after replacement schools were included.

1 National Desired Population does not correspond to International Desired Population.

2 Country surveyed the same cohort of students but at the beginning of the next school year.

▲ More than 10 percentage points above ICILS 2013 average

△ Significantly above ICILS 2013 average

▽ Significantly below ICILS 2013 average

▼ More than 10 percentage points below ICILS 2013 average

64 percent in both Australia and Ontario (Canada) and 77 percent in Newfoundland and Labrador (Canada).

We can reasonably expect that the more access students have to computers during school time, the greater their engagement and ability to participate in ICT learning activities will be. Trends observed from past crossnational surveys indicate that the number of students per available computer is decreasing over time (Law et al., 2008; Martin, Mullis, Gonzalez, Smith, & Kelly, 1999; Pelgrum & Anderson, 2001). The European Commission (2013) reported a tendency toward lower ratios for older students. In Chapter 2 of this current report, we noted that several of the ICILS countries have a national policy of establishing a 1:1 ratio between students and computers.

ICT-coordinators at the ICILS schools provided information about the numbers of computers at school available to students, while school principals reported the number of students enrolled at their school. We used these data to compute ratios of the number of students per computer. Low ratios indicate a well-resourced school; high numbers indicate a school with only a few computers available to its students.

Table 6.4 displays the average student–computer ratios for each participating country. It also provides the findings from our comparison of these ratios across rural schools (i.e., schools in communities with fewer than 15,000 inhabitants) and urban schools (communities with 15,000 or more inhabitants).[1]

The table shows considerable crossnational differences in the ratios. On average across all countries, every 18 students had access to one computer. However, the ratios ranged from two or three students per computer in Norway and Australia respectively to 80 students per computer in Turkey. Schools in rural areas in Croatia, the Czech Republic, Korea, Lithuania, Newfoundland and Labrador, Ontario, Poland, the Russian Federation, the Slovak Republic, and Turkey had significantly lower student–computer ratios (indicating greater access) than those in urban areas. The reason for this difference might be because of the smaller school and class sizes in rural areas or because of policies directed toward increasing ICT investment in rural schools.

ICT-coordinators at ICILS schools provided information on where computers used for Grade 8 teaching and learning were located in these schools. Table 6.5 shows the national percentages of students at schools where computers were available in the various locations specified in the ICT-coordinator questionnaire.

Typically, computers were located in computer laboratories. On average, 95 percent of students were enrolled at schools where this was the case. The national percentages ranged from 76 percent in Norway to 100 percent in a large number of countries. Majorities of students (64% on average) also tended to be studying at schools where computers were located in the library. Here, the national percentages ranged from 28 percent in the Czech Republic to 94 percent in Lithuania. On average, about one third of students were attending schools with class sets of computers that could be moved across classrooms (34% on average, with national percentages ranging from 6% in Croatia to 68% in Norway). Almost the same proportion of students (33% on average) could be found in schools where their classrooms had computers. The national percentages ranged from 12 percent in Chile to 81 percent in Slovenia.

---

1 Information on community size was typically provided by school principals.

Table 6.4: National student–computer ratios at schools by school location

Country	School Location Differences for Student—Computer Ratios			
	All students	Urban	Rural	Differences (urban - rural)*
Australia	3 (0.3)	2 (0.3)	3 (1.0)	-1 (1.0)
Chile	22 (4.7)	18 (1.2)	34 (22.0)	-16 (22.0)
Croatia	26 (0.8)	30 (1.5)	23 (1.3)	**7** (2.3)
Czech Republic	10 (0.3)	10 (0.5)	9 (0.5)	2 (0.7)
Germany[†]	11 (0.8)	11 (0.7)	12 (1.9)	0 (2.1)
Korea, Republic of	20 (2.3)	21 (2.5)	7 (1.2)	**14** (2.7)
Lithuania	13 (0.7)	16 (1.2)	10 (0.7)	**6** (1.4)
Norway (Grade 9)[1]	2 (0.1)	3 (0.1)	2 (0.2)	0 (0.2)
Poland	10 (0.5)	13 (0.8)	8 (0.4)	**5** (0.9)
Russian Federation[2]	17 (1.0)	19 (1.4)	13 (1.3)	**6** (1.8)
Slovak Republic	9 (0.5)	11 (0.7)	8 (0.5)	**3** (0.9)
Slovenia	15 (0.5)	16 (0.9)	15 (0.6)	2 (1.2)
Thailand[2]	14 (0.9)	15 (1.4)	13 (1.0)	2 (1.7)
Turkey	80 (16.0)	97 (22.5)	41 (9.1)	**56** (24.4)
ICILS 2013 average	18 (1.2)	20 (1.6)	14 (1.7)	**6** (2.4)
Countries not meeting sample requirements				
Denmark	4 (0.4)	5 (0.6)	4 (0.6)	0 (0.8)
Hong Kong SAR	8 (0.8)	8 (0.8)		
Netherlands	5 (0.8)	5 (1.0)	5 (0.7)	0 (1.2)
Switzerland	7 (0.6)	6 (0.7)	7 (0.8)	-1 (1.0)
Benchmarking participants				
Newfoundland and Labrador, Canada	6 (0.0)	6 (0.0)	5 (0.0)	**2** (0.0)
Ontario, Canada	6 (0.3)	7 (0.4)	5 (0.5)	**2** (0.6)
Benchmarking participant not meeting sample requirements				
City of Buenos Aires, Argentina	33 (9.4)	33 (9.4)		

Notes:

* Statistically significant ($p < .05$) coefficients in **bold**.

() Standard errors appear in parentheses. Because some results are rounded to the nearest whole number, some totals may appear inconsistent.

[†] Met guidelines for sampling participation rates only after replacement schools were included.

[1] National Desired Population does not correspond to International Desired Population.

[2] Country surveyed the same cohort of students but at the beginning of the next school year.

Minorities of students were studying at schools where computers resided in other places, such as cafeterias, auditoriums, and study areas (17% on average) and/or where students brought their own computers to class (18% on average). However, there were notable differences across countries with regard to use of the latter. While in some countries about half of the students were enrolled at a school where they could bring their own computers to class, in many countries the corresponding national averages were below 10 percent.

Table 6.5: National percentages of students at schools with school computers at different locations

Country	In Most Classrooms (80% or More)	In Computer Laboratories	As Class Sets of Computers That Can Be Moved Between Classrooms	In the Library	In Other Places Accessible to Students (e.g., Cafeteria, Auditorium, Study Area)	Student Computers (School-Provided or Student-Owned) Brought by Students to Class
Australia	20 (2.6) ▲	85 (2.5) ▽	58 (3.7) ▲	90 (2.1) ▲	24 (3.0) △	53 (3.9) ▲
Chile	12 (3.0) ▲	98 (0.8) △	47 (4.1) ▲	64 (4.1) ▲	6 (1.9) ▲	20 (3.3)
Croatia	24 (3.2) ▽	100 (0.0) △	6 (1.7) ▼	56 (3.6) ▽	7 (2.4) ▲	7 (2.3) ▼
Czech Republic	27 (3.7) ▲	100 (0.0) △	12 (2.5) ▼	28 (3.4) ▲	23 (3.0)	7 (1.7) ▼
Germany†	17 (3.4) ▲	100 (0.0) △	44 (4.6) ▲	44 (4.3) ▲	23 (4.1)	18 (3.4)
Korea, Republic of	40 (3.3) △	87 (2.5) ▽	41 (4.2) ▲	80 (3.4) ▲	21 (3.2)	4 (1.6) ▼
Lithuania	55 (4.4) ▲	98 (1.4) △	22 (3.7) ▼	94 (1.8) ▲	12 (2.7)	11 (2.5) ▽
Norway (Grade 9)[1]	39 (4.7) ▽	76 (3.6) ▼	68 (4.3) ▲	56 (4.4) ▲	26 (4.3)	48 (4.3) ▲
Poland	24 (3.6) ▽	100 (0.0) △	33 (3.8)	87 (3.0) ▲	20 (3.4)	6 (1.9) ▲
Russian Federation[2]	56 (4.2) ▲	99 (0.5) △	42 (3.5) △	71 (3.5)	24 (2.6) △	15 (2.5)
Slovak Republic	14 (3.0) ▲	100 (0.0) △	20 (3.7) ▲	30 (3.5) ▲	8 (2.3) ▽	6 (2.0) ▲
Slovenia	81 (3.7) ▲	100 (0.0) △	43 (3.9) △	82 (3.1) ▲	11 (2.1) ▽	9 (2.5) ▽
Thailand[2]	13 (3.5) ▲	100 (0.0) △	23 (4.5) ▲	87 (3.0) ▲	20 (3.9) ▽	37 (4.7) ▲
Turkey	37 (4.4)	84 (2.7) ▼	23 (4.0) ▲	33 (4.2) ▲	16 (3.4)	10 (2.8) ▽
ICILS 2013 average	33 (1.0)	95 (0.4)	34 (1.0)	64 (0.9)	17 (0.8)	18 (0.8)
Countries not meeting sample requirements						
Denmark	26 (6.3)	71 (5.4)	72 (6.2)	62 (5.4)	34 (6.1)	83 (3.6)
Hong Kong SAR	84 (4.3)	100 (0.0)	32 (4.8)	93 (2.7)	34 (5.3)	11 (3.4)
Netherlands	38 (6.1)	89 (4.1)	39 (7.2)	65 (6.4)	54 (6.3)	33 (6.9)
Switzerland	43 (8.0)	98 (2.3)	44 (7.5)	43 (6.0)	18 (6.0)	16 (6.1)
Benchmarking participants						
Newfoundland and Labrador, Canada	51 (0.3)	100 (0.0)	56 (0.3)	91 (0.1)	12 (0.2)	52 (0.3)
Ontario, Canada	60 (4.8)	75 (3.4)	64 (5.0)	82 (3.5)	8 (2.9)	56 (5.2)
Benchmarking participant not meeting sample requirements						
City of Buenos Aires, Argentina	15 (7.3)	80 (8.9)	22 (8.1)	47 (9.6)	9 (4.7)	51 (6.4)

▲ More than 10 percentage points above ICILS 2013 average
△ Significantly above ICILS 2013 average
▽ Significantly below ICILS 2013 average
▼ More than 10 percentage points below ICILS 2013 average

Notes:
() Standard errors appear in parentheses. Because some results are rounded to the nearest whole number, some totals may appear inconsistent.
† Met guidelines for sampling participation rates only after replacement schools were included.
[1] National Desired Population does not correspond to International Desired Population.
[2] Country surveyed the same cohort of students but at the beginning of the next school year.

School policies and practices for using ICT

The ICILS principal questionnaire contained a question that asked principals if their schools or school systems had procedures in place regarding the following aspects of ICT use:

- Setting up security measures to prevent unauthorized system access or entry;
- Restricting the number of hours students are allowed to sit at a computer;
- Giving students access to school computers outside class hours (but during school hours);
- Giving students access to school computers outside school hours;
- Honoring intellectual property rights (e.g., software copyright);
- Prohibiting access to inappropriate material (e.g., pornography, violence);
- Playing games on school computers;
- Giving the local community (parents and/or others) access to school computers and/or the internet; and
- Providing students with their own laptop computers and/or other mobile learning devices for use at school and at home.

The percentages of students who were attending schools where these procedures were implemented are presented in Table 6.6. Setting up security measures at school was found almost universally. On average, 94 percent of students were enrolled in schools with security measures in place. The national percentages ranged from 85 percent to 100 percent.

Approximately half of the students across countries were enrolled at schools with restrictions on the amount of time that students could sit at a computer. National percentages of students ranged from 18 percent in Australia to 92 percent in the Russian Federation.

On average, four out of five students were studying at schools that had a policy in relation to access to computers outside class time (but still during school time). National percentages ranged from 68 percent in Ontario to 93 percent in Thailand. However, there was wide variation across countries with respect to the presence of this policy. While approximately half of all students internationally were at schools with such a policy, the national percentages ranged from 27 percent in Poland to 86 percent in the Russian Federation.

Procedures at schools to ensure compliance with intellectual property rights were evident for 89 percent of students on average across the ICILS countries, with the national average percentages ranging from 77 percent in Chile and Poland to 96 percent in the Czech Republic. The overwhelming majority of students (on average 97%) across all countries were in schools that had procedures regarding access to inappropriate material. The national percentages ranged from 90 percent in Lithuania to 100 percent in Newfoundland and Labrador, Ontario, and the Russian Federation.

The majority of students in all countries were at schools that had protocols regarding playing games on school computers (68%). The exceptions were the Russian Federation and Turkey (39% and 34% respectively). The highest percentage was reported in Australia (90%).

Table 6.6: National percentages of students at schools with procedures regarding different aspects of ICT

Country	Setting Up Security Measures To Prevent Unauthorized System Access or Entry	Restricting the Number of Hours Students Are Allowed To Sit at a Computer	Student Access to School Computers Outside Class Hours (but During School Hours)	Student Access to School Computers Outside School Hours	Honoring of Intellectual Property Rights (e.g., Software Copyright)	Prohibiting Access to Inappropriate Material (e.g., Pornography, Violence)	Playing Games on School Computers	Giving the Local Community (Parents and/or Others) Access to School Computers and/or the Internet	Providing Students With Their Own Laptop Computers and/or Other Mobile Learning Devices for Use at School and at Home
Australia	100 (0.0) △	18 (3.1) ▼	77 (3.3)	63 (3.6) ▲	95 (1.5) △	99 (0.6) △	90 (2.7) ▲	35 (3.7) ▼	80 (3.2) ▲
Chile	91 (2.6)	67 (4.0) ▲	83 (2.7)	47 (4.8)	77 (3.9) ▼	99 (1.2)	64 (4.2)	47 (4.4)	21 (3.7) ▼
Croatia	92 (2.6)	50 (4.2)	71 (4.1) ▽	55 (4.1)	90 (2.5)	98 (1.0)	71 (3.3)	24 (3.5) ▼	20 (3.6) ▼
Czech Republic	98 (1.0) △	42 (3.9) ▼	71 (3.5) ▽	52 (3.7) ▼	96 (1.5) △	99 (0.4) △	79 (3.1) ▲	29 (3.7) ▼	18 (2.8) ▼
Germany†	99 (0.6) △	42 (4.6) ▼	76 (4.2)	32 (4.7) ▼	92 (2.3)	97 (1.7)	69 (4.5)	47 (4.5)	26 (3.7) ▽
Korea, Republic of	97 (1.4)	64 (3.9) ▲	71 (3.3) ▽	66 (4.0) ▲	95 (1.7) △	96 (1.4)	66 (3.6)	72 (3.7) ▲	33 (3.7)
Lithuania	88 (2.9)	57 (4.3)	90 (2.6) ▽	28 (3.9) ▼	87 (2.3)	90 (2.5) ▽	70 (4.1)	72 (4.1) ▲	13 (2.9) ▼
Norway (Grade 9)[1]	100 (0.0) △	32 (5.0) ▼	81 (4.4)	67 (4.8) ▲	88 (3.4)	93 (2.6)	81 (4.1) ▲	38 (4.8)	76 (4.3) ▲
Poland	93 (2.4)	36 (3.8) ▼	76 (3.8)	27 (4.2) ▼	77 (3.8) ▼	97 (1.5)	68 (4.2)	33 (3.6) ▼	7 (2.2) ▼
Russian Federation[2]	99 (0.9) △	92 (2.1) ▲	89 (2.5) △	86 (2.3) ▲	92 (1.8)	100 (0.0) △	39 (3.4) ▼	33 (2.9) ▼	15 (2.8) ▼
Slovak Republic	98 (1.5) △	51 (4.1)	86 (3.3)	27 (4.1) ▼	91 (2.4)	98 (1.4)	75 (3.7)	45 (4.8)	27 (4.1)
Slovenia	92 (1.7)	39 (4.4) ▼	84 (3.2)	54 (4.4)	85 (2.8)	94 (1.7)	74 (3.1)	52 (4.0)	22 (4.0) ▲
Thailand[2]	87 (3.1) ▽	71 (4.3) ▲	93 (2.7) ▲	68 (3.9) ▲	92 (2.9)	97 (1.5)	74 (4.9)	72 (4.2) ▲	61 (4.6) ▲
Turkey	85 (2.9) ▽	71 (4.1) ▲	75 (3.2)	51 (4.0)	85 (3.0)	94 (2.0)	34 (4.2) ▼	58 (4.0) ▲	71 (4.1) ▲
ICILS 2013 average	94 (0.5)	52 (1.1)	80 (0.9)	52 (1.1)	89 (0.7)	97 (0.4)	68 (1.0)	47 (1.1)	35 (1.0)
Countries not meeting sample requirements									
Denmark	86 (4.3)	4 (2.1)	69 (5.7)	47 (5.9)	86 (5.1)	56 (5.4)	52 (6.4)	36 (5.1)	79 (4.9)
Hong Kong SAR	100 (0.0)	33 (5.8)	87 (3.7)	72 (4.5)	100 (0.0)	100 (0.0)	77 (4.4)	39 (5.4)	43 (5.6)
Netherlands	97 (2.7)	5 (1.7)	70 (5.6)	46 (6.0)	87 (4.3)	95 (3.2)	85 (4.7)	65 (5.4)	55 (5.6)
Switzerland	100 (0.2)	25 (5.2)	72 (6.4)	33 (5.8)	86 (5.1)	97 (2.0)	71 (6.5)	48 (8.2)	32 (6.9)
Benchmarking participants									
Newfoundland and Labrador, Canada	99 (0.0)	36 (0.2)	73 (0.3)	52 (0.3)	84 (0.3)	100 (0.0)	87 (0.2)	25 (0.2)	29 (0.3)
Ontario, Canada	97 (2.0)	29 (4.8)	68 (4.6)	41 (5.3)	95 (1.6)	100 (0.0)	82 (4.4)	41 (5.5)	69 (4.6)
Benchmarking participant not meeting sample requirements									
City of Buenos Aires, Argentina	84 (6.7)	36 (8.8)	67 (7.7)	29 (8.6)	76 (7.4)	93 (4.8)	55 (6.4)	28 (7.7)	49 (6.9)

▲ More than 10 percentage points above ICILS 2013 average
△ Significantly above ICILS 2013 average
▽ Significantly below ICILS 2013 average
▼ More than 10 percentage points below ICILS 2013 average

Notes:
() Standard errors appear in parentheses. Because some results are rounded to the nearest whole number, some totals may appear inconsistent.
† Met guidelines for sampling participation rates only after replacement schools were included.
1 National Desired Population does not correspond to International Desired Population.
2 Country surveyed the same cohort of students but at the beginning of the next school year.

On average, just under half of all ICILS students were attending schools where procedures were in place for giving people in the local community access to school computers. National percentages ranged from 24 percent in Croatia to 72 percent in Korea, Lithuania, and Thailand.

On average across countries, 35 percent of students were in schools where they had their own laptop and/or other mobile learning devices for use at school and at home. There was a large degree of crosscountry variation in this provision, with national percentages ranging from seven percent in Poland to 80 percent in Australia.

Principals were asked to rate the level of priority ("high priority," "medium priority," "low priority," "not a priority") in their school for the following methods of facilitating ICT use in teaching and learning:

- Increasing the numbers of computers per student in the school;
- Increasing the number of computers connected to the internet;
- Increasing the bandwidth of internet access for the computers connected to the internet;
- Increasing the range of digital learning resources;
- Establishing or enhancing an online learning support platform;
- Providing for participation in professional development on pedagogical use of ICT;
- Increasing the availability of qualified technical personnel to support the use of ICT;
- Providing teachers with incentives to integrate ICT use in their teaching;
- Providing more time for teachers to prepare lessons in which ICT is used; and
- Increasing the professional learning resources for teachers on using ICT.

Table 6.7 shows the percentages of students in schools where principals gave "medium" or "high" priority ratings to these ways of facilitating ICT use in teaching and learning. Principals tended to accord medium to high priority to increasing the computers per student ratio. On average across the countries, 88 percent of students were enrolled in schools where principals recorded these levels of priority. The national percentages ranged from 64 percent to 99 percent.

Principals gave similar ratings to increasing the number of computers connected to the internet and increasing the internet bandwidth of internet-connected computers. Crossnationally, an average of 89 percent of students were enrolled at schools where principals accorded medium or high priority to these ways of facilitating ICT use. National percentages ranged from 66 percent (Germany) to 99 percent (Slovak Republic) for the former and 71 percent (Germany) to 99 percent (Slovenia) for the latter. Principals considered a range of digital learning resources to be of medium to high priority on average at schools attended by 93 percent of students, with national percentages ranging from 82 percent in Germany to 100 percent in Slovenia.

Establishing or enhancing an online learning support platform was a medium to high priority at schools representing 79 percent of students on average across participating countries (with national percentages ranging from 54% in Germany to 97% in Slovenia). All countries had provision for participation in professional development on using ICT for pedagogical purposes. The schools where this was the case typically represented between 88 and 100 percent of students (with the exception of Germany, where this situation represented only 63% of students). The ICILS 2013 average was 91 percent.

Table 6.7: National percentages of students at schools where medium or high priority is given to different ways of facilitating ICT use in teaching and learning

Country	Increasing the Numbers of Computers per Student in the School	Increasing the Number of Computers Connected to the Internet	Increasing the Bandwidth of Internet Access for the Computers Connected to the Internet	Increasing the Range of Digital Learning Resources	Establishing or Enhancing an Online Learning Support Platform	Providing for Participation in Professional Development on Pedagogical Use of ICT	Increasing the Availability of Qualified Technical Personnel to Support the Use of ICT	Providing Teachers With Incentives to Integrate ICT Use in Their Teaching	Providing More Time for Teachers to Prepare Lessons in Which ICT Is Used	Increasing the Professional Learning Resources for Teachers in the Use of ICT
Australia	81 (2.8) ▽	79 (3.0) ▼	84 (2.6) ▽	93 (2.0)	90 (2.1) ▲	97 (1.2) △	80 (2.8)	68 (3.6) ▼	54 (4.0) ▼	90 (2.2)
Chile	91 (2.5)	94 (1.9) △	95 (1.7) △	95 (1.9)	86 (2.8) △	93 (2.3)	81 (3.6)	56 (4.0) ▼	70 (3.5) ▽	90 (2.6)
Croatia	95 (1.8) △	98 (0.9) △	96 (1.5) △	90 (2.4)	74 (3.5)	88 (3.0)	87 (3.1)	99 (0.9) ▲	87 (2.6) △	93 (2.0)
Czech Republic	83 (3.0)	87 (2.7)	87 (2.9)	92 (2.1)	65 (4.0) ▼	92 (2.0)	80 (3.2)	96 (1.4) ▲	70 (3.3) ▽	96 (1.4) △
Germany†	64 (4.7) ▼	66 (4.7) ▼	71 (4.8) ▼	82 (4.0) ▼	54 (4.5) ▼	63 (4.5) ▼	62 (4.6) ▼	56 (4.6) ▼	45 (4.9) ▼	68 (3.9) ▼
Korea, Republic of	65 (3.6) ▼	71 (3.5) ▼	75 (3.8) ▼	89 (2.7)	94 (2.0) ▲	89 (2.5)	84 (3.1)	90 (2.6)	87 (2.7) △	96 (1.7) △
Lithuania	94 (2.2) △	90 (2.3)	89 (2.8)	93 (1.9)	55 (4.5) ▼	91 (2.3)	82 (3.4)	98 (1.2) ▲	89 (2.5) ▲	88 (2.8)
Norway (Grade 9)¹	91 (2.8)	89 (3.0)	86 (3.5)	96 (2.0)	86 (3.1) △	94 (2.5)	77 (4.5)	71 (4.2) ▼	60 (4.8) ▼	76 (4.0) ▼
Poland	96 (1.7) △	95 (1.6) △	92 (2.6)	84 (3.7) ▽	79 (4.0)	93 (2.5)	84 (3.1)	85 (3.5)	79 (4.1)	94 (2.1)
Russian Federation²	94 (1.7) △	95 (1.6) △	97 (1.3) △	96 (1.5)	72 (3.0) ▽	97 (1.0) △	95 (1.6) ▲	93 (2.0) △	75 (3.4)	93 (1.7)
Slovak Republic	97 (1.0) △	99 (0.7) △	97 (1.3) △	98 (1.1) △	76 (3.7)	97 (1.3) △	93 (2.1) △	99 (0.8) ▲	88 (2.8) ▲	96 (1.6) △
Slovenia	94 (2.7) △	95 (2.4) △	99 (0.3) △	100 (0.0) △	97 (1.8) ▲	100 (0.0) △	93 (2.3) △	99 (0.0) ▲	91 (2.7) ▲	98 (0.7) △
Thailand²	99 (0.9) △	98 (0.9) △	97 (1.5) △	96 (1.7)	96 (1.4) ▲	95 (1.7) △	92 (2.7) △	94 (2.7) △	94 (2.6) ▲	94 (2.5)
Turkey	83 (3.3)	94 (2.0)	88 (2.7)	93 (2.2)	82 (3.4)	91 (2.6)	84 (3.3)	98 (1.1) ▲	96 (1.6) ▲	97 (1.4) △
ICILS 2013 average	88 (0.7)	89 (0.7)	89 (0.7)	93 (0.6)	79 (0.9)	91 (0.6)	84 (0.9)	86 (0.7)	78 (0.9)	91 (0.6)
Countries not meeting sample requirements										
Denmark	90 (3.7)	87 (4.6)	87 (4.1)	97 (1.9)	81 (4.2)	91 (3.4)	82 (4.5)	96 (2.4)	28 (5.2)	93 (3.0)
Hong Kong SAR	50 (4.3)	74 (5.1)	84 (3.9)	83 (4.3)	87 (3.3)	79 (3.7)	68 (5.0)	69 (4.8)	55 (6.0)	80 (4.1)
Netherlands	74 (4.7)	76 (5.0)	81 (4.6)	93 (3.5)	82 (4.4)	83 (4.1)	50 (5.8)	28 (4.7)	26 (5.2)	77 (4.6)
Switzerland	61 (6.8)	63 (8.2)	71 (6.6)	74 (5.6)	66 (7.3)	57 (7.5)	46 (7.7)	51 (7.3)	24 (5.9)	39 (7.1)
Benchmarking participants										
Newfoundland and Labrador, Canada	97 (0.1)	91 (0.1)	92 (0.1)	96 (0.1)	88 (0.3)	95 (0.1)	84 (0.3)	71 (0.3)	80 (0.3)	95 (0.1)
Ontario, Canada	90 (3.0)	84 (3.9)	77 (3.8)	93 (2.7)	68 (4.0)	86 (3.4)	76 (4.2)	67 (4.7)	55 (5.2)	84 (3.4)
Benchmarking participant not meeting sample requirements										
City of Buenos Aires, Argentina	92 (5.1)	94 (4.8)	86 (5.3)	92 (4.6)	84 (6.4)	93 (4.5)	87 (5.5)	95 (4.0)	76 (6.2)	88 (5.5)

Notes:
() Standard errors appear in parentheses. Because some results are rounded to the nearest whole number, some totals may appear inconsistent.
† Met guidelines for sampling participation rates only after replacement schools were included.
¹ National Desired Population does not correspond to International Desired Population.
² Country surveyed the same cohort of students but at the beginning of the next school year.

▲ More than 10 percentage points above ICILS 2013 average
△ Significantly above ICILS 2013 average
▽ Significantly below ICILS 2013 average
▼ More than 10 percentage points below ICILS 2013 average

Increasing the availability of qualified technical personnel to support the use of ICT was a medium to high priority for schools representing 84 percent of students on average (with the range extending from 62 percent in Germany to 95 percent in the Russian Federation).

On average across the ICILS countries, 86 percent of students were in schools where principals accorded medium or high priority to providing teachers with incentives to integrate ICT use in their teaching (with national percentages ranging from 56% in Chile and Germany to 99% in Croatia, the Slovak Republic, and Slovenia). Seventy-eight percent of students were enrolled at schools where principals gave priority to providing teachers with more time to prepare lessons encompassing ICT use. The national percentages ranged from 45 percent in Germany to 96 percent in Turkey.

More than 90 percent of students (on average) were attending schools that placed a medium or high priority on offering their teachers more professional learning resources focused on ICT. The national percentages ranged from 68 percent in Germany to 98 percent in Slovenia.

Perceptions of school ICT learning environments

Perspectives from SITES Module 2 (Kozma, 2003b) and the School Net 2013 Survey (European Commission, 2013) suggest that teachers use ICT more frequently when their school culture supports technology in particular and innovation in general. ICILS asked teachers to rate their agreement or disagreement ("strongly agree," "agree," "disagree," "strongly disagree") with the following five statements about aspects of their school's approach to using ICT.

- I work together with other teachers on improving the use of ICT in classroom teaching.
- There is a common set of rules in the school about how ICT should be used in classrooms.
- I systematically collaborate with colleagues to develop ICT-based lessons based on the curriculum.
- I observe how other teachers use ICT in teaching.
- There is a common set of expectations in the school about what students will learn about ICT.

Table 6.8 records the percentages of agreement ("strongly agree" or "agree") with each of these statements. The statement "I work together with other teachers on improving the use of ICT in classroom teaching" attracted an average level of agreement of 71 percent. The lowest level of agreement was found in Korea (45%) and the highest in Thailand (91%). The item "I observe how other teachers use ICT in teaching" attracted an average agreement of 69 percent, with the range extending from 45 percent in the Czech Republic to 92 percent in the Russian Federation. The statement that "There is a common set of expectations in the school about what students will learn about ICT" attracted agreement from schools representing 63 percent of students on average, with agreement ranging from 35 percent in Slovenia to 92 percent in Thailand.

The two items that attracted the least agreement were "There is a common set of rules in the school about how ICT should be used in classrooms" (on average 58%, with national percentages ranging from 31% in Slovenia to 92% in Thailand), and "I

Table 6.8: National percentages of teachers who agree with statements regarding collaborative use of ICT in teaching and learning

Country	I Work Together with Other Teachers on Improving the Use of ICT in Classroom Teaching		There Is a Common Set of Rules in the School About How ICT Should Be Used in Classrooms		I Systematically Collaborate With Colleagues To Develop ICT-Based Lessons Based on the Curriculum		I Observe How Other Teachers Use ICT in Teaching		There is a Common Set of Expectations in the School about What Students Will Learn about ICT	
Australia	72	(1.7)	58	(1.8)	48	(2.1) ▽	64	(2.4) ▽	48	(1.9) ▼
Chile	52	(2.0) ▼	49	(2.0) ▽	44	(2.1) ▽	49	(2.0) ▼	56	(2.3) ▽
Croatia	56	(1.4) ▼	34	(1.2) ▼	31	(1.1) ▼	53	(1.3) ▼	39	(1.5) ▼
Czech Republic	69	(1.4)	68	(1.5) △	36	(1.3) ▼	45	(2.0) ▼	73	(1.4) △
Korea, Republic of	45	(2.3) ▼	59	(2.3)	44	(1.9) ▽	71	(1.0) △	48	(1.4) ▼
Lithuania	83	(1.0) ▲	49	(1.4) ▽	62	(1.2) △	74	(1.1) △	71	(1.4) △
Poland	69	(1.3)	45	(1.9) ▼	41	(1.8) ▼	69	(1.6)	62	(1.6)
Russian Federation[1]	81	(1.3) ▲	81	(1.2) ▲	74	(1.9) ▲	92	(0.9) ▲	80	(1.3) ▲
Slovak Republic	80	(1.1) △	73	(1.5) ▲	60	(1.6) △	78	(1.1) △	80	(1.4) ▲
Slovenia	67	(1.2) ▽	31	(1.1) ▼	37	(1.4) ▼	61	(1.4) ▽	35	(1.6) ▼
Thailand	91	(1.6) ▲	92	(1.6) ▲	91	(1.7) ▲	89	(1.9) ▲	92	(1.6) ▲
Turkey	82	(1.4) ▲	60	(2.6)	71	(1.7) ▲	77	(1.5) △	71	(1.9) △
ICILS 2013 average	71	(0.4)	58	(0.5)	53	(0.5)	69	(0.5)	63	(0.5)
Countries not meeting sample requirements										
Denmark	60	(2.4)	35	(2.1)	27	(1.7)	60	(2.0)	48	(2.9)
Germany	30	(1.6)	56	(2.3)	12	(1.4)	41	(2.8)	54	(2.0)
Hong Kong SAR	57	(1.5)	57	(1.7)	39	(1.6)	61	(1.9)	54	(1.6)
Netherlands	55	(2.2)	41	(2.2)	26	(1.8)	47	(2.2)	25	(2.0)
Norway (Grade 9)	52	(2.1)	48	(2.7)	21	(1.8)	52	(2.4)	47	(2.6)
Benchmarking participant										
Newfoundland and Labrador, Canada	67	(2.3)	47	(2.6)	36	(1.9)	66	(2.8)	38	(2.8)
Benchmarking participant not meeting sample requirements										
Ontario, Canada	67	(2.8)	54	(2.8)	46	(4.0)	69	(2.4)	38	(3.3)

Notes:
() Standard errors appear in parentheses. Because some results are rounded to the nearest whole number, some totals may appear inconsistent.
[1] Country surveyed teachers retrospectively to the previous school year when they were teaching the target grade.

▲ More than 10 percentage points above ICILS 2013 average
△ Significantly above ICILS 2013 average
▽ Significantly below ICILS 2013 average
▼ More than 10 percentage points below ICILS 2013 average

systematically collaborate with colleagues to develop ICT-based lessons based on the curriculum." The international average for this second statement was 53 percent, and the national percentages ranged from 31 percent in Croatia to 91 percent in Thailand.

We used the above five items to form a scale relating to collaborative approaches to using ICT. With a coefficient alpha of 0.80, the scale had sound reliability.[2] Table 6.9 records the national average scores on this scale as well as for teachers 40 years of age or more and those younger than 40 years.

National average scores on the *ICT collaboration scale* ranged from 45 scale score points (Croatia) to 58 such points (Thailand). The Russian Federation (55 points) and Turkey (53) had notably high scores, whereas Slovenia (46) and Chile (47) had notably low

---

2 We used the Rasch partial credit model to construct the scale and standardized the item response theory (IRT) scores to have an ICILS 2013 average score of 50 points and a standard deviation of 10 points. This metric was used for most of the questionnaire-based scales derived from the ICILS data. The standard deviation of 10 points is appropriate for the numbers of items in most of these scales. However, we used a standard deviation of 100 for the CIL achievement scale because it had many more items than the questionnaires had.

Table 6.9: National averages for teachers collaborating when using ICT overall and by age group

Country	Collaboration Among Teachers When Using ICT by Age Group				Score Distribution by Age Group
	All teachers	Under 40	40 and over	Differences (40 and over – under 40)*	
Australia	49 (0.5) ▽	50 (0.3)	49 (0.7)	-1 (0.7)	
Chile	47 (0.5) ▶	46 (0.6)	48 (0.6)	2 (0.7)	
Croatia	45 (0.2) ▶	43 (0.4)	46 (0.3)	2 (0.6)	
Czech Republic	49 (0.4)	47 (0.5)	51 (0.5)	3 (0.5)	
Korea, Republic of	47 (0.3) ▽	47 (0.4)	48 (0.3)	1 (0.4)	
Lithuania	51 (0.3) △	50 (0.5)	52 (0.3)	2 (0.5)	
Poland	48 (0.3) ▽	47 (0.5)	49 (0.4)	2 (0.7)	
Russian Federation[1]	55 (0.3) ◀	54 (0.4)	55 (0.4)	1 (0.5)	
Slovak Republic	52 (0.3) △	52 (0.4)	53 (0.3)	1 (0.4)	
Slovenia	46 (0.3) ▶	45 (0.5)	46 (0.3)	2 (0.4)	
Thailand	58 (0.9) ◀	59 (1.2)	57 (0.8)	-2 (1.1)	
Turkey	53 (0.6) ◀	53 (0.7)	55 (0.9)	2 (1.0)	
ICILS 2013 average	50 (0.1)	49 (0.2)	51 (0.1)	1 (0.2)	
Countries not meeting sample requirements					
Denmark	45 (0.4)	45 (0.7)	46 (0.4)	1 (0.6)	
Germany	41 (0.5)	40 (0.5)	41 (0.6)	1 (0.7)	
Hong Kong SAR	47 (0.3)	47 (0.4)	47 (0.4)	-1 (0.6)	
Netherlands	44 (0.4)	44 (0.4)	44 (0.5)	-1 (0.6)	
Norway (Grade 9)	45 (0.3)	44 (0.5)	45 (0.4)	1 (0.5)	
Benchmarking participant					
Newfoundland and Labrador, Canada	47 (0.4)	47 (0.7)	47 (0.5)	0 (0.9)	
Benchmarking participant not meeting sample requirements					
Ontario, Canada	49 (0.8)	49 (1.0)	48 (1.5)	-1 (1.9)	

◀ More than three score points above ICILS 2013 average
△ Significantly above ICILS 2013 average
▽ Significantly below ICILS 2013 average
▶ More than three score points below ICILS 2013 average

■ Under 40 average score +/− confidence interval
■ Over 40 average score +/− confidence interval

On average, teachers with a score in the range indicated by this color have more than a 50% probability of responding to the statements about collaboration between teachers in using ICT with:

Disagreement to positive, agreement to negative items

Agreement to positive, disagreement to negative items

Notes:
* Statistically significant (*p* <0.05) coefficients in **bold**.
() Standard errors appear in parentheses. Because some results are rounded to the nearest whole number, some totals may appear inconsistent.
1 Country surveyed teachers retrospectively to the previous school year when they were teaching the target grade.

scores. Overall, the average scores on the ICT collaboration scale were about two scale points higher for teachers older than 40 than for teachers under 40 years of age.

ICT-coordinators were asked to indicate the extent ("a lot," "to some extent," "very little," or "not at all'") to which a range of different obstacles hindered using ICT in teaching and learning at their school. Table 6.10 presents the national percentages of students at schools where ICT-coordinators reported that ICT use for teaching and learning was hindered a lot or to some extent by each obstacle. Typically, majorities of students across the ICILS countries came from schools where, according to the ICT-coordinators, the following obstacles relating to personnel and teaching support limited ability to use ICT for pedagogical purposes:

- A lack of ICT skills among teachers (63% on average, with national percentages ranging from 27% in Korea to 80% in Ontario);

- Insufficient time for teachers to prepare lessons (63% on average, with national percentages ranging from 38% in Croatia to 81% in Thailand);

- A lack of effective professional learning resources for teachers (60% on average, with national percentages ranging from 43% to 78%);

- A lack of incentives for teachers to integrate ICT use in their teaching (60% on average, with national percentages ranging from 40% to 80%); and

- A lack of qualified technical personnel to support the use of ICT (53% on average, with national percentages ranging from 27% to 82%).

ICT-coordinators across countries generally perceived personnel-related hindrances to be more prevalent than those related to resources. The extent of this difference varied considerably from country to country, however, as the following international average percentages show.

- Fifty-five percent of students were enrolled at schools where ICT-coordinators reported a lack of sufficiently powerful computers for ICT use. The national percentages ranged from 27 percent in Australia to 85 percent in Turkey.

- Fifty-two percent of students were attending schools where ICT-coordinators reported that a lack of computers limited opportunity to use ICT for instructional purposes. The national percentages ranged from 26 percent in Australia to 81 percent in Turkey.

- Forty-five percent of students were enrolled at schools where insufficient internet bandwidth or speed was seen as a hindrance. The national percentages ranged from 21 percent in the Czech Republic and Lithuania to 89 percent in Thailand.

- Just under half (47%) of the ICILS students were at schools where the ICT-coordinators said insufficient computer software was hindering ICT use. National percentages ranged from 10 percent in Australia to 74 percent in Turkey.

- Approximately one third of students were attending schools that, according to the coordinators, had too few computers connected to the internet. The national percentages ranged from eight percent in Australia to 74 percent in Thailand.

ICILS asked teachers to report their perceptions of obstacles to using ICT in teaching. The study also asked teachers about the extent to which they collaborated with one another and how much they and their colleagues followed common procedures when using ICT in their teaching.

Table 6.10: National percentages of students at schools where different obstacles hinder using ICT in teaching and learning

Country	Too Few Computers Connected to the Internet	Insufficient Internet Bandwidth or Speed	Not Enough Computers for Instruction	Lack of Sufficiently Powerful Computers	Not Enough Computer Software	Lack of ICT Skills among Teachers	Insufficient Time for Teachers to Prepare Lessons	Lack of Effective Professional Learning Resources for Teachers	Lack of an Effective Online Learning Support Platform	Lack of Incentives for Teachers to Integrate ICT Use in Their Teaching	Lack of Qualified Technical Personnel to Support ICT Use
Australia	8 (2.0) ▶	39 (3.3)	26 (3.1) ▶	27 (3.4) ▶	10 (2.2) ▶	75 (2.9) ◀	67 (3.4)	51 (3.4) ▽	35 (3.5) ▶	51 (3.2) ▽	31 (3.0) ▶
Chile	25 (3.7)	52 (3.3) △	34 (4.1) ▶	46 (4.7)	53 (4.7)	71 (3.8) △	58 (4.6)	65 (4.2)	65 (4.6)	70 (4.2) ◀	45 (4.7)
Croatia	43 (4.0) ◀	35 (4.1) ▽	74 (3.6) ◀	66 (3.5) ◀	49 (4.0)	71 (3.8) △	38 (3.6) ▶	65 (3.7)	48 (4.3) ▽	57 (4.1)	67 (3.7) ◀
Czech Republic	13 (2.8) ▶	21 (3.8) ▶	32 (3.5) ▶	41 (3.8) ▶	40 (3.8)	56 (4.5)	59 (4.4)	43 (3.8) ▶	60 (4.2)	50 (4.1) ▽	37 (4.0) ▶
Germany†	41 (4.5)	49 (5.1)	54 (4.6)	44 (4.6) ▶	39 (4.0)	79 (3.7) ◀	76 (4.6) ◀	70 (4.2) ◀	52 (4.1)	80 (4.5) ◀	63 (5.2)
Korea, Republic of	12 (2.7) ▶	26 (3.7) ▶	30 (3.9) ▶	57 (4.1) ◀	37 (3.7) ▽	27 (3.7) ▶	63 (3.8)	50 (4.0) ▽	52 (4.2)	61 (4.0)	66 (3.9) ◀
Lithuania	11 (2.6) ▶	21 (3.4) ▶	49 (5.0)	58 (4.8) ◀	45 (4.7)	55 (4.8)	50 (4.4) ▶	60 (4.6)	57 (4.7)	40 (4.3) ▶	27 (3.8) ▶
Norway (Grade 9)¹	27 (4.5)	28 (4.1) ▶	65 (4.5) ◀	33 (4.4) ▶	26 (3.9) ▶	77 (4.0) ◀	57 (4.8)	52 (4.9)	50 (5.0)	62 (4.7)	36 (4.5) △
Poland	50 (4.1) ◀	53 (4.4)	65 (4.1) ◀	52 (4.0)	65 (4.2) ◀	56 (4.4)	66 (4.1)	64 (3.7)	63 (4.3)	59 (3.7)	63 (4.0) ◀
Russian Federation²	43 (3.4) ◀	62 (3.9) ◀	48 (3.2)	60 (3.0) ◀	51 (3.6)	55 (4.1)	56 (3.9)	63 (3.7)	57 (4.1) ▶	49 (3.7) ▶	59 (3.9)
Slovak Republic	24 (3.5) ▽	41 (4.2)	60 (4.5)	62 (4.0) ◀	48 (4.1)	53 (4.6) ▶	73 (3.9) ◀	51 (4.3)	56 (4.2)	43 (4.2) ▶	50 (4.5)
Slovenia	21 (3.6) ▶	35 (3.7) ▽	45 (4.3)	64 (4.1) △	46 (4.0)	69 (3.3)	74 (3.5) ◀	56 (4.4)	53 (4.3)	59 (4.1)	41 (4.6) ▶
Thailand²	74 (4.5) ◀	89 (3.3) ◀	73 (3.9) ◀	77 (3.9) ◀	71 (3.8) ◀	72 (4.4)	81 (3.6) ◀	78 (4.0) ◀	84 (3.7) ◀	76 (4.2) ◀	82 (4.3) ◀
Turkey	64 (4.0) ◀	77 (3.3) ◀	81 (3.2) ◀	85 (2.9) ◀	74 (3.8) ◀	66 (3.7)	61 (3.9)	70 (3.8) ◀	78 (3.6) ◀	78 (3.5) ◀	82 (3.2) ◀
ICILS 2013 average	33 (1.0)	45 (1.0)	52 (1.1)	55 (1.1)	47 (1.1)	63 (1.1)	63 (1.1)	60 (1.1)	58 (1.1)	60 (1.1)	53 (1.1)
Countries not meeting sample requirements											
Denmark	20 (4.3)	34 (6.2)	64 (5.2)	40 (5.9)	25 (5.2)	80 (4.5)	56 (5.5)	57 (5.2)	29 (5.6)	54 (6.2)	43 (5.9)
Hong Kong SAR	22 (4.7)	39 (5.6)	26 (4.0)	55 (4.7)	48 (4.5)	52 (5.6)	87 (4.1)	73 (5.8)	51 (5.4)	77 (4.8)	53 (5.2)
Netherlands	17 (5.0)	34 (6.4)	20 (5.9)	27 (6.2)	26 (5.7)	83 (5.6)	71 (6.0)	66 (6.5)	55 (6.8)	72 (6.2)	28 (5.5)
Switzerland	38 (6.8)	39 (7.9)	50 (6.0)	22 (6.9)	14 (4.2)	82 (6.1)	57 (7.1)	61 (7.2)	41 (6.8)	60 (8.2)	55 (6.1)
Benchmarking participants											
Newfoundland and Labrador, Canada	41 (0.3)	35 (0.3)	55 (0.3)	39 (0.3)	29 (0.3)	63 (0.3)	79 (0.3)	77 (0.3)	69 (0.3)	67 (0.3)	70 (0.3)
Ontario, Canada	29 (4.5)	52 (4.9)	66 (5.0)	59 (5.5)	30 (4.6)	80 (4.3)	59 (5.4)	58 (5.1)	48 (4.9)	64 (4.8)	54 (4.9)
Benchmarking participant not meeting sample requirements											
City of Buenos Aires, Argentina	37 (9.8)	51 (8.5)	66 (7.2)	47 (8.4)	32 (8.2)	60 (10.4)	67 (9.3)	64 (8.7)	60 (9.6)	68 (8.3)	52 (9.3)

▲ More than 10 percentage points above ICILS 2013 average
△ Significantly above ICILS 2013 average
▽ Significantly below ICILS 2013 average
▼ More than 10 percentage points below ICILS 2013 average

Notes:
() Standard errors appear in parentheses. Because some results are rounded to the nearest whole number, some totals may appear inconsistent.
† Met guidelines for sampling participation rates only after replacement schools were included.
1 National Desired Population does not correspond to International Desired Population.
2 Country surveyed the same cohort of students but at the beginning of the next school year.

To gain teachers' perceptions about obstacles, the ICILS teacher questionnaire asked teachers to consider a number of statements and to use the following response key to state their level of agreement with each one: "strongly agree," "agree," "disagree," and "strongly disagree." Table 6.11 records the percentages of teachers who expressed agreement with each of the statements. On average, just over half of the teachers considered ICT to be a teaching priority in their school. The national average percentages ranged from less than a third of teachers in Slovenia to 87 percent of teachers in Newfoundland and Labrador.

Forty-two percent of the ICT equipment resources at schools were deemed insufficient. In the Czech Republic, less than a quarter of teachers thought this. In Thailand, however, approximately three quarters of teachers held this view.

Russian and Thai teachers were those most likely crossnationally to indicate a lack of access to digital learning resources as an issue. The respective percentages were 47 percent and 45 percent. Czech and Slovak teachers were least likely to identify this lack as an issue (only 8%). Across all ICILS countries, 22 percent of teachers thought the lack was a problem.

There was some inter-country variability in the percentages of teachers who said that limited internet connectivity presented a barrier to them using ICT for their teaching. On average, we recorded a 40 percent agreement internationally with this concern and majority agreement with it in Chile (54%), the Russian Federation (55%), Thailand (73%), and Turkey (59%).

On average across the ICILS countries, 38 percent of teachers agreed that their school computer equipment was out of date. The national percentages ranged from 22 percent in the Czech Republic to 60 percent in Thailand.

The most common issue that the teachers identified was insufficient time to prepare lessons encompassing ICT use. Fifty-seven percent of teachers, on average, endorsed this view. Except for the Czech Republic and Lithuania, with 46 percent and 44 percent agreement respectively, the majority of teachers in all countries specified lack of time as problematic.

Majorities of teachers from Korea (68%), Thailand (67%), Turkey (57%), and the Canadian province of Newfoundland and Labrador (66%) indicated insufficient provision for them to develop ICT-related expertise (the ICILS 2013 average was 39%). Fewer than half of the teachers in the remaining countries reported this lack as a problem.

On average crossnationally, 45 percent of teachers expressed agreement with the statement that they did not have sufficient technical support to maintain ICT resources. The highest national percentages of agreement were found in Turkey (65%) and Thailand (77%); the lowest such percentage was recorded in the Czech Republic (13%).

We used six of the eight items listed to form a scale reflecting teachers' perceptions of ICT resource limitations at their school.[3] The *ICT resource limitations at school scale,*

---

3 The items making up this scale were:
  • My school does not have sufficient ICT equipment (e.g., computers).
  • My school does not have access to digital learning resources.
  • My school has limited connectivity (e.g., slow or unstable speed) to the internet.
  • The computer equipment in our school is out of date.
  • There is not sufficient provision for me to develop expertise in ICT.
  • There is not sufficient technical support to maintain ICT resources.
  The remaining two items were concerned with priorities ("ICT is not considered a priority for use in teaching") and time ("There is not sufficient time to prepare lessons that incorporate ICT").

Table 6.11: National percentages of teachers who agree with statements about the use of ICT in their school

Country	ICT Is Not Considered a Priority for Use in Teaching	My School Does Not Have Sufficient ICT Equipment (e.g., Computers)	My School Does Not Have Access to Digital Learning Resources	My School Has Limited Connectivity (e.g., Slow or Unstable Speed) to the Internet	The Computer Equipment in Our School Is Out of Date	There Is Not Sufficient Time to Prepare Lessons that Incorporate ICT	There Is Not Sufficient Provision for Me to Develop Expertise in ICT	There Is Not Sufficient Technical Support to Maintain ICT Resources
Australia	17 (1.2) ▼	32 (1.7) ▼	13 (1.1) ▽	37 (1.6) ▽	28 (1.7) ▼	54 (1.2) ▽	48 (1.7) △	37 (1.8) ▽
Chile	36 (2.2) ▼	33 (2.7) ▽	21 (2.4)	54 (2.4) ▲	34 (2.7)	68 (2.1) ▲	38 (2.2)	42 (2.6)
Croatia	66 (1.8) ▲	43 (2.3)	25 (1.7)	39 (1.8)	46 (2.2) △	51 (1.6) ▽	43 (1.6)	54 (2.0) △
Czech Republic	55 (1.6) △	22 (1.8) ▼	8 (0.9) ▼	23 (1.5) ▼	22 (1.7) ▼	46 (1.4) ▼	17 (1.0) ▼	13 (1.3) ▼
Korea, Republic of	45 (2.2)	46 (4.0)	30 (2.0) △	35 (1.8) ▽	48 (1.8) ▲	70 (1.9) ▲	68 (2.3) ▲	62 (1.6) ▲
Lithuania	27 (1.4) ▼	49 (2.8) △	17 (1.6) ▽	30 (2.1) ▼	39 (2.4)	44 (1.4) ▲	25 (1.2) ▼	33 (2.3) ▼
Poland	63 (1.3) ▲	42 (2.2)	11 (1.1) ▼	32 (1.9) ▽	39 (2.4)	54 (1.5)	30 (1.5) ▽	44 (2.0)
Russian Federation[1]	44 (1.7)	45 (3.1)	47 (2.9) ▲	55 (2.3) ▲	34 (2.7)	52 (2.0) ▽	32 (1.9) ▽	48 (2.3)
Slovak Republic	42 (1.6) ▽	28 (2.3) ▼	8 (1.0) ▼	26 (1.9) ▲	28 (2.4) ▽	57 (1.6)	27 (1.6) ▼	33 (2.3) ▼
Slovenia	69 (1.4) ▲	34 (1.7) ▽	10 (0.8) ▼	16 (1.1) ▼	26 (1.6) ▼	68 (1.1) ▲	22 (1.1) ▼	28 (1.5) ▼
Thailand	28 (2.8) ▼	75 (2.4) ▲	43 (3.5) ▲	73 (2.3) ▲	60 (3.0) ▲	65 (2.9) △	65 (2.4) ▲	77 (2.4) ▲
Turkey	63 (2.5) ▲	58 (3.0) ▲	35 (2.9) ▲	59 (2.6) ▲	52 (2.4) ▲	57 (2.1)	57 (2.4) ▲	65 (2.4) ▲
ICILS 2013 average	46 (0.5)	42 (0.7)	22 (0.6)	40 (0.6)	38 (0.7)	57 (0.5)	39 (0.5)	45 (0.6)
Countries not meeting sample requirements								
Denmark	12 (1.5)	50 (4.5)	12 (1.5)	38 (3.5)	39 (4.1)	54 (2.5)	55 (2.7)	44 (2.7)
Germany	61 (1.8)	42 (2.4)	28 (2.0)	46 (3.4)	43 (2.9)	57 (1.9)	49 (1.8)	51 (2.3)
Hong Kong SAR	38 (1.8)	23 (1.9)	14 (1.5)	27 (2.1)	39 (2.4)	63 (1.4)	51 (1.8)	46 (2.0)
Netherlands	29 (2.6)	56 (2.5)	13 (1.2)	35 (2.2)	41 (2.4)	53 (1.7)	37 (1.6)	38 (2.1)
Norway (Grade 9)	24 (2.2)	53 (3.3)	11 (1.3)	43 (2.5)	34 (2.9)	50 (1.8)	52 (2.3)	49 (3.1)
Benchmarking participant								
Newfoundland and Labrador, Canada	13 (1.8)	35 (2.5)	22 (2.7)	35 (2.8)	29 (2.5)	68 (2.9)	66 (3.0)	59 (2.8)
Benchmarking participant not meeting sample requirements								
Ontario, Canada	20 (2.5)	56 (4.8)	31 (3.9)	49 (4.4)	49 (3.8)	60 (4.5)	62 (4.3)	57 (5.1)

() Standard errors appear in parentheses. Because some results are rounded to the nearest whole number, some totals may appear inconsistent.

[1] Country surveyed teachers retrospectively to the previous school year when they were teaching the target grade.

▲ More than 10 percentage points above ICILS 2013 average
△ Significantly above ICILS 2013 average
▽ Significantly below ICILS 2013 average
▼ More than 10 percentage points below ICILS 2013 average

which we constructed via the Rasch partial credit model, had a reliability (coefficient alpha) of 0.83 and IRT scores standardized to an ICILS 2013 average score of 50 points and a standard deviation of 10 points. The higher scores on the scale represent stronger perceptions of inadequate resourcing. Table 6.12 presents the mean scores on this scale for all teachers overall, for teachers under 40 years, and for teachers over 40 years of age.

Teachers from the Czech Republic and Slovenia scored more than three points lower than the ICILS 2013 average, indicating a perception that the school had relatively adequate ICT resources. In comparison, Thailand and Turkey both had scale scores more than three points above the ICILS 2013 average, indicating that teachers saw ICT resourcing at their schools as inadequate.

In general, we found little difference between the scale scores of teachers under and the scale scores of teachers over the age of 40. However, we did record significantly higher scale scores for teachers 40 years of age and under (compared to the 40 and over group) in Croatia and Turkey.

Teachers' professional development in using ICT for pedagogical purposes

Two sources of information provided perspectives on teachers' professional development in the pedagogical use of ICT. One of these was the school principal, who provided information on the extent to which teachers in his or her school had participated in various forms of professional development. The other source of information was the teachers themselves. They identified the forms of professional development they had participated in over the past two years.

School perspectives

The ICILS school questionnaire asked principals to indicate the extent to which teachers in their respective schools had participated in different forms of professional development focused on using ICT for teaching and learning. The response categories were "none or almost none," "some," "many," and "all or almost all." Table 6.13 shows the national percentages of students attending schools where many or all or almost all of the teachers had taken part in various forms of professional development.

Participation in courses is a traditional form of professional development. These are typically provided by the school in which the teacher is located, by an external agency or expert, or as a program delivered online. About two thirds of the schools (the ICILS 2013 average was 68%) indicated that many teachers had participated "in courses on the use of ICT in teaching provided by the school." This type of participation was by far the most prevalent among the various forms of professional development listed. In the following countries, 79 percent or more of the ICILS students were studying at schools where many or almost all teachers had participated in a course on using ICT in their teaching: Slovenia, Lithuania, Croatia, Thailand, the Russian Federation, Australia, and the Slovak Republic. In four other countries—Chile, Germany, Turkey, and the Canadian province of Ontario—less than half of the students were enrolled at schools that had this level of participation in such a course.

Smaller proportions of students were studying at schools where many or almost all of their teachers had taken part in "courses conducted by an external agency or expert" (a crossnational average of 39%) or in "professional learning programs delivered through ICT" (also 39%).

Table 6.12: National averages for teachers' perceptions of ICT resources at their school overall and by school characteristics

Country	All teachers		Teacher Perceptions of ICT Teaching by Age Group				Score Distribution by Age Group
			Under 40	40 and over	Differences (40 and over – under 40)*		
Australia	49 (0.4)	▽	49 (0.4)	48 (0.4)	0	(0.4)	
Chile	49 (0.7)		49 (0.8)	50 (0.7)	0	(0.9)	
Croatia	51 (0.4)	△	52 (0.5)	51 (0.5)	–1	(0.5)	
Czech Republic	42 (0.4)	▶	42 (0.5)	41 (0.4)	0	(0.5)	
Korea, Republic of	53 (0.4)	△	53 (0.4)	53 (0.6)	1	(0.7)	
Lithuania	49 (0.4)		50 (0.6)	49 (0.4)	0	(0.6)	
Poland	49 (0.5)		49 (0.6)	49 (0.7)	0	(0.8)	
Russian Federation[1]	52 (0.5)	△	52 (0.5)	52 (0.5)	0	(0.5)	
Slovak Republic	48 (0.4)	▽	47 (0.5)	48 (0.4)	1	(0.5)	
Slovenia	46 (0.4)	▶	46 (0.5)	47 (0.4)	1	(0.5)	
Thailand	58 (0.8)	◀	58 (0.9)	57 (0.8)	0	(0.8)	
Turkey	54 (0.7)	◀	55 (0.7)	53 (1.1)	–2	(1.1)	
ICILS 2013 average	50 (0.1)		50 (0.2)	50 (0.2)	0	(0.2)	
Countries not meeting sample requirements							
Denmark	51 (0.6)		51 (0.7)	51 (0.7)	–1	(0.7)	
Germany	50 (0.7)		52 (0.8)	49 (0.7)	–2	(0.9)	
Hong Kong SAR	50 (0.4)		49 (0.5)	51 (0.4)	2	(0.5)	
Netherlands	51 (0.3)		50 (0.5)	51 (0.4)	0	(0.5)	
Norway (Grade 9)	51 (0.5)		51 (0.6)	51 (0.6)	0	(0.7)	
Benchmarking participant							
Newfoundland and Labrador, Canada	51 (0.6)		51 (0.9)	52 (0.7)	1	(1.2)	
Benchmarking participant not meeting sample requirements							
Ontario, Canada	54 (1.4)		53 (1.2)	54 (1.9)	0	(1.3)	

Legend:

■ Under 40 average score +/– confidence interval
■ Over 40 average score +/– confidence interval

On average, teachers with a score in the range indicated by this color have more than a 50% probability of responding to the statements about perceptions of ICT teaching at their school with:

□ Disagreement to positive, agreement to negative items
▨ Agreement to positive, disagreement to negative items

▲ More than three score points above ICILS 2013 average
△ Significantly above ICILS 2013 average
▽ Significantly below ICILS 2013 average
▶ More than three score points below ICILS 2013 average

Notes:
* Statistically significant (*p* <.05) coefficients in **bold**.
() Standard errors appear in parentheses. Because some results are rounded to the nearest whole number, some totals may appear inconsistent.
[1] Country surveyed teachers retrospectively to the previous school year when they were teaching the target grade.

Table 6.13: National percentages of students at schools where teachers participate in professional development about ICT for teaching and learning

Country	Participating in School-Provided Courses on the Use of ICT in Teaching	Working With Another Teacher Who Has Attended a Course and Then Trains Other Teachers	Discussing the Use of ICT in Education as a Regular Item During Meetings of the Teaching Staff	Observing Colleagues Using ICT in Their Teaching	Discussion Within Groups of Teachers About Using ICT in Their Teaching	Participating in a [Community of Practice] Concerned with ICT in Teaching	Participating in Courses Conducted by an External Agency or Expert	Participating in Professional Learning Programs Delivered Through ICT
Australia	80 (2.6) ◄	67 (3.6) ◄	75 (2.8) ◄	55 (3.6) ◄	72 (3.2) ◄	44 (3.6) ◄	41 (3.4)	58 (3.0) ◄
Chile	44 (4.6) ►	31 (4.8) ►	39 (4.4) ►	41 (3.7) ►	42 (4.5) ►	23 (3.9)	23 (4.1) ►	20 (4.0) ►
Croatia	85 (2.9) ◄	50 (3.9)	39 (3.6) ►	36 (3.6) ▽	51 (3.9)	27 (2.8)	45 (4.2)	47 (4.1)
Czech Republic	75 (3.5)	44 (4.1)	39 (4.5) ►	21 (3.3) ►	44 (4.3) ►	13 (3.1) ►	37 (3.9)	23 (3.4) ►
Germany†	42 (4.7) ►	22 (3.9) ►	22 (4.1) ►	4 (1.7) ►	37 (4.4) ►	5 (2.0) ►	13 (2.9) ►	10 (3.6) ►
Korea, Republic of	61 (4.3)	48 (4.2)	36 (3.7) ►	60 (4.1) ◄	37 (4.4) ►	25 (3.8)	34 (4.1)	45 (4.0)
Lithuania	86 (3.0) ◄	54 (4.8)	67 (4.5) ◄	57 (4.7) ◄	76 (3.8) ◄	36 (4.5)	31 (4.4)	35 (4.6)
Norway (Grade 9)[1]	58 (4.5) ►	52 (4.9)	62 (5.1)	22 (4.2) ►	65 (5.2)	7 (2.5) ►	10 (2.5) ►	19 (3.9) ►
Poland	56 (4.0) ►	53 (4.4)	45 (4.7)	48 (4.4)	60 (4.0)	28 (4.2)	38 (4.3)	13 (2.6) ►
Russian Federation[2]	82 (2.8) ◄	62 (3.4) ◄	85 (3.2) ◄	85 (2.6) ◄	86 (3.0) ◄	77 (3.2) ◄	72 (3.6) ◄	64 (3.2) ◄
Slovak Republic	79 (3.3) ◄	48 (4.4)	66 (4.3) ◄	44 (4.3)	60 (3.9)	9 (2.5) ►	47 (3.9) △	45 (4.1) ◄
Slovenia	87 (3.0) ◄	35 (3.9) ►	60 (3.7)	32 (2.7) ►	56 (4.1)	27 (4.0)	71 (3.9) ◄	59 (4.1) ◄
Thailand[2]	83 (2.9) ◄	78 (3.8) ◄	60 (4.7)	59 (4.8) ◄	63 (4.9)	64 (5.0) ◄	58 (4.9) ◄	65 (4.0) ◄
Turkey	41 (4.4) ►	20 (3.1) ►	51 (4.3)	52 (4.4)	29 (3.6) ►	24 (3.7)	22 (3.7) ►	38 (4.0)
ICILS 2013 average	68 (1.0)	47 (1.1)	53 (1.1)	44 (1.0)	56 (1.1)	29 (1.0)	39 (1.0)	39 (1.0)
Countries not meeting sample requirements								
Denmark	63 (5.8)	40 (6.3)	56 (6.2)	20 (4.3)	52 (6.3)	37 (5.6)	36 (5.5)	27 (4.8)
Hong Kong SAR	39 (5.6)	15 (4.4)	18 (4.5)	36 (5.3)	19 (4.4)	11 (3.9)	21 (4.6)	26 (5.2)
Netherlands	58 (5.4)	36 (5.6)	53 (5.8)	13 (4.0)	40 (5.9)	8 (3.4)	20 (4.4)	10 (3.4)
Switzerland	42 (6.7)	26 (6.4)	44 (7.7)	21 (7.0)	42 (6.8)	10 (2.5)	11 (5.1)	13 (5.6)
Benchmarking participants								
Newfoundland and Labrador, Canada	53 (0.3)	63 (0.3)	67 (0.3)	51 (0.3)	58 (0.3)	44 (0.3)	21 (0.1)	24 (0.3)
Ontario, Canada	49 (5.1)	43 (5.7)	53 (5.8)	43 (5.2)	53 (5.0)	34 (4.7)	15 (4.0)	24 (4.8)
Benchmarking participant not meeting sample requirements								
City of Buenos Aires, Argentina	26 (7.0)	20 (7.8)	62 (8.1)	24 (8.3)	36 (8.4)	12 (5.8)	20 (5.2)	11 (5.7)

◄ More than 10 percentage points above ICILS 2013 average
△ Significantly above ICILS 2013 average
▽ Significantly below ICILS 2013 average
► More than 10 percentage points below ICILS 2013 average

Notes:
() Standard errors appear in parentheses. Because some results are rounded to the nearest whole number, some totals may appear inconsistent.
† Met guidelines for sampling participation rates only after replacement schools were included.
[1] National Desired Population does not correspond to International Desired Population.
[2] Country surveyed the same cohort of students but at the beginning of the next school year.

The percentage of students at schools with higher levels of teacher participation in externally provided courses was significantly higher than the ICILS 2013 average in the Russian Federation (72%), Slovenia (71%), and Thailand (58%). The percentages of students at schools with teacher participation at this level in learning programs delivered online was significantly higher than the ICILS 2013 average in Thailand (65%), the Russian Federation (64%), Slovenia (59%), and Australia (58%).

Other forms of professional development involve collaboration among teachers in various forums. Schools representing more than half of the student population reported that many or all of their teachers had participated in discussions "within groups of teachers about using ICT in their teaching" (56%) or in discussions about "the use of ICT in education as a regular item during meetings of the teaching staff" (53%). These forms of professional development for teachers were reported also by schools representing high percentages of students (above the ICILS 2013 average) in the Russian Federation (86% and 85% respectively for the two statements), Australia (72% and 75%), and Lithuania (76% and 67%).

Collaborative learning with colleagues, such as "working with another teacher who has attended a course" and "observing colleagues using ICT in their teaching," was reported by schools representing less than half of the student population: 47 and 44 percent respectively. The percentages of students at schools where many or all teachers had worked with another teacher were significantly higher than the ICILS 2013 average in Thailand (78%), Australia (67%), and the Russian Federation (62%). In five countries, schools representing proportions of the student population larger than the ICILS average said that many or all of their teachers had observed colleagues using ICT in their teaching. These countries were the Russian Federation (85%), Korea (60%), Thailand (59%), Lithuania (57%), and Australia (55%).

Only 29 percent of students were enrolled at schools where many or all teachers had participated in a "community of practice concerned with ICT in teaching." The percentage of students at schools where teachers participated in this type of community was significantly higher than the ICILS 2013 average in the Russian Federation (77%), Thailand (64%), and Australia (44%).

Teacher perspectives

The teacher questionnaire included a question that asked teachers about their participation ("yes" or "no") in a range of professional development activities. Table 6.14 provides information on the types of professional development programs teachers had participated in during the previous two years.

The most common form of participation involved observing other teachers using ICT. On average across countries, 46 percent of teachers reported this type of participation. The countries whose teachers most frequently reported observing their colleagues' use of ICT were Lithuania (60%), Australia (57%), and Korea (57%). The next most widely reported form of professional development concerned integrating ICT into teaching and learning. On average, 43 percent of teachers across the ICILS countries had participated in such a course. The highest percentages were recorded in Slovenia (64%) and Australia (57%).

Table 6.14: National percentages of teachers participating in ICT-related professional development activities

Country	Introductory Course on General Applications (e.g., Basic Wordprocessing, Spreadsheets, Databases)	Advanced Course on General Applications (e.g., Advanced Wordprocessing, Spreadsheets, Databases)	Introductory Course on Internet Use (e.g., Compiling Internet Searches, Digital Resources)	Advanced Course on Internet Use (e.g., Creating Websites, Building Web-Based Resources)	Course on Integrating ICT into Teaching and Learning	Training on Subject-Specific Software	Observing Other Teachers Using ICT in Teaching	Course on Multimedia Involving Use of Digital Video/Audio Equipment	Course on Subject-Specific Digital Resources	An ICT-Mediated Discussion or Forum on Teaching and Learning	Sharing and Evaluating Digital Resources with Others within a Collaborative Work Space
Australia	23 (1.1) ▶	14 (0.7) ▽	23 (1.2) ▽	18 (0.9)	57 (1.5) ◀	45 (1.7) ◀	57 (1.5) ◀	23 (1.0)	30 (1.3) △	35 (1.3) △	48 (1.5) ◀
Chile	34 (1.9)	15 (0.9) ▽	33 (1.8)	15 (1.1) ▽	39 (2.1)	21 (1.7) ▽	37 (1.9) ▽	18 (1.3) ▽	19 (1.6) ▽	26 (1.7)	29 (1.5)
Croatia	53 (1.7) ◀	23 (1.4)	61 (2.0) ◀	14 (0.9) ▽	45 (1.8)	18 (1.1) ▶	36 (1.4) ▶	15 (1.0) ▽	15 (0.9) ▽	19 (0.8) ▽	14 (0.8) ▶
Czech Republic	25 (1.7) ▽	21 (1.6)	16 (1.1) ▶	11 (0.9) ▽	36 (1.8) ▽	28 (1.7)	27 (1.8) ▶	24 (1.4)	18 (1.2) ▽	21 (1.3) ▽	31 (1.4)
Korea, Republic of	36 (2.2)	21 (1.2)	31 (1.3)	15 (0.9) ▽	42 (1.7)	32 (1.3)	57 (2.0) ◀	35 (1.0) ◀	28 (1.3) △	20 (1.3) ▽	23 (1.3) ▽
Lithuania	31 (1.7)	30 (1.8) △	30 (1.8)	23 (2.1) △	54 (1.5) ◀	49 (1.5) ◀	60 (1.4) ◀	23 (1.2)	28 (1.4) △	28 (1.0)	16 (1.3) ▶
Poland	15 (1.0) ▶	12 (1.1) ▽	12 (1.0) ▶	11 (0.9) ▽	29 (1.4) ▶	29 (1.3)	43 (1.4) ▽	36 (1.6) ◀	18 (1.4) ▽	22 (1.5) ▽	23 (1.4) ▽
Russian Federation[1]	47 (2.0) ◀	29 (1.7) △	46 (1.9) ◀	17 (1.3)	44 (1.7)	34 (1.3) △	83 (1.2) ◀	24 (1.8)	40 (1.6) ◀	39 (2.2) ◀	57 (1.9) ◀
Slovak Republic	32 (1.5)	25 (1.3) △	26 (1.2) △	8 (0.7) ▽	40 (1.4)	21 (1.0) ▽	33 (1.4) ▽	23 (1.3)	20 (1.1) ▽	21 (1.2) ▽	15 (1.1) ▽
Slovenia	26 (2.2) ▽	26 (1.3) △	19 (1.0) ▶	26 (1.4) △	64 (1.6) ◀	41 (1.5) ◀	47 (1.4)	25 (1.1)	27 (1.1) △	40 (1.6) ◀	29 (1.1)
Thailand	48 (3.3) ◀	32 (3.6) ◀	59 (2.6) ◀	33 (2.7) ◀	50 (2.8) ◀	36 (2.2) △	53 (2.3) △	36 (2.7) ◀	32 (2.7) ◀	45 (3.2) ◀	40 (2.8) ◀
Turkey	27 (2.2) ▽	13 (1.1) ▽	22 (1.8) ▽	13 (1.2) ▽	14 (1.6) ▶	12 (1.3) ▶	23 (1.5) ▶	9 (0.9) ▶	9 (1.0) ▶	17 (1.4) ▶	23 (1.8) ▽
ICILS 2013 average	33 (0.6)	22 (0.5)	32 (0.5)	17 (0.4)	43 (0.5)	30 (0.4)	46 (0.5)	24 (0.4)	24 (0.4)	28 (0.5)	29 (0.5)
Countries not meeting sample requirements											
Denmark	19 (2.3)	15 (2.0)	19 (1.9)	14 (1.5)	43 (2.8)	39 (2.8)	25 (1.7)	21 (3.0)	36 (3.5)	27 (1.8)	27 (1.8)
Germany	10 (1.1)	7 (0.9)	8 (1.0)	5 (0.8)	18 (1.6)	28 (2.3)	19 (1.9)	14 (1.4)	10 (1.1)	8 (1.2)	9 (1.1)
Hong Kong SAR	21 (1.5)	14 (1.3)	20 (1.6)	14 (1.4)	34 (1.9)	24 (1.5)	41 (1.6)	22 (1.5)	13 (1.2)	26 (1.4)	26 (1.3)
Netherlands	13 (1.6)	7 (1.3)	8 (1.0)	7 (1.3)	35 (2.2)	27 (1.6)	24 (1.7)	13 (1.2)	26 (2.0)	15 (1.1)	23 (1.6)
Norway (Grade 9)	25 (1.7)	10 (1.1)	16 (1.4)	7 (1.0)	28 (1.9)	35 (2.1)	31 (2.1)	12 (1.3)	22 (1.6)	37 (1.8)	35 (1.8)
Benchmarking participant											
Newfoundland and Labrador, Canada	11 (2.0)	5 (1.4)	13 (2.0)	23 (2.6)	44 (3.2)	42 (2.4)	47 (3.3)	17 (2.2)	25 (2.7)	28 (2.5)	47 (3.2)
Benchmarking participant not meeting sample requirements											
Ontario, Canada	12 (2.4)	7 (1.9)	13 (2.6)	20 (3.2)	44 (3.6)	47 (3.7)	44 (3.2)	21 (3.0)	24 (3.4)	27 (3.6)	41 (3.9)

◀ More than 10 percentage points above ICILS 2013 average
△ Significantly above ICILS 2013 average
▽ Significantly below ICILS 2013 average
▶ More than 10 percentage points below ICILS 2013 average

Notes:

() Standard errors appear in parentheses. Because some results are rounded to the nearest whole number, some totals may appear inconsistent.

[1] Country surveyed teachers retrospectively to the previous school year when they were teaching the target grade.

On average across countries, teachers took part in introductory courses on the following topics: general ICT applications (33%), internet use (32%), and subject-specific software (30%). The highest rates of participation in introductory courses on general applications were recorded in Croatia (53%), Thailand (48%), and the Russian Federation (47%). These countries also reported the highest levels of participation in introductory courses on internet use (61%, 57%, and 46% respectively). Training on subject-specific software was reported most frequently in Lithuania (49%), Australia (45%), and Newfoundland and Labrador (42%).

Two activities involving collaboration attracted lesser mention. Twenty-nine percent of teachers across the ICILS countries reported "sharing and evaluating digital resources with others using a collaborative work space." The highest percentages were 57 percent in the Russian Federation and 48 percent in Australia. Corresponding percentages for participating in "an ICT-mediated discussion or forum on teaching and learning" were 28 percent (the ICILS 2013 average), 46 percent in Thailand, and 40 percent in Slovenia.

Relatively few teachers crossnationally mentioned the following professional development courses focused on more advanced aspects of ICT:

- Course on multimedia involving use of digital video/audio equipment (24%);
- Course on subject-specific digital resources (24%);
- Advanced course on general applications (e.g., advanced wordprocessing, spreadsheets, databases) (22%); and
- Advanced course on internet use (e.g., creating websites, building web-based resources) (17%).

No more than a quarter of teachers said they had taken part in these courses. None of the ICILS countries recorded a large proportion of teachers who said they had engaged in these activities.

Conclusion

Data from the ICILS ICT-coordinator and principal questionnaires confirmed that schools in most of the participating countries had access to computer and ICT resources. Unsurprisingly, the provision of such infrastructure had increased in comparison to the levels seen in earlier IEA studies on ICT use in education (Law et al., 2008; Pelgrum & Anderson, 2001). However, in keeping with these studies, ICILS 2013 still showed considerable crosscountry variation in the relative abundance of resources.

Resourcing included ICT that could be used to support collaborative work. It also included learning management systems, portable computing devices, and specialized software, such as data-logging and monitoring tools and simulations and modeling software. Student to computer ratios varied from two or three students per computer in some countries to more than 20 students per computer in other countries (and 80 in one of the countries), with lower ratios reported on average in schools in rural areas. On average, students from countries with better student to computer ratios gained higher scores on the CIL assessment.

Some aspects of school policy, such as setting up security measures and restricting inappropriate online material, were almost universally applied in schools, whereas policies such as providing students with laptops and allowing the local community access to school computers had far greater inter-country variation. In general, schools reported that they accorded medium to high priority to facilitating ICT as teaching and learning tools. Also, according to teachers, ICT generally enabled them to work collaboratively with their colleagues.

However, schools identified a number of obstacles to using ICT pedagogically. ICT-coordinators varied in their ratings of such hindrances. In general, personnel issues featured as more of a concern than did those related to resources. Teachers also varied in their perceptions of whether the resources available to them (both in terms of ICT infrastructure and pedagogical support) were sufficient.

The main forms of teacher professional development with respect to the pedagogical use of ICT typically operated at school level, either through participation in school-organized professional development activities or through teachers observing one another using these resources. Teachers were more likely to attend professional development activities conducted outside the school if these encompassed less advanced aspects of ICT use.

Overall, the results from this chapter provide insight into the school-related contexts for students' use of ICT. Despite the global increase in ICT-infrastructure uptake, all of the ICILS countries reported challenges in their delivery of ICT-related education. Understandably, those countries with relatively lower levels of infrastructure were those most likely to have both teachers and ICT-coordinators reporting this lack as a barrier to this type of education.

However, even those countries with well-established infrastructure for ICT use in teaching and learning activities reported barriers, such as lack of skills, training, time available, and incentive to integrate ICT in educational practice. These findings suggest that more needs to be done in terms of nonphysical ICT resourcing. In particular, there seems to be a need for much greater pedagogical support. It is not enough to simply provide the physical resources that are needed for ICT in teaching and learning activities; the appropriate procedures and training also need to be in place to complement that infrastructure.

CHAPTER 7:

Teaching with and about Information and Communication Technologies

Introduction

This chapter focuses not only on the extent to which the teachers who participated in ICILS 2013 were using information and communication technology (ICT) in their classrooms but also on the classroom contexts for acquisition of computer and information literacy (CIL). The chapter's content pertains to ICILS Research Question 2: *What aspects of schools and education systems are related to student achievement in computer and information literacy with respect to (a) school and teaching practices, (b) teacher attitudes to and proficiency in using computers, (c) access to ICT in schools, and (d) teacher professional development?*

We begin the chapter by exploring the integration of technology into classroom practice (i.e., teaching with ICT). We review how often teachers were using ICT in their pedagogical practice, look at the characteristics of teachers who were frequently using ICT when teaching, and consider how teachers were actually using ICT in their classrooms. We then focus on the emphasis that the ICILS teachers placed on developing student computer and information literacy (CIL). From there, we look at the extent to which the participating teachers emphasized the development of CIL and the factors that were seemingly associated with them placing strong emphasis on CIL. Finally, we investigate several other details about pedagogical use of ICT. These include the tools that the teachers were using, the learning activities through which ICT was being integrated into classroom practice, and ICT-based teaching practices.

Background

As we have emphasized in earlier chapters, ensuring that school students can use computers and other forms of ICT has become an increasingly important aspect of preparing them for adult life. Many countries have adopted policies directed toward helping schools and teachers use ICT for pedagogical purposes (Bakia, Murphy, Anderson, & Trinidad, 2011; Plomp, Anderson, Law, & Quale, 2009). Many of those policies are predicated on the belief that ICT use facilitates changes in approaches to teaching, especially changes that result in a more collaborative, student-centered and student-shaped pedagogy. However, research shows that teachers' uptake of ICT varies greatly within as well as across countries (European Commission, 2013; Law, Pelgrum, & Plomp, 2008).

Although ICILS 2013 did not investigate the relationship between ICT use in schools or classrooms and achievement in academic learning areas such as language, mathematics, and science, a recent meta-analysis conducted by Tamin, Bernard, Borokhovski, Abrami, and Schmid (2011) points to positive associations between pedagogical use of ICT and achievement in various learning areas. Findings such as these doubtless also prompt the growing emphasis on ICT use in educational contexts.

A considerable body of research has looked at the benefits of integrating ICT in teaching, but some research has also considered barriers to using ICT in teaching. Ertmer (1999), for example, proposed a distinction between first-order and second-order barriers. First-order barriers include factors such as resources (both hardware and software) and ICT-related training and support. Second-order factors are those that relate to teachers' expertise and interest, such as confidence in using ICT, beliefs about student learning, and perceptions about the value of ICT in education.

When conducting their study of computer integration in the classrooms of 185 primary and 204 secondary school teachers, Mueller, Wood, Willoughby, Ross, and Specht (2008) used discriminant function analysis to identify factors that distinguished between teachers who integrated computers in their classroom teaching and teachers who did not. The major distinguishing factors the authors identified were teachers' previous positive teaching experience with computers, how comfortable teachers were with computers, the beliefs they held about the value of computers in education (in terms of both instruction and motivation), and the support they received with respect to using computers. The authors also identified several general factors, such as teachers' sense of efficacy, beliefs about teaching, and attitudes to work. Participation in professional development workshops was identified as a relevant factor for primary school but not for secondary school teachers.

The European Commission (2013) concluded from its survey of schools, teachers, and students in 31 countries that although most of the participating teachers were familiar with ICT for teaching and learning, they used these technologies mainly for preparing lessons and only to a limited extent during their classroom work with students. The authors of the European Commission report also concluded that student use of ICT in lessons is most likely to occur and be successful when teachers are confident about using ICT, view ICT use in education positively, and are in school environments that support pedagogical ICT use. The authors furthermore emphasized that although teachers had become more confident users of ICT between 2008 and 2013, and computer resources were more abundant than in 2008, active use of ICT in lessons had barely increased.

The Second International Technology in Education Study (SITES) 2006, conducted by the International Association for the Evaluation of Educational Achievement (IEA), also concluded that teachers were more likely to use ICT if they were confident users of these tools, if they had participated in ICT-related professional development, and if there were relatively few contextual obstacles (infrastructure, digital learning resources, ICT access) to that use (Law et al., 2008). In addition, the results from SITES 2006 showed that the percentage of teachers reporting ICT use was significantly higher among science teachers than among mathematics teachers. Other studies have reported similar findings (Jones, 2004; Kozma & McGhee, 2003). One inference we can draw from these results is that the subject (or discipline) context may be an important aspect determining uptake of ICT in teaching.

An earlier iteration of SITES highlighted ways in which ICT can support pedagogical innovation. This international study, known as SITES Module 2 (SITES-M2), involved a detailed examination of various pedagogical practices that, according to expert opinion, used ICT in innovative ways (Kozma, 2003b). Twenty-eight education systems took part in the study, which generated a set of 174 qualitative case studies of innovative pedagogical practices. The SITES researchers then used qualitative and quantitative methods based on a common framework to conduct an intensive analysis of each case. The results identified seven patterns of innovation involving ICT use: tool use, student collaboration, information management, teacher collaboration, communication with outside authorities, product creation, and tutorial practice (Kozma, 2003b).

Ertmer, Ottenbreit-Leftwich, Sadik, Sendurur, and Sendurur (2012) conducted an indepth study focused on a small number of teachers recognized as notable users of technology. Findings indicated that the teachers' general beliefs about teaching influenced how they used the technology as did their interest in the technology itself. According to Aubusson, Burke, Schuck, and Kearney (2014), learning technologies can influence how teachers adopt "rich tasks" (extended project work) in their classes. The authors argue that engagement with learning technologies "moderates teachers' perceptions about the use of rich tasks" (p. 219). Aubusson and colleagues (2014), however, point to the complexity of factors mediating pedagogical use of technology, as well as to the range of factors that influence teachers' decisions to adopt technology in the first place.

Teachers' familiarity with ICT

In this section, we look at several aspects relevant to how and why the ICILS teachers were using ICT as part of their teaching practice. Of particular interest is the extent to which teachers' pedagogical use of ICT was associated with their use of computers in other settings and their experience of using computers in general.

Experience with and use of computers

The ICILS teacher questionnaire asked teachers to use the following response categories to indicate how much experience they had in using computers for teaching purposes: "never," "less than two years," and "two years or more." The questionnaire also asked teachers how frequently they used computers in various settings: at school when teaching, at school for other purposes, and outside of school. The response categories for each place were "never," "less than once a month," "at least once a month but not every week," "at least once a week but not every day," and "every day." In the discussion of computer use based on Table 7.1, we defined frequent computer use as at least once a week (i.e., the last two response categories indicating the highest frequencies).

Table 7.1 presents the data for teacher experience with computers in terms of the percentages of teachers who said they were using computers in each of the categories. The table also records the percentages of teachers who said they frequently used computers at school when teaching, at school for other work-related purposes, and outside school for any purpose.

The majority of teachers in all countries (an ICILS 2013 average of 84%) reported having at least two years of experience using computers. The national percentages ranged from a high of 94 percent in the Canadian province of Newfoundland and Labrador to a low of 71 percent in Croatia. Eleven percent of teachers crossnationally had less than two years' experience; only five percent of teachers had no experience using computers. Teacher experience in using computers for teaching purposes was, on average, moderately strongly associated with frequency of use ($r = 0.34$).

According to the survey data, teachers were most frequently using computers outside of school (the ICILS 2013 average was 90%), followed by use at school for work-related purposes other than teaching (84%), and finally use at school when teaching (62%). Teachers from the Canadian province of Newfoundland and Labrador were the most frequent users of ICT in all three settings.

The percentage of teachers who said they frequently used computers when teaching is of particular interest in the context of ICILS. In Newfoundland and Labrador as well as

Table 7.1: National percentages of teachers' computer experience and use in different settings (at school teaching, at school for other purposes, outside school)

Country	Teacher Experience in Using Computers			Teachers Using a Computer at Least Once a Week		
	Never	Less than two years	Two years or more	At school when teaching	At school for other work-related purposes	Outside school for any purpose
Australia	0 (0.1)	7 (0.7)	92 (0.7)	90 (0.8) ◀	98 (0.4) ◀	97 (0.3) △
Chile	3 (0.6)	12 (1.0)	86 (1.2)	62 (2.0)	83 (1.8)	93 (1.2) △
Croatia	15 (0.8)	14 (0.9)	71 (1.1)	41 (1.5) ▶	72 (1.3) ▶	91 (1.0)
Czech Republic	4 (0.5)	11 (0.9)	85 (1.0)	66 (1.7) △	92 (0.8) △	96 (0.5) △
Korea, Republic of	3 (0.9)	10 (1.0)	88 (0.7)	76 (1.7) ◀	94 (0.8) ◀	83 (1.3) ▽
Lithuania	3 (0.4)	7 (0.8)	91 (0.9)	66 (1.7) △	89 (1.1) △	93 (0.7) △
Poland	7 (0.8)	8 (0.7)	86 (1.0)	41 (1.5) ▶	77 (1.7) ▽	98 (0.4) △
Russian Federation[1]	3 (0.4)	10 (1.1)	87 (1.1)	76 (1.6) ◀	86 (1.1)	84 (1.6) ▽
Slovak Republic	7 (0.8)	14 (0.8)	78 (1.1)	58 (1.7) ▽	84 (1.0)	93 (0.7) △
Slovenia	8 (0.7)	12 (1.0)	80 (1.3)	66 (1.4) △	93 (0.7) △	96 (0.5) △
Thailand	8 (1.6)	14 (1.9)	78 (2.6)	50 (2.5) ▶	74 (2.8) ▶	71 (2.8) ▶
Turkey	5 (0.7)	13 (1.4)	82 (1.7)	47 (3.4) ▶	65 (1.9) ▶	91 (1.1)
ICILS 2013 average	5 (0.2)	11 (0.3)	84 (0.4)	62 (0.5)	84 (0.4)	90 (0.3)
Countries not meeting sample requirements						
Denmark	0 (0.1)	4 (0.9)	95 (0.9)	79 (2.3)	99 (0.4)	98 (0.8)
Germany	6 (0.8)	9 (1.0)	85 (1.2)	34 (2.3)	65 (2.2)	97 (0.5)
Hong Kong SAR	1 (0.3)	8 (0.9)	91 (1.0)	79 (1.6)	95 (0.9)	94 (0.7)
Netherlands	2 (0.3)	9 (1.1)	88 (1.1)	77 (1.7)	97 (0.5)	99 (0.4)
Norway (Grade 9)	1 (0.2)	7 (0.9)	92 (0.9)	78 (1.7)	98 (0.6)	98 (0.4)
Benchmarking participant						
Newfoundland and Labrador, Canada	0 (0.0)	6 (1.3)	94 (1.3)	93 (1.4)	99 (0.4)	99 (0.4)
Benchmarking participant not meeting sample requirements						
Ontario, Canada	0 (0.0)	4 (1.1)	95 (1.1)	89 (1.4)	98 (0.9)	100 (0.2)

◀ More than 10 percentage points above ICILS 2013 average
△ Significantly above ICILS 2013 average
▽ Significantly below ICILS 2013 average
▶ More than 10 percentage points below ICILS 2013 average

Notes:
() Standard errors appear in parentheses. Because some results are rounded to the nearest whole number, some totals may appear inconsistent.
[1] Country surveyed teachers retrospectively to the previous school year when they were teaching the target grade.

in Australia, the two percentages (93% and 90% respectively) were much higher than the ICILS 2013 average. Fewer than half of all teachers in Croatia (41%), Poland (41%), and Turkey (47%) reported using a computer at least once a week at school when teaching. We found only moderate correlations between frequent computer use when teaching and frequent computer use for other school-related purposes and frequent computer use outside school. The associations tended to be strongest when computer use for teaching was less extensive.

The ICILS 2013 average for the percentage of teachers frequently using computers (62%) was similar to the ICILS 2013 average for the percentage of students frequently using computers (56%). However, when we compare the data in Table 7.1 with those in Table 5.2, we can see that teachers in some countries were more likely than their students to report more frequent use of computers.[1] The correlations between school averages for teachers' weekly computer use and school averages for students' weekly computer use were relatively weak. Across countries, the school-level correlation coefficients between the aggregated data of these indicators averaged about 0.2.

There are several possible reasons why teachers' and students' use of computers in classrooms might differ. One is that teachers use computers as part of their teaching practice even though their students do not use them during class time. This occurrence could be due to scarce resources or teacher-centered pedagogy. A second reason is that teachers and students undertake different activities in classrooms so that, for example, students use ICT for activities while teachers do not. A third reason may have to do with the correspondence between questions eliciting data. The ICILS student questionnaire asked students if they used computers at school whereas the teacher questionnaire asked teachers if they used computers when teaching. Thus, the ICILS students may have been using computers at school but outside of lessons (classroom time). The point being made here is that recorded teacher use of ICT may not necessarily correspond with recorded student use of ICT.

Teachers' views about ICT

In this section, we report the ICILS teachers' perceptions of the benefits of using ICT in school education. We also record the teachers' self-expressed confidence in using ICT and their views on how well their school environments supported pedagogical use of ICT.

Benefits of ICT in school education

Debates about the benefits of widespread adoption of ICT by schools tend to be characterized by different and often strongly held views. Various stakeholders maintain that these technologies develop, among other attributes, 21st-century skills (including CIL) that are central to life in modern societies, facilitate access to resources, provide rich learning materials that engage student interest, and support more effective curriculum design and planning (Kozma & McGhee, 2003). Others, however, argue that these technologies draw attention away from the traditional core educational tasks of reading and mathematics, limit the time spent on the direct contact with materials that is essential for concept formation, provide artificial views of the real/natural world, and encourage uncritical acceptance of views that may not be based in evidence (Cuban,

---

1 This discrepancy was greatest in Korea (57 percentage points), Slovenia (40 percentage points), Newfoundland and Labrador (39 percentage points), and Poland (38 percentage points).

2001). We were interested in determining if the ICILS teachers' views on the advantages and disadvantages of ICT in school education had any association with the extent to which they were using computers in their classrooms.

The ICILS teacher questionnaire asked teachers to rate their level of agreement ("strongly agree," "agree," "disagree," "strongly disagree") with a series of statements that presented both positive and negative aspects of using ICT for teaching and learning at school. Table 7.2 shows the national percentages of teachers expressing agreement (i.e., either strongly agree or agree) with each of these statements. It also shows whether each national percentage was significantly above or below the ICILS 2013 average for the item.

With regard to the statements reflecting positive aspects of ICT use for teaching and learning, almost all teachers across participating countries (an ICILS 2013 average of 96%) agreed that ICT use enables students to access better sources of information. The

Table 7.2: National percentages of teachers agreeing with statements about ICT teaching and learning in schools

Country	Enables Students to Access Better Sources of Information	Results in Poorer Writing Skills among Students	Helps Students to Consolidate and Process Information More Effectively	Only Introduces Organizational Problems for Schools	Helps Students Learn to Collaborate With Other Students	Impedes Concept Formation Better Done with Real Objects than Computer Images
Australia	95 (0.6)	64 (1.4)	78 (1.0) ▼	18 (1.1)	72 (1.2) ▽	32 (1.1) ▽
Chile	97 (0.5) △	55 (2.1) ▼	94 (0.8) △	11 (1.1) ▽	90 (1.0) ▲	24 (1.7) ▼
Croatia	95 (0.7)	65 (1.0)	86 (0.8) ▽	15 (0.9) ▽	79 (0.9)	42 (1.0) △
Czech Republic	97 (0.5)	75 (1.2) △	92 (0.8)	7 (0.6) ▽	62 (1.4) ▼	48 (1.2) △
Korea, Republic of	95 (0.6)	76 (1.6) △	90 (1.1)	42 (1.3) ▲	69 (1.3) ▽	51 (2.1) ▲
Lithuania	97 (0.4) △	73 (1.4) △	94 (0.5) △	16 (1.0)	80 (1.0)	37 (1.3) ▽
Poland	96 (0.4)	68 (1.7)	93 (0.7) △	7 (0.8) ▼	85 (1.1) △	33 (1.2) ▽
Russian Federation[1]	89 (1.1) ▽	63 (1.9)	95 (0.7) △	15 (1.3)	84 (1.2) △	46 (2.4) △
Slovak Republic	98 (0.3) △	71 (1.4) △	87 (1.0) ▽	12 (1.0) ▽	77 (1.3)	29 (1.1) ▼
Slovenia	93 (0.6) ▽	79 (1.0) ▲	94 (0.7) △	10 (0.8) ▽	67 (1.0) ▼	55 (1.1) ▲
Thailand	99 (0.6) △	52 (3.7) ▼	93 (1.2)	32 (2.9) ▲	90 (2.1) ▲	42 (3.0)
Turkey	98 (0.3) △	59 (1.7) ▽	94 (0.8) △	20 (1.4)	79 (1.4)	38 (1.6)
ICILS 2013 average	96 (0.2)	67 (0.5)	91 (0.3)	17 (0.4)	78 (0.4)	40 (0.5)
Countries not meeting sample requirements						
Denmark	98 (0.8)	23 (2.4)	91 (1.6)	20 (2.8)	70 (1.7)	21 (2.0)
Germany	90 (0.9)	52 (1.7)	65 (1.3)	34 (1.7)	50 (1.9)	38 (1.7)
Hong Kong SAR	97 (0.5)	62 (1.6)	86 (1.1)	19 (1.4)	85 (1.0)	71 (1.4)
Netherlands	91 (0.9)	62 (1.5)	79 (1.4)	13 (1.5)	52 (1.8)	30 (1.5)
Norway (Grade 9)	97 (0.5)	30 (1.6)	92 (1.1)	17 (1.9)	61 (1.8)	23 (1.5)
Benchmarking participant						
Newfoundland and Labrador, Canada	98 (0.8)	39 (2.8)	91 (1.9)	13 (1.9)	85 (2.3)	20 (2.2)
Benchmarking participant not meeting sample requirements						
Ontario, Canada	98 (0.7)	29 (2.1)	92 (1.9)	12 (1.9)	82 (2.5)	20 (2.9)

Notes:
() Standard errors appear in parentheses. Because some results are rounded to the nearest whole number, some totals may appear inconsistent.
[1] Country surveyed teachers retrospectively to the previous school year when they were teaching the target grade.

lowest rate of agreement was found in Russia (89%) and the highest rate in Thailand (99%). Similarly, more than 90 percent of teachers, on average crossnationally, indicated that using ICT helped students consolidate and process information more effectively. National percentages of agreement ranged from 78 percent in Australia to 95 percent in the Russian Federation.

On average across the participating countries, 78 percent of teachers agreed that ICT helps students learn to collaborate with one another, and 68 percent believed that ICT helps students communicate more effectively with others. Percentages of agreement for countries ranged from 62 percent to 90 percent for the former statement, and from 57 percent to 88 percent for the latter.

Almost 80 percent of teachers on average across participating countries agreed that ICT helps students develop greater interest in learning. The national percentages ranged from 66 percent in the Czech Republic to 92 percent in Thailand. Across countries, four

Table 7.2: National percentages of teachers agreeing with statements about ICT teaching and learning in schools (contd.)

Enables Students to Communicate More Effectively with Others	Only Encourages Copying Material from Published Internet Sources	Helps Students Develop Greater Interest in Learning	Helps Students Work at a Level Appropriate to Their Learning Needs	Limits the Amount of Personal Communication among Students	Helps Students Develop Skills in Planning and Self-Regulating Their Work	Results in Poorer Calculation and Estimation Skills among Students	Improves Academic Performance of Students	Only Distracts Students from Learning
57 (1.0) ▼	46 (1.3) ▽	86 (0.9) △	80 (1.0)	43 (1.1) ▼	60 (1.3) ▽	41 (1.6) ▽	61 (1.2) ▽	23 (1.5)
78 (1.3) △	40 (1.7) ▽	86 (1.4) △	86 (1.3) △	46 (1.7) ▼	78 (1.3) ▲	35 (1.9) ▼	82 (1.6) ▲	13 (0.9) ▼
57 (1.1) ▼	51 (1.2)	72 (1.0) ▽	69 (1.4) ▼	63 (1.2) △	54 (1.2) ▼	49 (1.1)	53 (2.1) ▼	25 (1.0)
58 (1.2) ▼	59 (1.5) △	66 (1.3) ▼	74 (1.4) ▽	71 (1.2) ▲	41 (1.4) ▼	46 (1.3)	53 (1.6) ▼	28 (1.4) △
63 (2.2) ▽	48 (1.8)	90 (0.7) ▲	79 (2.1)	56 (1.2)	62 (1.6)	64 (1.1) ▲	64 (1.7) ▽	31 (1.2) △
71 (1.2) △	56 (1.3) △	79 (1.0)	83 (0.9) △	57 (1.3)	55 (1.5) ▼	46 (1.3)	72 (1.0) △	27 (1.4)
83 (0.9) ▲	31 (1.3) ▼	65 (1.6) ▼	75 (1.3) ▽	59 (1.3)	64 (1.4)	46 (1.3)	72 (1.2) △	16 (0.9) ▽
73 (1.6) △	40 (1.9) ▽	80 (1.6)	87 (1.4) △	57 (2.0)	67 (2.1)	61 (2.0) ▲	64 (1.6) ▽	18 (1.5) ▽
70 (1.3)	46 (1.4) ▽	70 (1.6) ▽	79 (1.6)	60 (1.6)	67 (1.6)	44 (1.4) ▽	58 (1.6) ▽	26 (1.2)
59 (1.1) ▽	46 (1.3) ▽	68 (1.5) ▼	69 (1.4) ▼	68 (1.3) △	69 (1.3) △	49 (1.2)	56 (1.2) ▼	11 (0.8) ▼
88 (1.6) ▲	68 (2.4) ▲	92 (2.0) ▲	93 (1.3) ▲	56 (3.1)	88 (1.9) ▲	46 (3.9)	93 (1.4) ▲	48 (2.5) ▲
64 (1.4) ▽	61 (1.5) ▲	91 (0.8) ▲	87 (1.4) △	61 (1.8)	81 (1.4) ▲	51 (1.5)	85 (1.4) ▲	19 (1.3) ▽
68 (0.4)	49 (0.5)	79 (0.4)	80 (0.4)	58 (0.5)	65 (0.4)	48 (0.5)	68 (0.4)	24 (0.4)
82 (1.7)	36 (2.7)	87 (1.7)	82 (1.2)	24 (2.6)	75 (2.2)	17 (1.7)	83 (1.5)	14 (1.7)
34 (1.7)	76 (1.7)	64 (1.3)	57 (1.6)	52 (1.6)	48 (1.8)	41 (1.6)	39 (1.6)	29 (1.5)
69 (1.7)	45 (2.0)	86 (0.9)	83 (1.3)	25 (1.7)	66 (1.9)	40 (1.6)	59 (1.8)	35 (1.8)
53 (2.7)	64 (1.7)	82 (1.4)	83 (1.3)	52 (1.9)	60 (2.0)	33 (1.9)	59 (2.1)	19 (1.5)
77 (1.6)	31 (1.7)	89 (1.2)	76 (1.8)	32 (1.8)	64 (1.7)	22 (1.4)	75 (1.6)	15 (1.5)
75 (2.6)	38 (2.6)	94 (1.5)	86 (2.1)	34 (3.0)	73 (3.1)	30 (2.8)	81 (2.6)	14 (1.6)
71 (2.6)	33 (2.9)	95 (0.9)	88 (1.9)	35 (3.3)	76 (2.7)	33 (2.9)	82 (2.9)	11 (1.5)

▲ More than 10 percentage points above ICILS 2013 average
△ Significantly above ICILS 2013 average
▽ Significantly below ICILS 2013 average
▼ More than 10 percentage points below ICILS 2013 average

out of five teachers agreed or strongly agreed that ICT helps students work at a level appropriate to their learning. The lowest levels of teacher agreement with this statement were recorded in Croatia and Slovenia (69%), and the highest in Thailand (93%).

There was less support for statements concerned with the impact of ICT on academic performance, planning, and self-regulation. Approximately two thirds of teachers (the ICILS 2013 average was 68%) agreed with the proposition that ICT improves students' academic performance. The level of agreement was highest in Thailand and Turkey (93% and 85% respectively) and lowest in the Czech Republic and Croatia (53% each). A similar percentage of teachers (65%) believed, on average, that ICT helps students plan and self-regulate their work. Agreement was less extensive among teachers from the Czech Republic, where less than half of the teachers agreed with this statement (41%). In contrast, 88 percent of teachers from Thailand either strongly agreed or agreed with this statement.

Teachers' views of statements reflecting negative aspects of the use of ICT in teaching and learning generally attracted less support than statements reflecting positive aspects. However, the statement that ICT use results in poorer writing skills amongst students attracted agreement from two thirds of teachers. A majority of teachers in each country indicated that they believed this to be the case. An exception was in Newfoundland and Labrador (Canada), where only 39 percent of teachers expressed agreement with the statement. Slovenia had the highest percentage of teachers expressing agreement with this statement (79%). Similarly, almost half of teachers internationally (the ICILS 2013 average was 48%) endorsed the view that using ICT results in poorer calculation and estimation skills among students. The national percentages of agreement ranged from 30 percent in Newfoundland and Labrador (Canada) to 64 percent in Korea.

On average across the ICILS countries, teachers rejected the statement that ICT "only introduces organizational problems for schools" (the ICILS 2013 average was 17%). Only seven percent of teachers in both the Czech Republic and Poland agreed with this assertion whereas 42 percent of teachers in Korea endorsed this view.

Across the ICILS countries, 40 percent of teachers, on average, said they agreed with the view that "ICT impedes concept formation better done with real objects than computer images." Percentages of agreement ranged from 20 percent in Newfoundland and Labrador (Canada) to 55 percent in Slovenia.

Internationally, almost half of all teachers (the ICILS 2013 average was 49%) thought that ICT "only encourages copying material from published internet sources." Poland recorded the lowest rate of agreement with this statement (31%); two thirds of teachers in Thailand (66%) endorsed this view.

With the exception of teachers in Australia (43%), Chile (46%), and Newfoundland and Labrador (34%), majorities of teachers in each country believed that ICT "limits the amount of personal communication among students" (an ICILS 2013 average of 58%). The highest percentage of agreement with this statement was recorded in the Czech Republic (71%).

Majorities of teachers in all participating countries rejected the notion that ICT only distracts students from learning (on average 76% of teachers disagreed with this statement). Thailand had the highest percentage of teachers believing that ICT is a distraction (46%); Slovenia had the lowest such percentage (11%).

We found that the items in the question about possible consequences of using ICT in teaching and learning at school actually represented two separate dimensions (see Fraillon, Schulz, Friedman, Ainley, & Gebhardt, forthcoming)—one reflecting the positive aspects of using ICT in teaching and learning at school and the other reflecting negative perceptions.[2] We accordingly formed two scales reflecting teachers' views on ICT use in schools. The first contained positively worded items. The second contained negatively worded items.

We used the Rasch partial credit model to construct the *positive views on using ICT in teaching and learning scale*. This scale was standardized to have an ICILS 2013 average score of 50 points and a standard deviation of 10 points, and it had an average reliability (coefficient alpha) of 0.83.[3] Table 7.3 presents the average scale scores, with the higher values reflecting more positive views, by country and age group (teachers under 40 years of age and those over).

Teachers from Chile, Thailand, and Turkey had average scale scores that were more than three points higher than the ICILS 2013 average for the scale, a finding which suggests that the teachers in these countries held a relatively more positive opinion of the value that ICT offers teaching and learning. Teachers in Slovenia scored three points lower than the average, suggesting that they held less positive views on the value of ICT for teaching and learning than their colleagues in the other ICILS countries. Overall, there were no differences in views between the two age groups. However, older teachers from the Czech Republic and Slovak Republic had slightly more positive views than the younger teachers of the value of using ICT; the scale score differences between the two were statistically significant.

The second scale, *negative views of using ICT in teaching and learning,*[4] was constructed in the same way as the other scales described in this report. It had an average reliability (coefficient alpha) of 0.80 and was standardized to have an ICILS 2013 average score of 50 points and a standard deviation of 10 points. The higher scores on the scale reflect more negative views of ICT use at school. Table 7.4 shows the national average scores for all teachers and within the two age groups for each participating country.

We observed little variation among countries in the extent to which teachers held negative views about ICT use in teaching and learning. Teachers in Chile, whose mean scale score was more than five points lower than the ICILS 2013 average scale score, were the least negative of all teachers across the participating countries. No country recorded an average scale score more than three points higher than the ICILS 2013 average.

---

2 It is possible, and our analyses confirmed this, for individuals to simultaneously hold both positive and negative views of the use of ICT in school given they are not necessarily polar opposites.

3 The items making up this scale were:
   - Enables students to access better sources of information;
   - Helps students to consolidate and process information more effectively;
   - Helps students learn to collaborate with other students;
   - Enables students to communicate more effectively with others;
   - Helps students develop greater interest in learning;
   - Helps students work at a level appropriate to their learning needs;
   - Helps students develop skills in planning and self-regulation of their work; and
   - Improves academic performance of students.

4 The items making up this scale were:
   - Results in poorer writing skills among students;
   - Only introduces organizational problems for schools;
   - Impedes concept formation better done with real objects than computer images;
   - Only encourages copying material from published internet sources;
   - Limits the amount of personal communication among students;
   - Results in poorer calculation and estimation skills among students; and
   - Only distracts students from learning.

Table 7.3: National averages for teachers with positive views on using ICT in teaching and learning overall and by age group

| Country | Positive Views on Using ICT in Teaching and Learning by Age Group | | | | Score Distribution by Age Group |
	All teachers	Under 40	40 and over	Differences (40 and over — under 40)*	
Australia	48 (0.3) ▽	48 (0.3)	48 (0.4)	0 (0.5)	
Chile	55 (0.5) ◀	56 (0.7)	55 (0.6)	-1 (0.9)	
Croatia	47 (0.3) ▽	47 (0.3)	47 (0.3)	0 (0.4)	
Czech Republic	47 (0.3) ▽	46 (0.3)	48 (0.4)	1 (0.4)	
Korea, Republic of	48 (0.3) ▽	49 (0.5)	48 (0.5)	-1 (0.9)	
Lithuania	49 (0.2) ▽	49 (0.5)	49 (0.2)	0 (0.5)	
Poland	50 (0.3)	49 (0.3)	50 (0.4)	0 (0.4)	
Russian Federation[1]	50 (0.4)	50 (0.5)	50 (0.4)	0 (0.5)	
Slovak Republic	48 (0.3) ▽	47 (0.4)	48 (0.3)	1 (0.4)	
Slovenia	47 (0.3) ▶	46 (0.4)	47 (0.3)	1 (0.5)	
Thailand	56 (0.7) ◀	56 (0.7)	57 (0.9)	0 (0.7)	
Turkey	54 (0.4) ◀	54 (0.4)	54 (0.8)	0 (0.9)	
ICILS 2013 average	50 (0.1)	50 (0.1)	50 (0.1)	0 (0.2)	
Countries not meeting sample requirements					
Denmark	51 (0.4)	51 (0.6)	51 (0.5)	0 (0.7)	
Germany	43 (0.3)	43 (0.5)	43 (0.3)	0 (0.6)	
Hong Kong SAR	48 (0.2)	48 (0.3)	48 (0.4)	0 (0.5)	
Netherlands	46 (0.3)	46 (0.4)	45 (0.4)	-1 (0.3)	
Norway (Grade 9)	49 (0.3)	50 (0.5)	49 (0.3)	-1 (0.5)	
Benchmarking participant					
Newfoundland and Labrador, Canada	53 (0.7)	52 (0.9)	54 (1.0)	2 (1.2)	
Benchmarking participant not meeting sample requirements					
Ontario, Canada	54 (0.9)	55 (1.1)	53 (1.4)	-2 (1.6)	

Notes:

* Statistically significant (*p*<0.05) coefficients in **bold**.

() Standard errors appear in parentheses. Because some results are rounded to the nearest whole number, some totals may appear inconsistent.

[1] Country surveyed teachers retrospectively to the previous school year when they were teaching the target grade.

▲ More than three score points above ICILS 2013 average

△ Significantly above ICILS 2013 average

▽ Significantly below ICILS 2013 average

▶ More than three score points below ICILS 2013 average

■ Under 40 average score +/−confidence interval
■ Over 40 average score +/− confidence interval

On average, teachers with a score in the range indicated by this color have more than a 50% probability of responding to the statements about positive views on using ICT in teaching and learning with:

Disagreement to positive, agreement to negative statements

Agreement to positive, disagreement to negative items

Table 7.4: National averages for teachers with negative views on using ICT in teaching and learning overall and by age group

Country	Negative Views on Using ICT in Teaching and Learning by Age Group				Score Distribution by Age Group
	All teachers	Under 40	40 and over	Differences (40 and over – under 40)*	
Australia	49 (0.3) ▽	49 (0.4)	48 (0.4)	-1 (0.5)	
Chile	45 (0.5) ▶	44 (0.8)	46 (0.6)	2 (0.9)	
Croatia	51 (0.2) △	49 (0.3)	52 (0.3)	2 (0.4)	
Czech Republic	50 (0.3)	49 (0.4)	51 (0.4)	2 (0.5)	
Korea, Republic of	53 (0.3) △	51 (0.6)	53 (0.6)	2 (1.1)	
Lithuania	51 (0.3) △	49 (0.7)	51 (0.3)	2 (0.7)	
Poland	49 (0.3) ▽	48 (0.4)	49 (0.4)	1 (0.4)	
Russian Federation[1]	50 (0.4)	49 (0.6)	51 (0.4)	1 (0.5)	
Slovak Republic	50 (0.3)	50 (0.5)	50 (0.3)	0 (0.5)	
Slovenia	51 (0.3) △	50 (0.4)	51 (0.3)	1 (0.4)	
Thailand	51 (1.2)	51 (1.1)	51 (1.5)	-1 (1.1)	
Turkey	51 (0.4)	50 (0.3)	53 (0.8)	3 (0.7)	
ICILS 2013 average	50 (0.1)	49 (0.2)	51 (0.2)	1 (0.2)	
Countries not meeting sample requirements					
Denmark	42 (0.6)	42 (0.8)	42 (0.7)	0 (0.8)	
Germany	50 (0.4)	52 (1.0)	49 (0.7)	-3 (1.5)	
Hong Kong SAR	50 (0.3)	50 (0.4)	51 (0.3)	1 (0.5)	
Netherlands	49 (0.3)	49 (0.4)	49 (0.3)	-1 (0.5)	
Norway (Grade 9)	44 (0.4)	44 (0.4)	44 (0.5)	0 (0.6)	
Benchmarking participant					
Newfoundland and Labrador, Canada	45 (0.7)	46 (0.8)	44 (1.0)	-2 (1.2)	
Benchmarking participant not meeting sample requirements					
Ontario, Canada	43 (0.9)	43 (1.2)	43 (1.1)	0 (1.6)	

Notes:

* Statistically significant (*p*<0.05) coefficients in **bold**.

( ) Standard errors appear in parentheses. Because some results are rounded to the nearest whole number, some totals may appear inconsistent.

[1] Country surveyed teachers retrospectively to the previous school year when they were teaching the target grade.

▲ More than three score points above ICILS 2013 average

△ Significantly above ICILS 2013 average

▽ Significantly below ICILS 2013 average

▶ More than three score points below ICILS 2013 average

Under 40 average score +/− confidence interval

Over 40 average score +/− confidence interval

On average, teachers with a score in the range indicated by this color have more than a 50% probability of responding to the statements about negative views on using ICT in teaching and learning with:

Disagreement to positive, agreement to negative statements

Agreement to positive, disagreement to negative items

Teachers over 40 years of age tended to report significantly more negative attitudes toward ICT use than did their colleagues under 40 years of age. This finding featured in eight of the 13 countries that met sampling requirements. The only teachers under the age of 40 who held more negative views than their older colleagues about pedagogical use of ICT were those in Newfoundland and Labrador (Canada).

Confidence in using ICT

As studies such as SITES 2006 (Law et al., 2008) and the School Net 2013 survey (European Commission, 2013) indicate, teachers who are confident users of ICT are more likely than unconfident teachers to adopt ICT as part of their teaching. The ICILS teacher questionnaire invited teachers to rate their confidence ("I know how to do this," "I could work out how to do this," or "I do not think I could do this") in their ability to complete various tasks on a computer by themselves. The tasks listed were ones further developed from an item set used in SITES 2006 (Law et al., 2008).

Table 7.5 reports the percentages of teachers who said they knew how to do each of these tasks. The tasks that teachers felt most comfortable with were finding useful resources on the internet (92% of teachers crossnationally), producing a letter using a word

Table 7.5: National percentages of teachers expressing confidence in doing different computer tasks

Country	Producing a Letter Using a Wordprocessing Program	Emailing a File as an Attachment	Storing Digital Photos on a Computer	Filing Digital Documents in Folders and Subfolders	Monitoring Students' Progress	Using a Spreadsheet Program (e.g., [Lotus 1 2 3 ®, Microsoft Excel ®]) for Keeping Records or Analyzing Data
Australia	98 (0.3) △	98 (0.3) △	93 (0.5) ▲	94 (0.6) △	86 (0.8) ▲	74 (1.2) ▲
Chile	90 (1.2)	92 (1.2)	84 (1.5)	89 (1.3) △	62 (1.9)	57 (1.7)
Croatia	90 (0.7)	86 (0.8) ▽	77 (0.8) ▽	79 (0.8) ▽	54 (1.5) ▼	45 (1.4) ▼
Czech Republic	97 (0.4) △	96 (0.5) △	79 (1.3) ▽	90 (0.7) △	49 (1.5) ▼	58 (1.3)
Korea, Republic of	95 (0.8) △	97 (0.9) △	96 (0.9) ▲	94 (0.7) △	62 (1.7)	69 (1.1) △
Lithuania	92 (0.8) △	91 (1.1)	82 (1.1)	81 (1.2) ▽	83 (1.6) ▲	53 (1.3) ▽
Poland	97 (0.5) △	95 (0.7) △	80 (1.0) ▽	82 (1.2)	66 (1.9)	66 (1.4) △
Russian Federation[1]	90 (1.0)	76 (1.9) ▼	81 (1.3)	88 (1.4) △	68 (2.1)	64 (1.4) △
Slovak Republic	95 (0.6) △	93 (0.8) △	78 (1.1) ▽	71 (1.1) ▼	59 (1.1) ▽	68 (1.1) △
Slovenia	97 (0.6) △	97 (0.5) △	82 (1.0)	84 (1.0)	67 (1.0)	55 (1.5) ▽
Thailand	46 (3.1) ▼	69 (1.8) ▼	72 (1.8) ▼	73 (1.9) ▼	50 (2.6) ▼	55 (2.7)
Turkey	76 (1.5) ▼	81 (1.8) ▽	84 (1.5)	83 (1.6)	73 (1.3) △	43 (1.8) ▼
ICILS 2013 average	89 (0.3)	89 (0.3)	82 (0.3)	84 (0.3)	65 (0.5)	59 (0.4)
Countries not meeting sample requirements						
Denmark	99 (0.4)	99 (0.4)	90 (1.4)	92 (1.6)	84 (2.2)	55 (2.4)
Germany	99 (0.3)	94 (0.9)	87 (1.4)	93 (0.9)	51 (1.5)	52 (1.9)
Hong Kong SAR	94 (1.1)	97 (0.6)	93 (1.0)	92 (0.9)	52 (1.5)	74 (1.5)
Netherlands	99 (0.4)	98 (0.4)	93 (0.7)	95 (0.7)	96 (0.7)	58 (1.4)
Norway (Grade 9)	98 (0.4)	97 (0.7)	90 (1.1)	92 (0.7)	71 (2.0)	52 (1.7)
Benchmarking participant						
Newfoundland and Labrador, Canada	99 (0.4)	98 (0.8)	92 (1.7)	92 (1.7)	89 (1.5)	56 (2.7)
Benchmarking participant not meeting sample requirements						
Ontario, Canada	99 (0.5)	98 (0.8)	90 (1.8)	88 (1.9)	77 (2.8)	60 (2.8)

Notes:

() Standard errors appear in parentheses. Because some results are rounded to the nearest whole number, some totals may appear inconsistent.

[1] Country surveyed teachers retrospectively to the previous school year when they were teaching the target grade.

processing program (89%), and emailing a file as an attachment (89%). More than 80 percent of teachers across the participating countries were confident of their ability to file digital documents in folders and subfolders (84%) and to store their digital photos on a computer (82%).

On average internationally, more than half, but under four fifths, of the teachers expressed confidence in carrying out a series of other tasks. These were using the internet for online purchases and payments (77%), producing presentations with simple animation functions (76%), preparing lessons involving student use of ICT (73%), using a spreadsheet for keeping records or analyzing data (59%), and contributing to a discussion forum/user group on the internet (58%).

Approximately two thirds of teachers across participating countries were confident about their ability to use computers for the following two aspects of teaching. Seventy-one percent expressed confidence in their ability to use ICT for assessing student learning, and 65 percent were confident that they could use a computer for monitoring students' progress. Less than half of the teachers (on average across participating countries) felt confident about installing software (47%) and collaborating with others using shared resources (44%).

Table 7.5: National percentages of teachers expressing confidence in doing different computer tasks (contd.)

Contributing to a Discussion Forum/ User Group on the Internet (e.g., a Wiki or Blog)	Producing Presentations (e.g., [Microsoft PowerPoint®] or a Similar Program), with Simple Animation Functions	Using the Internet for Online Purchases and Payments	Preparing Lessons That Involve the Use of ICT by Students	Finding Useful Teaching Resources on the Internet	Assessing Student Learning	Collaborating With Others Using Shared Resources such as [Google Docs®]	Installing Software
60 (1.1)	87 (0.6) ▲	95 (0.5) ▲	90 (0.7) ▲	96 (0.5) △	83 (0.9) ▲	48 (1.8) △	69 (1.1) ▲
55 (1.7)	87 (1.2) ▲	76 (1.9)	83 (1.6) △	95 (0.8) △	75 (1.7) △	54 (2.0) △	57 (2.2) ▲
49 (1.6) ▽	73 (1.1) ▽	66 (1.3) ▼	52 (1.8) ▼	92 (0.8)	59 (1.2) ▼	39 (1.6) ▽	42 (1.2) ▽
56 (1.4)	78 (1.2) △	89 (0.8) ▲	81 (1.2) △	97 (0.4) △	66 (1.3) ▽	29 (1.2) ▼	43 (1.4) ▽
66 (1.5) △	68 (2.0) ▽	94 (0.8) ▲	84 (1.2) ▲	95 (1.8)	82 (2.0) ▲	35 (1.1) ▽	66 (1.8) ▲
64 (1.3) △	70 (1.1) ▽	81 (1.0) △	85 (1.2) ▲	94 (0.8) △	84 (1.7) ▲	47 (1.6)	24 (1.2) ▼
68 (1.6) △	72 (1.5) ▽	88 (1.1) ▲	73 (1.6)	98 (0.3) △	67 (1.7) ▽	60 (1.9) ▲	54 (1.2) △
46 (2.0) ▼	79 (1.3) △	57 (2.0) ▼	82 (1.2) △	92 (0.6)	69 (1.9)	43 (1.9)	32 (1.2) ▼
63 (1.5) △	85 (0.9) △	85 (0.9) △	81 (1.0) △	94 (0.6) △	75 (1.1) △	38 (1.2) ▽	38 (1.4) ▽
63 (1.4) △	84 (0.9) △	75 (1.5)	78 (1.1) △	93 (0.7)	65 (1.2) ▽	45 (1.6)	39 (1.1) ▽
51 (2.5) ▽	60 (2.3) ▼	47 (2.1) ▼	41 (2.5) ▼	72 (1.9) ▼	55 (2.4) ▼	45 (3.0)	33 (2.0) ▼
58 (1.9)	63 (1.9) ▼	73 (2.2)	52 (1.6) ▼	87 (1.1) ▽	72 (1.7)	41 (2.4)	62 (2.0) ▲
58 (0.5)	76 (0.4)	77 (0.4)	73 (0.4)	92 (0.3)	71 (0.5)	44 (0.5)	47 (0.4)
55 (2.3)	84 (2.0)	98 (0.8)	93 (1.4)	98 (0.6)	75 (2.6)	49 (2.7)	66 (2.4)
47 (1.5)	74 (1.8)	92 (1.0)	67 (1.7)	97 (0.5)	51 (1.7)	24 (1.6)	70 (1.6)
66 (1.6)	92 (0.8)	80 (1.2)	74 (1.2)	94 (0.6)	58 (1.4)	45 (1.5)	69 (1.5)
55 (1.5)	87 (1.3)	97 (0.5)	78 (1.6)	95 (0.5)	47 (1.8)	34 (2.1)	69 (1.4)
53 (2.1)	83 (1.5)	96 (0.6)	91 (1.1)	96 (0.9)	78 (1.6)	34 (1.7)	59 (2.4)
71 (3.0)	86 (2.0)	96 (1.0)	72 (2.7)	98 (0.6)	85 (2.2)	69 (2.0)	75 (2.1)
64 (3.2)	87 (2.1)	96 (1.2)	72 (3.1)	97 (0.6)	80 (2.6)	64 (2.5)	75 (2.3)

▲ More than 10 percentage points above ICILS 2013 average △ Significantly above ICILS 2013 average
▽ Significantly below ICILS 2013 average ▼ More than 10 percentage points below ICILS 2013 average

We used the 14 items[5] on teachers' confidence in performing these ICT tasks to derive a scale called the *ICT self-efficacy scale*. It had an average reliability (coefficient alpha) of 0.87 and scores set to an ICILS 2013 average of 50 with a standard deviation of 10 points. The higher values on the scale reflect greater levels of confidence. Table 7.6 records the national averages for the confidence scale overall and by two age groups (teachers under 40 and teachers over 40 years of age).

We noted several differences in the average scale scores across the ICILS countries. Teachers in Australia (55 scale score points) and Korea (53) recorded average scores five and three scale points respectively above the ICILS 2013 average. The national average scores in Chile (52) and Poland (51) were also above the ICILS 2013 average by a statistically significant amount. Teachers in Thailand (45) recorded a national average score that was five points below the ICILS 2013 average. Other countries that had average scores lower than the ICILS 2013 average were Croatia (47), the Russian Federation (49), and Turkey (49).

It was also evident that teachers under the age of 40 years were more confident than those over 40 years of age in carrying out the specified tasks. The score point differences were statistically significant in all countries that satisfied sampling requirements. On average, the difference between the two groups was six scale points across the ICILS countries. The largest difference, eight scale points, was recorded in Croatia.

Associations between ICT use and teachers' views

We investigated the associations between the frequency with which the teachers were using computers (defined as at least once per week) and the various attitudes teachers held about ICT use in schools. The latter included teachers' confidence (self-efficacy) in using ICT, how positive teachers felt about that use, and how negative. We also included in these investigations two aspects of the ICT environment in schools: the presence or otherwise of resource-related obstacles to using ICT in teaching,[6] and the extent to which teachers were collaborating and following common procedures when using ICT in their teaching.[7] We used the Rasch partial credit model to construct a scale for each

---

5 The items were:
   • Producing a letter using a wordprocessing program;
   • Emailing a file as an attachment;
   • Storing your [the teacher's] digital photos on a computer;
   • Filing digital documents in folders and subfolders;
   • Monitoring students' progress;
   • Using a spreadsheet program for keeping records or analyzing data;
   • Contributing to a discussion forum/user group on the internet (e.g., a wiki or blog);
   • Producing presentations (e.g., [Microsoft PowerPoint®] or a similar program), with simple animation functions;
   • Using the internet for online purchases and payments;
   • Preparing lessons that involve the use of ICT by students;
   • Finding useful teaching resources on the internet;
   • Assessing student learning;
   • Collaborating with others using shared resources such as [Google Docs®]; and
   • Installing software.
6 Chapter 6 describes and discusses the responses to the items making up this scale, which had an average reliability (coefficient alpha) across countries of 0.83. The six items were:
   • My school does not have sufficient ICT equipment (e.g., computers);
   • My school does not have access to digital learning resources;
   • My school has limited connectivity (e.g., slow or unstable speed) to the internet;
   • The computer equipment in our school is out of date;
   • There is not sufficient provision for me to develop expertise in ICT; and
   • There is not sufficient technical support to maintain ICT resources.
7 Chapter 5 describes and discusses the responses to the items making up this scale, which had an average reliability (coefficient alpha) across countries of 0.79. The five items were:
   • I work together with other teachers on improving the use of ICT in classroom teaching;
   • There is a common set of rules in the school about how ICT should be used in classrooms;
   • I systematically collaborate with colleagues to develop ICT-based lessons based on the curriculum;
   • I observe how other teachers use ICT in teaching; and
   • There is a common set of expectations in the school about what students will learn about ICT.

Table 7.6: National averages for teachers' ICT self-efficacy overall and by age group

Country	Teachers' ICT Self-Efficacy by Age Group				Score Distribution by Age Group
	All teachers	Under 40	40 and over	Differences (40 and over – under 40)*	
Australia	55 (0.2) ◄	57 (0.2)	53 (0.3)	-4 (0.3)	
Chile	52 (0.4) △	55 (0.3)	48 (0.6)	-7 (0.7)	
Croatia	47 (0.3) ▽	52 (0.4)	43 (0.4)	-8 (0.6)	
Czech Republic	50 (0.3)	53 (0.3)	47 (0.3)	-6 (0.4)	
Korea, Republic of	53 (0.3) ◄	55 (0.3)	52 (0.5)	-4 (0.6)	
Lithuania	50 (0.3)	55 (0.5)	48 (0.3)	-6 (0.7)	
Poland	51 (0.3) △	54 (0.4)	50 (0.4)	-5 (0.5)	
Russian Federation[1]	49 (0.4) ▽	52 (0.5)	48 (0.4)	-4 (0.5)	
Slovak Republic	50 (0.2)	53 (0.3)	47 (0.3)	-6 (0.4)	
Slovenia	50 (0.3)	54 (0.5)	47 (0.3)	-7 (0.5)	
Thailand	45 (0.6) ▶	48 (0.6)	42 (0.8)	-7 (0.7)	
Turkey	49 (0.5) ▽	50 (0.5)	45 (1.0)	-5 (1.0)	
ICILS 2013 average	50 (0.1)	53 (0.1)	47 (0.1)	-6 (0.2)	
Countries not meeting sample requirements					
Denmark	53 (0.5)	55 (0.7)	52 (0.5)	-2 (0.7)	
Germany	49 (0.3)	53 (0.4)	47 (0.4)	-5 (0.6)	
Hong Kong SAR	52 (0.3)	54 (0.3)	50 (0.4)	-4 (0.5)	
Netherlands	52 (0.2)	54 (0.3)	50 (0.3)	-3 (0.5)	
Norway (Grade 9)	52 (0.4)	55 (0.4)	49 (0.4)	-6 (0.5)	
Benchmarking participant					
Newfoundland and Labrador, Canada	55 (0.4)	56 (0.6)	54 (0.7)	-2 (0.9)	
Benchmarking participant not meeting sample requirements					
Ontario, Canada	54 (0.5)	56 (0.6)	52 (1.0)	-3 (1.2)	

Under 40 average score +/– confidence interval
Over 40 average score +/– confidence interval

On average, teachers with a score in the range indicated by this color have more than a 50% probability of responding to the statements about ICT self-efficacy with:

Disagreement to positive, agreement to negative statements

Agreement to positive, disagreement to negative items

Notes:

* Statistically significant (*p*<0.05) coefficients in **bold**.

() Standard errors appear in parentheses. Because some results are rounded to the nearest whole number, some totals may appear inconsistent.

1 Country surveyed teachers retrospectively to the previous school year when they were teaching the target grade.

◄ More than three score points above ICILS 2013 average

△ Significantly above ICILS 2013 average

▽ Significantly below ICILS 2013 average

▶ More than three score points below ICILS 2013 average

of these aspects and standardized their respective IRT (item response theory) scores to have an ICILS 2013 average score of 50 points and a standard deviation of 10 points.

Table 7.7 records the average scale scores for these dimensions for frequent and infrequent computer users in each country. These data reveal a substantial difference between the ICT confidence (self-efficacy) scores of frequent and infrequent users of computers when teaching. On average, the difference between these two groups was six scale points (or 0.6 of a standard deviation). The difference was statistically significant in every country and ranged from 10 scale points (one standard deviation) in the Russian Federation to four scale points in Korea. While it is not possible to infer causality from these cross-sectional data, it is worth noting that the gap is large.

The data in Table 7.7 also present information on the extent to which teachers who frequently used computers and those who infrequently used them differed in their general views about ICT use in school. The frequent users had stronger positive views about the effects of ICT than did the infrequent computer users. On average across countries, the difference was three scale points (or one third of a standard deviation). The difference was statistically significant in every ICILS country that satisfied sampling requirements and ranged from six (Australia) to two (Lithuania) scale points.

Frequent users of computers for teaching also expressed less negative views than infrequent users about the outcomes of using ICT in school. On average, the difference was three scale points (one third of a standard deviation). The difference was statistically significant in most countries and ranged from one scale point (Turkey and Hong Kong SAR) to four scale points (Chile and Croatia).

The data in Table 7.8 show that, compared to infrequent users of computers for teaching, frequent users reported better ICT resourcing (i.e., fewer obstacles) and a stronger sense of shared collaboration regarding ICT use in their schools. On average, the scale score difference between the two groups was three scale points (one third of a standard deviation). The largest differences (four score points) were recorded in Poland, the Russian Federation, and Turkey (as well as in Denmark, one of the countries that did not meet ICILS sampling requirements).

The extent of reported collaboration among teachers also differed between frequent and infrequent pedagogical computer users. The average international difference was three scale points, while the national differences ranged from two scale points in Korea, Lithuania, and Slovenia to five scale points in Australia, Thailand, and Turkey.

Teaching with and about ICT

Teachers of students enrolled in the ICILS target grade are often, but not always, specialists in a subject area and so teach several different classes, including classes at other grades. The ICILS research team considered that it was important to focus the investigation on one class per teacher, with that class selected from among the classes the teacher was teaching. Teachers were asked to base their responses regarding their teaching practices on their experiences with this particular "reference" class. To help teachers select this class, ICILS provided the following instruction:

> This is the first [target grade] class that you teach for a regular subject (i.e., other than home room, assembly etc.) on or after Tuesday following the last weekend before you first accessed this questionnaire. You may, of course, teach the class at other times during the week as well. If you did not teach a [target grade] class on that Tuesday, please use the [target grade] class that you taught on the first day after that Tuesday.

Table 7.7: National mean scale teacher attitude scores for frequent and infrequent users of ICT when teaching

Country	ICT Self-Efficacy			Positive ICT Views			Negative ICT Views		
	Frequent user	Infrequent user	Difference (infrequent - frequent users)*	Frequent user	Infrequent user	Difference (infrequent - frequent users)*	Frequent user	Infrequent user	Difference (infrequent - frequent users)*
Australia	55 (0.2)	49 (0.9)	**-6** (1.0)	49 (0.3)	43 (0.7)	**-6** (0.7)	48 (0.3)	52 (0.7)	**3** (0.7)
Chile	53 (0.4)	49 (0.6)	**-4** (0.6)	56 (0.6)	54 (0.8)	**-3** (1.0)	44 (0.6)	48 (0.8)	**4** (1.0)
Croatia	52 (0.4)	44 (0.4)	**-8** (0.5)	50 (0.3)	45 (0.3)	**-4** (0.4)	48 (0.3)	52 (0.3)	**4** (0.4)
Czech Republic	52 (0.3)	45 (0.5)	**-7** (0.6)	48 (0.4)	46 (0.4)	**-3** (0.5)	49 (0.5)	53 (0.5)	**3** (0.7)
Korea, Republic of	54 (0.3)	50 (1.4)	**-4** (1.6)	49 (0.3)	46 (0.9)	**-3** (0.9)	52 (0.3)	55 (1.1)	**3** (1.2)
Lithuania	52 (0.3)	46 (0.5)	**-5** (0.6)	50 (0.3)	48 (0.3)	**-2** (0.4)	50 (0.3)	52 (0.5)	**2** (0.6)
Poland	55 (0.4)	49 (0.4)	**-6** (0.6)	51 (0.5)	48 (0.4)	**-3** (0.7)	47 (0.5)	50 (0.4)	**3** (0.7)
Russian Federation[1]	51 (0.4)	42 (0.8)	**-10** (0.8)	51 (0.4)	47 (0.8)	**-4** (0.8)	49 (0.4)	53 (0.6)	**3** (0.6)
Slovak Republic	53 (0.3)	46 (0.4)	**-7** (0.6)	49 (0.4)	46 (0.3)	**-3** (0.4)	49 (0.3)	52 (0.4)	**3** (0.4)
Slovenia	51 (0.3)	47 (0.4)	**-5** (0.4)	48 (0.3)	45 (0.5)	**-3** (0.5)	50 (0.3)	53 (0.3)	**3** (0.4)
Thailand	49 (0.9)	41 (0.7)	**-8** (1.0)	59 (0.8)	54 (0.8)	**-4** (0.8)	50 (1.5)	52 (1.0)	**2** (1.0)
Turkey	51 (0.6)	47 (0.5)	**-5** (0.7)	56 (0.7)	53 (0.5)	**-3** (0.9)	50 (0.6)	51 (0.5)	**1** (0.8)
ICILS 2013 average	52 (0.1)	46 (0.2)	**-6** (0.2)	51 (0.1)	48 (0.2)	**-3** (0.2)	49 (0.2)	52 (0.2)	**3** (0.2)
Countries not meeting sample requirements									
Denmark	54 (0.4)	49 (1.2)	**-5** (1.1)	52 (0.5)	49 (0.7)	**-3** (1.0)	41 (0.6)	45 (1.3)	**4** (1.4)
Germany	54 (0.4)	47 (0.3)	**-7** (0.5)	46 (0.5)	41 (0.3)	**-4** (0.6)	47 (0.6)	51 (0.6)	**4** (0.9)
Hong Kong SAR	53 (0.3)	49 (0.5)	**-3** (0.6)	48 (0.3)	46 (0.4)	**-2** (0.5)	50 (0.4)	51 (0.6)	**1** (0.7)
Netherlands	52 (0.3)	50 (0.7)	**-2** (0.8)	46 (0.4)	45 (0.5)	-1 (0.6)	48 (0.4)	50 (0.5)	**2** (0.8)
Norway	53 (0.4)	47 (0.5)	**-5** (0.6)	50 (0.3)	47 (0.5)	**-4** (0.6)	43 (0.4)	47 (0.8)	**3** (0.8)
Benchmarking participant									
Newfoundland & Labrador, Canada	55 (0.5)	50 (2.4)	**-5** (2.5)	54 (0.7)	47 (1.7)	**-7** (1.6)	45 (0.7)	48 (1.6)	**4** (1.5)
Benchmarking participant not meeting sample requirements									
Ontario, Canada	55 (0.5)	48 (1.1)	**-7** (1.2)	55 (1.0)	52 (2.0)	-2 (2.1)	42 (1.0)	52 (1.6)	**10** (2.0)

Notes:

* Statistically significant (*p*<0.05) coefficients in **bold**.

() Standard errors appear in parentheses. Because some results are rounded to the nearest whole number, some totals may appear inconsistent.

[1] Country surveyed teachers retrospectively to the previous school year when they were teaching the target grade.

Table 7.8: National mean scale teacher environment scores for frequent and infrequent users of ICT when teaching

Country	ICT Resources			ICT Collaboration		
	Frequent user	Infrequent user	Difference (infrequent – frequent users)*	Frequent user	Infrequent user	Difference (infrequent – frequent users)*
Australia	48 (0.4)	51 (0.7)	3 (0.7)	49 (0.5)	45 (0.9)	-5 (0.9)
Chile	49 (0.7)	51 (0.9)	2 (0.9)	48 (0.6)	45 (0.6)	-4 (0.7)
Croatia	50 (0.6)	52 (0.4)	2 (0.5)	46 (0.4)	44 (0.2)	-3 (0.4)
Czech Republic	41 (0.5)	43 (0.5)	2 (0.6)	50 (0.5)	47 (0.6)	-4 (0.7)
Korea, Republic of	53 (0.4)	54 (0.9)	1 (0.9)	48 (0.3)	46 (0.4)	-2 (0.4)
Lithuania	48 (0.5)	52 (0.5)	3 (0.5)	52 (0.3)	50 (0.4)	-2 (0.5)
Poland	47 (0.7)	51 (0.4)	4 (0.6)	50 (0.4)	47 (0.4)	-3 (0.5)
Russian Federation[1]	51 (0.5)	55 (0.4)	4 (0.6)	56 (0.4)	52 (0.7)	-4 (0.8)
Slovak Republic	46 (0.5)	49 (0.5)	3 (0.5)	54 (0.4)	51 (0.3)	-3 (0.5)
Slovenia	45 (0.4)	48 (0.5)	3 (0.5)	46 (0.4)	44 (0.4)	-2 (0.5)
Thailand	58 (0.7)	57 (1.1)	-1 (0.9)	60 (0.9)	56 (1.0)	-5 (0.9)
Turkey	52 (0.9)	57 (0.6)	4 (0.9)	56 (0.9)	51 (0.4)	-5 (1.0)
ICILS 2013 average	49 (0.2)	52 (0.2)	3 (0.2)	51 (0.2)	48 (0.2)	-3 (0.2)
Countries not meeting sample requirements						
Denmark	50 (0.7)	54 (0.7)	4 (1.0)	46 (0.4)	41 (0.7)	-5 (0.8)
Germany	48 (0.8)	51 (0.8)	3 (0.8)	44 (0.7)	39 (0.6)	-5 (0.8)
Hong Kong SAR	49 (0.5)	51 (0.5)	1 (0.6)	47 (0.3)	46 (0.6)	-2 (0.6)
Netherlands	50 (0.3)	52 (0.6)	2 (0.6)	44 (0.4)	43 (0.6)	-1 (0.7)
Norway	51 (0.6)	53 (0.7)	2 (0.6)	46 (0.3)	42 (0.6)	-3 (0.7)
Benchmarking participant						
Newfoundland and Labrador, Canada	51 (0.5)	51 (4.2)	0 (4.1)	47 (0.4)	43 (1.4)	-4 (1.5)
Benchmarking participant not meeting sample requirements						
Ontario, Canada	53 (1.3)	55 (3.0)	1 (2.1)	49 (0.8)	45 (2.6)	-4 (2.5)

Notes:

* Statistically significant (p<.05) coefficients in **bold**.

() Standard errors appear in parentheses. Because some results are rounded to the nearest whole number, some totals may appear inconsistent.

[1] Country surveyed teachers retrospectively to the previous school year when they were teaching the target grade.

The teacher questionnaire asked teachers to indicate not only whether they had used ICT in their teaching of the reference class during the current year but also what emphasis they had placed on developing the CIL of the students in that class. In addition, the questionnaire asked teachers about the subject they were teaching their reference class, their use of specified ICT tools in that class, the learning activities for which their students were using ICT, and which of their teaching practices featured ICT use.

Prevalence of ICT use

Table 7.9 shows the national percentages of teachers who said they used ICT in the reference class. On average across the ICILS countries, just over three quarters (76%) of the teachers indicated that they used ICT in the reference class. National percentages in Australia (94%), Chile (83%), the Russian Federation (82%), Slovenia (81%), Korea (81%), and Lithuania (80%) were significantly above the ICILS 2013 average, while those in the Slovak Republic (71%), Poland (71%), Thailand (68%), Croatia (64%), and Turkey (58%) were significantly below the ICILS 2013 average.

Table 7.9 also shows the national percentages of teachers who reported using ICT in the reference class, with that class defined, for the purposes of this question, according to the subject being taught in it. On average crossnationally, the percentage of teachers using ICT was greatest for reference classes focused on information technology or computer studies (95%). However, it was also very high for the (natural) sciences (84%) and for human sciences or humanities (also 84%). Of the teachers teaching the language of the ICILS student assessment or a foreign language in their reference class, 79 percent reported using ICT in their teaching. Across countries, three quarters of teachers whose reference class involved the creative arts, and 71 percent whose class focused on mathematics, were using ICT in their teaching. In practical and vocational education, 69 percent of teachers said they used ICT when teaching their class. The corresponding figure for teachers teaching subjects classified as "other" was 54 percent.

Another perspective on ICT use by subject area can be gained by looking at the national percentages for each area and then comparing them across countries.[8] The data in Table 7.9 show a very high prevalence of ICT use in information technology or computer studies in most countries except for Chile. In the subject area (natural) sciences, ICT was most prevalent in Australia (99%) and Slovenia (95%) and least prevalent in Turkey (72%) and Croatia (73%). Using ICT during teaching was also widespread in the human sciences or humanities. In classes in this subject area, usage was again most prevalent in Australia (100%) and least prevalent in Turkey (62%) and Thailand (68%).

ICT use in teaching language arts was high in Australia (98%), the Russian Federation (91%) and Korea (90%) but low in Croatia (63%), the Slovak Republic (69%), Thailand (67%), and Turkey (52%). Similar patterns across countries were evident in the use of ICT in teaching foreign and other national languages.

With respect to mathematics, ICT use in teaching was relatively low in the Slovak Republic (60%) and Turkey (53%) but high in Australia (94%), Lithuania (84%), and Slovenia (83%). In the creative arts, using ICT when teaching was of relatively low prevalence in Croatia (49%) and Turkey (60%) but high in the Russian Federation

---

8 There are no data for Denmark or Norway regarding an information technology or computer studies subject. The item was not administered in those countries because such a subject is not offered in schools at the target grade. Similarly, there are no data for Ontario regarding practical or vocational subjects, as these subjects are not provided in Grade 8, which forms part of primary schooling in that province.

Table 7.9: National percentages of teachers using ICT in teaching and learning by learning areas

Country	Is ICT Ever Used in the Teaching and Learning Activities of the Reference Class?	[Language Arts: Test Language]	[Language Arts: Foreign and Other National Languages]	Mathematics	Sciences (General Science and/or Physics, Chemistry, Biology, Geology, Earth Sciences)	Human Sciences/Humanities (History, Geography, Civic and Citizenship, Law, Economics, etc.)	Creative Arts (Visual Arts, Music, Dance, Drama, etc.)	[Information Technology, Computer Studies, or Similar]	Practical and Vocational Subjects (Preparation for a Specific Occupation)	Other (Morals/Ethics, Physical Education, Home Economics, Personal and Social Development)
Australia	94 (0.6)	97 (1.1) ◄	98 (1.1) ◄	94 (1.7) ◄	99 (0.5) ◄	100 (0.2) ◄	89 (2.1) ◄	98 (1.5) △	81 (4.0) ◄	87 (1.6) ◄
Chile	83 (1.6)	88 (3.8) △	90 (2.9) ◄	76 (4.5)	91 (2.5) △	96 (1.6) ◄	83 (3.9) △	84 (5.0) ►	72 (20.6)	72 (2.9) ◄
Croatia	64 (1.4)	63 (5.0) ►	64 (3.4) ►	64 (4.1)	73 (2.8) ►	81 (2.7)	49 (3.4) ►	97 (1.4)	78 (5.0)	37 (2.6) ►
Czech Republic	75 (1.4)	77 (3.7)	77 (2.5)	69 (4.0)	85 (2.1)	86 (2.3)	68 (4.2)	100 (0.0) △	66 (8.3)	47 (4.3)
Korea, Republic of	81 (1.1)	90 (1.9) ◄	91 (2.7) ◄	71 (3.8)	92 (1.6) △	84 (3.2)	87 (3.7) ◄	88 (3.3)	60 (27.0)	65 (4.4) ◄
Lithuania	80 (1.1)	84 (4.1)	85 (1.9) △	84 (2.8) ◄	86 (2.6)	88 (3.0)	80 (3.6)	100 (0.5) △	75 (4.0)	53 (3.1)
Poland	71 (1.3)	82 (2.9)	70 (2.6) ►	65 (4.6)	79 (2.6) ▽	79 (3.5)	72 (4.4)	90 (3.0)	100 (0.1) ◄	50 (3.4)
Russian Federation[1]	82 (0.9)	91 (1.8) ◄	79 (2.8)	77 (3.1)	85 (2.1)	91 (1.1) △	92 (2.0) ◄	98 (1.9)	70 (4.6)	61 (3.2)
Slovak Republic	71 (1.7)	69 (3.7) ►	75 (2.6)	60 (4.7) ►	81 (2.3)	81 (2.7)	74 (5.9)	100 (0.0) △	75 (6.0)	43 (2.9) ►
Slovenia	81 (1.1)	88 (1.9) △	90 (2.1) ◄	83 (2.9) ◄	95 (1.0) ◄	94 (2.1) △	76 (3.3)	97 (2.2)	72 (7.6)	40 (3.2) ►
Thailand	68 (2.2)	67 (4.7) ►	67 (5.0)	61 (5.2)	75 (4.2) ▽	68 (7.9) ►	69 (5.3)	93 (3.0)	45 (9.4) ►	50 (5.1)
Turkey	58 (2.2)	52 (3.2) ►	63 (4.7) ►	53 (4.9) ►	72 (3.9) ►	65 (4.0) ►	60 (5.5) ►	93 (3.5)	27 (13.3) ►	47 (3.4) ▽
ICILS 2013 average	76 (0.4)	79 (1.0)	79 (0.9)	71 (1.1)	84 (0.7)	84 (1.0)	75 (1.2)	95 (0.7)	68 (3.4)	54 (1.0)
Countries not meeting sample requirements										
Denmark	93 (1.4)	96 (2.3)	98 (0.9)	100 (0.0)	93 (3.9)	93 (4.9)	54 (10.8)		100 (0.0)	45 (10.9)
Germany	57 (1.7)	60 (4.4)	47 (4.2)	58 (4.6)	57 (3.7)	59 (5.1)	53 (6.5)	92 (8.5)	83 (7.6)	50 (5.4)
Hong Kong SAR	83 (1.5)	85 (3.0)	81 (4.8)	74 (4.0)	88 (4.1)	87 (2.7)	90 (3.8)	93 (2.7)	73 (25.2)	68 (4.2)
Netherlands	88 (0.9)	95 (2.3)	93 (1.8)	89 (3.0)	95 (1.6)	98 (1.5)	93 (2.8)	88 (13.2)	92 (4.1)	46 (4.5)
Norway (Grade 9)	90 (1.0)	96 (1.6)	95 (1.9)	93 (2.3)	99 (0.7)	96 (2.2)	71 (4.2)			78 (3.7)
Benchmarking participant										
Newfoundland and Labrador, Canada	85 (2.1)	86 (4.1)	99 (1.0)	91 (4.1)	91 (3.8)	92 (3.4)	79 (7.9)	100 (0.0)	23 (20.9)	52 (6.8)
Benchmarking participant not meeting sample requirements										
Ontario, Canada	83 (2.4)	85 (4.6)	80 (8.9)	84 (4.8)	93 (5.2)	88 (7.1)	73 (13.1)	100 (0.0)		62 (10.6)

◄ More than 10 percentage points above ICILS 2013 average
△ Significantly above ICILS 2013 average
▽ Significantly below ICILS 2013 average
► More than 10 percentage points below ICILS 2013 average

Notes:
() Standard errors appear in parentheses. Because some results are rounded to the nearest whole number, some totals may appear inconsistent.
[1] Country surveyed teachers retrospectively to the previous school year when they were teaching the target grade.

(92%), Australia (89%), and Korea (87%). Using ICT when teaching was not very prevalent in practical and vocational subjects, except in Poland and Australia, where the percentages were 100 percent and 81 percent respectively. The prevalence of ICT use in practical and vocational subjects was notably low for Thailand (45%) and Turkey (27%).

Developing computer and information literacy

Teachers who use ICT in their classes can be expected to use those technologies not only to teach the substance of their subject more effectively but also to develop their students' computer and information literacy (CIL). The teacher questionnaire invited all teachers who said they used ICT in their teaching to indicate how much emphasis they placed on developing their students' CIL. More specifically, teachers were asked to indicate with regard to their reference class how much emphasis ("strong," "some," "little," "no emphasis") they had given to developing several specified ICT-based capabilities.[9] Teachers who said they did not use ICT in the reference class were assigned the category of no emphasis for the purpose of computing national percentages, thus ensuring that each country estimate encompassed the whole population of Grade 8 teachers.

Table 7.10 records the national percentages of teachers who placed some or strong emphasis (i.e., the combination of the first two categories) on developing each of the specified ICT-based capabilities. The capability most widely emphasized in their teaching was "accessing information efficiently." Overall across countries, 63 percent (the ICILS 2013 average) of teachers said they emphasized this skill in their teaching. The highest national percentage was recorded in Australia (76%) and the lowest in Lithuania (40%).

The ICT capabilities emphasized by more than half of the teachers were the following:

- Using computer software to construct digital work products (e.g., presentations, documents, images, and diagrams) (56% of teachers);
- Displaying information for a given audience/purpose (54%);
- Exploring a range of digital resources when searching for information (53%);
- Evaluating the relevance of digital information (52%);
- Evaluating the credibility of digital information (52%);
- Understanding the consequences of making information publically available online (51%); and
- Validating the accuracy of digital information (51%).

---

9 The capabilities were:
  - Accessing information efficiently;
  - Evaluating the relevance of digital information;
  - Displaying information for a given audience/purpose;
  - Evaluating the credibility of digital information;
  - Validating the accuracy of digital information;
  - Sharing digital information with others;
  - Using computer software to construct digital work products (e.g., presentations, documents, images, and diagrams);
  - Self-evaluating their [students'] approach to information searches;
  - Providing digital feedback on the work of others (such as classmates);
  - Exploring a range of digital resources when searching for information;
  - Providing references for digital information sources; and
  - Understanding the consequences of making information publically available online.

Table 7.10: National percentages of teachers giving strong or some emphasis to ICT-based capabilities in their students

Country	Accessing Information Efficiently	Evaluating the Relevance of Digital Information	Displaying Information for a Given Audience/Purpose	Evaluating the Credibility of Digital Information	Validating the Accuracy of Digital Information	Sharing Digital Information with Others	Using Computer Software to Construct Digital Work Products (e.g., Presentations, Documents, Images, and Diagrams)	Evaluating Their Approach to Information Searches	Providing Digital Feedback on the Work of Others (such as Classmates)	Exploring a Range of Digital Resources When Searching for Information	Providing References for Digital Information Sources	Understanding the Consequences of Making Information Publically Available Online
Australia	76 (1.0) ◀	66 (0.9) ◀	70 (1.0) ◀	62 (1.0) △	58 (0.9) △	53 (1.3) △	72 (1.1) ◀	53 (1.1) △	28 (1.7) ▽	62 (1.1) △	58 (1.3) △	51 (1.6)
Chile	72 (1.7) △	65 (2.0) ◀	63 (2.1) △	61 (2.1) △	61 (2.2) △	55 (2.2) ◀	62 (2.1) △	57 (2.4) △	47 (2.2) ◀	64 (1.9) ◀	58 (2.3) △	54 (2.5)
Croatia	62 (1.3)	53 (1.4)	57 (1.5) △	54 (1.2)	55 (1.3) △	49 (1.3) △	58 (1.3)	53 (1.3) △	41 (1.1) △	47 (1.3) ▽	44 (1.1) ▽	58 (1.3) △
Czech Republic	64 (1.4)	55 (1.5)	53 (1.6)	56 (1.4) △	49 (1.2)	33 (1.4) ▶	55 (1.8)	43 (1.5) ▽	26 (1.2) ▽	57 (1.3) △	54 (1.4) △	49 (1.3)
Korea, Republic of	62 (1.4)	55 (1.5)	50 (1.3) ▽	51 (1.8)	50 (1.6)	50 (1.4) △	54 (1.7)	48 (2.8)	40 (1.5) △	57 (1.2) △	56 (1.1) △	47 (1.1) ▽
Lithuania	40 (1.5) ▶	27 (1.2) ▶	34 (1.3) ▶	25 (1.0) ▶	24 (1.1) ▶	29 (1.3) ▶	35 (1.3) ▶	23 (1.0) ▶	18 (1.0) ▶	38 (1.2) ▶	34 (1.1) ▶	32 (1.2) ▶
Poland	61 (1.4)	49 (1.5) ▽	50 (1.5) ▽	52 (1.5)	52 (1.4)	36 (1.4) ▽	55 (1.7)	56 (1.4) △	25 (1.1) ▽	52 (1.3)	44 (1.5) ▽	59 (1.6) △
Russian Federation[1]	68 (1.7) △	54 (1.7)	60 (2.0) △	65 (1.5) ◀	65 (1.5) ◀	43 (2.1)	65 (1.6) △	51 (2.1)	35 (1.7)	58 (1.6) △	51 (1.7)	58 (1.9) △
Slovak Republic	66 (1.7)	55 (1.6)	55 (1.5)	55 (1.4)	53 (1.6)	42 (1.5)	58 (1.6)	47 (1.7)	32 (1.5)	57 (1.6)	52 (1.6)	54 (1.7)
Slovenia	67 (1.1) △	45 (1.4) ▽	49 (1.3) ▽	41 (1.5) ▶	40 (1.1) ▶	32 (1.2) ▶	49 (1.5) ▽	40 (1.2) ▽	25 (1.0) ▽	42 (1.2) ▶	39 (1.0) ▶	51 (1.1)
Thailand	59 (2.0)	49 (2.7)	52 (3.3)	50 (2.6)	51 (2.0)	49 (2.8)	52 (2.0)	51 (2.4)	47 (2.0) ◀	52 (2.3)	54 (2.1) △	55 (2.3)
Turkey	56 (2.3) ▽	53 (2.2)	53 (2.3)	52 (2.0)	52 (2.1)	50 (2.2) △	53 (2.1)	49 (2.2)	45 (2.3) ◀	51 (2.3)	49 (2.2)	47 (2.1)
ICILS 2013 average	63 (0.5)	52 (0.5)	54 (0.5)	52 (0.5)	51 (0.5)	43 (0.5)	56 (0.5)	48 (0.5)	34 (0.5)	53 (0.5)	49 (0.5)	51 (0.5)
Countries not meeting sample requirements												
Denmark	78 (1.7)	72 (2.1)	72 (2.2)	70 (2.0)	61 (2.9)	54 (2.8)	68 (2.7)	49 (2.6)	26 (2.1)	55 (2.8)	54 (2.7)	48 (2.4)
Germany	36 (2.3)	28 (1.2)	30 (2.0)	29 (1.4)	23 (1.2)	15 (1.2)	29 (1.6)	27 (1.7)	9 (1.6)	27 (2.0)	32 (1.7)	26 (1.2)
Hong Kong SAR	53 (1.7)	36 (1.6)	42 (1.5)	36 (1.6)	36 (1.5)	38 (1.8)	51 (1.6)	36 (1.5)	27 (1.5)	33 (1.6)	40 (1.4)	45 (2.0)
Netherlands	49 (1.9)	37 (1.6)	35 (1.8)	34 (1.6)	36 (1.6)	27 (1.6)	52 (1.9)	17 (1.2)	11 (1.2)	43 (1.5)	18 (1.4)	27 (1.8)
Norway (Grade 9)	72 (1.7)	65 (2.3)	70 (1.8)	67 (2.1)	61 (2.2)	47 (1.5)	72 (2.0)	44 (2.3)	22 (1.7)	49 (2.5)	62 (1.8)	55 (2.0)
Benchmarking participant												
Newfoundland and Labrador, Canada	75 (2.5)	65 (2.6)	69 (2.7)	62 (2.4)	58 (3.0)	62 (2.9)	70 (2.3)	57 (2.8)	30 (2.5)	60 (2.4)	52 (2.4)	60 (2.8)
Benchmarking participant not meeting sample requirements												
Ontario, Canada	74 (2.6)	66 (3.5)	71 (2.6)	66 (3.4)	65 (3.3)	62 (3.0)	73 (2.7)	55 (3.0)	31 (3.3)	61 (3.0)	59 (3.2)	66 (3.3)

Notes:

( ) Standard errors appear in parentheses. Because some results are rounded to the nearest whole number, some totals may appear inconsistent.

[1] Country surveyed teachers retrospectively to the previous school year when they were teaching the target grade.

◀ More than 10 percentage points above ICILS 2013 average
△ Significantly above ICILS 2013 average
▽ Significantly below ICILS 2013 average
▶ More than 10 percentage points below ICILS 2013 average

The capabilities emphasized by less than half of the teachers included these ones:

- Providing references for digital information sources (49%);
- Students self-evaluating their approach to information searches (48%);
- Sharing digital information with others (43%); and
- Providing digital feedback on the work of others (such as classmates) (34%).

In general, these findings suggest that more than half of the teachers at the ICILS target grade were intent on developing most of the ICT capabilities (listed in the questionnaire) of their students. This emphasis was most evident for the capabilities associated with accessing and evaluating digital information and least evident for the capabilities associated with sharing digital information.

Factors associated with emphasis on developing CIL

We used the 12 items denoting teacher emphasis on *developing students' CIL* to obtain a highly reliable scale (the coefficient alpha was 0.93). As for previously described scales, we used the Rasch partial credit model to construct the scale and standardized its scores to have an ICILS 2013 average score of 50 points and a standard deviation of 10 points. The higher values on this scale reflect stronger levels of emphasis. We used this scale to explore the extent to which emphasis was associated with other characteristics of the teachers and their classes.

Table 7.11 reports the results of the regression analyses that we conducted for each ICILS country. The dependent variable in these analyses was the emphasis teachers placed on developing the ICT-based capabilities (seen here as equivalent to CIL) of their students. The independent variables were teachers' ICT self-efficacy, teachers' perceptions of whether or not the school environment had a collaborative approach to ICT use, positive teacher-held views of the value of using ICT in education,[10] and the extent to which teachers considered lack of resources impeded ICT use.

The independent variable that had the strongest correlation with the dependent variable was ICT self-efficacy. Thus, teachers who were confident about their own ICT capability were more likely than their less-confident colleagues to place a greater degree of emphasis on developing their students' ICT-related skills. The ICILS 2013 average for the regression coefficient was 0.32, which means that one (international) standard deviation difference in ICT self-efficacy (10 scale points) was associated with one third of a standard deviation in emphasis on developing student CIL (3.2 scale points). This association was statistically significant in all participating countries. Among those countries that satisfied the ICILS sampling requirements, the regression coefficients ranged from 0.20 (in Australia) to 0.43 (in Croatia), making for a consistent, moderately sized association across countries.

After we had allowed for the other influences incorporated in the analysis, we found that the teachers who were working in schools they saw as supporting ICT use through a planned collaborative approach were the teachers most likely to emphasize the development of student CIL. The ICILS 2013 average for the regression coefficient was 0.19. This means that one (international) standard deviation difference in planned ICT collaboration was associated with a difference in emphasis on developing students' CIL of about one fifth of a standard deviation.

---

10 A preliminary analysis showed that seeing the value of using ICT in education in negative terms was not a significant predictor of emphasis on developing CIL.

Table 7.11: Multiple regression analyses of predictors of teacher emphasis on developing computer and information literacy

Country	Unstandardized Regression Coefficients*				
	Student characteristics				
	ICT self-efficacy	Positive views of ICT	Collaboration about ICT use	Lack of ICT resources at school	Variance explained (%)
Australia	**0.20** (0.03)	**0.17** (0.03)	**0.19** (0.02)	0.02 (0.02)	20
Chile	**0.32** (0.03)	**0.14** (0.03)	**0.16** (0.02)	0.01 (0.03)	21
Croatia	**0.43** (0.02)	**0.18** (0.04)	**0.12** (0.03)	-0.05 (0.03)	24
Czech Republic	**0.31** (0.03)	**0.12** (0.02)	**0.16** (0.03)	0.00 (0.02)	18
Korea, Republic of	**0.33** (0.04)	**0.29** (0.04)	**0.16** (0.07)	-0.01 (0.02)	26
Lithuania	**0.32** (0.03)	**0.06** (0.03)	**0.16** (0.03)	**-0.06** (0.02)	24
Poland	**0.36** (0.02)	0.02 (0.03)	**0.33** (0.04)	-0.06 (0.03)	24
Russian Federation[1]	**0.33** (0.02)	**0.06** (0.02)	**0.22** (0.03)	**-0.09** (0.02)	32
Slovak Republic	**0.36** (0.02)	**0.11** (0.04)	**0.20** (0.03)	-0.03 (0.04)	19
Slovenia	**0.29** (0.02)	**0.17** (0.03)	**0.19** (0.03)	-0.03 (0.02)	23
Thailand	**0.34** (0.04)	**0.13** (0.06)	**0.21** (0.08)	-0.05 (0.07)	24
Turkey	**0.28** (0.05)	**0.15** (0.04)	**0.23** (0.05)	**-0.21** (0.04)	19
ICILS 2013 average	**0.32** (0.01)	**0.13** (0.01)	**0.19** (0.01)	**-0.05** (0.01)	23
Countries not meeting sample requirements					
Denmark	**0.22** (0.03)	**0.14** (0.05)	**0.18** (0.03)	0.03 (0.04)	17
Germany	**0.31** (0.03)	**0.15** (0.03)	**0.09** (0.03)	-0.05 (0.03)	19
Netherlands	**0.15** (0.03)	**0.12** (0.04)	**0.18** (0.03)	0.02 (0.03)	11
Norway (Grade 9)	**0.25** (0.03)	0.01 (0.04)	**0.19** (0.03)	0.03 (0.03)	12
Hong Kong SAR	**0.22** (0.03)	**0.19** (0.05)	**0.23** (0.04)	-0.01 (0.04)	19
Benchmarking participant					
Newfoundland and Labrador, Canada	**0.32** (0.06)	**0.16** (0.04)	0.03 (0.07)	-0.09 (0.07)	18
Benchmarking participant not meeting sample requirements					
Ontario, Canada	**0.40** (0.08)	0.00 (0.09)	**0.26** (0.09)	0.00 (0.04)	26

Notes:

* Statistically significant (*p*<.05) coefficients in **bold**.

() Standard errors appear in parentheses. Because some results are rounded to the nearest whole number, some totals may appear inconsistent.

[1] Country surveyed teachers retrospectively to the previous school year when they were teaching the target grade.

While we might consider this effect a small one, it was statistically significant in all participating countries that met sampling requirements. In the Canadian province of Newfoundland and Labrador, the value of the coefficient was close to zero. The magnitude of the coefficients among those countries that met the ICILS participation requirements ranged from 0.16 in Chile, the Czech Republic, Korea, and Lithuania to 0.33 in Poland.

Teacher positivity about the value of using ICT in school education was also consistently related to teacher emphasis on developing students' CIL. The regression coefficient was statistically significant in all countries except one (Poland) that met participation requirements. The ICILS 2013 average for the regression coefficient was 0.13. One (international) standard deviation difference in positive views of ICT was thus associated with one eighth of a standard deviation difference in the emphasis on developing students' CIL, making for a relatively weak association.

We found no consistent association between teachers stating that their schools lacked ICT resources and an emphasis on developing students' CIL. The only three countries where we did record statistically significant regression coefficients were Turkey, the Russian Federation, and Lithuania. The negative sign in Table 7.11 indicates that schools in these countries not only had insufficient resources, as perceived by teachers, but also had teachers who placed relatively less emphasis on developing students' CIL. However, we can regard the lack of an association in most countries as an indication that, internationally, the development of ICT in schools has progressed to a point where resources can no longer be seen as an explanation for teachers failing to develop their students' CIL.

The combination of factors considered in our analysis accounted for 23 percent of the variance in the emphasis on CIL among the ICILS 2013 countries that met sampling requirements. The percentages of explained variance ranged from 18 in the Czech Republic to 32 percent in the Russian Federation.

We also investigated the extent to which emphases on CIL development differed across the ICILS countries and across the specified subject areas. Table 7.12 records the national average scores for each country overall and for each subject area within each country. The data also show the percentage distribution of the reference-class subject areas for each country. The data in Table 7.12 indicate that the strongest emphasis on developing CIL was evident in Australia and Chile (a national average of 53 scale points for each) and the least emphasis was evident in Lithuania (a national average of 47 scale points).

In order to indicate the extent to which the emphasis on developing CIL differed across subject areas, the last column of Table 7.12 shows the percentages of the variance in CIL emphasis attributable to the subject area of the reference class. The ICILS 2013 average for this difference was 12 percent, and the national percentages ranged from five percent in Turkey to 22 percent in Slovenia. What these two national percentages tell us is that there was little variation in emphasis across subjects in Turkey but relatively large differences in emphasis across subjects in Slovenia.

Across all ICILS countries, the emphasis was greatest in information technology or computer studies classes (the ICILS 2103 average was 58 scale points) and less so in (natural) sciences and human sciences and humanities classes (the ICILS 2013 average was 52 scale points). Emphasis on fostering CIL learning was least evident in classes concerned with mathematics (the ICILS 2013 average was 48 scale points) and in classes focused on the variety of subjects included under the heading "other" (morals/ethics, physical education, home economics, personal and social development). The ICILS 2013 average for this collection of subjects was 45 scale points.

The emphasis on students' CIL learning in information technology or computer studies was significantly greater than the emphasis in any other subject area. We found no differences in the emphases given to CIL learning across the subject areas of science, human sciences/humanities, and language arts. However, emphasis on students' CIL learning in science was significantly greater than the emphases in the creative arts, practical subjects, mathematics, and "other" subjects. We also recorded significantly greater emphases on CIL learning in the subject area human sciences and humanities than in the areas foreign language teaching, the creative arts, mathematics, and "other" subjects.

Table 7.12: National means for emphasis on developing computer and information literacy by subject area

Country	Emphasis on Developing Computer and Literacy Mean	SE	[Language Arts: Test Language] %	Mean scale score	[Language Arts: Foreign and Other National Languages] %	Mean scale score	Mathematics %	Mean scale score	Sciences (General Science and/or Physics, Chemistry, Biology, Geology Earth Sciences) %	Mean scale score	Human Sciences/Humanities (History, Geography, Civic and Citizenship, Law, Economics, etc.) %	Mean scale score	Creative Arts (Visual Arts, Music, Dance, Drama, etc.) %	Mean scale score	[Information Technology, Computer Studies, or Similar] %	Mean scale score	Practical and Vocational Subjects (Preparation for a Specific Occupation) %	Mean scale score	Other (Morals/Ethics, Physical Education, Home Economics, Personal and Social Development) %	Mean scale score	Effect of Subject Area on Emphasis on Developing Computer and Information Literacy Variance explained
Australia	53	(0.2)	14	55 (0.4)	7	53 (0.6)	15	48 (0.6)	12	54 (0.4)	13	57 (0.3)	12	51 (0.6)	3	58 (0.8)	6	50 (1.0)	18	51 (0.4)	15 (1.3)
Chile	53	(0.5)	15	55 (1.0)	11	54 (0.9)	13	50 (1.1)	12	55 (0.8)	11	56 (0.7)	11	53 (1.0)	6	54 (1.6)	0	57 (7.3)	21	49 (0.6)	7 (1.5)
Croatia	50	(0.3)	11	50 (1.3)	16	50 (0.7)	10	49 (1.0)	16	52 (0.7)	13	54 (0.8)	11	46 (0.8)	5	61 (0.6)	4	55 (1.3)	15	44 (0.6)	12 (1.2)
Czech Republic	49	(0.3)	8	52 (0.9)	21	49 (0.5)	8	46 (0.7)	20	51 (0.5)	15	52 (0.5)	10	48 (0.8)	5	58 (0.4)	2	49 (1.8)	11	44 (0.9)	12 (1.5)
Korea, Republic of	50	(0.2)	12	53 (0.6)	16	52 (0.9)	14	47 (0.8)	12	52 (0.6)	10	51 (0.7)	10	50 (0.7)	4	53 (0.9)	3	47 (5.0)	19	47 (0.8)	7 (1.5)
Lithuania	47	(0.2)	9	47 (0.7)	22	46 (0.3)	9	47 (0.4)	13	48 (0.6)	12	49 (0.5)	9	47 (0.6)	4	56 (0.8)	7	47 (0.7)	16	43 (0.5)	13 (1.8)
Poland	49	(0.3)	11	52 (0.7)	21	49 (0.6)	10	47 (0.9)	18	51 (0.6)	9	51 (1.0)	6	51 (1.2)	6	57 (1.2)	1	56 (1.1)	18	44 (0.6)	11 (1.7)
Russian Federation[1]	51	(0.3)	11	52 (0.5)	14	50 (0.6)	10	49 (0.6)	18	51 (0.5)	16	53 (0.3)	6	52 (0.7)	7	56 (0.4)	6	48 (0.9)	14	46 (0.7)	11 (1.5)
Slovak Republic	50	(0.3)	10	50 (0.8)	22	50 (0.6)	9	47 (1.0)	16	52 (0.5)	15	52 (0.6)	4	49 (1.2)	6	59 (0.5)	3	51 (1.5)	15	44 (0.6)	12 (1.2)
Slovenia	49	(0.2)	14	51 (0.6)	18	49 (0.5)	13	47 (0.6)	15	51 (0.4)	12	53 (0.5)	10	48 (0.7)	2	59 (1.0)	2	47 (1.6)	14	40 (0.5)	22 (1.6)
Thailand	49	(0.5)	11	50 (1.1)	12	49 (1.1)	13	47 (1.0)	13	51 (0.8)	13	49 (1.6)	10	49 (1.1)	11	59 (0.9)	3	45 (2.0)	15	45 (0.9)	12 (2.4)
Turkey	50	(0.6)	18	48 (1.0)	13	51 (1.3)	13	49 (1.3)	12	54 (1.2)	11	53 (1.1)	10	52 (1.5)	3	62 (1.7)	1	43 (3.2)	20	47 (0.9)	5 (1.4)
ICILS 2013 average	50	(0.1)	12	51 (0.2)	16	50 (0.2)	11	48 (0.3)	15	52 (0.2)	12	52 (0.2)	9	50 (0.3)	5	58 (0.3)	3	50 (0.9)	16	45 (0.2)	12 (0.5)
Countries not meeting sample requirements																					
Denmark	53	(0.4)	22	55 (0.7)	23	53 (0.5)	18	53 (0.6)	18	53 (0.8)	11	55 (1.3)	2	43 (1.9)	0	35 (0.0)	0	59 (0.0)	5	42 (1.3)	19 (6.0)
Germany	44	(0.3)	11	44 (0.6)	17	42 (0.7)	10	42 (1.0)	15	43 (0.6)	14	45 (0.9)	10	43 (1.1)	4	54 (2.1)	2	48 (1.7)	17	42 (0.6)	8 (2.5)
Hong Kong SAR	48	(0.3)	21	48 (0.6)	12	47 (0.7)	12	45 (0.8)	9	48 (0.9)	17	50 (0.6)	8	49 (1.0)	8	55 (1.0)	1	46 (2.1)	13	46 (0.9)	8 (1.9)
Netherlands	47	(0.3)	12	50 (0.7)	23	46 (0.5)	10	42 (0.6)	20	48 (0.7)	9	51 (0.7)	9	47 (0.6)	1	52 (1.1)	4	49 (1.4)	12	40 (0.8)	20 (3.0)
Norway (Grade 9)	51	(0.3)	17	55 (0.6)	24	53 (0.7)	13	51 (0.6)	10	53 (0.5)	9	54 (0.5)	8	45 (1.0)	0	0 (0.0)	0	0 (0.0)	19	48 (0.7)	15 (3.0)
Benchmarking participant																					
Newfoundland and Labrador, Canada	52	(0.5)	18	54 (1.4)	10	54 (0.9)	17	50 (1.1)	14	52 (0.9)	12	54 (1.0)	7	50 (1.8)	6	58 (1.3)	1	41 (8.0)	15	45 (1.3)	15 (4.0)
Benchmarking participant not meeting sample requirements																					
Ontario, Canada	53	(0.7)	42	55 (1.3)	4	51 (2.3)	24	50 (1.3)	8	55 (1.4)	9	56 (1.9)	4	47 (2.2)	1	69 (10.8)	0	0 (0.0)	8	47 (2.2)	12 (4.3)

Notes:

() Standard errors appear in parentheses. Because some results are rounded to the nearest whole number, some totals may appear inconsistent.

[1] Country surveyed teachers retrospectively to the previous school year when they were teaching the target grade.

The ICT tools teachers were using

The ICILS teachers who were using ICT in their teaching said they used a variety of ICT tools for this purpose. The teacher questionnaire asked the teachers to identify the ICT tools they used, the learning activities in which they deployed these tools, and the teaching practices in which they incorporated them.

Types of tools

The teacher questionnaire specified a number of ICT tools and asked teachers to indicate how much they used each one in their reference class. The response categories were "never," "in some lessons," "in most lessons," and in "every or almost every lesson." When computing the national percentages of teacher responses for each item, we assigned the category of never to teachers who said they did not use any form of ICT in their reference class. This approach ensured that the national estimates referred to the whole population of participating Grade 8 teachers.

Table 7.13 records the national percentages of teachers using each of the ICT tools while teaching most or almost all of their lessons to the reference class. The most or almost all category combines the two questionnaire response categories indicating most frequent use.

The ICT tools that teachers were most widely using on average across countries were wordprocessing and presentation software. Across all ICILS countries, 30 percent of teachers said they used these tools in most or all lessons. The prevalence of use of these utilities was greatest, by more than 10 percentage points above the ICILS 2013 average, in Korea (47%), the Russian Federation (44%), and Australia (41%). The lowest prevalence recorded was for Poland (13%).

Nearly one quarter (23%) of teachers said they used computer-based information resources (e.g., websites, wikis, and encyclopedias) in most or all lessons. National percentages of teachers reporting use of these resources were highest in Lithuania (32%), Australia (31%), Chile (28%), and the Russian Federation (28%) and lowest in Croatia (16%).

On average across the ICILS countries, 15 percent of teachers who made ICT part of their teaching practice were using interactive digital learning resources (e.g., learning objects) in most or all lessons. This use was most prevalent in Chile (21%), the Slovak Republic (21%), and the Russian Federation (20%) and least prevalent in Croatia (8%) and Poland (9%). Fifteen percent of teachers on average crossnationally said they were using tutorial software or practice programs in their lessons with the reference class. This usage was most prevalent in Korea (28%) and least prevalent in Australia (7%).

The ICILS data showed that those teachers using ICT were rarely using the following ICT tools when teaching their respective reference classes: simulation and modeling software (3% on average across countries), e-portfolios (4%), concept-mapping software (4%), and social media (4%). Digital learning games and data-logging and monitoring tools were also being used by only small percentages of teachers (5% and 6% respectively). Interesting exceptions to these low-prevalence tools were social media in Thailand (17%) and graphing and drawing software in Korea (20%).

Table 7.13: National percentages of teachers using ICT tools for teaching in most lessons

Country	Tutorial Software or [Practice Programs]	Digital Learning Games	Wordprocessors or Presentation Software (e.g., [Microsoft Word ®], [Microsoft PowerPoint ®])	Spreadsheets (e.g., [Microsoft Excel®])	Multimedia Production Tools (e.g., Media Capture and Editing, Web Production)	Concept Mapping Software (e.g., [Inspiration ®], [Webspiration ®])
Australia	7 (0.6) ▽	6 (0.6)	41 (1.2) ▲	5 (0.5) ▽	10 (0.6)	2 (0.3) ▽
Chile	13 (1.1)	6 (0.9)	37 (1.4) △	5 (0.8) ▽	11 (0.9) △	7 (1.0) △
Croatia	11 (0.8) ▽	3 (0.4) ▽	26 (1.1) ▽	5 (0.5) ▽	4 (0.6) ▽	1 (0.2) ▽
Czech Republic	12 (1.1) ▽	2 (0.3) ▽	23 (1.4) ▽	3 (0.4) ▽	1 (0.3) ▽	0 (0.1) ▽
Korea, Republic of	28 (1.9) ▲	7 (1.0)	47 (1.9) ▲	10 (0.8) △	17 (2.0) △	3 (0.7)
Lithuania	19 (1.0) △	4 (0.6)	29 (1.4)	5 (0.5) ▽	9 (0.8)	1 (0.3) ▽
Poland	9 (0.9) ▽	2 (0.4) ▽	13 (0.9) ▼	3 (0.4) ▽	6 (0.8) ▽	1 (0.4) ▽
Russian Federation[1]	19 (1.2) △	7 (0.6) △	44 (1.6) ▲	12 (1.0) △	9 (0.8)	6 (0.7) △
Slovak Republic	15 (1.1)	4 (0.5)	25 (1.4) ▽	8 (0.6)	3 (0.4) ▽	3 (0.5)
Slovenia	22 (1.4) △	5 (0.6)	31 (1.3)	3 (0.3) ▽	9 (0.7)	1 (0.2) ▽
Thailand	10 (1.3) ▽	6 (1.0)	26 (1.4) ▽	16 (2.1) △	12 (1.6) △	9 (1.1) △
Turkey	15 (1.9)	9 (1.4) △	23 (1.8) ▽	7 (1.3)	10 (1.4)	8 (0.9) △
ICILS 2013 average	15 (0.4)	5 (0.2)	30 (0.4)	7 (0.3)	8 (0.3)	4 (0.2)
Countries not meeting sample requirements						
Denmark	7 (1.2)	3 (0.8)	31 (2.8)	6 (1.2)	4 (0.7)	1 (0.3)
Germany	1 (0.4)	0 (0.1)	10 (1.4)	3 (0.6)	2 (0.6)	0 (0.2)
Hong Kong SAR	22 (1.2)	3 (0.6)	52 (1.9)	9 (1.0)	11 (1.0)	3 (0.6)
Netherlands	15 (1.3)	5 (0.8)	33 (1.9)	3 (0.7)	4 (0.6)	1 (0.3)
Norway (Grade 9)	3 (0.7)	2 (0.8)	19 (1.5)	1 (0.4)	1 (0.3)	0 (0.2)
Benchmarking participant						
Newfoundland and Labrador, Canada	11 (1.8)	7 (1.5)	42 (2.5)	1 (0.3)	10 (1.6)	2 (1.0)
Benchmarking participant not meeting sample requirements						
Ontario, Canada	13 (2.5)	10 (2.7)	41 (3.6)	5 (2.2)	17 (2.8)	5 (1.4)

Notes:

() Standard errors appear in parentheses. Because some results are rounded to the nearest whole number, some totals may appear inconsistent.

[1] Country surveyed teachers retrospectively to the previous school year when they were teaching the target grade.

Use in learning activities

In addition to asking teachers about the tools they used, ICILS asked them to indicate whether they required their students in the reference class to use ICT when engaged in various learning activities. As was the case for the question about ICT tools, we assigned, for the purpose of computing national percentages, the category of never to teachers who said they did not use ICT in the reference class. Again, doing this ensured that the national estimates referred to the whole population of Grade 8 teachers.

Table 7.14 records the percentages of teachers who said they often required their students to use ICT when carrying out the activities specified in the relevant teacher questionnaire item. The activities in which ICT was most widely used were those concerned with searching for information, completing reports, and doing assessments over certain periods of time. The relevant activities as listed in the teacher questionnaire were:

- Searching for information on a topic using outside resources (29% of teachers across the ICILS countries required their students to engage in this activity);

- Working on short assignments (i.e., within one week) (20%);

Table 7.13: National percentages of teachers using ICT tools for teaching in most lessons (contd.)

Data-Logging and Monitoring Tools	Simulations and Modeling Software	Social Media (e.g., Facebook, Twitter)	Communication Software (e.g., Email, Blogs)	Computer-Based Information Resources (e.g., Websites, Wikis, Encyclopedias)	Interactive Digital Learning Resources (e.g., Learning Objects)	Graphing or Drawing Software	E-portfolios
5 (0.5)	4 (0.5)	1 (0.3) ▽	15 (1.4) △	31 (1.1) △	15 (0.8)	5 (0.5) ▽	3 (0.4) ▽
9 (0.9) △	4 (0.7)	6 (0.8) △	15 (1.1) △	28 (1.5) △	21 (1.4) △	7 (0.8)	4 (0.7)
3 (0.4) ▽	2 (0.4) ▽	1 (0.2) ▽	3 (0.4) ▽	16 (0.9) ▽	8 (0.8) ▽	3 (0.5) ▽	1 (0.3) ▽
2 (0.4) ▽	0 (0.1) ▽	1 (0.2) ▽	4 (0.5) ▽	19 (1.3) ▽	16 (1.3)	3 (0.4) ▽	2 (0.3) ▽
5 (0.9)	6 (0.7) △	5 (0.8) △	12 (1.2)	20 (1.0) ▽	11 (0.6) ▽	20 (2.4) ▲	6 (0.9)
12 (0.7) △	2 (0.4) ▽	2 (0.5) ▽	16 (1.0) △	32 (1.3) △	13 (0.9)	5 (0.7) ▽	10 (0.8) △
2 (0.4) ▽	1 (0.2) ▽	1 (0.3) ▽	6 (1.1) ▽	17 (1.0) ▽	9 (0.9) ▽	3 (0.5) ▽	1 (0.4) ▽
13 (0.9) △	5 (0.5) △	4 (0.6)	10 (1.0)	28 (1.4) △	20 (1.2) △	12 (0.9) △	7 (0.6) △
3 (0.5) ▽	2 (0.3) ▽	2 (0.6) ▽	8 (1.1) ▽	20 (1.4)	21 (1.8) △	5 (0.8)	2 (0.4) ▽
2 (0.3) ▽	2 (0.4) ▽	1 (0.2) ▽	7 (0.6) ▽	22 (1.1)	12 (1.2) ▽	3 (0.4) ▽	1 (0.2) ▽
8 (1.0) △	5 (0.8) △	18 (2.2) ▲	17 (1.6) △	26 (1.5)	16 (2.1)	11 (1.8) △	9 (1.7) △
8 (0.9) △	5 (0.7) △	3 (0.5)	8 (1.1) ▽	19 (1.9) ▽	15 (1.5)	8 (0.9)	4 (0.9)
6 (0.2)	3 (0.1)	4 (0.2)	10 (0.3)	23 (0.4)	15 (0.4)	7 (0.3)	4 (0.2)
1 (0.3)	1 (0.4)	2 (1.1)	10 (1.7)	31 (2.1)	21 (2.1)	6 (0.9)	2 (0.5)
2 (0.3)	1 (0.3)	1 (0.2)	1 (0.3)	9 (1.3)	3 (0.7)	3 (0.5)	0 (0.1)
3 (0.6)	3 (0.5)	3 (0.6)	9 (1.1)	13 (1.0)	13 (1.1)	6 (0.7)	2 (0.4)
15 (1.2)	1 (0.3)	1 (0.3)	8 (1.1)	25 (1.7)	18 (1.4)	4 (0.8)	1 (0.4)
1 (0.2)	0 (0.1)	1 (0.3)	3 (0.8)	14 (1.3)	6 (0.8)	2 (0.7)	2 (0.5)
6 (1.7)	4 (1.3)	3 (0.9)	13 (1.8)	28 (2.5)	17 (2.2)	8 (1.7)	5 (1.3)
9 (2.0)	6 (1.9)	7 (1.8)	20 (3.3)	32 (3.2)	18 (2.7)	7 (2.0)	5 (1.9)

▲ More than 10 percentage points above ICILS 2013 average
△ Significantly above ICILS 2013 average
▽ Significantly below ICILS 2013 average
▼ More than 10 percentage points below ICILS 2013 average

- Submitting completed work for assessment (18%); and
- Working individually on learning materials at their [the students'] own pace (16%).

On average across countries, between 10 and 15 percent of teachers said they often asked their students to undertake extended and shared work that involved ICT use and included evaluating and processing information. The relevant activities were:

- Evaluating information resulting from a search (14%);
- Working on extended projects (i.e., over several weeks) (12%);
- Explaining and discussing ideas with other students (12%);
- Processing and analyzing data (11%); and
- Planning a sequence of learning activities for themselves (11%).

On average, fewer than 10 percent of teachers from the ICILS countries said they often had students engaged in the following activities requiring ICT use:

- Undertaking open-ended investigations or field work (8%);
- Seeking information from experts outside the school (7%);

Table 7.14: National percentages of teachers often using ICT for learning activities in classrooms

Country	Working on Extended Projects (i.e., over Several Weeks)		Working on Short Assignments (i.e., within One Week)		Explaining and Discussing Ideas with Other Students		Submitting Completed Work for Assessment		Working Individually on Learning Materials at Their Own Pace	
Australia	31 (1.3)	▲	31 (1.5)	▲	15 (1.0)	△	32 (1.3)	▲	28 (1.2)	▲
Chile	13 (1.3)		28 (2.0)	△	13 (1.5)		28 (1.9)	▲	19 (1.6)	△
Croatia	8 (0.7)	▽	12 (0.8)	▽	7 (0.7)	▽	8 (0.9)	▽	10 (0.8)	▽
Czech Republic	9 (0.9)	▽	17 (1.1)	▽	7 (0.5)	▽	12 (0.9)	▽	11 (0.9)	▽
Korea, Republic of	9 (1.3)	▽	13 (1.4)	▽	8 (0.9)	▽	11 (0.9)	▽	11 (1.2)	▽
Lithuania	15 (1.0)	△	19 (1.1)		13 (1.1)		14 (0.9)	▽	15 (1.1)	
Poland	5 (0.6)	▽	25 (1.4)	△	21 (1.0)	△	32 (1.6)	▲	21 (1.0)	△
Russian Federation[1]	13 (0.8)		27 (1.6)	△	18 (1.0)	△	27 (1.6)	△	21 (1.3)	△
Slovak Republic	12 (0.9)		20 (1.1)		10 (0.9)		17 (1.0)		15 (1.0)	
Slovenia	10 (0.6)	▽	16 (0.8)	▽	8 (0.6)	▽	7 (0.6)	▼	7 (0.6)	▽
Thailand	8 (1.0)	▽	14 (1.6)	▽	10 (1.4)		16 (2.3)		18 (1.8)	
Turkey	13 (1.4)		20 (1.9)		8 (1.1)	▽	6 (1.1)	▼	10 (1.2)	▽
ICILS 2013 average	12 (0.3)		20 (0.4)		12 (0.3)		18 (0.4)		16 (0.3)	
Countries not meeting sample requirements										
Denmark	29 (2.2)		40 (2.3)		21 (1.7)		43 (2.7)		32 (1.9)	
Germany	11 (1.2)		10 (1.2)		4 (0.6)		6 (0.7)		5 (1.1)	
Hong Kong SAR	12 (1.1)		5 (0.7)		5 (0.7)		7 (0.8)		5 (0.6)	
Netherlands	15 (1.6)		19 (2.0)		4 (0.7)		15 (1.4)		16 (1.6)	
Norway (Grade 9)	27 (1.9)		26 (1.6)		5 (1.0)		34 (2.1)		15 (1.6)	
Benchmarking participant										
Newfoundland and Labrador, Canada	24 (2.4)		26 (2.3)		14 (2.0)		21 (2.4)		16 (2.0)	
Benchmarking participant not meeting sample requirements										
Ontario, Canada	43 (3.0)		39 (3.7)		19 (2.4)		32 (3.7)		23 (2.9)	

Notes:

() Standard errors appear in parentheses. Because some results are rounded to the nearest whole number, some totals may appear inconsistent.

[1] Country surveyed teachers retrospectively to the previous school year when they were teaching the target grade.

- Reflecting on their learning experiences (e.g., by using a learning log) (6%); and
- Communicating with students in other schools on projects (3%).

Use in teaching practices

Teachers who used ICT when teaching their reference class were asked how frequently ("never," "sometimes," "often") they used ICT in a set of teaching practices. Teachers who said they did not use ICT in the reference class were assigned the category of never for the purpose of computing national percentages.

Table 7.15 records the percentages of teachers who often used ICT in each of these teaching practices. The two teaching practices most widely used across the participating countries were "presenting information through direct class instruction" (an ICILS 2013 international average percentage of 33%) and "reinforcing learning of skills through repetition of examples" (an ICILS 2013 international average percentage of 21%). Presenting information was most prevalent in Australia (46%) and least prevalent in Turkey (22%). Reinforcing learning of skills was most evident in the Russian Federation (34%) and least evident in Croatia (16%) and the Czech Republic (16%).

Table 7.14: National percentages of teachers often using ICT for learning activities in classrooms (contd.)

Undertaking Open-Ended Investigations or Field Work	Reflecting on Their Learning Experiences (e.g., by Using a Learning Log)	Communicating with Students in Other Schools on Projects	Seeking Information from Experts Outside the School	Planning a Sequence of Learning Activities for Themselves	Processing and Analyzing Data	Searching for Information on a Topic Using Outside Resources	Evaluating Information Resulting from a Search
16 (1.0) △	6 (0.6)	4 (0.5)	4 (0.4) ▽	3 (0.4) ▽	7 (0.7) ▽	32 (1.4) △	15 (0.9)
19 (1.6) ▲	8 (1.2)	3 (0.6)	10 (1.5) △	17 (1.3) △	14 (1.2) △	30 (2.1)	18 (1.7)
11 (0.8) △	2 (0.3) ▽	3 (0.4)	4 (0.5) ▽	4 (0.4) ▽	5 (0.7) ▽	22 (1.1) ▽	6 (0.8) ▽
2 (0.3) ▽	1 (0.2) ▽	1 (0.2) ▽	2 (0.4) ▽	3 (0.4) ▽	5 (0.5) ▽	21 (1.2) ▽	11 (0.8) ▽
5 (0.7) ▽	4 (0.6) ▽	4 (0.7)	15 (1.7) △	5 (0.8) ▽	10 (1.4)	19 (2.1) ▽	7 (1.0) ▽
13 (0.8) △	16 (1.4) ▲	4 (0.5)	3 (0.4) ▽	12 (0.9)	14 (0.9) △	36 (1.2) △	18 (1.2) △
1 (0.2) ▽	3 (0.4) ▽	2 (0.3) ▽	4 (0.7) ▽	11 (0.8)	17 (1.1) △	35 (1.5) △	22 (1.1) △
4 (0.4) ▽	7 (0.6)	4 (0.5)	5 (0.6) ▽	21 (1.3) ▲	20 (1.2) △	38 (1.8) △	23 (1.3) △
1 (0.4) ▽	3 (0.5) ▽	2 (0.4) ▽	10 (0.8) △	10 (0.9)	9 (0.9) ▽	28 (1.5)	15 (1.2)
2 (0.3) ▽	2 (0.3) ▽	2 (0.3) ▽	6 (0.6)	13 (0.9) △	10 (0.7)	30 (1.3)	10 (0.7) ▽
14 (1.8) △	18 (2.2) ▲	9 (1.0) △	19 (1.5) ▲	20 (2.4) △	16 (2.9)	28 (2.4)	17 (2.1)
11 (1.2) △	6 (0.9)	4 (0.9)	5 (1.0) ▽	8 (1.2) ▽	5 (0.9) ▽	22 (1.6) ▽	11 (1.3) ▽
8 (0.3)	6 (0.3)	3 (0.2)	7 (0.3)	11 (0.3)	11 (0.4)	29 (0.5)	14 (0.4)
8 (1.2)	4 (1.1)	1 (0.3)	6 (0.9)	6 (0.9)	11 (1.6)	20 (1.8)	22 (1.9)
3 (0.4)	1 (0.2)	1 (0.3)	0 (0.2)	1 (0.3)	1 (0.3)	14 (1.3)	5 (0.7)
3 (0.7)	2 (0.5)	2 (0.6)	2 (0.5)	2 (0.6)	5 (0.8)	11 (1.2)	4 (0.8)
6 (1.0)	2 (0.6)	1 (0.2)	2 (0.5)	11 (1.3)	5 (0.9)	22 (1.6)	7 (0.7)
5 (0.9)	2 (0.5)	1 (0.3)	3 (0.7)	3 (0.7)	4 (0.9)	22 (1.7)	14 (1.1)
7 (1.5)	5 (1.2)	2 (0.8)	3 (0.7)	3 (1.0)	4 (1.0)	27 (2.7)	14 (2.0)
17 (2.3)	8 (2.6)	8 (2.5)	9 (2.6)	5 (1.8)	10 (1.9)	40 (3.0)	22 (2.5)

▲ More than 10 percentage points above ICILS 2013 average
△ Significantly above ICILS 2013 average
▽ Significantly below ICILS 2013 average
▼ More than 10 percentage points below ICILS 2013 average

Several teaching practices incorporating ICT were each being used by about 16 percent (i.e., from 14% to 17%) of the ICILS teachers on average across countries. These were:

- Providing feedback to students;
- Assessing students' learning through tests;
- Supporting collaboration among students;
- Providing remedial or enrichment support to individual students or small groups of students;
- Enabling student-led whole-class discussions and presentations; and
- Supporting inquiry learning.

We recorded notably higher percentages of teachers in Thailand using ICT to support collaboration among students and to support inquiry learning (national averages of 30% and 31% respectively).

Teaching practices with a relatively low prevalence of ICT use were:

- Collaborating with parents or guardians in order to support students' learning (10% of teachers on average crossnationally),

Table 7.15: National percentages of teachers often using ICT for teaching practices in classrooms

Country	Presenting Information through Direct Class Instruction	Providing Remedial or Enrichment Support to Individual Students or Small Groups of Students	Enabling Student-Led Whole-Class Discussions and Presentations	Assessing Students' Learning through Tests	Providing Feedback to Students	Reinforcing Learning of Skills through Repetition of Examples	Supporting Collaboration among Students	Mediating Communication between Students and Experts or External Mentors	Enabling Students to Collaborate with Other Students (within or outside School)	Collaborating With Parents or Guardians in Supporting Students' Learning	Supporting Inquiry Learning
Australia	46 (1.6) ▲	19 (0.9) △	18 (0.9) △	10 (0.8) ▽	17 (0.8)	20 (1.1)	14 (1.0) ▽	3 (0.4) ▽	7 (0.6)	9 (0.7)	18 (1.0) △
Chile	43 (2.1) △	20 (1.4) △	22 (1.9) △	22 (1.5) △	33 (1.9) ▲	29 (2.0) △	27 (2.1) ▲	6 (1.0) △	12 (1.3) △	11 (1.7)	28 (1.8) ▲
Croatia	28 (1.3) ▽	10 (0.6) ▽	14 (0.9)	5 (0.4) ▼	8 (0.6) ▽	14 (0.9) ▽	9 (0.7) ▽	3 (0.5) ▽	3 (0.5) ▽	2 (0.3) ▽	12 (0.8) ▽
Czech Republic	31 (1.5)	4 (0.6) ▼	7 (0.7) ▽	8 (0.7) ▽	11 (0.8) ▽	14 (1.0) ▽	8 (0.8) ▽	1 (0.2) ▽	3 (0.4) ▽	6 (0.7) ▽	2 (0.3) ▼
Korea, Republic of	42 (1.9) △	22 (1.0) △	10 (1.2) ▽	12 (0.7) ▽	15 (1.7)	20 (2.0)	8 (1.0) ▽	5 (0.9)	8 (0.8)	4 (0.8) ▽	10 (1.4) ▽
Lithuania	36 (1.3) △	15 (1.1)	15 (1.0)	14 (1.0)	17 (0.9)	19 (1.1) ▽	12 (0.9) ▽	3 (0.5)	5 (0.7) ▽	22 (1.3) ▲	6 (0.7) ▽
Poland	23 (1.2) ▼	19 (1.1) △	10 (0.8) ▽	28 (1.4) ▲	28 (1.3) ▲	24 (1.2) △	24 (1.2) △	3 (0.5) ▽	5 (0.6) ▽	16 (1.1) △	18 (1.2) △
Russian Federation[1]	43 (1.6) △	21 (1.3) △	24 (1.6) △	33 (1.7) ▲	16 (1.1)	34 (1.7) ▲	26 (1.3) ▲	5 (0.6)	10 (0.9) △	21 (1.7) ▲	19 (1.3) △
Slovak Republic	29 (1.5) ▽	10 (0.9) ▽	13 (1.1)	9 (1.0) ▽	11 (0.9) ▽	18 (1.2) ▽	10 (0.9) ▽	3 (0.4) ▽	3 (0.5) ▽	6 (0.9) ▽	7 (1.0) ▽
Slovenia	35 (1.6)	15 (1.3)	19 (1.0) △	7 (0.6) ▽	13 (0.8) ▽	21 (1.3)	12 (0.7) ▽	3 (0.4) ▽	5 (0.4) ▽	5 (0.7) ▽	8 (0.7) ▽
Thailand	22 (2.0) ▼	13 (1.4)	14 (2.0)	25 (2.6) △	19 (2.2)	21 (2.5)	30 (2.6) ▲	10 (1.2) △	18 (1.8) ▲	13 (1.5) ▽	31 (2.4) ▲
Turkey	22 (2.1) ▼	15 (2.1)	15 (2.0)	20 (2.0)	17 (1.9)	20 (2.0)	11 (1.4) ▽	7 (1.1) △	7 (1.0)	6 (1.0) ▽	13 (1.7)
ICILS 2013 average	33 (0.5)	15 (0.3)	15 (0.4)	16 (0.4)	17 (0.4)	21 (0.5)	16 (0.4)	4 (0.2)	7 (0.3)	10 (0.3)	14 (0.4)
Countries not meeting sample requirements											
Denmark	41 (2.5)	22 (1.9)	23 (2.1)	18 (1.3)	21 (2.6)	16 (1.8)	16 (2.0)	4 (1.0)	4 (0.9)	23 (1.9)	15 (1.7)
Germany	13 (1.4)	4 (1.0)	5 (0.8)	3 (0.5)	4 (0.7)	4 (0.7)	4 (0.6)	1 (0.2)	2 (0.3)	3 (0.6)	4 (0.7)
Hong Kong SAR	38 (1.6)	9 (0.9)	8 (0.8)	12 (1.1)	15 (1.5)	16 (1.3)	8 (0.9)	3 (0.5)	5 (0.7)	3 (0.6)	6 (0.7)
Netherlands	44 (2.1)	14 (1.3)	11 (1.1)	15 (1.3)	10 (1.1)	26 (1.6)	11 (1.1)	1 (0.4)	3 (0.6)	8 (1.0)	8 (1.2)
Norway (Grade 9)	33 (2.1)	12 (1.2)	9 (1.1)	14 (1.6)	25 (2.2)	11 (1.3)	6 (1.0)	1 (0.4)	5 (0.9)	9 (1.2)	5 (0.9)
Benchmarking participant											
Newfoundland and Labrador, Canada	45 (2.5)	18 (2.6)	19 (2.6)	9 (1.7)	15 (2.1)	22 (2.2)	16 (2.3)	3 (0.9)	10 (1.8)	21 (2.4)	18 (2.0)
Benchmarking participant not meeting sample requirements											
Ontario, Canada	49 (3.0)	25 (2.7)	33 (2.7)	13 (2.5)	17 (3.0)	24 (2.5)	20 (2.6)	9 (1.7)	12 (2.2)	22 (2.6)	24 (2.8)

Notes:

() Standard errors appear in parentheses. Because some results are rounded to the nearest whole number, some totals may appear inconsistent.

[1] Country surveyed teachers retrospectively to the previous school year when they were teaching the target grade.

▲ More than 10 percentage points above ICILS 2013 average
△ Significantly above ICILS 2013 average
▽ Significantly below ICILS 2013 average
▼ More than 10 percentage points below ICILS 2013 average

- Enabling students to collaborate with other students (within or outside school) (7%); and
- Mediating communication between students and experts or external mentors (4%).

Conclusion

In general, the ICILS data considered in this chapter confirm substantial use of ICT in teaching and learning. Across the ICILS 2013 countries, three out five teachers were using computers at least once per week when teaching, and four out of five were using computers on a weekly basis for other work at their schools. It is not possible to judge whether the level of use was appropriate, but it was certainly extensive.

Teachers in most countries were experienced users of ICT and generally recognized the positive aspects of using ICT in teaching and learning at school, especially in terms of accessing and managing information. On balance, teachers reported generally positive attitudes toward the use of these technologies despite reporting awareness of some potentially negative aspects of using them (e.g., for writing, calculation, and estimation).

Generally, teachers were confident regarding their ability to use a variety of computer applications, with two-thirds expressing confidence in their ability to use ICT for assessing and monitoring student progress. There were differences among countries in the level of confidence that teachers expressed with regard to using computer technologies, and it was evident that younger teachers were a little more confident than their older colleagues.

A substantial majority of teachers across the participating ICILS countries were using ICT in their teaching. Teachers were most likely to use these technologies when they were confident about their expertise in this regard, worked in school environments where there was collaboration about and planning of ICT use, and where there were fewer resource-based obstacles to using ICT. These were also the conditions that supported teaching about CIL. This finding suggests that if CIL is to be developed to the greatest extent possible, then teacher expertise in ICT use needs to be developed and supported by collaborative environments that incorporate institutional planning.

ICT use was reported in most subject areas. However, outside of information technology subjects, its use was more prevalent in the (natural) sciences and in the human sciences or humanities than in other areas. The ICILS results also show that ICT use in teaching was less prevalent in mathematics and in practical and vocational education. It seems that these latter subject areas are those in which teachers give less emphasis to developing their students' CIL capabilities.

The ICT tools that teachers were most frequently using in their classrooms were wordprocessing and presentation software as well as computer-based information resources such as websites, wikis, and encyclopedias. According to teachers' responses on the ICILS teacher survey, students were most commonly using ICT to search for information, work on short assignments, and carry out individual work on learning materials. The survey data also suggest that teachers were often using ICT to present information and reinforce skills. In general, the teachers appear to have been using ICT most frequently for relatively simple tasks rather than for more complex tasks.

CHAPTER 8:

Investigating Variations in Computer and Information Literacy

In previous chapters, we described several associations between students' computer and information literacy (CIL) and selected variables such as gender and home background. Our aim in this chapter is to investigate the combined influence of a number of variables on variations in CIL, including individual (student-level) as well as contextual (school-level) variables. The ICILS research questions that we address in this chapter are the following:

- Research Question 2: *What aspects of schools and education systems are related to student achievement in computer and information literacy?*

- Research Question 3: *What characteristics of students' levels of access to, familiarity with, and self-reported proficiency in using computers are related to student achievement in computer and information literacy?*

- Research Question 4: *What aspects of students' personal and social backgrounds (such as gender, socioeconomic background, and language background) are related to computer and information literacy?*

We used multilevel models to review the extent to which different factors at the student and school level are associated with variations in CIL. Factors of interest include those related to access to, use of, and familiarity with information and communication technology (ICT) as well as other variables reflecting students' personal and social backgrounds.

A model for explaining variation in CIL

When developing this model, we drew on research literature as well as the contextual framework for ICILS (Fraillon, Schulz, & Ainley, 2013) to determine which predictors of variation in CIL to include in our multivariate analyses.

Prior to ICILS, research into CIL learning outcomes and factors influencing student knowledge in this area was generally limited to national studies. Sample surveys carried out as part of the Australian National Assessment Program (NAP) for ICT Literacy showed that students' gender (female), socioeconomic background, and experience with and current use of computers were positive predictors of ICT literacy (Australian Curriculum, Assessment and Reporting Authority, 2012; Ministerial Council for Education, Early Childhood Development and Youth Affairs, 2010; Ministerial Council on Education, Employment, Training and Youth Affairs, 2007).

The Chilean national assessment program SIMCE TIC also assessed ICT literacy. Multilevel analyses of this body of data illustrated considerable variation among schools as well as effects of cultural background, socioeconomic status, and school characteristics (private/public, subsidies) on digital competencies (Román & Murrillo, 2013). Further analyses also provided evidence of strong effects of prior achievement in reading and mathematics on digital competence (San Martin, Claro, Cabello, & Preiss, 2013).

© International Association for the Evaluation of Educational Achievement (IEA) 2014
J. Fraillon et al., *Preparing for Life in a Digital Age,* DOI 10.1007/978-3-319-14222-7_9

As part of its Programme in International Student Assessment (PISA), the OECD assessed the performance of 15-year-old students in digital reading across 16 countries (OECD, 2011). Although this international study assessed reading competences in a digital environment, it also reflected CIL-based skills. Study results showed that socioeconomic background as well as computer use had statistically significant effects on students' digital reading skills. However, no clear association was found between these skills and computer use at school.

The ICILS contextual framework (Fraillon et al., 2013) postulated that students' CIL is influenced by context variables located at different levels (wider community, schools/classrooms, individual learner, and home), with these levels featuring antecedent as well as process-related factors. When conducting the analysis of CIL presented in this chapter, we included variables pertaining to the school/classroom context, the context of the individual learner, and the home context.

Another distinction, one that we introduced into the analyses in this report, can be made between variables associated with (1) ICT and learning about CIL, and (2) personal and social background factors in addition to the ICT-related variables. If we use only the first group of variables in a multivariate model (i.e., Model 1), we obtain results that indicate the effects of the ICT-related variables by themselves. Contrasting these results with those from a second model (Model 2), which contains all predictor variables, including those reflecting social and personal background factors, provides us with an indication of the net effects of the ICT-related variables as well as the net effects of background.

The models we chose for our analyses included several predictors that we classified into the following broad categories:

- *ICT resources and use at home:* These predictors were ICT resources at home, personal experience with ICT, students' use of ICT at home and school, and students' experiences with learning about ICT at school. We included these variables at the student level in Models 1 and 2.

- *ICT resources and use at school:* ICILS 2013 collected information on schools' ICT resources through its ICT-coordinator and teacher questionnaires. The school's CIL learning context includes experience at school with using ICT in teaching and learning, the extent to which students at school are regular users of computers, and students' perceptions of their having learned CIL skills at school. We included these variables at the school level in Models 1 and 2.

- *Personal and social background:* Previous research and results from other analyses conducted during ICILS (see Chapter 4) illustrate the extent to which gender, students' expectations of their own educational attainment, and parental socioeconomic status are associated with students' CIL. We included these variables at the student level in Model 2.

- *Social context of schools:* At the school level, the average socioeconomic status of the student body is a factor that, as numerous studies show, is associated with many different learning outcomes. We included this variable at the school level in Model 2.

We used the following variables to indicate home ICT resources:

- *Internet access at home:* For the purpose of our analysis, we coded students who reported having internet access at home as 1 and all others as 0.

- *Number of computers at home:* We coded the indicator variable resulting from students' reports of the number of desktop and portable computers in their homes as 0 (no computer), 1 (one computer), 2 (two computers), or 3 (three or more computers).

This next batch of variables relates to students' individual learning contexts.

- *Experience with computers:* This variable reflected how long each ICILS student had been using computers. We coded it in approximate years (with values of 0, 2, 4, and 6) so that the regression coefficient would reflect the change in CIL score points for one additional year of experience.

- *Weekly use of computers at home:* This variable reflected the frequency with which the students were using computers at home and was coded 1 for at least weekly use and 0 for less frequent use. This meant that the regression coefficient would reflect the change in CIL score points between students with at least weekly use of a computer at home and students with less frequent use after we had controlled for all other variables in the model.

- *Weekly use of computers at school:* This variable reflected the frequency with which students were using computers at school. We coded it 1 for at least weekly use and 0 for less frequent use so that the regression coefficient would reflect the change in CIL score points between students with at least weekly use of a computer at home and students with less frequent use after we had controlled for all other variables in the model.

- *Students' reports on learning CIL tasks at school:* We based this index on a set of eight items that required the ICILS students to indicate whether they had learned about different CIL tasks at school.[1] The values were IRT (item response theory) scores, which we standardized for our analyses within each country to have a mean of 0 and a standard deviation of 1. We centered these values on the school averages so that the individual values would indicate the difference from the average index score in each school.

The following school-level predictors reflect ICT resources at school but from different perspectives:

- *Availability of ICT resources for teaching and learning:* This measure, based on responses from the ICT-coordinators, was computed using ICILS questionnaire data on the availability of nine different computer and ICT resources.[2] We coded the

---

1 The tasks were:
   - Providing references to internet sources;
   - Accessing information with a computer;
   - Presenting information for a given audience or purpose with a computer;
   - Working out whether to trust information from the internet;
   - Deciding what information is relevant to include in school work;
   - Organizing information obtained from internet sources;
   - Deciding where to look for information about an unfamiliar topic; and
   - Looking for different types of digital information on a topic.
2 The following ICT resources were used for scaling:
   - Interactive digital learning resources (e.g., learning objects);
   - Tutorial software or [practice programs];
   - Digital learning games;
   - Multimedia production tools (e.g., media capture and editing, web production);
   - Data-logging and monitoring tools;
   - Simulations and modeling software;
   - Graphing or drawing software;
   - Space on a school network for students to store their work; and
   - A school intranet with applications and workspaces for students to use (e.g., [Moodle]).

items dichotomously (1 = available, 0 = not available) and then estimated the IRT scale scores. The higher values indicate more ICT resources at school.

- *ICT resource limitations for teaching and learning:* This index reflected the extent to which the ICILS teachers thought their schools had insufficient ICT resources.[3] We based the IRT scale scores on teacher survey data aggregated at the school level and standardized them for this analysis to have a mean of 0 and a standard deviation of 1 across weighted schools in each education system.

The following school-level predictors reflect the school learning context:

- *School experience with using ICT for teaching and learning:* School ICT-coordinators reported on the amount of time their school had been using computers for teaching and learning. We coded the four response categories as 0 for "not using computers," 2.5 for "fewer than 5 years," 7.5 for "at least 5 but fewer than 10 years," and 12.5 for "10 years or more" so that the regression coefficients would reflect the approximate increase per year of computer experience.

- *Percentage of students reporting at least weekly use of computers at home:* This index reflected the extent to which students were in a home context where computers were commonly used. At schools where majorities of students tend to use computers at home, we can expect that individual student learning will be fostered by an environment where exchanging ideas about ICT is common.

- *School average of students who said they had learned CIL tasks at school:* This measure, derived as the average student score on perceptions of having learned CIL tasks at schools, provided a school-level measure of the extent to which CIL-related content was being used at the school. We standardized the school-level index so that 0 was the mean and 1 the standard deviation of weighted school averages within the participating education systems.

The personal and social student background characteristics included in our analyses were:

- *Students' gender:* We coded this variable as 1 for females and 0 for males.

- *Students' expected educational attainment:* Although this variable is more than a simple background factor, it does reflect home-based expectations regarding students' ongoing education as well as students' educational aspirations with respect to fields beyond the domain of the (in this case, ICILS) assessment. For the present analyses, this factor was reflected in three indicator variables of expected highest educational attainment, namely, lower-secondary, post-secondary nonuniversity, and university education (each coded as 1 = expected or 0 = not expected). Expectation of attaining an upper-secondary qualification served as a reference category.

- *Students' socioeconomic background:* This variable was a composite index that we standardized to have a mean of 0 and a standard deviation of 1 within each country and centered on school averages so that it would indicate the effect of socioeconomic

---

3 Teachers were asked to rate their agreement or disagreement with the following statements:
   - My school does not have sufficient ICT equipment (e.g., computers);
   - My school does not have access to digital learning resources;
   - My school has limited connectivity (e.g., slow or unstable speed) to the internet;
   - The computer equipment in our school is out of date;
   - There is not sufficient provision for me to develop expertise in ICT;
   - There is not sufficient technical support to maintain ICT resources.

background within schools. The index consisted of factor scores derived from a principal component analysis of:

- highest parental occupation (ISEI scores);
- highest parental education (categorical variable with 0 = lower-secondary or below, 1 = upper-secondary, 2 = post-secondary nonuniversity education, and 3 = university education); and
- number of books at home (categorical variable with 0 = 0–10 books, 1 = 11–25 books, 2 = 26–100 books, and 3 = more than 100 books).

We used the following variable to measure the schools' "social intake":

- *School socioeconomic context:* This variable reflected the average of student scores on the composite index of socioeconomic background. It indicated the social (student) intake of schools and the social context in which the ICILS students were learning. We standardized the index to have a mean of 0 and a standard deviation of 1 across weighted schools within each participating education system.

During multivariate analyses, any issues relating to missing data tend to become more prevalent than in other forms of analysis because of the simultaneous inclusion of numerous variables. To address the missing data issue, we first excluded from the analyses the small proportion of students for whom there were no student questionnaire data. We were able to take this approach because only small proportions of students had missing data for the student-level variables.

Because there were higher proportions of missing data for the variables derived from the ICT-coordinator questionnaire (ICT resources at school and ICT experience at school) and the ICILS teacher survey, we needed to treat these by setting the missing values to national mean or median values, respectively, and then adding a missing indicator variable for missing school data and another one for missing teacher data. We chose this approach (see Cohen & Cohen, 1975) because of its simplicity and because of the relatively limited number of missing values.

On average, data from about 97 percent of tested students were included in the analysis. The only country where this proportion was somewhat lower, at 93 percent, was Germany. The ICILS technical report (Fraillon, Schulz, Friedman, Ainley, & Gebhardt, forthcoming) provides detailed information on the multilevel modeling and treatment of missing data.

The hierarchical nature of the data lent itself to multivariate multilevel regression analysis (see Raudenbush & Bryk, 2002). We estimated, for each national sample, two-level hierarchical models, with students nested within schools. We used the software package MPlus (Version 7; see Muthén & Muthén, 2012) to carry out the analyses and obtained estimates after applying sampling weights at the student and school levels.

We excluded from the analyses some countries and benchmarking participants that had insufficient data. The extremely low participation rates for the teacher survey in the City of Buenos Aires (Argentina) and Switzerland led to the exclusion of their data, while data from the Netherlands had to be excluded because of the missing information on parental occupation that was needed to derive the composite index of students' socioeconomic background.

When interpreting results from a multilevel analysis, it is important to be aware that first-level (i.e., student-level) variables have a different meaning from those in a single-level regression analysis. This is because student-level coefficients reflect the effect a variable has within schools. Consequently, with respect to ICILS, effects at this level may differ from the findings that emerged from the bivariate analyses reported in previous chapters.

Multilevel analysis also allows estimation of not only random effects models, where within-school effects vary across schools, but also interaction effects between school-level predictors and the slopes of student-level predictors within schools. However, in these first analyses of ICILS data focused on factors influencing CIL, we estimated all student-level effects as fixed effects that varied little across schools.

When conducting the multilevel analysis of CIL, we estimated three different models:

- Model 0 (the "null model"), which included no predictor variables other than school intercepts;
- Model 1, which included, as student-level and school-level predictors, only variables related to ICT;
- Model 2, which, added to the above variables, reflected the personal and social background of students as well as the average socioeconomic background of schools' student intakes.

Because Model 0 provided estimates of the variance at each level (within and between schools) before the inclusion of predictors, it established the point from which we could determine how much the subsequent models explained the variance. Model 1 included only those predictors directly related to ICT (resources, familiarity, learning context), while Model 2 provided information about how much of the variance over and above the Model 1 predictors was explained when students' personal and social backgrounds were taken into account.

Influences on variation in CIL

Student-level influences

Table 8.1 shows the unstandardized regression coefficients for student-level variables from both analysis models for the ICILS 2013 participating countries and benchmarking participants.[4] The coefficients reflect the effect of each ICT-related factor within schools before and after we controlled for personal and social background. The overall results for countries meeting sample participation requirements in ICILS 2013 should be interpreted with some caution, however, as they reflect average regression coefficients that are only meaningful for factors that have consistently positive or negative effects across countries.

For Model 1, the number of computers at home had statistically significant associations with CIL in about half of the participating education systems. The effects ranged from 3.7 CIL score points (per additional computer) in the Czech Republic to 16.5 such points in Newfoundland and Labrador (Canada). However, after controlling for personal and social background (Model 2), we observed statistically significant

---

4 Two countries that met sample participation requirements for the student but not the teacher survey were included in the main table with an annotation. We regarded this approach as appropriate given that the teacher survey data were limited to one indicator variable aggregated at the school level.

Table 8.1: Student-level results: ICT-related context factors

Country	Home ICT Resources						Students' ICT Familiarity					
	Numbers of computers at home		Internet access at home		Years of experience with computers		Use of home computers at least once a week		Use of school computers at least once a week		Students' learning experience at school	
	Model 1	Model 2	Model 1	Model 2	Model 1	Model 2	Model 1	Model 2	Model 1	Model 2	Model 1	Model 2
Australia	**9.2** (4.0)	5.4 (3.9)	**27.9** (10.0)	**21.2** (10.4)	**5.6** (0.9)	**4.6** (0.8)	**26.2** (9.9)	**23.0** (8.9)	3.5 (4.6)	4.1 (4.4)	**7.7** (1.9)	**6.2** (1.7)
Chile	4.1 (2.2)	0.0 (2.1)	-0.1 (7.3)	-1.0 (6.8)	**3.6** (0.8)	**2.5** (0.8)	**26.1** (5.7)	**26.8** (5.5)	0.3 (4.8)	-0.7 (4.3)	3.1 (1.8)	2.2 (1.8)
Croatia	**8.7** (3.1)	3.4 (2.8)	**30.8** (10.8)	**23.7** (10.3)	**7.5** (1.2)	**5.8** (1.1)	6.7 (9.5)	5.5 (9.2)	**22.6** (4.6)	**20.6** (4.0)	**8.9** (1.9)	**4.9** (1.7)
Czech Republic	**3.7** (1.8)	1.0 (1.7)	18.1 (12.5)	9.4 (11.7)	**1.5** (0.7)	**2.2** (0.6)	13.4 (7.3)	12.5 (7.5)	4.5 (3.7)	3.6 (3.4)	0.2 (1.4)	0.3 (1.4)
Germany†,††	1.7 (3.3)	2.3 (3.1)	^	^	1.2 (1.3)	1.1 (1.2)	7.2 (11.0)	10.1 (10.3)	-2.0 (6.9)	-2.5 (6.6)	-2.6 (2.2)	-2.1 (2.1)
Korea, Republic of	1.5 (5.0)	-2.2 (4.3)	**96.6** (40.1)	**60.1** (27.5)	**7.0** (1.0)	**6.3** (1.0)	**16.1** (6.6)	**24.1** (6.7)	10.6 (8.1)	6.0 (7.7)	**7.3** (2.7)	**5.4** (2.1)
Lithuania	2.0 (2.4)	-0.1 (2.5)	24.8 (14.9)	20.3 (13.5)	**6.2** (0.8)	**4.5** (0.9)	**42.3** (9.8)	**32.4** (9.3)	**17.6** (6.1)	**16.8** (5.3)	2.0 (2.3)	1.5 (2.1)
Norway (Grade 9)¹,††	2.3 (4.4)	-1.0 (4.5)	^	^	**4.8** (1.2)	**4.7** (1.1)	**18.2** (8.5)	**20.6** (8.2)	1.8 (4.0)	2.3 (3.6)	2.9 (2.2)	1.0 (2.1)
Poland	**7.2** (2.4)	0.9 (2.4)	19.9 (12.6)	13.1 (12.5)	**8.3** (1.3)	**6.0** (1.2)	**33.2** (16.3)	31.0 (16.0)	11.7 (6.6)	6.3 (5.7)	-1.6 (2.0)	0.9 (1.8)
Russian Federation²	**6.5** (2.4)	3.8 (2.3)	**21.9** (10.0)	14.6 (10.9)	**4.2** (1.0)	**3.1** (1.0)	**14.3** (6.6)	**18.0** (6.1)	**9.7** (3.8)	**8.3** (3.6)	2.8 (1.7)	2.3 (1.6)
Slovak Republic	**5.8** (2.2)	-0.8 (2.1)	**40.4** (14.1)	**32.9** (11.9)	**4.8** (1.0)	**3.6** (0.9)	**27.5** (12.6)	**27.8** (12.0)	3.1 (5.2)	5.7 (4.8)	3.1 (1.9)	2.9 (1.7)
Slovenia	**9.6** (1.8)	2.8 (1.5)	**36.0** (12.4)	**24.2** (11.1)	**2.4** (0.8)	**2.7** (0.7)	12.0 (7.0)	10.4 (6.2)	-6.1 (3.2)	0.5 (3.3)	**3.8** (1.7)	2.4 (1.4)
Thailand²	**9.3** (3.5)	**6.8** (3.4)	5.5 (6.1)	3.5 (6.6)	**4.1** (1.1)	**3.7** (1.1)	**14.8** (7.5)	**15.6** (7.7)	**16.6** (4.9)	**16.3** (4.6)	1.9 (3.4)	2.2 (3.3)
Turkey	1.8 (2.9)	0.5 (2.8)	**12.0** (4.6)	8.7 (4.9)	**6.0** (0.9)	**5.4** (1.0)	4.9 (6.8)	7.1 (6.7)	9.0 (5.8)	10.4 (5.7)	**7.2** (2.3)	**6.1** (2.3)
ICILS 2013 average	**5.3** (0.8)	**1.6** (0.8)	**27.8** (3.9)	**19.2** (3.2)	**4.8** (0.3)	**4.0** (0.3)	**18.8** (2.5)	**18.9** (2.4)	**7.4** (1.4)	**7.0** (1.3)	**3.3** (0.6)	**2.6** (0.5)
Countries not meeting sample requirements												
Denmark††	3.6 (8.4)	4.3 (7.8)	^	^	**2.5** (1.0)	**2.0** (1.0)	9.8 (9.9)	12.1 (9.3)	6.7 (5.8)	5.9 (5.7)	1.1 (2.2)	0.9 (2.1)
Hong Kong SAR††	3.9 (2.4)	4.6 (2.4)	^	^	1.5 (1.2)	1.9 (1.1)	**16.4** (5.7)	**17.2** (5.2)	**7.7** (3.5)	**7.9** (3.5)	**8.5** (2.2)	**7.4** (2.0)
Benchmarking participants												
Newfoundland and Labrador, Canada	**16.5** (3.1)	**10.6** (3.0)	^	^	**5.8** (1.2)	**4.3** (1.1)	**21.2** (7.7)	**17.1** (6.4)	2.5 (4.4)	2.3 (4.1)	**9.8** (2.2)	**8.0** (2.0)
Ontario, Canada††	**9.0** (3.4)	5.8 (3.2)	11.5 (13.6)	3.2 (13.5)	**4.2** (1.2)	**3.5** (1.1)	**22.8** (7.2)	**18.9** (6.4)	-6.6 (4.7)	-4.7 (4.3)	**5.9** (2.2)	**5.4** (2.1)

Notes:

* Statistically significant (*p*<.05) coefficients in **bold.**

( ) Standard errors appear in parentheses. Because some results are rounded to the nearest whole number, some totals may appear inconsistent.

† Met guidelines for student survey sampling participation rates only after replacement schools were included.

†† Did not meet sampling participation rates for teacher survey.

¹ National Desired Population does not match International Desired Population.

² Country surveyed the same cohort of students but at the beginning of the next school year.

^ Subgroup sample size too small for reporting reliable estimate.

effects only in Thailand (with 6.8 CIL score points) and Newfoundland and Labrador (10.6 score points). This outcome seems plausible given that we can expect computer acquisition to be highly correlated with socioeconomic background.

Internet access was positively associated with CIL in a number of countries. In Model 1, this factor was associated with increases in score points ranging from 12 in Turkey to almost 97 in Korea. In all but two countries (Russian Federation and Turkey), the (within-school) effects remained statistically significant after we had controlled for personal and social background (in Model 2).

Years of computer experience was consistently and positively associated with CIL in all but two countries (Germany and Hong Kong SAR). In Model 1, on average across the ICILS countries, one year of additional computer experience was associated with about five CIL score points, with the range extending from 1.5 in the Czech Republic to 8.3 in Poland. Model 2 results show that even after we had controlled for other background variables, the estimated effect was only slightly smaller and remained statistically significant across countries.

In many countries, students' weekly use of computers at home was also positively associated with CIL. In Model 1, statistically significant effects ranged from 14.3 CIL score points (as the estimated difference between students who used home computers at least weekly and others) in the Russian Federation to 42.3 in Lithuania. These effects remained statistically significant for all countries (with the exception of Poland) after we had controlled for personal and social background factors (in Model 2); in some countries, slightly larger effects were recorded. Weekly use of school computers had statistically significant associations with CIL in only five countries—Croatia, Lithuania, the Russian Federation, Thailand, and Hong Kong SAR. These associations were of similar size in both models.

In Model 1, student reports on having learned about ICT at school had statistically significant positive effects in eight education systems (Australia, Croatia, Korea, Slovenia, Turkey, Hong Kong SAR, and the two Canadian provinces), with the effects ranging in strength from 3.8 CIL score points (per national standard deviation) in Slovenia to 9.8 in Newfoundland and Labrador (Canada). Except for Slovenia, these effects remained statistically significant after we had controlled for personal and social background variables (in Model 2).

School-level influences

Table 8.2 records the effects for ICT-related school-level factors for both models. The availability of ICT resources (as reported by the ICT-coordinators) had a statistically significant effect only in the Russian Federation, an outcome that remained unchanged after we controlled for background variables (in Model 2).

When estimating Model 1, we found teachers' perceptions of ICT resource limitations for teaching at their school had statistically significant negative effects on CIL in four countries—Australia, Korea, Poland, and the Russian Federation. The effects ranged from -4.7 CIL points (per national standard deviation) in Australia to -10.2 and -10.3 CIL points respectively in Korea and the Russian Federation. However, these effects remained statistically significant only in Korea after we controlled for schools' socioeconomic context.

For Model 1, students' school-based experience with ICT was recorded as a statistically significant predictor in Chile and Turkey only (estimated respectively as effects of 12.3

Table 8.2: School-level results: ICT-related factors

| Country | School ICT Resources | | | | | | Schools' ICT Learning Context | | | |
| | Availability of ICT resources | | ICT resource limitations for teaching | | Years of experience with computers at school | | Percentage of students with weekly use of home computers | | Students' average of learning ICT tasks at school | |
	Model 1	Model 2	Model 1	Model 2	Model 1	Model 2	Model 1	Model 2	Model 1	Model 2
Australia	-1.8 (4.3)	0.3 (3.1)	**-4.7** (2.3)	1.7 (2.3)	3.2 (4.3)	0.6 (3.5)	**1.4** (0.3)	**0.6** (0.3)	**14.3** (3.4)	**10.3** (2.8)
Chile	2.3 (4.1)	-1.5 (3.0)	-9.3 (6.0)	-3.7 (3.8)	**12.3** (4.9)	4.8 (3.7)	**1.5** (0.2)	**0.4** (0.2)	11.1 (6.9)	**11.1** (3.4)
Croatia	-5.2 (3.3)	-3.0 (3.6)	-0.1 (3.3)	-2.4 (3.0)	-2.0 (4.6)	2.3 (4.3)	0.7 (0.8)	-0.3 (0.8)	3.1 (4.2)	5.7 (4.1)
Czech Republic	4.7 (3.9)	0.8 (3.1)	-2.2 (3.0)	-3.4 (2.7)	0.8 (5.2)	1.3 (4.4)	0.9 (0.6)	0.1 (0.5)	-2.8 (3.1)	3.0 (2.7)
Germany[1],[tt]	2.0 (6.6)	3.7 (4.3)	16.5 (12.5)	9.4 (8.2)	-12.3 (14.6)	-10.2 (8.8)	**2.0** (0.8)	0.5 (0.4)	-10.1 (9.4)	-5.4 (5.3)
Korea, Republic of	-7.1 (5.1)	-4.7 (3.6)	**-10.2** (4.0)	**-9.6** (3.9)	-0.4 (5.9)	0.6 (4.4)	-0.1 (0.5)	0.0 (0.4)	-7.6 (5.3)	-5.0 (4.2)
Lithuania	-0.9 (3.6)	-0.3 (3.4)	-2.7 (3.7)	-2.5 (3.1)	-4.6 (5.5)	-7.1 (5.5)	**2.8** (0.7)	**2.4** (0.8)	-3.7 (4.5)	-1.7 (4.0)
Norway (Grade 9)[1],[tt]	4.9 (2.9)	1.9 (3.0)	-2.6 (2.9)	-4.7 (3.0)	0.9 (6.2)	2.2 (5.2)	0.7 (0.6)	0.6 (0.5)	5.1 (2.9)	4.0 (2.5)
Poland	1.0 (3.3)	-0.9 (2.4)	**-5.4** (2.6)	-0.2 (2.1)	2.1 (4.9)	1.1 (3.6)	**1.6** (0.7)	**0.8** (0.4)	**-16.9** (4.5)	0.5 (4.0)
Russian Federation[2]	**9.1** (3.9)	**8.7** (3.6)	**-10.3** (4.5)	-8.5 (5.1)	4.7 (5.7)	3.0 (5.6)	0.0 (0.3)	-0.2 (0.3)	-1.2 (4.0)	-1.1 (3.8)
Slovak Republic	1.8 (4.3)	1.1 (4.1)	-1.2 (4.9)	-3.3 (4.0)	5.3 (6.3)	3.6 (5.8)	**3.3** (0.6)	**2.2** (0.6)	3.4 (3.3)	4.4 (2.9)
Slovenia	2.4 (3.2)	1.4 (3.0)	-2.6 (2.3)	-2.4 (2.0)	-4.1 (4.6)	-7.0 (4.1)	-0.4 (0.5)	-0.4 (0.4)	5.2 (3.1)	**7.3** (2.9)
Thailand[2]	-1.3 (7.1)	-2.2 (6.4)	-4.0 (9.2)	-0.8 (7.8)	-2.6 (10.7)	1.5 (9.3)	0.5 (0.4)	-0.4 (0.5)	13.4 (8.4)	12.1 (7.2)
Turkey	5.0 (6.5)	8.5 (6.8)	-12.4 (6.4)	-9.0 (6.6)	**15.8** (6.9)	12.8 (7.2)	0.4 (0.3)	0.2 (0.3)	11.6 (8.7)	11.5 (8.1)
ICILS 2013 average	1.2 (1.2)	1.0 (1.1)	**-3.6** (1.5)	**-2.8** (1.2)	1.4 (1.9)	0.7 (1.5)	**1.1** (0.1)	**0.5** (0.1)	1.8 (1.5)	**4.0** (1.2)
Countries not meeting sample requirements										
Denmark[tt]	3.9 (3.7)	0.6 (3.0)	-0.1 (3.4)	-0.5 (3.0)	-3.6 (6.6)	-2.6 (5.3)	0.9 (0.5)	0.4 (0.5)	6.8 (3.7)	2.3 (3.1)
Hong Kong SAR[tt]	7.6 (7.1)	6.8 (6.6)	-5.6 (7.0)	-3.0 (6.4)	2.3 (11.8)	7.9 (11.5)	1.0 (0.6)	**1.2** (0.6)	**40.3** (7.2)	**31.7** (6.9)
Benchmarking participant not meeting sample requirements										
Newfoundland & Labrador, Canada	1.3 (4.0)	-0.3 (3.3)	-2.2 (4.0)	-2.6 (3.5)	13.6 (10.7)	12.8 (8.5)	0.3 (0.4)	0.2 (0.3)	**11.3** (3.2)	**10.5** (2.8)
Ontario, Canada[tt]	1.5 (4.4)	3.6 (3.4)	2.2 (2.9)	3.8 (2.4)	-0.4 (5.7)	-3.6 (4.4)	0.8 (0.4)	0.4 (0.3)	7.8 (4.5)	5.5 (3.9)

Notes:
* Statistically significant ($p<.05$) coefficients in **bold**.
() Standard errors appear in parentheses. Because some results are rounded to the nearest whole number, some totals may appear inconsistent.
[†] Met guidelines for student survey sampling participation rates only after replacement schools were included.
[††] Did not meet sampling participation rates for teacher survey.
[1] National Desired Population does not match International Desired Population.
[2] Country surveyed the same cohort of students but at the beginning of the next school year.

and 15.8 CIL score points per year of experience). However, these effects were no longer significant in these countries after we had controlled for the socioeconomic background of the student cohort in the school (in Model 2).

In six countries we recorded statistically significant context effects for the percentages of students who said they used computers at home at least once a week. In Model 1, these effects ranged from 1.4 CIL score points (per percentage point) in Australia to 3.3 points in the Slovak Republic. In five of six countries, these effects remained significant after we controlled for personal and social background variables. In Germany, however, the effect was no longer statistically significant.

In Model 1, aggregate scores of the index reflecting student reports on having learned about ICT tasks at school had statistically significant positive effects in four education systems (Australia, Poland, Hong Kong SAR, and Newfoundland and Labrador), and a significant negative effect in the Russian Federation. After controlling for the socioeconomic context of schools in Model 2, we observed statistically positive effects in Australia, Chile, Slovenia, Hong Kong SAR, and Newfoundland and Labrador. This finding suggests that school education related to CIL can affect students' achievement in this area beyond the influence of the socioeconomic context.

Student-level and school-level background influences

Table 8.3 shows the regression coefficients for indicators of students' personal and social backgrounds as well as the social context of the schools, as measured by the average index of students' socioeconomic background. These indicators were included in Model 2 only.

Female gender was a statistically significant positive predictor in a majority of countries. On average, after controlling for other variables, we found female students scoring about 12 CIL points higher than male students, with effects ranging from 7.5 in the Czech Republic to 35.7 points in Korea.

Expected educational attainment, which is likely to be associated with previous academic performance as well as parental background, was also significantly associated with CIL in all participating countries. While students who expected to attain educational qualifications no higher than lower-secondary tended to have lower CIL scores than those expecting to complete upper-secondary education (the reference category), students in several countries who expected to gain a post-secondary nonuniversity qualification had significantly higher CIL scores than those expecting to go no further than upper-secondary education.

Expected university education was consistently and significantly associated with CIL. After we had controlled for other factors, we observed that, on average across the ICILS countries, the achievement of students in this category was 36 CIL points higher than the score of students expecting to secure only upper-secondary qualifications. The statistically significant within-school effects ranged from 11.2 points in Germany to 61.0 in Croatia.

Within schools, students' individual socioeconomic background had statistically significant positive effects in a majority of countries, with the effects ranging from 4.1 score points in the Russian Federation to 12.1 in both Norway and Newfoundland and Labrador (Canada). The average socioeconomic background of schools was also a statistically significant predictor in all but three ICILS countries (Lithuania, the Russian

Table 8.3: Student and school-level results: personal and social background

Country	Gender (Female)	Student Expectations of Educational Attainment			Students' Socioeconomic Background	School Average of Students' Socioeconomic Background
		Lower-secondary education	Post-secondary nonuniversity education	University education		
Australia	13.5 (4.2)	-32.0 (8.2)	-1.8 (7.8)	27.4 (4.0)	6.8 (3.2)	17.1 (2.4)
Chile	17.7 (3.2)	^	23.2 (6.3)	45.1 (5.5)	8.4 (2.3)	30.2 (3.2)
Croatia	8.8 (3.6)	-27.6 (11.9)	39.5 (4.7)	61.0 (4.3)	7.2 (2.3)	10.5 (3.6)
Czech Republic	7.5 (2.5)	-12.7 (8.6)	17.6 (5.1)	28.8 (3.2)	5.9 (1.4)	16.3 (1.8)
Germany†,††	13.1 (5.2)	-16.2 (7.8)	3.1 (7.5)	11.2 (5.2)	2.3 (3.4)	39.8 (5.3)
Korea, Republic of	35.7 (7.2)	-42.9 (19.4)	10.6 (11.9)	31.6 (7.7)	11.0 (2.7)	11.4 (4.1)
Lithuania	9.8 (5.1)	-11.0 (8.5)	21.3 (5.9)	48.6 (6.2)	5.0 (2.7)	4.4 (5.6)
Norway (Grade 9)1,††	21.8 (3.9)	-18.4 (13.0)	8.7 (7.5)	25.2 (6.0)	12.1 (2.1)	10.7 (2.3)
Poland	3.4 (3.4)	-40.4 (10.0)	32.2 (6.2)	48.6 (4.4)	8.8 (2.6)	20.7 (4.5)
Russian Federation2	6.2 (3.4)	-9.1 (7.7)	10.6 (6.5)	38.0 (5.8)	4.1 (1.7)	5.6 (5.6)
Slovak Republic	8.9 (3.4)	-28.4 (10.8)	37.4 (5.7)	44.3 (3.9)	9.3 (2.2)	13.6 (5.3)
Slovenia	23.2 (3.1)	-25.3 (8.4)	26.8 (3.5)	46.1 (4.0)	10.6 (1.7)	7.8 (3.4)
Thailand2	2.2 (6.4)	-13.7 (8.8)	15.9 (11.5)	26.2 (7.6)	-0.7 (3.4)	28.3 (8.5)
Turkey	-2.2 (4.3)	-3.7 (9.0)	7.2 (6.9)	26.8 (7.0)	3.0 (3.1)	9.3 (6.3)
ICILS 2013 average	12.1 (1.2)	-21.6 (2.7)	18.0 (1.9)	36.4 (1.5)	6.7 (0.7)	16.1 (1.3)
Countries not meeting sample requirements						
Denmark††	15.7 (4.2)	-23.7 (8.2)	12.1 (6.4)	20.0 (4.5)	10.2 (2.2)	18.1 (4.9)
Hong Kong SAR††	10.0 (4.1)	-7.3 (10.3)	17.3 (8.8)	21.4 (8.0)	-6.3 (2.4)	15.4 (5.3)
Benchmarking participants						
Newfoundland & Labrador, Canada	31.8 (4.0)	-7.2 (10.3)	10.9 (10.0)	37.1 (8.0)	12.1 (2.2)	14.1 (2.8)
Ontario, Canada††	28.0 (4.0)	-14.3 (10.7)	10.3 (13.0)	29.3 (6.4)	11.4 (2.1)	12.5 (3.2)

Notes:
* Statistically significant (*p*<.05) coefficients in **bold**.
() Standard errors appear in parentheses. Because some results are rounded to the nearest whole number, some totals may appear inconsistent.
† Met guidelines for student survey sampling participation rates only after replacement schools were included.
†† Did not meet sampling participation rates for teacher survey.
1 National Desired Population does not match International Desired Population.
2 Country surveyed the same cohort of students but at the beginning of the next school year.
^ Subgroup sample size too small for reporting reliable estimate.

Federation, and Turkey). Statistically significant positive effects ranged from 7.8 score points (per national standard deviation across schools) in Slovenia to almost 40 points in Germany. These results possibly reflect the varying degrees of differentiation across study programs or school types within the different ICILS education systems.

Summary of influences on CIL

Table 8.4 provides a summary of the results from our comparison of the two models. It shows the number of statistically significant positive or negative effects for each indicator in both models. Although the variables reflecting students' ICT familiarity emerged as statistically significant predictors in many countries in both models, the effects of home ICT resources were often no longer significant once we had taken the social background of families into account. This finding is a plausible one given that families with higher socioeconomic status tend to be in a better position to acquire ICT equipment.

Table 8.4: Summary of statistically significant effects across countries

Predictor Variables	MODEL 1: Number of Countries or Benchmarking Participants Where the Predictor Had a Statistically Significant ...		MODEL 2: Number of Countries or Benchmarking Participants Where the Predictor Had a Statistically Significant ...	
	Positive effect	Negative effect	Positive effect	Negative effect
ICT resources at home				
Number of computers	10	0	2	0
Internet access	7	0	5	0
ICT familiarity of students				
Years of computer experience	16	0	16	0
Weekly use of home computers	12	0	11	0
Weekly use of school computers	5	0	5	0
Learning experience at school	8	0	7	0
ICT resources at school				
Availability of ICT resources	1	0	1	0
ICT resource limitations for teaching	0	4	0	1
School ICT learning context				
Experience with computers at school	2	0	0	0
Percent weekly use of home computers	6	0	6	0
ICT learning at school	3	1	5	0
Students' personal and social background				
Gender (female)			13	0
Expected lower-secondary qualification			0	8
Expected post-secondary nonuniversity education			7	0
Expected university education			18	0
Socioeconomic background			13	1
Schools' social intake				
Average socioeconomic background			15	0

In Model 1, school-level indicators of ICT resources and experience with computers at school had significant effects in only a few countries. After we had controlled for the socioeconomic context, we found that these effects were generally no longer significant, a result which suggests that schools with students from higher income strata tend to be better resourced than schools with students from lower strata. However, this finding does not necessarily mean that resource indicators have no impact on student learning of CIL. Rather, it shows that socioeconomic context is a powerful explanatory variable reflecting a range of conditions (e.g., resources, climate, peer support) that positively influence student learning.

It is interesting to note that, in some countries, student context variables, such as the percentage of students who reported frequent computer use or the percentage of students who said they learned about ICT at school, remained significant predictors after we had controlled for the social context. This finding suggests that what schools teach regarding ICT use has an influence on CIL. As such, the finding is worth further investigation.

Table 8.5 shows the variance estimates for each country overall and at each level. The table also shows the extent to which Model 1 (ICT-related factors) and Model 2 (ICT-related factors and personal/social background factors) explained the variance in CIL scores. This information is displayed as a bar chart in the table. The longer bars reflect larger overall variance. Note that each bar's position relative to the vertical axis indicates whether more variance was found within schools (left-hand side of the axis) or between schools (right-hand side). Shading with darker colors at each side of the vertical axis indicates how much of the variance Model 1 explained (darkest color) and how much additional variance Model 2 explained (darkest and second-darkest colors). The lighter shaded sections of the bars show the variance that remained unexplained by the models.

As is evident in Table 8.5, the overall variance explained varied considerably across countries. The proportions of variance between schools (in the fourth column) also varied substantially among countries, from 11 percent in Norway and Slovenia to 53 percent in Germany (with an average of 30 percent and an inter-quartile range of 18 to 38 percent).

In line with results from other international studies of educational achievement, countries with comprehensive education systems, such as Norway, Denmark, and Slovenia, tended to have lower proportions of variance in CIL across schools. The education systems with differentiated provision through distinct study programs, such as Germany and the Slovak Republic, or with higher levels of social segregation, such as Chile, Thailand, and Turkey, recorded higher proportions of CIL variance across schools.

Model 1 explained, on average crossnationally, seven percent of the variance in CIL, with the highest proportion of variance explained (12%) recorded in Croatia. School-level predictors explained 37 percent of the variation in CIL, with the range extending from eight percent in Slovenia to 63 percent in Australia.

After we had controlled for personal and social background as well as schools' socioeconomic intake, Model 2 explained, on average, 17 percent of the student-level and 58 percent of the school-level variance in CIL. In Australia, Chile, Germany, and Poland, the ICT-related variables and personal and social background factors explained more than two thirds of the variation across schools.

Table 8.5: Total and explained variance in computer and information literacy

Country	Variance Estimates (Model 0)				Percent of Variance Explained by Model 1		Percent of Variance Explained by Model 2		Variance within Schools / Variance between Schools
	Total variance	Within schools	Between schools	Percent between schools	Within schools	Between schools	Within schools	Between schools	
Australia	5757	4241	1515	26	8	63	19	81	
Chile	7446	4626	2819	38	5	55	13	84	
Croatia	6562	5587	975	15	12	12	28	33	
Czech Republic	3718	2790	929	25	1	16	10	60	
Germany†,††	7680	3640	4040	53	2	22	4	74	
Korea, Republic of	8583	7135	1448	17	10	22	19	51	
Lithuania	7808	4910	2897	37	11	62	22	65	
Norway (Grade 9)1,††	5058	4493	565	11	6	33	18	49	
Poland	6351	5107	1243	20	9	49	23	80	
Russian Federation2	6038	3896	2142	35	6	32	13	39	
Slovak Republic	8504	5286	3218	38	6	49	19	59	
Slovenia	4698	4124	574	12	3	8	22	22	
Thailand2	8561	5142	3419	40	9	35	13	51	
Turkey	9261	4654	4608	50	9	60	13	61	
ICILS 2013 average	6859	4688	2171	30	7	37	17	58	
Countries not meeting sample requirements									
Denmark††	4394	3809	585	13	1	28	11	63	
Hong Kong SAR††	9073	4647	4426	49	5	45	8	53	
Benchmarking participants									
Newfoundland & Labrador, Canada	6419	5404	1014	16	9	34	21	60	
Ontario, Canada††	5098	4343	754	15	5	27	15	47	

Legend:
- Within-school variance explained by Model 1 predictors
- Additional within-school variance explained by Model 2 predictors
- Within-school variance *not* explained by model predictors
- Between-school variance explained by Model 1 predictors
- Additional between-school variance explained by Model 2 predictors
- Between-school variance *not* explained by model predictors

Notes:
† Met guidelines for sampling participation rates only after replacement schools were included.
†† Did not meet sampling participation rates for teacher survey.
1 National Desired Population does not match International Desired Population.
2 Country surveyed the same cohort of students but at the beginning of the next school year.

Conclusion

Our results show that students' experience with computers as well as regular use of computers at home had significant positive effects on CIL achievement in many of the ICILS countries even after we had controlled for the influence of personal and social context. This pattern suggests that familiarity with ICT, reflecting what students do and have done, contributes to students' CIL achievement.

The availability of ICT resources at home, measured as the number of computers and having access to internet, was associated with CIL achievement. However, ICT resources, in particular the number of computers at home, had hardly any effect after socioeconomic background had been taken into account (although internet access remained significant in five of the 14 countries that satisfied sampling requirements). The probable reason behind this finding is that level of ICT resources in homes is associated with socioeconomic background.

We observed statistically significant effects of ICT-related school-level factors on CIL achievement in only a few countries. In a number of education systems, we recorded evidence of limited effects on CIL of the school average of students' computer use (at home) and the extent to which students reported learning about ICT-related tasks at school. Because ICILS represents an initial exploration into the influences of school-level and student-level factors on CIL learning, these findings deserve further analysis in future research. The notion that school learning is an important aspect of developing CIL is a particularly important consideration and therefore worth investigating in greater detail.

Some of the effects of ICT-related factors that were no longer significant after we had controlled for the socioeconomic context of school could be considered proxies for other variables (resources, school climate, peer influences). In some countries, these effects may also reflect differences between school types and study programs.

CHAPTER 9:

Conclusions and Discussion

The International Computer and Information Literacy Study 2013 (ICILS 2013) investigated the ways in which young people have developed the computer and information literacy (CIL) that enables them to participate fully in the digital age. This study, the first in international research to investigate students' acquisition of CIL, has been groundbreaking in two ways. The first is its establishment of a crossnationally agreed definition and explication of CIL in terms of its component knowledge, skills, and understandings. The second is its operationalization of CIL as a crossnationally comparable measurement tool and marker of digital literacy.

The CIL construct was developed with reference to decades of research into the knowledge, skills, and understanding involved in effective use of information and communication technology (ICT). Various terms with similar but not identical meanings such as *information literacy, computer literacy, digital literacy*, and *ICT literacy* have been used to characterize this set of competences.

The CIL construct is described and explained in detail in the *ICILS Assessment Framework* (Fraillon, Schulz, & Ainley, 2013). The framework, developed in consultation with ICILS national research coordinators (NRCs) and other people expert in digital and ICT literacy, guided all aspects of the ICILS instrument development and data collection stages. One important outcome of this work has been the establishment of a crossnational, empirical foundation for describing the competencies underpinning the CIL construct.

The ICILS assessment of CIL is unique in the field of crossnational assessment because it comprises tasks grouped into self-contained, computer-based "modules" that reflect school-based research and communication. Included in each module is at least one "open" task wherein students create an information product (such as a poster, presentation, or website) using purpose-built software that applies the conventions of software interface design. The ICILS assessment is thus similar to classroom-based assessments that allow students freedom to work with a range of software tools on open-ended tasks.

However, in order to ensure standardization of students' experience and comparability of the resultant data, the ICILS 2013 assessment required students to work in a contained test environment, designed to prevent differential exposure to digital resources from outside that environment. Such exposure could have confounded the comparability (a necessary feature of instruments used in large-scale assessments) of the student data.

The previous chapters in this international report on ICILS 2013 provided information on CIL achievement across countries, the contexts in which CIL was being taught and learned, and the relationship of CIL as a learning outcome to student characteristics and school contexts.

To provide an overview in this current chapter of these earlier recorded results, we summarize the main study outcomes with respect to each of the four research questions that guided the study. We also discuss country-level outcomes concerned with aspects of ICT use in education as well as the findings from our bivariate and multivariate analyses designed to explore associations between CIL and student and school factors.

© International Association for the Evaluation of Educational Achievement (IEA) 2014
J. Fraillon et al., *Preparing for Life in a Digital Age*, DOI 10.1007/978-3-319-14222-7_10

We then consider a number of implications of the study's findings for educational policy and practice. We conclude the chapter by suggesting future directions for international research on CIL education.

ICILS guiding questions

The four research questions that guided the study were these:

1. What variations exist between countries, and within countries, in student computer and information literacy?

2. What aspects of schools and education systems are related to student achievement in computer and information literacy with respect to:
   (a) The general approach to computer and information literacy education;
   (b) School and teaching practices regarding the use of technologies in computer and information literacy;
   (c) Teacher attitudes to and proficiency in using computers;
   (d) Access to ICT in schools; and
   (e) Teacher professional development and within-school delivery of computer and information literacy programs.

3. What characteristics of students' levels of access to, familiarity with, and self-reported proficiency in using computers are related to student achievement in computer and information literacy?
   (a) How do these characteristics differ among and within countries?
   (b) To what extent do the strengths of the relations between these characteristics and measured computer and information literacy differ among countries?

4. What aspects of students' personal and social backgrounds (such as gender, socioeconomic background, and language background) are related to computer and information literacy?

Student proficiency in using computers

Student CIL proficiency was measured using an instrument comprising four thematic modules, each of which included discrete tasks[1] and each of which typically took less than a minute to complete. These tasks were followed by a large task that typically took 15 to 20 minutes to complete. The following discussion of student CIL proficiency includes examples taken from the After-School Exercise assessment module. The large task from this module required students to use given digital resources to create a poster advertising an after-school exercise program. Chapter 3 of this report provides a more detailed discussion, along with illustrative examples, of CIL proficiency.

The computer and information literacy (CIL) scale

The ICILS CIL scale, which has an average score set to 500 and a standard deviation of 100, comprises four proficiency levels. Accounts of what students should be able to achieve at each level serve to describe the scale.

Students working at Level 1 demonstrate familiarity with the basic range of software commands that enable them to access files and complete routine text and layout editing when directed to do so. Students can recognize some basic software conventions as well as the potential for misuse of computers by unauthorized users. Figure 9.1 provides an

---

1 These tasks can be described as discrete because, although they are connected by the common narrative, students can complete each one sequentially without having to explicitly refer to other tasks.

Figure 9.1: Example Level 1 task

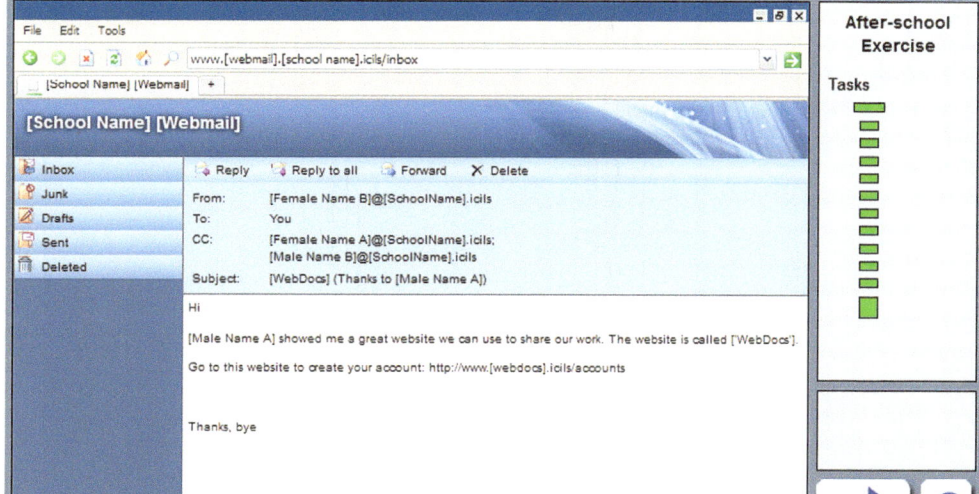

example of a Level 1 task. This task required students to identify the recipients of an email displaying the "From," "To," and "Cc" fields. The task assessed students' familiarity with the conventions used to display the sender and recipients of emails.

The work involved in doing the large task (creating a poster) contained in the After-School Exercise module provides another example of achievement at Level 1. The Level 1 aspect of the task required students to provide evidence of planning the poster in terms of selecting colors that would denote the roles of the poster's text, background, and images.

Students working at Level 2 demonstrate basic use of computers as information resources. Students are able to locate explicit information in simple electronic resources, select and add content to information products, and demonstrate some control of layout and formatting of text and images in information products. They demonstrate awareness of the need to protect access to some electronic information and of some possible consequences of unwanted access to information. Figure 9.2 provides an example of a Level 2 task.

The task shown in the figure required students to allocate "can edit" rights in the collaborative workspace to another student with whom, according to the module narrative, students were "collaborating" on the task. To complete this nonlinear skills task,[2] students needed to navigate within the website to the "settings" menu and then use its options to allocate the required user access. The Level 2 aspect of the module's large task required students to produce a relevant title for the poster, and then format the title to make its role clear. Ability to use formatting tools to some degree in order to show the role of different text elements is thus an indicator of achievement at Level 2.

---

2 Nonlinear skills tasks require students to execute a software command (or reach a desired outcome) by executing subcommands in a number of different sequences. The *ICILS Assessment Framework* (Fraillon et al., 2013) provides further information about the ICILS task and question types.

Figure 9.2: Example Level 2 task

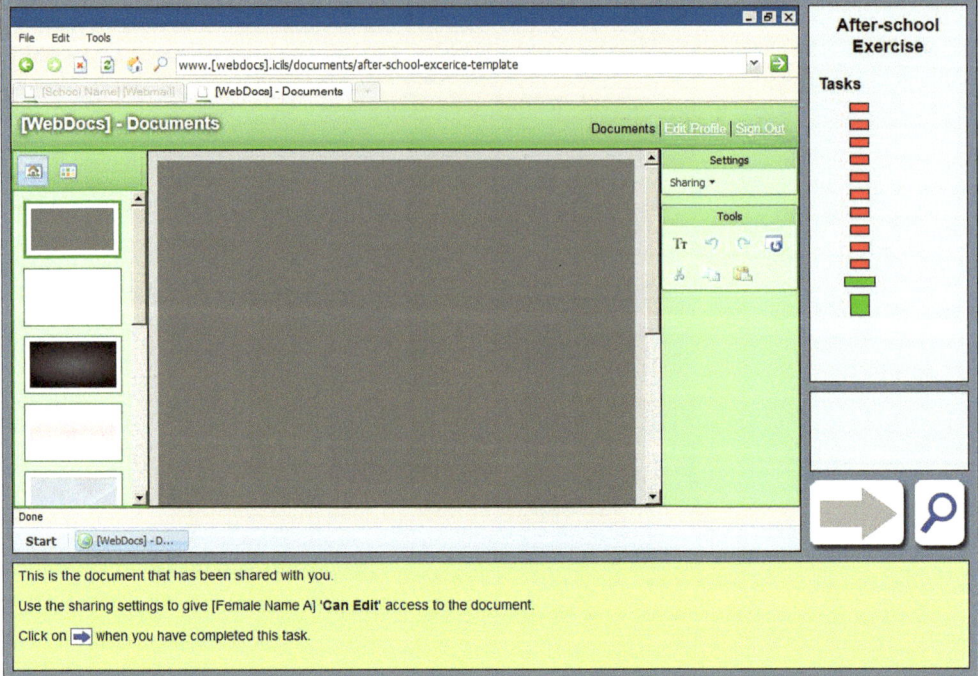

Students working at Level 3 demonstrate sufficient knowledge, skills, and understanding to independently search for and locate information and then edit it to suit the audience for, and the purpose of, the information products they create. Students at this level are able to select relevant information from within electronic resources and develop information products that exhibit controlled layout and design. They also demonstrate awareness that the information they access may be biased, inaccurate, or unreliable. Figure 9.3 provides an example of a Level 3 task.

Figure 9.3: Example Level 3 task

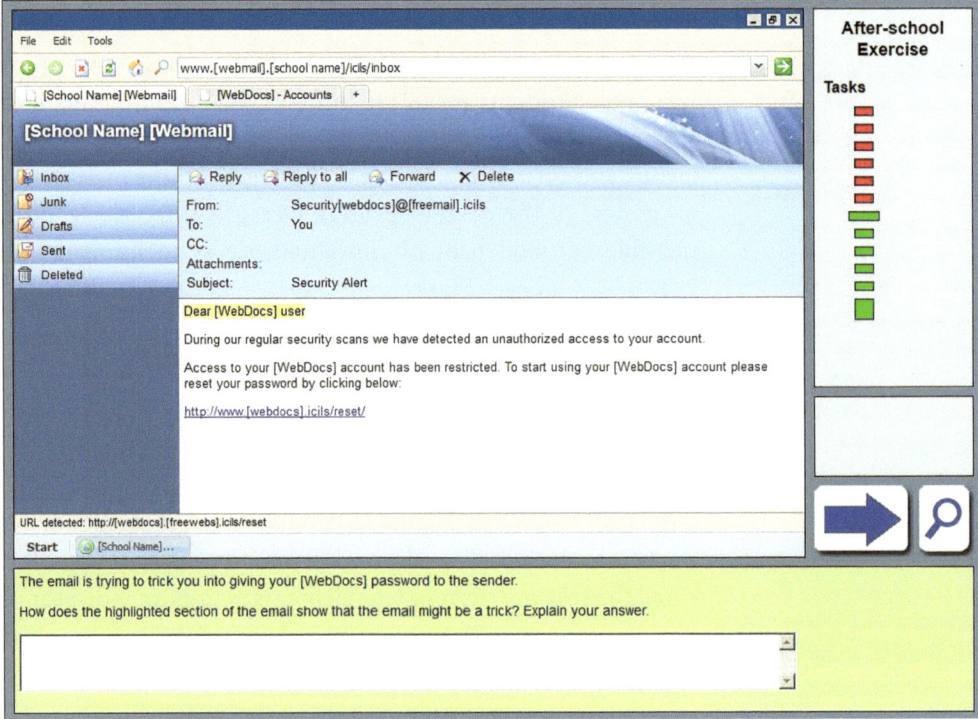

The task shown in Figure 9.3 required students to explain how the greeting (highlighted in the email) might be evidence that the email is trying to "trick" them. Ability to recognize that a generic (rather than personalized) greeting is one possible piece of evidence is an example of achievement at Level 3. Examples of Level 3 achievements in the large-task poster include students being able to complete some adaptation of information from resources (as opposed to directly copying and pasting information) and ability to include images that are well aligned with the poster's other elements.

Students working at Level 4 execute control and evaluative judgment when searching for information and creating information products. They also demonstrate awareness of audience and purpose when searching for information, selecting information to include in information products, and formatting and laying out the information products they create. They furthermore demonstrate awareness of the potential for information to be a commercial and malleable commodity and of issues relating to the use of electronically sourced third-party intellectual property. Figure 9.4 provides an example of a Level 4 task.

Figure 9.4: Example Level 4 task

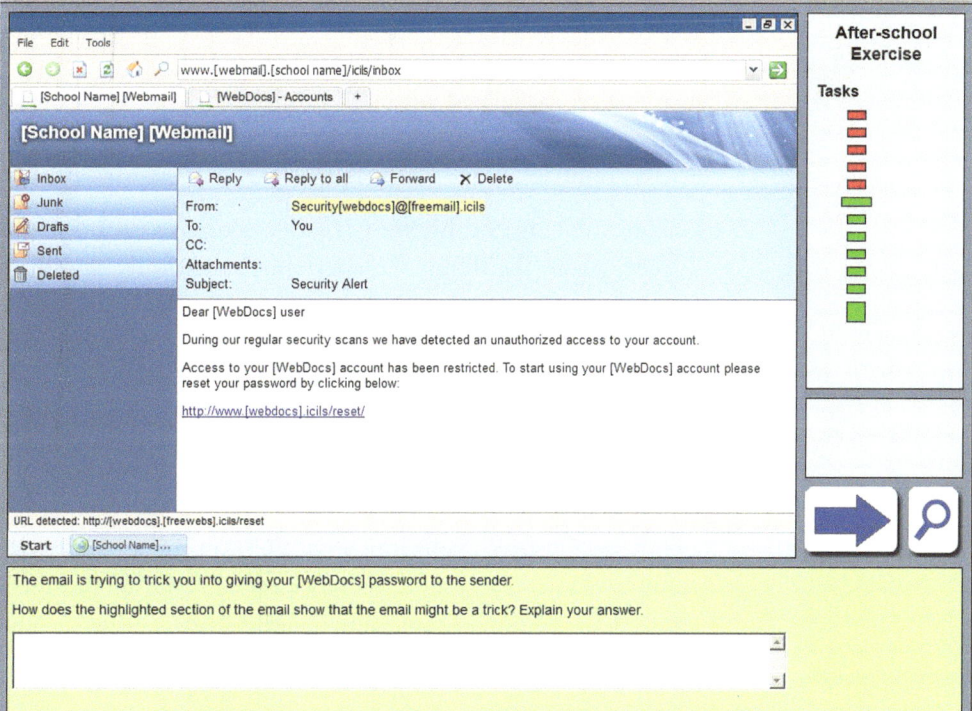

As with the task shown in Figure 9.3, the task in Figure 9.4 asked students to explain how the email address of the sender (highlighted in the email) might be evidence of the email trying to "trick" them. Students who recognize that the email is from a "freemail" account (and not a company account) or that the email address does not match the root of the hyperlink are achieving at Level 4 rather than lower levels because they demonstrate a more sophisticated understanding of email protocols with respect to safe and secure use. Examples of Level 4 achievements in the After-School Exercise poster task include students rephrasing the key points from source information and using formatting tools consistently throughout the poster so that the roles of the different text elements are clear to the reader.

Student achievement on the CIL scale

We can interpret and compare students' CIL by referring to their CIL scale scores and the proficiency levels of the scale.

Student CIL varied considerably across the ICILS countries. The average national scores on the scale ranged from 361 to 553 scale points, a span that extends from below Level 1 to a standard of proficiency within Level 3. This range was equivalent to almost two standard deviations. However, we need to acknowledge that the distribution of country CIL means was skewed because of the means of three countries being significantly below the ICILS 2013 average and the means of 12 other countries being significantly above the ICILS 2013 average.

Eighty-one percent of students achieved scores that placed them within CIL Levels 1, 2, and 3. In all but two countries, Turkey and Thailand, the highest percentage of students was in Level 2.

Students' computer use and CIL

A long conducted and established research literature shows that students' social background characteristics[3] and students' personal characteristics[4] are associated with student achievement across a range of learning areas. These same student-level factors were associated with CIL proficiency in ICILS. Characteristics reflecting higher socioeconomic status were associated with higher CIL proficiency both within and across countries.

Female students had higher CIL scale scores in all but two countries (Thailand and Turkey, where the differences were not statistically significant). This finding was not unexpected given that CIL is heavily reliant on text-based reading skills and given past research showing that females tend to outperform males on tests of reading. Similarly, students who spoke the language of the CIL test (which is also the language of instruction in their country) also performed better on the assessment.

When we took the associations between these various student factors into account using multiple regression techniques, we found that the following variables had statistically significant positive associations with CIL in most countries: students' gender (female compared to male), students' expected educational attainment, parental educational attainment, parental occupational status, the number of books in the home, and ICT home resources.

ICILS also investigated student access to, familiarity with, and confidence in using computers. Students were asked a range of questions relating to their access to and use of computers at home, at school, and in other places. There is an assumption that the generation of young people that includes the ICILS target grade students (i.e., Grade 8) has grown up with computers as a ubiquitous part of their lives. However, questions remain as to how such access relates to their CIL.

Almost all ICILS students reported that they were experienced users of computers and had access to them at home and at school. On average across the ICILS countries, more than one third of the Grade 8 students said they had been using computers for seven

---

3 Especially those related to socioeconomic status, which include measures of parental occupational status, parental educational attainment, and the number of books in the home.

4 Such as gender, students' expected highest level of education, and whether or not the language of testing/instruction is also spoken at home.

or more years, with a further 29 percent reporting that they had been using computers for between five and seven years. Ninety-four percent of the students on average crossnationally reported having at least one computer (desktop, laptop, notebook, or tablet device) at home, while 48 percent reported having three or more computers at home. Ninety-two percent of students stated that they had some form of internet connection at home. Both number of computers students had at home and access to a home internet connection were positively associated with CIL scores.

The ICILS student questionnaire also asked students a range of questions about their frequency of computer use, the types of tasks they completed using computers, and their attitudes toward using computers. These questions were underpinned by hypotheses that increased computer use, and focused use, would be positively associated with CIL.

Students across the ICILS countries reported using computers more frequently at home than elsewhere. On average, 87 percent said they used a computer at home at least once a week, whereas 54 percent and 13 percent reported this same frequency of computer use at school and other places respectively.

Computer use outside school

ICILS 2013 data indicate that students were making widespread and frequent use of digital technologies when outside school. Students tended to use the internet for social communication and exchange of information, computers for recreation, and software applications for school work and other purposes.

On average across the ICILS countries, three-quarters of the students said they communicated with others by way of messaging or social networks at least weekly. Just over half said that they used the internet for "searching for information for study or school work" at least once a week, and almost half indicated that they engaged in "posting comments to online profiles or blogs" at least once each week. On average, there was evidence of slightly more frequent use of the internet for social communication and exchanging information among females than among males.

Students were also frequently using computers for recreation. On average across the ICILS countries, 82 percent of students reported "listening to music" on a computer at least once a week, 68 percent reported "watching downloaded or streamed video (e.g., movies, TV shows, or clips)" on a weekly basis, and 62 percent said they used the internet to "get news about things of interest," also on a weekly basis. Just over half of all the ICILS students were "playing games" once a week or more. Overall, we recorded only a small, albeit statistically significant, gender difference in the extent of recreational use of computers, with males reporting slightly higher frequencies than females.

Students also reported using software applications outside school. Generally across the ICILS countries, the most extensive weekly use of software applications involved "creating or editing documents" (28% of students). Use of most other utilities was much less frequent. For example, only 18 percent of the students were "using education software designed to help with school study." We found no significant difference between female and male students with respect to using software applications outside school.

Use of ICT for school work

Crossnationally, just under half (45%) of the ICILS students, on average, were using computers to "prepare reports or essays" at least once a week. We recorded a similar extent of use for "preparing presentations" (44%). Forty percent of students reported using ICT when working with other students from their own school at least weekly, and 39 percent of students reported using a computer once a week or more to complete worksheets or exercises.

Two school-related uses of computers were reported by less than one fifth of the students. These were "writing about one's own learning," which referred to using a learning log, and "working with other students from other schools." Nineteen percent of students said they used a computer for the first of these tasks; 13 percent said they used a computer for the second.

The subject area in which computers were most frequently being used was, not surprisingly, information technology or computer studies (56%). On average, about one fifth of the students studying (natural) sciences said they used computers in most or all lessons. The same proportion reported using computers in most or all of their human sciences/humanities lessons. In language arts (the test language) and language arts (foreign languages), students were using computers a little less frequently: about one sixth of the students reported computer use in most or all lessons. Approximately one in seven students studying mathematics reported computer use in most mathematics lessons or almost every lesson. Of the students studying creative arts, just a little more than one in 10 reported computer use in most or all lessons.

The ICILS teacher questionnaire asked teachers to select one of their Grade 8 classes as a reference class and then to report their use of ICT in that class. The order of frequency of ICT use by subject was very similar to that reported by students. On average, the percentage of teachers using ICT was greatest if the reference class was being taught information technology or computer studies (95%), but it was also very high if the class was studying (natural) sciences (84%) or human sciences/humanities (84%). Seventy-nine percent of teachers whose reference class was engaged in language arts (test language) or language arts (foreign languages) reported using ICT in their teaching. Across countries, three quarters of teachers whose reference class was a creative arts class, and 71 percent of those teaching mathematics, said they used ICT in their teaching.

Students' perceptions of ICT

The ICILS student questionnaire also gathered information about two aspects of student perceptions of ICT. One concerned students' confidence in using computers (their ICT self-efficacy). The other was students' interest and enjoyment in using ICT. The questions relating to students' ICT self-efficacy formed two scales—*basic ICT skills* (such as searching for and finding a file) and *advanced ICT skills* (such as creating a database, computer program, or macro).

Some small gender differences were evident in basic ICT self-efficacy in seven countries, with males scoring lower than females in six of these countries. However, in the case of advanced ICT self-efficacy, males scored significantly and substantially higher than females in all 14 countries that met sampling requirements.

We found no consistent associations overall between advanced ICT self-efficacy and CIL scale scores, but did observe positive associations between basic ICT self-efficacy and CIL scale scores. This finding is not unexpected given the nature of the CIL assessment construct, which is made up of information literacy and communication skills that are not necessarily related to advanced computer skills such as programming or database management. Even though CIL is computer based, in the sense that students demonstrate CIL in the context of computer use, the CIL construct itself does not emphasize advanced computer-based technical skills.

Students were asked to indicate their agreement with a series of statements about their interest and enjoyment in using computers and doing computing. Overall, students expressed interest in computing and said they enjoyed it. Greater interest and enjoyment was associated with higher CIL scores, an effect that was statistically significant in nine of the 14 countries that met the ICILS sampling requirements.

Teacher, school, and education system characteristics relevant to CIL

General approaches to CIL education

The ICILS countries differed in terms of the characteristics of their education systems, their ICT infrastructure, and their approaches to ICT use.

Data from international databases show large differences among countries in their economies and (of particular relevance to this current study) ICT infrastructure. Data from the ICILS national context survey suggest that most of the participating countries were supportive at either the national or state/provincial level or both levels for using ICT in education. Plans and policies mostly included strategies for improving and supporting student learning and providing ICT resources.

International databases also show that countries differ with regard to including an ICT-related subject at the primary and lower-secondary levels of education. Although almost all of the ICILS countries had a subject or curriculum area equivalent to CIL at one or more levels of their respective education systems, fewer than half of the participating countries said their education system supported using ICT for student assessments. Across the countries, teaching CIL-related content was set within specific ICT-related subjects and was also regarded as a crosscurricular responsibility.

Teacher capacity to use ICT was rarely a requirement for teacher registration. However, teacher capacity to use ICT was often supported during preservice and inservice programs. In general, nearly all countries offered some form of support for teacher access to and participation in ICT-based professional development.

Teachers and CIL

Generally, the ICILS data confirm extensive use of ICT in school education. Across the ICILS countries, three out of every five teachers said they used computers at least once a week when teaching, while four out of every five reported using computers on a weekly basis for other work at their schools. As we commented in an earlier chapter, it is not possible to judge whether the reported level of use was appropriate, but we can agree that it was extensive.

Teachers in most countries were experienced users of ICT and generally recognized the positive aspects of using ICT in teaching and learning at school, especially with respect to accessing and managing information. On balance, teachers reported generally positive attitudes toward the use of ICT, although many teachers were aware that ICT use could have some detrimental aspects, such as adversely affecting students' development of writing, calculation, and estimation skills.

In general, teachers were confident about their ability to use many computer applications; two thirds of them expressed confidence in their ability to use these technologies for assessing and monitoring student progress. There were differences, however, among countries in the level of confidence that teachers expressed with regard to using computer technologies, and younger teachers tended to be more confident ICT users than their older colleagues.

A substantial majority of the ICILS teachers were using ICT in their teaching. This use was greatest among teachers who were confident about their ICT expertise and who were working in school environments where there was collaboration about and planning of ICT use, and where there were fewer resource limitations to that use. These were also the conditions that supported teaching CIL. These findings suggest that if schools are to develop students' CIL to the greatest possible extent, then teacher expertise in ICT use needs to be augmented, and ICT use needs to be supported by collaborative environments that incorporate institutional planning.

According to the ICILS teachers, the utilities (software) most frequently used in their respective reference classes were those concerned with wordprocessing, presentations, and computer-based information resources, such as websites, wikis, and encyclopedias. Teachers said that, within their classrooms, ICT was most commonly being used by their students to search for information, work on short assignments, and undertake individual work on learning materials. The survey data also suggest that ICT was often being used to present information in class and reinforce skills. Overall, teachers appeared to be using ICT most frequently for relatively simple tasks and less often for more complex tasks.

Schools and CIL

Data from the ICT-coordinator questionnaire showed that, in general, the schools participating in ICILS were well equipped in terms of internet-related and software resources. The types of computer resources available for use were more variable, however, with countries being less likely to have on hand tablet devices, a school intranet, internet-based applications for collaborative work, and a learning management system.

An examination of the ratio of number of students in a school per available computers showed substantial differences across countries. Ten of the 16 countries that met sampling requirements had more computers per student available in rural settings than in urban schools. We investigated the association between CIL and the ratio of students to computers in schools across countries and found that students from countries with greater access to computing in schools tended to have stronger CIL skills.

Computers in schools were most often located in computer laboratories and libraries. However, there was some variation among countries as to whether portable class-sets of computers or student computers brought to class were being used. Most schools had policies about the use of ICT, but there was substantial cross-country variation regarding policies relating to access to school computers for both students and members of the local community. The same can be said with regard to provision of laptops and other mobile learning devices for use at school or home.

The ICT-coordinators reported a range of hindrances to teaching and learning ICT. These typically related to resource provision and to personnel and teaching support. In general, the coordinators rated personnel and teaching support issues as more problematic than resource issues. However, there was considerable variation across schools within countries and across countries in the types of limitation arising from resource inadequacy.

Variation was also evident in the level of teachers' agreement with negatively worded statements about the use of ICT in teaching at school. Statements reflecting insufficient time to prepare ICT-related lessons, schools not viewing ICT as a priority, and insufficient technical support to maintain ICT resources all attracted relatively high levels of teacher agreement.

Both teachers and principals provided perspectives on the range of professional development activities relevant to pedagogical use of ICT. According to principals, teachers were most likely to participate in school-provided courses on pedagogical use of ICT, to talk about this type of use when they were within groups of teachers, and to discuss ICT use in education as a regular item during meetings of teaching staff. From the teachers' perspective, the most common professional development activities available included observing other teachers using ICT in their teaching, introductory courses on general applications, and sharing and evaluating digital resources with others via a collaborative work space.

Results from the multivariate analyses

These results showed that students' experience with computers as well as regular home-based use of computers had significant positive effects in many countries, even after we had controlled for the influence of personal and social context. ICT resources, particularly the number of computers at home, no longer had effects once we took socioeconomic background into account.

Only a few countries recorded significant influences of school-level variables on CIL, and some of these associations were not significant after we controlled for the effect of the school's socioeconomic context.

In a number of education systems, the extent of students' computer use (at home) and the extent to which students had learned about ICT-related tasks at school appeared to be influencing students' CIL. There is much potential here for secondary analyses directed toward further investigating the associations between CIL education and CIL outcomes within countries.

Reflections on policy and practice

The findings from ICILS 2013 can be considered to constitute two broad categories: the nature and measurement of CIL, and factors that relate to CIL proficiency.

ICILS has provided a description of the competencies underpinning CIL that incorporates the notions of being able to safely and responsibly access and use digital information as well as to produce and develop digital products. ICILS has also provided an empirically derived scale and description of the CIL learning progress that can be used to anchor interpretations of learning in this field. It furthermore provides a common language and framework that policymakers and scholars can use when deliberating about CIL education. This common framework and associated measurement scale also offer a basis for understanding variation in CIL at present and for monitoring change in the CIL that results from developments in policy and practice over time.

Some of the findings of this report are similar to those of crossnational studies in other learning areas. For example, students from economically and socially advantaged backgrounds typically have higher levels of achievement. However, other findings relate specifically to the development of CIL through education.

One question raised by the ICILS results relates to the place of CIL in the curriculum. While many countries have some form of subject and curriculum associated with CIL, responsibility for addressing and assessing the relevant learning outcomes is less clear. Countries generally appear to use a combination of information technology or computer studies classes together with the expectation that the learning outcomes associated with CIL are a crosscurricular responsibility shared across discipline-based subjects.

The ICILS data show that teaching emphases relating to CIL outcomes were most frequently being addressed in technology or computer studies classes and in (natural) sciences and human sciences or humanities classes. Teachers and students differed in their perceptions of computer use across the subjects. Queries remain, however, about how schools maintain the continuity, completeness, and coherence of their CIL education programs. This last concern had particular relevance in several ICILS countries, where there was only limited, nonobligatory assessment of CIL-related competences, or where assessment took place only at the school level.

A second question relates to the role of ICT resource availability and its relationship to CIL. Overall, the ICILS data suggest that increased access to ICT resources at home and school are associated with higher levels of CIL, but only up to a certain point, as is evident at the different levels of our analyses. At the student level, each additional computer at home was associated with an increase in CIL. At the national level, higher average levels of CIL were associated with higher country rankings on the ICT Development Index (see Chapter 1), and lower ratios of students to computers. These associations are somewhat difficult to interpret fully given that higher levels of CIL resourcing are typically associated with higher levels of economic development, which itself has a strong positive association with CIL.

The ICILS results also suggest that the knowledge, skills, and understandings that comprise CIL can and should be taught. To some extent, this conclusion challenges perspectives of young people as *digital natives* with a self-developed capacity to use digital technology. Even though we can discern in the ICILS findings high levels of access to ICT and high levels of use by young people in and (especially) outside school, we need to remain aware of the large variations in CIL proficiency within and across the ICILS countries.

The CIL construct combines information literacy, critical thinking, technical skills, and communication skills applied across a range of contexts and for a range of purposes. The variations in CIL proficiency show that while some of the young people participating in ICILS were independent and critical users of ICT, there were many who were not. As the volume of computer-based information available to young people continues to increase, so too will the onus on societies to critically evaluate the credibility and value of that information.

Changing and more sophisticated technologies (such as social media and mobile technologies) are increasing the ability of young people to communicate with one another and publish information to a worldwide audience in real time. This facility obliges individuals to consider what is ethically appropriate and to determine how to maximize the communicative efficacy of information products. The knowledge, skills, and understandings that are the basis of the receptive and productive aspects of CIL can and need to be taught and learned through coherent education programs. The knowledge, skills, and understandings described in the CIL scale show that, regardless of whether or not we consider young people to be digital natives, we would be naive to expect them to develop CIL in the absence of coherent learning programs.

One message from the ICILS teacher data is that a certain set of factors appears to influence their confidence in using ICT and integrating CIL in their teaching. It is therefore worth repeating here that teachers' ICT use was greatest when the teachers were confident about their expertise and were working in school environments that collaborated on and planned ICT use and had few if any resource limitations hindering that use. These were also the conditions that supported teachers' ability to teach CIL.

Once threshold levels of ICT resourcing have been met in a school, we suggest that system- and school-level resourcing and planning should focus on increasing teacher expertise in ICT use. Attention should also be paid to implementing supportive collaborative environments that incorporate institutional planning focused on using ICT and teaching CIL in schools.

ICILS also showed differences in teacher attitudes toward and self-efficacy in using ICT in their teaching. Older teachers typically held less positive views than younger teachers about using ICT and expressed lower confidence in their ability to use ICT in their teaching practice. Programs developed to support teachers gain the skills and confidence they need to use ICT effectively would be valuable for all teachers. Consideration should also be given to ensuring that these programs meet the requirements of older teachers and, in some instances, directly target these teachers.

The ICILS results also call into question some of the idealized images commonly associated with visions of ICT in teaching and learning. In ICILS, both students and teachers were asked about students' use of computers in classes. Students reported most frequently using computers to "prepare reports or essays" and "prepare presentations" in class, and using utilities to "create or edit documents" out of school. When teachers were asked to report on their own use of ICT in teaching, the two practices reported as most frequent were "presenting information through direct class instruction" and "reinforcing learning of skills through repetition of examples." Although teachers reported high levels of access to and use of ICT in their professional work, including in the classroom, the ICILS data suggest that computers were most commonly being used to access digital textbooks and workbooks rather than provide dynamic, interactive pedagogical tools.

In a similar vein, one of the intended benefits of ICT, particularly web-technologies, is to support collaboration on tasks. Overall, the school-based use of ICT to support collaboration was not extensive. Low prevalence of ICT use was reported by teachers for practices such as "collaborating with parents or guardians in supporting students' learning," "enabling students to collaborate with other students (within or outside school)," and "mediating communication between students and experts or external mentors." Furthermore, the majority of teachers (and in the majority of countries) who participated in ICILS reported that ICT "limits the amount of personal communication among students," a finding which suggests not only that teachers were not using ICT to support collaboration, but also that they believed ICT use inhibits communication among students.

Future directions for research

The ICILS data clearly show that the contexts for CIL education vary across countries, as do the influences of factors at the individual, school, and country levels on CIL. One approach to secondary analyses of the ICILS data by scholars could be to investigate, build, and test models that explain variations in CIL within ICILS countries. Examples of areas of interest are the impact of school and teaching approaches on the development of CIL in students and the related aspects of teacher professional learning that may contribute to building capacity for CIL education development.

One challenge in identifying the relationship between ICT resourcing and CIL proficiency is that, because ICT resourcing is expensive, it typically disappears as an explanatory factor in regression models once socioeconomic background factors are accounted for. This happens at the level of the student and also in the school. Further research using the ICILS data may uncover alternative ways of better describing the relationship between ICT resource availability and CIL proficiency.

Finally, ICILS has provided a baseline study for future measurement of CIL and CIL education across countries. A future cycle of ICILS could be developed to support measurement of trends in CIL as well as maintain the study's relevance to innovations in software, hardware, and delivery technologies. Some possibilities for future iterations of ICILS could include internet delivery of the assessment, accommodation of "bring your own device" (BYOD) in schools, adapting a version for use on tablet devices, and incorporating contemporary and relevant software environments, such as multimedia and gaming. The key to the future of such research is to maintain a strong link to the core elements of the discipline while accommodating the new contexts in which CIL achievement can be demonstrated.

Appendices

© International Association for the Evaluation of Educational Achievement (IEA) 2014
J. Fraillon et al., *Preparing for Life in a Digital Age*, DOI 10.1007/978-3-319-14222-7

APPENDIX A:

Samples and participation rates

Table A.1: Coverage of ICILS 2013 target population for the student survey

Country	International Target Population	Exclusions from Target Population		
	Coverage	School-level exclusions	Within-sample exclusions	Overall exclusions
Australia	100%	0.7%	4.3%	5.0%
Chile	100%	2.8%	1.7%	4.5%
Croatia	100%	1.1%	2.6%	3.7%
Czech Republic	100%	1.0%	0.6%	1.7%
Denmark	100%	2.9%	1.9%	4.8%
Germany	100%	0.8%	0.7%	1.5%
Hong Kong SAR	100%	5.1%	1.5%	6.5%
Korea, Republic of	100%	0.8%	0.5%	1.3%
Lithuania	100%	1.8%	1.5%	3.3%
Netherlands	100%	2.9%	1.9%	4.7%
Norway	100%	1.7%	4.4%	6.1%
Poland	100%	2.9%	1.7%	4.6%
Russian Federation	100%	2.9%	3.0%	5.9%
Slovak Republic	100%	2.6%	2.6%	5.1%
Slovenia	100%	1.3%	1.1%	2.3%
Switzerland	100%	2.2%	1.8%	3.9%
Thailand	100%	0.3%	0.8%	1.1%
Turkey	100%	2.0%	1.2%	3.2%
Benchmarking participants				
City of Buenos Aires, Argentina	100%	1.4%	0.2%	1.6%
Newfoundland and Labrador, Canada	100%	0.8%	6.8%	7.6%
Ontario, Canada	100%	0.6%	4.4%	5.0%

Note:
Because results are rounded to the nearest whole number, some totals may appear inconsistent.

Table A.2: Participation rates and sample sizes for student survey

Country	School Participation Rate			Total Number of Schools that Participated in Student Survey	Student Participation Rate (Weighted)	Total Number of Students Assessed	Overall Participation Rate	
	Before replacement (weighted)	After replacement (weighted)	After replacement (unweighted)				Before replacement (weighted)	After replacement (weighted)
Australia	97.5%	98.0%	96.0%	311	88.1%	5326	85.9%	86.3%
Chile	94.8%	100.0%	100.0%	174	93.4%	3180	88.5%	93.4%
Croatia	94.7%	94.7%	94.4%	170	85.6%	2850	81.1%	81.1%
Czech Republic	99.5%	100.0%	100.0%	170	93.7%	3066	93.3%	93.7%
Denmark	41.8%	73.0%	73.0%	103	87.8%	1767	36.7%	64.1%
Germany	70.9%	91.3%	91.3%	136	82.4%	2225	58.4%	75.2%
Hong Kong SAR	72.4%	77.0%	78.7%	118	89.1%	2089	64.5%	68.6%
Korea, Republic of	100.0%	100.0%	100.0%	150	96.3%	2888	96.3%	96.3%
Lithuania	90.9%	96.6%	93.1%	162	92.0%	2756	83.6%	88.8%
Netherlands	50.1%	81.9%	81.8%	121	87.7%	2197	44.0%	71.9%
Norway	84.8%	92.8%	92.6%	138	89.8%	2436	76.2%	83.4%
Poland	84.7%	99.3%	98.7%	156	87.0%	2870	73.6%	86.3%
Russian Federation	99.2%	99.2%	99.0%	206	93.6%	3626	92.8%	92.8%
Slovak Republic	94.9%	99.6%	98.8%	167	92.7%	2994	87.9%	92.3%
Slovenia	90.7%	98.4%	97.8%	218	91.5%	3740	83.0%	90.0%
Switzerland	30.3%	48.5%	58.7%	98	89.7%	3225	27.2%	43.5%
Thailand	89.5%	94.9%	94.7%	198	93.6%	3646	83.8%	88.8%
Turkey	93.3%	93.9%	94.0%	141	91.4%	2540	85.2%	85.8%
Benchmarking participants								
City of Buenos Aires, Argentina	67.5%	67.5%	68.0%	68	80.2%	1076	54.2%	54.2%
Newfoundland and Labrador, Canada	98.3%	98.3%	98.3%	118	87.8%	1556	86.3%	86.3%
Ontario, Canada	94.5%	96.7%	97.0%	193	92.1%	3377	87.0%	89.1%

Table A.3: Participation rates and sample sizes for teacher survey

Country	School Participation Rate			Total Number of Schools that Participated in Teacher Survey	Teacher Participation Rate (Weighted)	Total Number of Teachers Assessed	Overall Participation Rate	
	Before replacement (weighted)	After replacement (weighted)	After replacement (unweighted)				Before replacement (weighted)	After replacement (weighted)
Australia	90.9%	91.3%	90.7%	294	86.5%	3495	78.5%	79.0%
Chile	95.1%	100.0%	100.0%	174	95.9%	1800	91.2%	95.9%
Croatia	99.6%	99.6%	99.4%	179	96.5%	2578	96.0%	96.0%
Czech Republic	99.3%	100.0%	100.0%	170	99.9%	2126	99.2%	99.9%
Denmark	32.8%	58.2%	58.2%	82	85.5%	728	28.0%	49.7%
Germany	66.0%	81.7%	81.2%	121	79.5%	1386	52.5%	64.9%
Hong Kong SAR	65.0%	70.8%	71.3%	107	82.2%	1338	53.5%	58.3%
Korea, Republic of	100.0%	100.0%	100.0%	150	99.9%	2189	99.9%	99.9%
Lithuania	91.2%	96.8%	93.7%	163	88.4%	2171	80.7%	85.6%
Netherlands	41.6%	64.9%	64.9%	96	76.3%	1083	31.7%	49.5%
Norway	70.8%	77.6%	77.9%	116	83.1%	1158	58.9%	64.5%
Poland	86.4%	99.4%	99.4%	157	94.1%	2228	81.3%	93.6%
Russian Federation	99.9%	99.9%	99.5%	207	98.5%	2728	98.4%	98.4%
Slovak Republic	93.1%	99.5%	98.8%	167	98.2%	2145	91.4%	97.7%
Slovenia	88.2%	94.8%	96.0%	214	92.9%	2787	82.0%	88.1%
Switzerland	20.9%	36.6%	44.3%	74	74.2%	796	15.5%	27.2%
Thailand	79.8%	89.0%	88.0%	184	95.9%	2114	76.5%	85.4%
Turkey	99.1%	100.0%	100.0%	150	95.8%	1887	94.9%	95.8%
Benchmarking participants								
City of Buenos Aires, Argentina	49.5%	49.5%	49.0%	49	77.8%	591	38.6%	38.6%
Newfoundland and Labrador, Canada	85.8%	85.8%	85.8%	103	92.6%	403	79.4%	79.4%
Ontario, Canada	73.3%	77.4%	77.7%	153	92.9%	443	68.1%	71.9%

APPENDIX B:

Percentage correct by country for example large task scoring criteria

Table B.1: Percent correct in large task by country for Criterion 1

Criterion	Score/Max. Score	CIL Scale Difficulty	Descriptor	Assessment Framework Aspect
1. Title design	1/2	492	A relevant title has been added and placed in a prominent position.	2.2. Creating information
1. Title design	2/2	548	A relevant title has been added and formatted to make its role clear.	2.1. Transforming information

Country	Percent Correct Response	
	1/2	2/2
Australia	80 (1.1)	64 (1.2)
Chile	71 (1.5)	38 (1.9)
Croatia	76 (1.5)	59 (1.4)
Czech Republic	86 (0.9)	80 (1.2)
Germany[†]	76 (1.6)	60 (1.7)
Korea, Republic of	71 (1.5)	50 (1.7)
Lithuania	64 (1.8)	29 (1.5)
Norway[1]	75 (1.6)	60 (1.6)
Poland	71 (1.6)	61 (1.6)
Russian Federation[2]*	66 (1.6)	36 (1.3)
Slovak Republic	75 (1.7)	63 (2.0)
Slovenia	70 (1.8)	40 (1.6)
Thailand[2]	32 (2.1)	12 (1.3)
Turkey	23 (1.8)	11 (1.2)
Countries not meeting sample requirements		
Denmark*	84 (1.3)	72 (1.4)
Hong Kong SAR*	69 (2.7)	49 (2.8)
Netherlands*	73 (2.1)	56 (2.3)
Switzerland*	77 (2.0)	52 (2.1)
Benchmarking participants		
Newfoundland and Labrador, Canada	78 (1.9)	61 (2.7)
Ontario, Canada	83 (1.3)	67 (1.7)
Benchmarking participant not meeting sample requirements		
City of Buenos Aires, Argentina*	48 (3.5)	17 (2.7)

Notes:

* Country data not used for scaling for this criterion.

() Standard errors appear in parentheses. Because some results are rounded to the nearest whole number, some totals may appear inconsistent.

[†] Met guidelines for sampling participation rates only after replacement schools were included.

[1] National Desired Population does not correspond to International Desired Population.

[2] Country surveyed the same cohort of students but at the beginning of the next school year.

Table B.2: Percent correct in large task by country for Criterion 2

Criterion	Score/Max. Score	CIL Scale Difficulty	Descriptor	Assessment Framework Aspect
2. Image layout	1/1	591	One or more images are well aligned with the other elements on the page and appropriately sized.	2.2. Creating information

Country	Percent Correct Response
	1/1
Australia	50 (1.4)
Chile	35 (1.6)
Croatia	43 (1.7)
Czech Republic	52 (1.5)
Germany[†]	42 (1.9)
Korea, Republic of	49 (1.5)
Lithuania	35 (1.7)
Norway[1]	47 (1.5)
Poland	42 (1.9)
Russian Federation[2]	37 (1.5)
Slovak Republic	42 (2.1)
Slovenia	47 (1.6)
Thailand[2]	21 (1.5)
Turkey	11 (1.2)
Countries not meeting sample requirements	
Denmark*	42 (2.0)
Hong Kong SAR*	32 (2.3)
Netherlands*	43 (1.8)
Switzerland*	41 (3.0)
Benchmarking participants	
Newfoundland and Labrador, Canada	54 (2.2)
Ontario, Canada	55 (2.1)
Benchmarking participant not meeting sample requirements	
City of Buenos Aires, Argentina*	27 (2.6)

Notes:

* Country data not used for scaling for this criterion.

() Standard errors appear in parentheses. Because some results are rounded to the nearest whole number, some totals may appear inconsistent.

[†] Met guidelines for sampling participation rates only after replacement schools were included.

[1] National Desired Population does not correspond to International Desired Population.

[2] Country surveyed the same cohort of students but at the beginning of the next school year.

Table B.3: Percent correct in large task by country for Criterion 3

Criterion	Score/Max. Score	CIL Scale Difficulty	Descriptor	Assessment Framework Aspect
3. Text layout and formatting	1/2	553	Formatting tools have been used to some degree to show the role of the different text elements.	2.2. Creating information
3. Text layout and formatting	2/2	673	Formatting tools have been used consistently throughout the poster to show the role of the different text elements.	2.2. Creating information

Country	Percent Correct Response	
	1/2	2/2
Australia*	65 (1.7)	19 (1.1)
Chile	56 (1.8)	6 (0.7)
Croatia	67 (1.8)	27 (1.6)
Czech Republic	47 (1.5)	18 (1.1)
Germany[†]*	67 (1.6)	38 (1.5)
Korea, Republic of	73 (1.3)	27 (1.2)
Lithuania	42 (1.8)	12 (1.0)
Norway[1]*	56 (1.7)	20 (1.1)
Poland*	71 (1.4)	39 (1.3)
Russian Federation[2]*	60 (1.4)	16 (1.0)
Slovak Republic	55 (2.3)	29 (1.7)
Slovenia	34 (1.7)	8 (0.8)
Thailand[2]	20 (1.8)	3 (0.5)
Turkey	17 (1.4)	4 (0.7)
Countries not meeting sample requirements		
Denmark*	64 (2.3)	24 (1.8)
Hong Kong SAR*	52 (3.1)	11 (1.4)
Netherlands*	65 (2.0)	22 (1.6)
Switzerland*	66 (2.1)	13 (1.8)
Benchmarking participants		
Newfoundland and Labrador, Canada	67 (2.5)	27 (1.9)
Ontario, Canada	68 (1.5)	27 (1.4)
Benchmarking participant not meeting sample requirements		
City of Buenos Aires, Argentina*	35 (3.3)	11 (1.7)

Notes:

*   Country data not used for scaling for this criterion.

() Standard errors appear in parentheses. Because some results are rounded to the nearest whole number, some totals may appear inconsistent.

[†] Met guidelines for sampling participation rates only after replacement schools were included.

[1] National Desired Population does not correspond to International Desired Population.

[2] Country surveyed the same cohort of students but at the beginning of the next school year.

Table B.4: Percent correct in large task by country for Criterion 4

Criterion	Score/Max. Score	CIL Scale Difficulty	Descriptor	Assessment Framework Aspect
4. Color contrast	1/2	472	The text mostly contrasts sufficiently with the background to support reading.	2.2. Creating information
4. Color contrast	2/2	655	There is sufficient contrast to enable all text to be seen and read easily.	2.1. Transforming information

Country	Percent Correct Response	
	1/2	2/2
Australia	76 (1.1)	25 (0.9)
Chile	67 (1.6)	20 (1.3)
Croatia	68 (1.3)	18 (1.1)
Czech Republic	89 (0.9)	79 (1.2)
Germany[†]	72 (1.7)	22 (1.4)
Korea, Republic of	73 (1.2)	16 (1.0)
Lithuania	68 (1.8)	20 (1.2)
Norway[1]	74 (1.4)	21 (1.3)
Poland	75 (1.2)	20 (1.4)
Russian Federation[2]	70 (1.3)	20 (1.1)
Slovak Republic	73 (1.7)	23 (1.0)
Slovenia	82 (1.0)	23 (1.1)
Thailand[2]	39 (2.2)	7 (0.9)
Turkey	31 (2.0)	5 (0.7)
Countries not meeting sample requirements		
Denmark*	76 (1.7)	27 (1.6)
Hong Kong SAR*	66 (2.5)	11 (1.3)
Netherlands*	75 (1.7)	22 (1.3)
Switzerland*	74 (1.9)	26 (1.5)
Benchmarking participants		
Newfoundland and Labrador, Canada	79 (1.9)	25 (2.4)
Ontario, Canada	81 (1.3)	25 (1.3)
Benchmarking participant not meeting sample requirements		
City of Buenos Aires, Argentina*	57 (3.0)	17 (2.4)

Notes:

* Country data not used for scaling for this criterion.

() Standard errors appear in parentheses. Because some results are rounded to the nearest whole number, some totals may appear inconsistent.

[†] Met guidelines for sampling participation rates only after replacement schools were included.

[1] National Desired Population does not correspond to International Desired Population.

[2] Country surveyed the same cohort of students but at the beginning of the next school year.

Table B.5: Percent correct in large task by country for Criterion 5

Criterion	Score/Max. Score	CIL Scale Difficulty	Descriptor	Assessment Framework Aspect
5. Color consistency	1/1	417	The poster shows evidence of planning regarding the use of color to denote the role of the text, background, and images in the poster.	2.3. Sharing information

Country	Percent Correct Response
	1/1
Australia	67 (1.5)
Chile	77 (1.7)
Croatia	88 (1.2)
Czech Republic	90 (0.8)
Germany[†]	84 (1.3)
Korea, Republic of	76 (1.2)
Lithuania*	39 (1.7)
Norway[1]	79 (1.3)
Poland*	92 (0.9)
Russian Federation[2]*	42 (1.1)
Slovak Republic	79 (1.7)
Slovenia	84 (1.0)
Thailand[2]*	25 (1.9)
Turkey*	14 (1.4)
Countries not meeting sample requirements	
Denmark*	85 (1.6)
Hong Kong SAR*	76 (2.6)
Netherlands*	81 (1.6)
Switzerland*	76 (2.4)
Benchmarking participants	
Newfoundland and Labrador, Canada	84 (1.9)
Ontario, Canada	86 (1.3)
Benchmarking participant not meeting sample requirements	
City of Buenos Aires, Argentina*	37 (2.6)

Notes:

* Country data not used for scaling for this criterion.

() Standard errors appear in parentheses. Because some results are rounded to the nearest whole number, some totals may appear inconsistent.

[†] Met guidelines for sampling participation rates only after replacement schools were included.

[1] National Desired Population does not correspond to International Desired Population.

[2] Country surveyed the same cohort of students but at the beginning of the next school year.

Table B.6: Percent correct in large task by country for Criterion 6

Criterion	Score/Max. Score	CIL Scale Difficulty	Descriptor	Assessment Framework Aspect
6. Information adaptation	1/2	636	Some useful information has been copied from the resources and edited to improve ease of comprehension and relevance.	2.3. Sharing information
6. Information adaptation	2/2	722	The relevant key points from the resources have been rephrased using student's own words.	2.3. Sharing information

Country	Percent Correct Response	
	1/2	2/2
Australia*	52 (1.4)	13 (0.9)
Chile	14 (1.0)	3 (0.4)
Croatia	32 (1.3)	7 (0.6)
Czech Republic	35 (1.4)	6 (0.6)
Germany[†]*	48 (1.4)	7 (0.8)
Korea, Republic of	63 (1.4)	33 (1.3)
Lithuania	17 (1.2)	6 (0.8)
Norway[1]	25 (1.3)	6 (0.7)
Poland*	43 (1.5)	4 (0.6)
Russian Federation[2]*	45 (1.4)	8 (0.8)
Slovak Republic	22 (1.7)	7 (0.9)
Slovenia	38 (1.9)	4 (0.5)
Thailand[2]	14 (1.2)	2 (0.3)
Turkey	6 (0.7)	2 (0.4)
Countries not meeting sample requirements		
Denmark*	38 (2.5)	9 (1.3)
Hong Kong SAR*	8 (1.0)	1 (0.5)
Netherlands*	49 (1.9)	14 (1.3)
Switzerland*	63 (2.3)	14 (2.0)
Benchmarking participants		
Newfoundland and Labrador, Canada	43 (2.6)	5 (1.2)
Ontario, Canada	46 (1.9)	8 (0.9)
Benchmarking participant not meeting sample requirements		
City of Buenos Aires, Argentina*	19 (2.6)	5 (1.2)

Notes:
* Country data not used for scaling for this criterion.
() Standard errors appear in parentheses. Because some results are rounded to the nearest whole number, some totals may appear inconsistent.
[†] Met guidelines for sampling participation rates only after replacement schools were included.
[1] National Desired Population does not correspond to International Desired Population.
[2] Country surveyed the same cohort of students but at the beginning of the next school year.

Table B.7: Percent correct in large task by country for Criterion 7

Criterion	Score/Max. Score	CIL Scale Difficulty	Descriptor	Assessment Framework Aspect
7. Information completeness	1/2	539	Two of the three required pieces of information about the program (when, where, and what equipment is required) have been included in the poster.	1.2. Accessing and evaluating information
7. Information completeness	2/2	634	All required information about the program (when, where, and what equipment is required) have been included in the poster.	1.2. Accessing and evaluating information

Country	Percent Correct Response	
	1/2	2/2
Australia	65 (1.4)	40 (1.4)
Chile	56 (1.8)	17 (1.1)
Croatia	62 (1.5)	30 (1.3)
Czech Republic	79 (1.2)	53 (1.4)
Germany[†]	60 (1.7)	30 (1.5)
Korea, Republic of	63 (1.4)	31 (1.5)
Lithuania	40 (1.7)	11 (1.1)
Norway[1]	61 (1.7)	31 (1.5)
Poland	73 (1.5)	42 (1.7)
Russian Federation[2]*	46 (1.5)	17 (1.5)
Slovak Republic	56 (2.1)	35 (1.7)
Slovenia	78 (1.3)	28 (1.1)
Thailand[2]	12 (1.3)	3 (0.5)
Turkey	7 (0.9)	2 (0.4)
Countries not meeting sample requirements		
Denmark*	71 (2.1)	41 (2.3)
Hong Kong SAR*	51 (3.0)	16 (1.9)
Netherlands*	59 (2.3)	34 (2.0)
Switzerland*	58 (2.8)	32 (2.2)
Benchmarking participants		
Newfoundland and Labrador, Canada	67 (2.1)	32 (1.7)
Ontario, Canada	66 (1.5)	35 (1.8)
Benchmarking participant not meeting sample requirements		
City of Buenos Aires, Argentina*	27 (3.0)	7 (1.3)

Notes:

* Country data not used for scaling for this criterion.

() Standard errors appear in parentheses. Because some results are rounded to the nearest whole number, some totals may appear inconsistent.

[†] Met guidelines for sampling participation rates only after replacement schools were included.

[1] National Desired Population does not correspond to International Desired Population.

[2] Country surveyed the same cohort of students but at the beginning of the next school year.

Table B.8: Percent correct in large task by country for Criterion 8

Criterion	Score/Max. Score	CIL Scale Difficulty	Descriptor	Assessment Framework Aspect
8. Persuasiveness	1/1	643	Uses some emotive or persuasive language to make the program appealing to readers.	2.1. Transforming information

Country	Percent Correct Response
	1/1
Australia	38 (1.3)
Chile	26 (1.6)
Croatia	21 (1.1)
Czech Republic	35 (1.5)
Germany[†]	19 (1.3)
Korea, Republic of	60 (1.5)
Lithuania	23 (1.5)
Norway[1]	29 (1.3)
Poland*	12 (1.0)
Russian Federation[2]	24 (1.2)
Slovak Republic	28 (1.5)
Slovenia*	69 (1.1)
Thailand[2]	6 (0.8)
Turkey	3 (0.6)
Countries not meeting sample requirements	
Denmark*	51 (2.0)
Hong Kong SAR*	10 (1.3)
Netherlands*	40 (2.1)
Switzerland*	33 (2.3)
Benchmarking participants	
Newfoundland and Labrador, Canada	41 (2.3)
Ontario, Canada	46 (1.6)
Benchmarking participant not meeting sample requirements	
City of Buenos Aires, Argentina*	13 (2.4)

Notes:

* Country data not used for scaling for this criterion.

() Standard errors appear in parentheses. Because some results are rounded to the nearest whole number, some totals may appear inconsistent.

[†] Met guidelines for sampling participation rates only after replacement schools were included.

[1] National Desired Population does not correspond to International Desired Population.

[2] Country surveyed the same cohort of students but at the beginning of the next school year.

Table B.9: Percent correct in large task by country for Criterion 9

Criterion	Score/Max. Score	CIL Scale Difficulty	Descriptor	Assessment Framework Aspect
9. Use of full page	1/1	563	Uses full page when creating poster.	2.1. Transforming information

Country	Percent Correct Response
	1/1
Australia	61 (1.5)
Chile	37 (2.0)
Croatia	47 (1.8)
Czech Republic	52 (1.5)
Germany[†]	58 (1.9)
Korea, Republic of	57 (1.4)
Lithuania	42 (1.9)
Norway[1]	49 (1.4)
Poland	59 (1.5)
Russian Federation[2]	46 (1.5)
Slovak Republic	50 (2.1)
Slovenia	56 (1.6)
Thailand[2]	15 (1.4)
Turkey	17 (1.4)
Countries not meeting sample requirements	
Denmark*	57 (2.2)
Hong Kong SAR*	50 (2.9)
Netherlands*	59 (1.8)
Switzerland*	57 (2.9)
Benchmarking participants	
Newfoundland and Labrador, Canada	53 (3.0)
Ontario, Canada	57 (1.9)
Benchmarking participant not meeting sample requirements	
City of Buenos Aires, Argentina*	30 (3.0)

Notes:

* Country data not used for scaling for this criterion.

() Standard errors appear in parentheses. Because some results are rounded to the nearest whole number, some totals may appear inconsistent.

[†] Met guidelines for sampling participation rates only after replacement schools were included.

[1] National Desired Population does not correspond to International Desired Population.

[2] Country surveyed the same cohort of students but at the beginning of the next school year.

APPENDIX C:

Percentiles and standard deviations for computer and information literacy

Table C.1: Percentiles of computer and information literacy

Country	5th Percentile		25th Percentile		75th Percentile		95th Percentile	
Australia	404	(6.0)	497	(2.9)	595	(2.7)	656	(3.2)
Chile	330	(7.9)	435	(5.5)	548	(2.7)	608	(5.1)
Croatia	364	(7.6)	463	(4.6)	570	(2.8)	631	(2.6)
Czech Republic	445	(6.8)	516	(2.6)	595	(1.5)	648	(2.3)
Germany[†]	380	(10.6)	481	(4.6)	577	(2.2)	631	(3.9)
Korea, Republic of	375	(5.8)	481	(5.0)	600	(4.0)	664	(3.2)
Lithuania	346	(11.5)	442	(4.8)	553	(3.5)	619	(3.9)
Norway (Grade 9)[1]	409	(8.3)	494	(3.7)	585	(2.5)	645	(5.3)
Poland	399	(7.2)	491	(3.3)	591	(3.2)	651	(4.7)
Russian Federation[2]	381	(6.5)	465	(4.0)	572	(3.7)	635	(3.4)
Slovak Republic	343	(11.7)	468	(7.6)	580	(3.2)	640	(4.6)
Slovenia	385	(6.0)	470	(3.2)	559	(2.2)	612	(3.6)
Thailand[2]	219	(9.6)	307	(5.4)	439	(6.1)	535	(7.6)
Turkey	191	(10.0)	296	(6.4)	430	(5.7)	519	(7.3)
Countries not meeting sample requirements								
Denmark	418	(14.4)	501	(4.6)	590	(3.4)	643	(6.5)
Hong Kong SAR	334	(13.9)	451	(12.1)	578	(5.2)	644	(5.6)
Netherlands	381	(11.1)	488	(7.3)	592	(5.3)	653	(5.1)
Switzerland	399	(12.3)	481	(7.1)	576	(6.2)	636	(7.6)
Benchmarking participants								
Newfoundland and Labrador, Canada	390	(7.8)	477	(5.6)	584	(4.9)	652	(7.4)
Ontario, Canada	421	(6.9)	501	(4.6)	598	(3.3)	659	(5.8)
Benchmarking participant not meeting sample requirements								
City of Buenos Aires, Argentina	282	(17.0)	390	(11.4)	518	(8.9)	594	(8.1)

Notes:

() Standard errors appear in parentheses. Because some results are rounded to the nearest whole number, some totals may appear inconsistent.

[†] Met guidelines for sampling participation rates only after replacement schools were included.

[1] National Desired Population does not correspond to International Desired Population.

[2] Country surveyed the same cohort of students but at the beginning of the next school year.

Table C.2: Means and standard deviations for computer and information literacy

Country	All Students		Females		Males	
	Mean	Standard deviation	Mean	Standard deviation	Mean	Standard deviation
Australia	542 (2.3)	78 (1.6)	554 (2.8)	73 (1.8)	529 (3.3)	80 (2.2)
Chile	487 (3.1)	86 (2.5)	499 (3.9)	81 (2.9)	474 (3.9)	89 (3.1)
Croatia	512 (2.9)	82 (1.7)	520 (3.1)	80 (2.4)	505 (3.6)	83 (2.2)
Czech Republic	553 (2.1)	62 (1.6)	559 (2.0)	60 (1.7)	548 (2.8)	63 (2.0)
Germany[†]	523 (2.4)	78 (2.0)	532 (2.9)	75 (2.9)	516 (3.2)	79 (2.3)
Korea, Republic of	536 (2.7)	89 (1.5)	556 (3.1)	81 (2.0)	517 (3.7)	92 (2.4)
Lithuania	494 (3.6)	84 (2.6)	503 (4.2)	84 (3.2)	486 (3.8)	84 (2.9)
Norway (Grade 9)[1]	537 (2.4)	72 (1.6)	548 (2.8)	70 (2.1)	525 (3.1)	72 (1.9)
Poland	537 (2.4)	77 (1.7)	544 (2.9)	75 (2.2)	531 (3.1)	78 (2.0)
Russian Federation[2]	516 (2.8)	77 (1.7)	523 (2.8)	76 (2.0)	510 (3.4)	78 (2.1)
Slovak Republic	517 (4.6)	90 (3.3)	524 (4.8)	91 (3.7)	511 (5.1)	90 (3.6)
Slovenia	511 (2.2)	69 (1.2)	526 (2.8)	63 (2.1)	497 (2.8)	71 (2.0)
Thailand[2]	373 (4.7)	96 (2.6)	378 (5.7)	96 (3.6)	369 (5.3)	96 (2.8)
Turkey	361 (5.0)	100 (3.0)	362 (5.2)	100 (3.6)	360 (5.4)	100 (3.2)
Countries not meeting sample requirements						
Denmark	542 (3.5)	69 (2.0)	549 (4.7)	67 (3.4)	534 (4.1)	70 (2.4)
Hong Kong SAR	509 (7.4)	95 (4.8)	523 (7.5)	91 (3.5)	498 (9.2)	97 (6.4)
Netherlands	535 (4.7)	82 (2.9)	546 (5.1)	79 (3.7)	525 (5.4)	83 (3.1)
Switzerland	526 (4.6)	72 (2.6)	529 (5.5)	72 (3.5)	522 (4.6)	71 (2.7)
Benchmarking participants						
Newfoundland and Labrador, Canada	528 (2.8)	80 (2.3)	544 (4.1)	74 (2.4)	509 (3.7)	82 (3.4)
Ontario, Canada	547 (3.2)	73 (2.2)	560 (4.0)	70 (2.4)	535 (3.4)	75 (2.8)
Benchmarking participant not meeting sample requirements						
City of Buenos Aires, Argentina	450 (8.6)	94 (4.0)	453 (8.9)	95 (4.2)	448 (9.7)	93 (5.7)

Notes:

() Standard errors appear in parentheses. Because some results are rounded to the nearest whole number, some totals may appear inconsistent.

[†] Met guidelines for sampling participation rates only after replacement schools were included.

[1] National Desired Population does not correspond to International Desired Population.

[2] Country surveyed the same cohort of students but at the beginning of the next school year.

APPENDIX D:

The scaling of ICILS questionnaire items

ICILS used sets of student, teacher, and school questionnaire items to measure constructs relevant in the field of computer and information literacy. Usually, sets of Likert-type items with four categories (for example, "strongly agree," "agree," "disagree," and "strongly disagree") were used to obtain this information, but at times two-point or three-point rating scales were chosen (e.g., "Yes" and "No"; or "never," "sometimes," and "often"). The items were then recoded so that the higher scale scores reflected more positive attitudes or higher frequencies.

The Rasch Partial Credit Model (Masters & Wright, 1997) was used for scaling, and the resulting weighted likelihood estimates (Warm, 1989) were transformed into a metric with a mean of 50 and a standard deviation of 10 for equally weighted ICILS national samples that satisfied guidelines for sample participation. Details on scaling procedures will be provided in the ICILS technical report (Fraillon, Schulz, Friedman, Ainley, & Gebhardt, forthcoming).

The resulting ICILS scale scores can be interpreted with regard to the average across countries participating in ICILS, but they do not reveal the extent to which students endorsed the items used for measurement. However, use of the Rasch Partial Credit Model allows mapping of scale scores to item responses. Thus, it is possible for each scale score to predict the most likely item response for a respondent. (For an application of these properties in the IEA ICCS 2009 survey, see Schulz & Friedman, 2011.)

Appendix E provides item-by-score maps for each student, teacher, or school questionnaire scale presented in the report. The maps provide a prediction of the minimum coded score (e.g., 0 = "strongly disagree," 1 = "disagree," 2 = "agree," and 3 = "strongly agree") a respondent would obtain on a Likert-type item based on their questionnaire scale score. For example, for students with a certain scale score, one could predict that they would have a 50 percent probability of agreeing (or strongly agreeing) with a particular item (see example item-by-score map in Figure D.1). For each item, it is possible to determine Thurstonian thresholds, the points at which a minimum item score becomes more likely than any lower score and which determine the boundaries between item categories on the item-by-score map.

This information can also be summarized by calculating the average thresholds across all items in a scale. For four-point Likert-type scales, this was usually done for the second threshold, making it possible to predict how likely it would be for a respondent with a certain scale score to have (on average across items) responses in the two lower or upper categories. Use of this approach in the case of items measuring agreement made it possible to distinguish between scale scores with which respondents were most likely to agree or disagree with the average item used for scaling.

National average scale scores are depicted as boxes that indicate their mean values plus/minus sampling error in graphical displays (e.g., Table 5.4 in the main body of the text) that have two underlying colors. If national average scores are located in the area in light blue on average across items, students would have had responses in the lower item categories ("disagree or strongly disagree," "not at all or not very interested," "never or rarely"). If these scores are found in the darker blue area, then students' average item responses would have been in the upper item response categories ("agree or strongly agree," "quite or very interested," "sometimes or often").

Figure D.1: Example of questionnaire item-by-score map

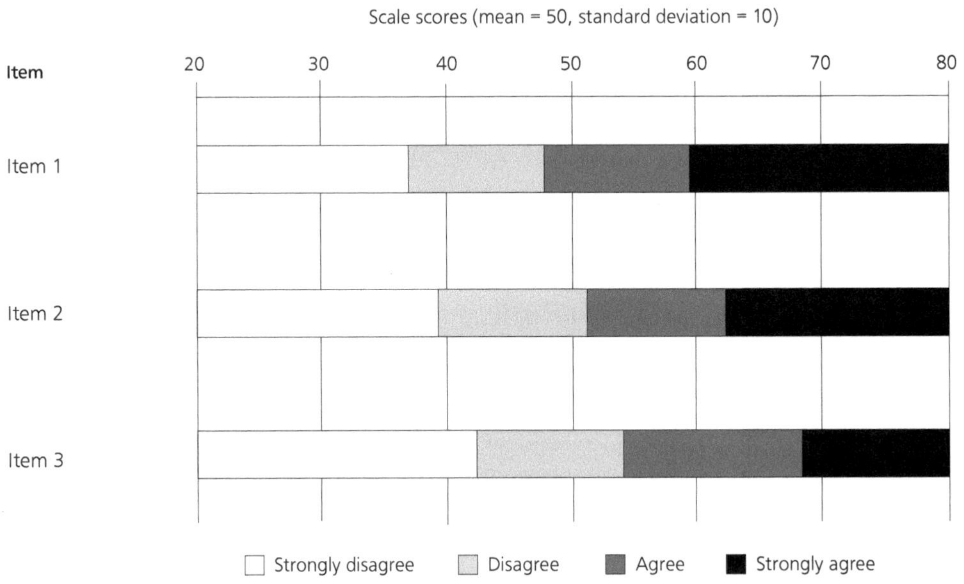

Scale scores (mean = 50, standard deviation = 10)

Example of how to interpret the item-by-score map

1:    A respondent with score 30 has more than a 50% probability of strongly disagreeing with all three items

2:    A respondent with score 40 has more than a 50% probability of **not** strongly disagreeing with Items 1 and 2 but of strongly disagreeing with Item 3

3:    A respondent with score 50 has more than a 50% probability of agreeing with Item 1 and of disagreeing with Items 2 and 3

4:    A respondent with score 60 has more than a 50% probability of strongly agreeing with Item 1 and of at least agreeing with Items 2 and 3

5:    A respondent with score 70 has more than a 50% probability of strongly agreeing with Items 1, 2, and 3

APPENDIX E:

Item-by-score maps

Figure E.1: Item-by-score map for students' use of specific ICT applications

How often do you use a computer outside of school for each of the following activities?

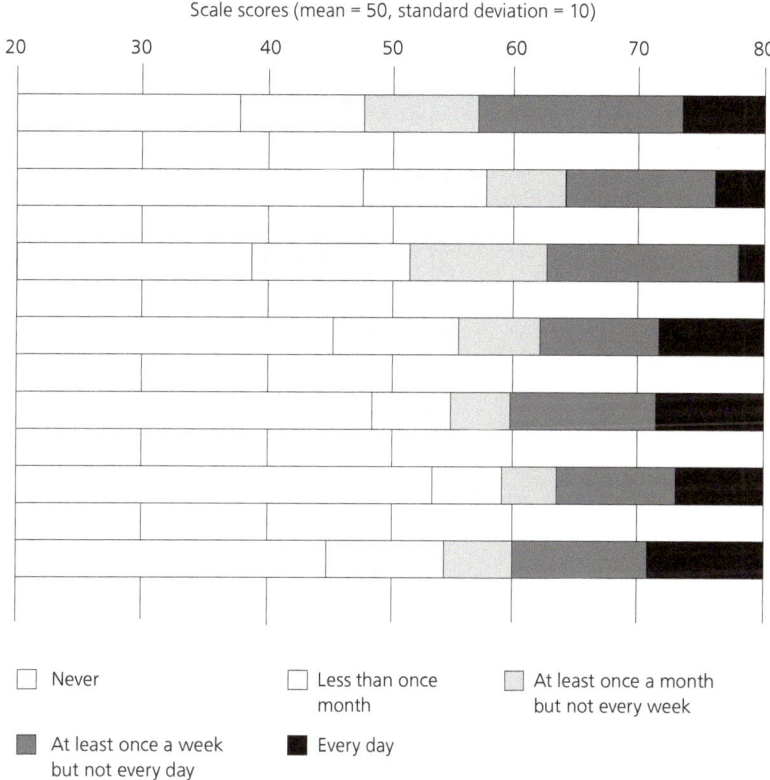

Scale scores (mean = 50, standard deviation = 10)

International Item Frequencies (row percentages)

Activity	Never	Less than once month	At least once a month but not every week	At least once a week but not every day	Every day	Sum
Creating or editing documents (e.g., to write stories or assignments)	16	26	30	23	5	100
Using a spreadsheet to do calculations, store data or plot graphs (e.g., using [Microsoft EXCEL ®])	41	32	16	9	2	100
Creating a simple "slideshow" presentation (e.g., using [Microsoft PowerPoint ®])	19	33	31	15	2	100
Creating a multimedia presentation (with sound, pictures, video)	34	33	18	11	4	100
Using education software that is designed to help with your school study (e.g., mathematics or reading software)	42	25	16	14	5	100
Writing computer programs, macros, or scripts (e.g., using [Logo, Basic or HTML])	58	21	11	7	3	100
Using drawing, painting, or graphics software	32	31	18	14	5	100

Note:
Average percentages for 14 equally weighted participating countries that met sample participation requirements. Because results are rounded to the nearest whole number, some totals may appear inconsistent.

Figure E.2: Item-by-score map for students' use of ICT for social communication

How often do you use the internet outside of school for each of the following activities?

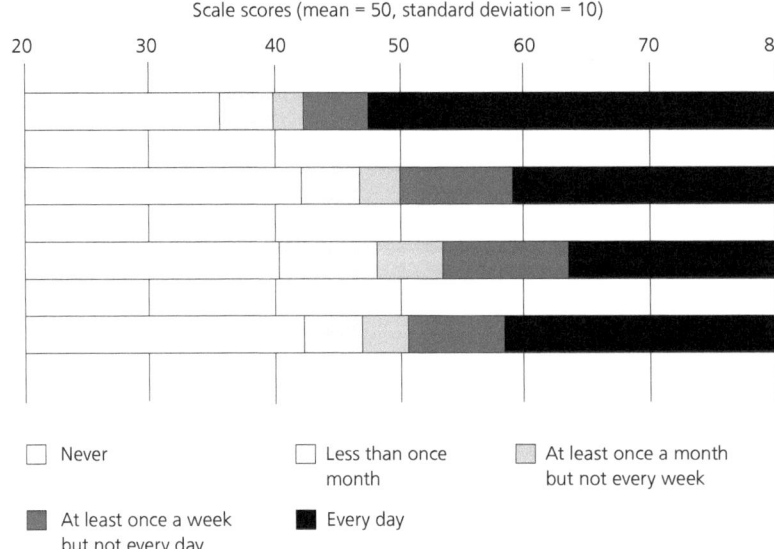

Scale scores (mean = 50, standard deviation = 10)

Communicating with others using messaging or social networks (e.g., instant messaging or [status updates])

Posting comments to online profiles or blogs

Uploading images or video to an [online profile] or [online community] (e.g., Facebook or YouTube)

Using voice chat (e.g., Skype) to chat with friends or family online

☐ Never   ☐ Less than once a month   ▨ At least once a month but not every week

▨ At least once a week but not every day   ■ Every day

International Item Frequencies (row percentages)

Sum

Activity	Never	Less than once a month	At least once a month but not every week	At least once a week but not every day	Every day	Sum
Communicating with others using messaging or social networks (e.g., instant messaging or [status updates])	10	7	8	20	56	100
Posting comments to online profiles or blogs	23	14	14	25	24	100
Uploading images or video to an [online profile] or [online community] (e.g., Facebook or YouTube)	21	21	20	23	15	100
Using voice chat (e.g., Skype) to chat with friends or family online	24	14	14	23	25	100

Note:
Average percentages for 14 equally weighted participating countries that met sample participation requirements. Because results are rounded to the nearest whole number, some totals may appear inconsistent.

Figure E.3: Item-by-score map for students' use of ICT for exchanging information

How often do you use the internet outside of school for each of the following activities?

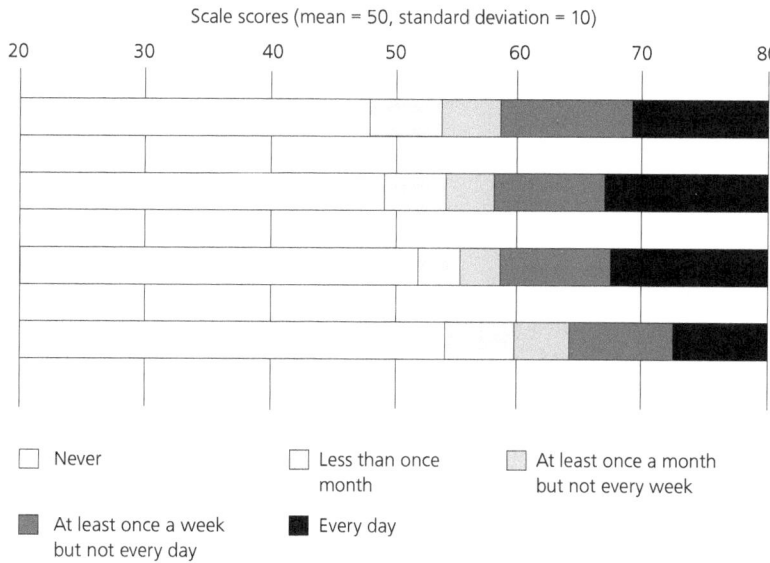

Scale scores (mean = 50, standard deviation = 10)

Asking questions on forums or [question and answer] websites

Answering other people's questions on forums or websites

Writing posts for your own blog

Building or editing a webpage

☐ Never ☐ Less than once a month ☐ At least once a month but not every week

■ At least once a week but not every day ■ Every day

International Item Frequencies (row percentages)

						Sum
Asking questions on forums or [question and answer] websites	45	19	14	14	9	100
Answering other people's questions on forums or websites	48	18	11	14	10	100
Writing posts for your own blog	56	13	9	12	9	100
Building or editing a webpage	61	18	9	7	4	100

Note:
Average percentages for 14 equally weighted participating countries that met sample participation requirements. Because results are rounded to the nearest whole number, some totals may appear inconsistent.

Figure E.4: Item-by-score map for students' use of ICT for recreation

How often do you use a computer for each of the following out-of-school activities?

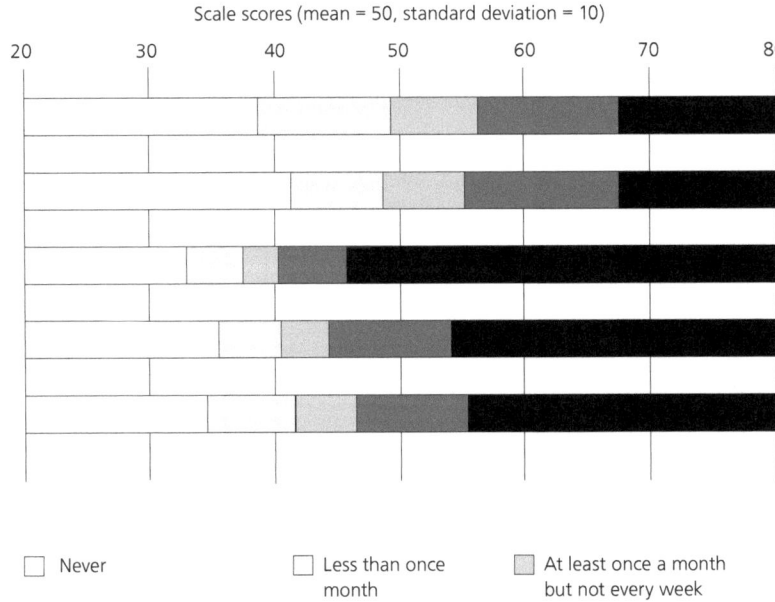

Scale scores (mean = 50, standard deviation = 10)

☐ Never   ☐ Less than once a month   ☐ At least once a month but not every week

■ At least once a week but not every day   ■ Every day

International Item Frequencies (row percentages)

						Sum
Accessing the internet to find out about places to go or activities to do	19	30	23	20	8	100
Reading reviews on the internet of things you might want to buy	24	23	23	22	9	100
Listening to music	5	6	7	21	61	100
Watching downloaded or streamed video (e.g., movies, TV shows, or clips)	9	10	14	32	36	100
Using the internet to get news about things I am interested in	9	13	17	30	32	100

Note:
Average percentages for 14 equally weighted participating countries that met sample participation requirements. Because results are rounded to the nearest whole number, some totals may appear inconsistent.

Figure E.5: Item-by-score map for students' use of ICT for study purposes

How often do you use computers for the following school-related purposes?

Scale scores (mean = 50, standard deviation = 10)

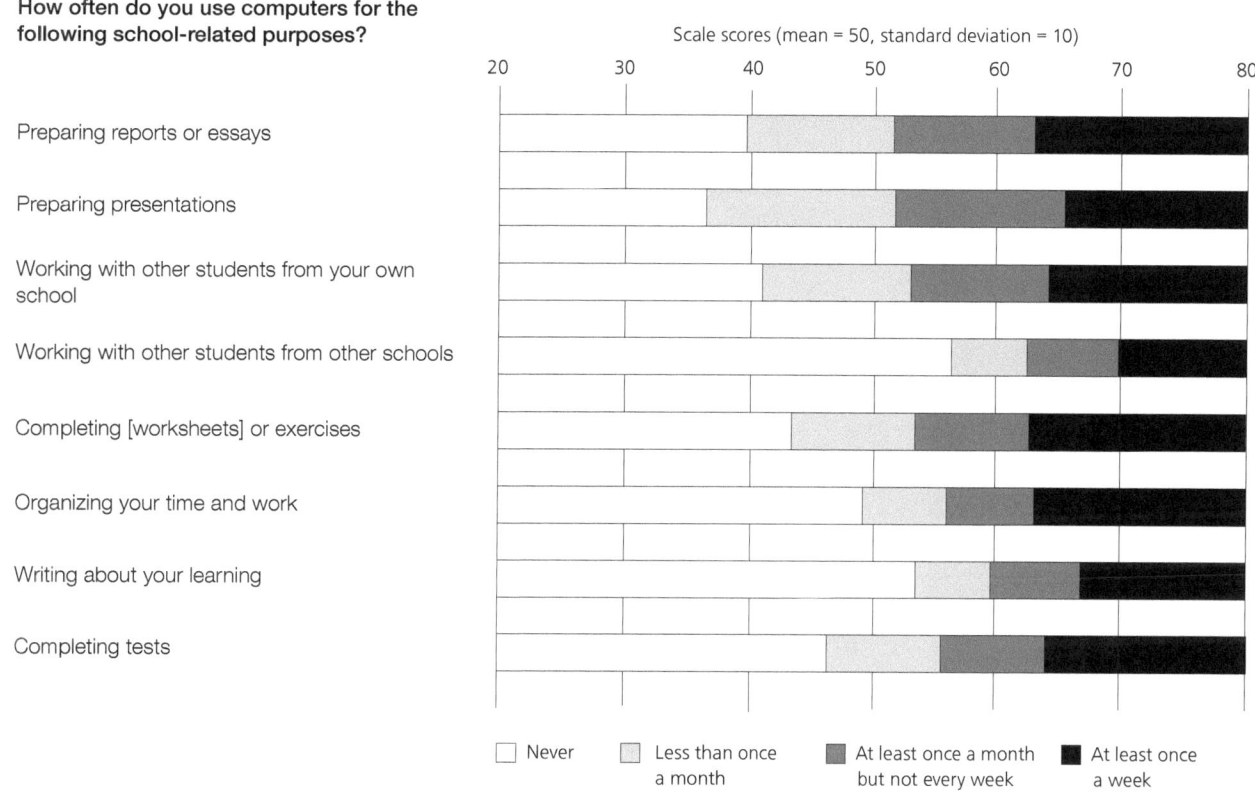

| | Never | Less than once a month | At least once a month but not every week | At least once a week |

International Item Frequencies (row percentages)

	Never	Less than once a month	At least once a month but not every week	At least once a week	Sum
Preparing reports or essays	20	35	30	15	100
Preparing presentations	15	40	33	11	100
Working with other students from your own school	23	37	28	13	100
Working with other students from other schools	68	19	9	4	100
Completing [worksheets] or exercises	29	32	25	15	100
Organizing your time and work	45	25	18	13	100
Writing about your learning	59	22	12	7	100
Completing tests	35	32	21	12	100

Note:
Average percentages for 14 equally weighted participating countries that met sample participation requirements. Because results are rounded to the nearest whole number, some totals may appear inconsistent.

Figure E.6: Item-by-score map for students' learning of ICT tasks at school

At school, have you learned how to do the following tasks?

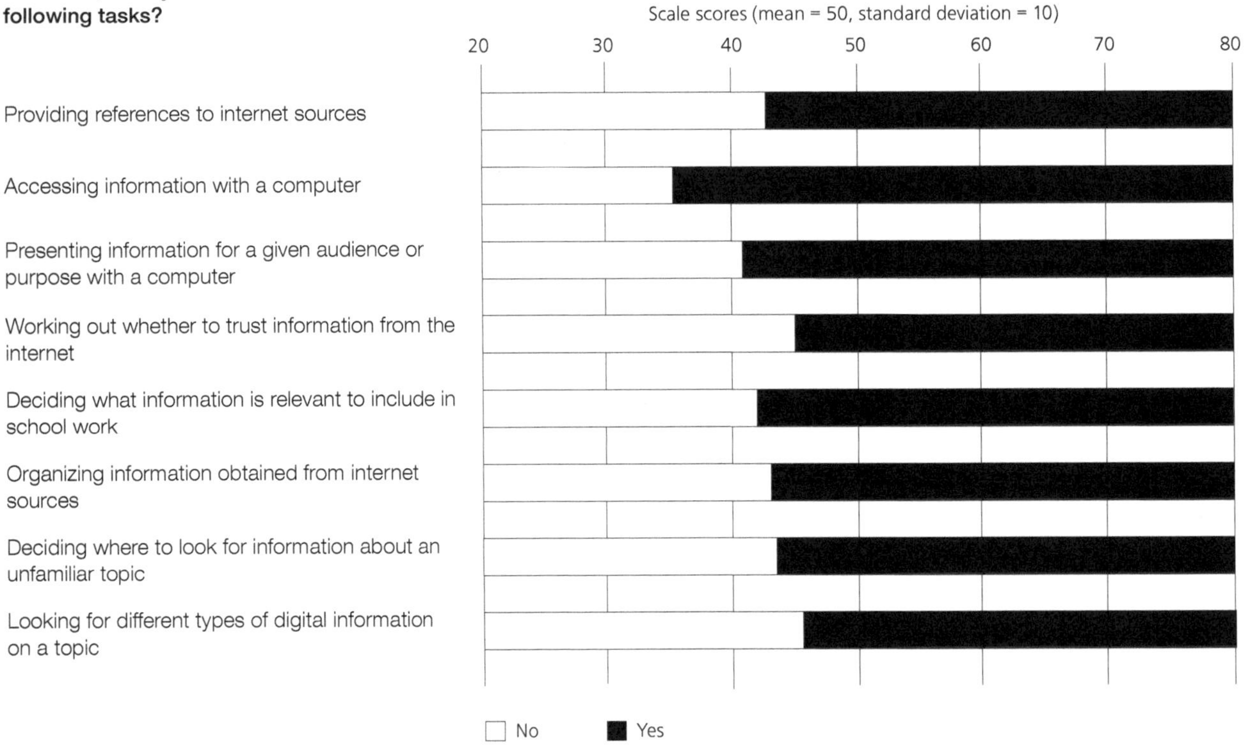

Scale scores (mean = 50, standard deviation = 10)

| | Providing references to internet sources | Accessing information with a computer | Presenting information for a given audience or purpose with a computer | Working out whether to trust information from the internet | Deciding what information is relevant to include in school work | Organizing information obtained from internet sources | Deciding where to look for information about an unfamiliar topic | Looking for different types of digital information on a topic |

☐ No   ■ Yes

International Item Frequencies (row percentages)

	No	Yes	Sum
Providing references to internet sources	27	73	100
Accessing information with a computer	15	85	100
Presenting information for a given audience or purpose with a computer	24	76	100
Working out whether to trust information from the internet	30	70	100
Deciding what information is relevant to include in school work	25	75	100
Organizing information obtained from internet sources	27	73	100
Deciding where to look for information about an unfamiliar topic	28	72	100
Looking for different types of digital information on a topic	33	68	100

Note:
Average percentages for 14 equally weighted participating countries that met sample participation requirements. Because results are rounded to the nearest whole number, some totals may appear inconsistent.

Figure E.7: Item-by-score map for students' ICT self-efficacy basic skills

How well can you do each of these tasks on a computer?

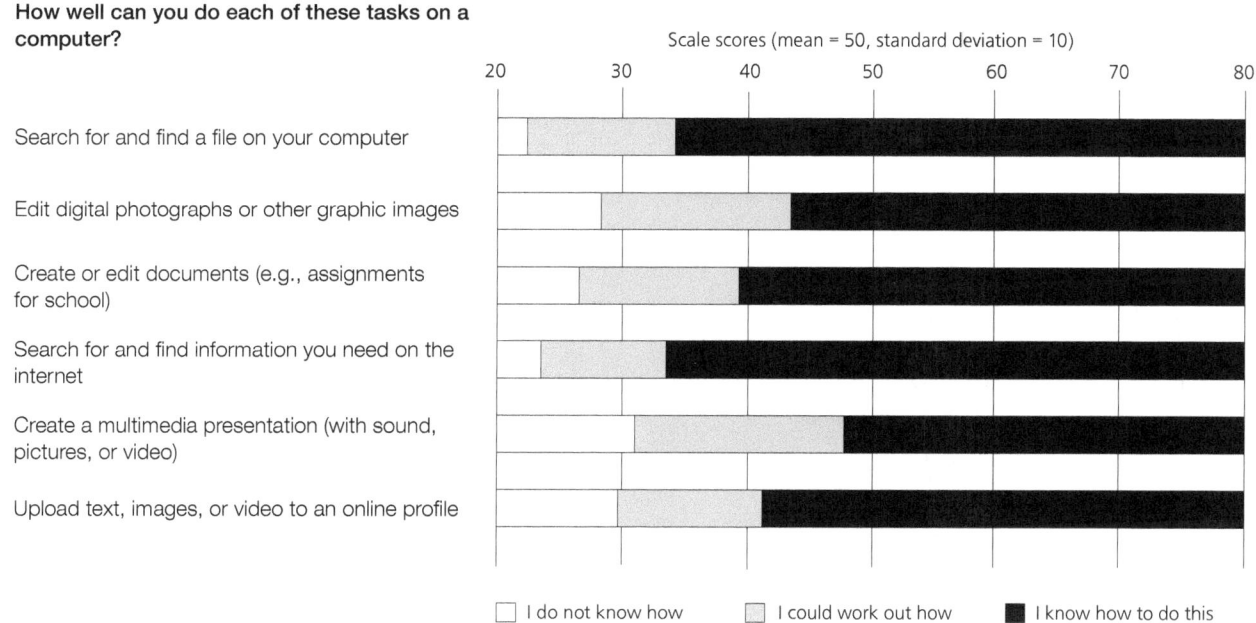

Scale scores (mean = 50, standard deviation = 10)

| | 20 | 30 | 40 | 50 | 60 | 70 | 80 |

Search for and find a file on your computer

Edit digital photographs or other graphic images

Create or edit documents (e.g., assignments for school)

Search for and find information you need on the internet

Create a multimedia presentation (with sound, pictures, or video)

Upload text, images, or video to an online profile

□ I do not know how to do this   ▨ I could work out how to do this   ■ I know how to do this

International Item Frequencies (row percentages)

				Sum
Search for and find a file on your computer	3	10	87	100
Edit digital photographs or other graphic images	6	21	73	100
Create or edit documents (e.g., assignments for school)	4	15	81	100
Search for and find information you need on the internet	3	9	89	100
Create a multimedia presentation (with sound, pictures, or video)	8	28	64	100
Upload text, images, or video to an online profile	6	17	77	100

Note:
Average percentages for 14 equally weighted participating countries that met sample participation requirements. Because results are rounded to the nearest whole number, some totals may appear inconsistent.

Figure E.8: Item-by-score map for students' ICT self-efficacy advanced skills

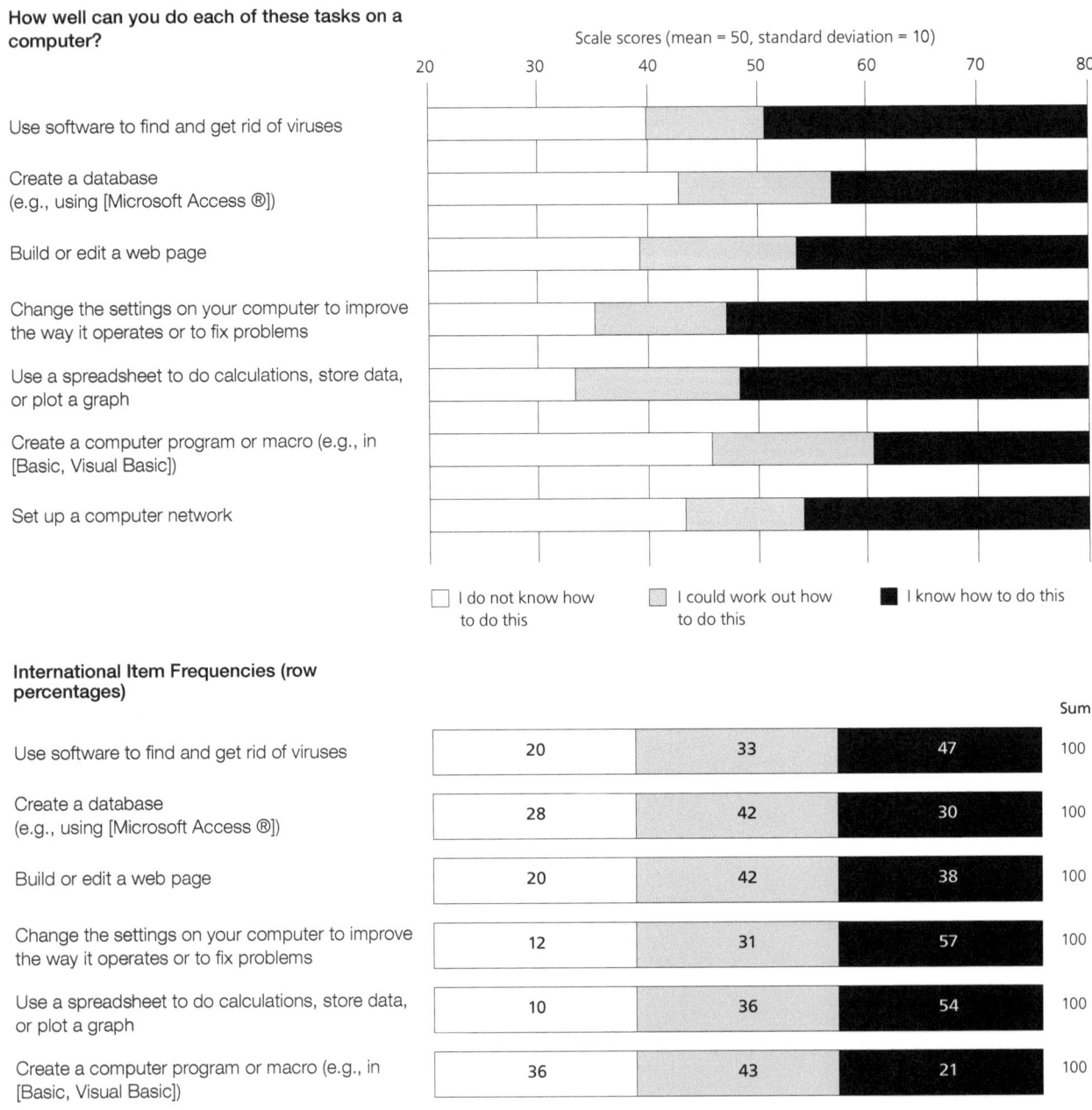

How well can you do each of these tasks on a computer?

Scale scores (mean = 50, standard deviation = 10)

Use software to find and get rid of viruses

Create a database
(e.g., using [Microsoft Access ®])

Build or edit a web page

Change the settings on your computer to improve
the way it operates or to fix problems

Use a spreadsheet to do calculations, store data,
or plot a graph

Create a computer program or macro (e.g., in
[Basic, Visual Basic])

Set up a computer network

☐ I do not know how   ☐ I could work out how   ■ I know how to do this
to do this   to do this

International Item Frequencies (row percentages)

	I do not know how to do this	I could work out how to do this	I know how to do this	Sum
Use software to find and get rid of viruses	20	33	47	100
Create a database (e.g., using [Microsoft Access ®])	28	42	30	100
Build or edit a web page	20	42	38	100
Change the settings on your computer to improve the way it operates or to fix problems	12	31	57	100
Use a spreadsheet to do calculations, store data, or plot a graph	10	36	54	100
Create a computer program or macro (e.g., in [Basic, Visual Basic])	36	43	21	100
Set up a computer network	29	35	36	100

Note:
Average percentages for 14 equally weighted participating countries that met sample participation requirements. Because results are rounded to the nearest whole number, some totals may appear inconsistent.

Figure E.9: Item-by-score map for students' ICT interest and enjoyment

Thinking about your experience with computers: To what extent do you agree or disagree with the following statements?

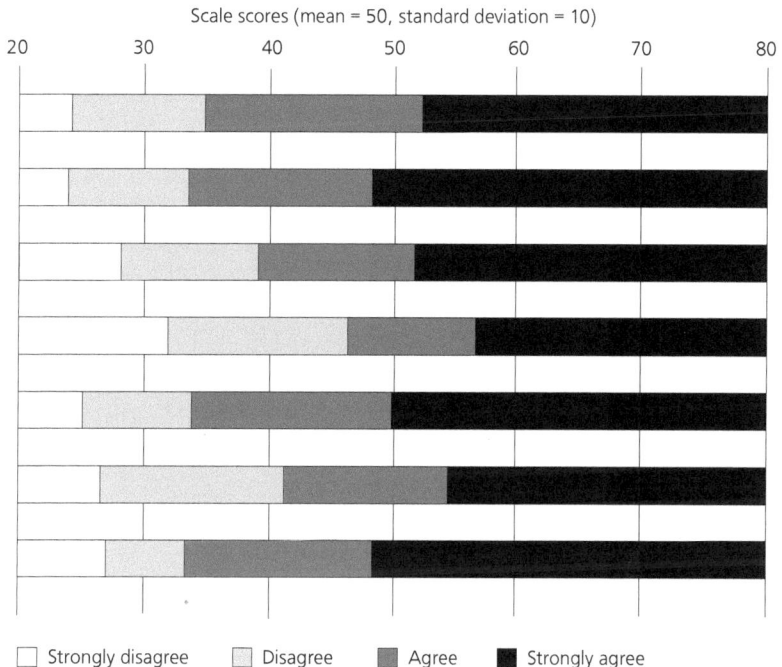

Scale scores (mean = 50, standard deviation = 10)

It is very important to me to work with a computer.

I think using a computer is fun.

It is more fun to do my work using a computer than without a computer.

I use a computer because I am very interested in the technology.

I like learning how to do new things using a computer.

I often look for new ways to do things using a computer.

I enjoy using the internet to find out information.

☐ Strongly disagree ☐ Disagree ◼ Agree ◼ Strongly agree

International Item Frequencies (row percentages)

Statement	Strongly disagree	Disagree	Agree	Strongly agree	Sum
It is very important to me to work with a computer.	2	9	45	44	100
I think using a computer is fun.	1	8	38	53	100
It is more fun to do my work using a computer than without a computer.	3	15	39	44	100
I use a computer because I am very interested in the technology.	8	29	34	29	100
I like learning how to do new things using a computer.	2	7	41	50	100
I often look for new ways to do things using a computer.	3	20	42	36	100
I enjoy using the internet to find out information.	2	6	38	55	100

Note:
Average percentages for 14 equally weighted participating countries that met sample participation requirements. Because results are rounded to the nearest whole number, some totals may appear inconsistent.

Figure E.10: Item-by-score map for teachers' collaboration in using ICT

To what extent do you agree or disagree with the following practices and principles in relation to the use of ICT in teaching and learning?

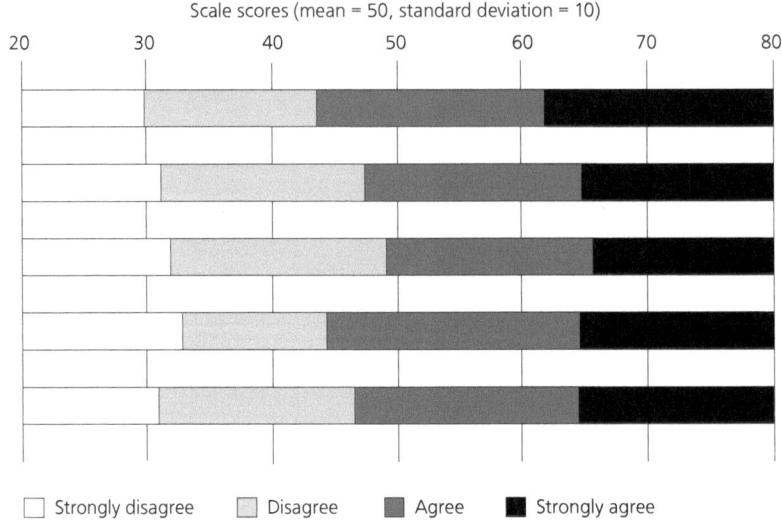

Scale scores (mean = 50, standard deviation = 10)

I work together with other teachers on improving the use of ICT in classroom teaching.

There is a common set of rules in the school about how ICT should be used in classrooms.

I systematically collaborate with colleagues to develop ICT-based lessons based on the curriculum.

I observe how other teachers use ICT in teaching.

There is a common set of expectations in the school about what students will learn about ICT.

☐ Strongly disagree   ☐ Disagree   ■ Agree   ■ Strongly agree

International Item Frequencies (row percentages)

	Strongly disagree	Disagree	Agree	Strongly agree	Sum
I work together with other teachers on improving the use of ICT in classroom teaching.	4	26	55	15	100
There is a common set of rules in the school about how ICT should be used in classrooms.	5	37	48	11	100
I systematically collaborate with colleagues to develop ICT-based lessons based on the curriculum.	6	41	44	9	100
I observe how other teachers use ICT in teaching.	6	25	57	11	100
There is a common set of expectations in the school about what students will learn about ICT.	5	32	52	11	100

Note:
Average percentages for 12 equally weighted participating countries that met sample participation requirements. Because results are rounded to the nearest whole number, some totals may appear inconsistent.

Figure E.11: Item-by-score map for teachers' lack of computer resources at school

To what extent do you agree or disagree with the following statements about the use of ICT in teaching at your school?

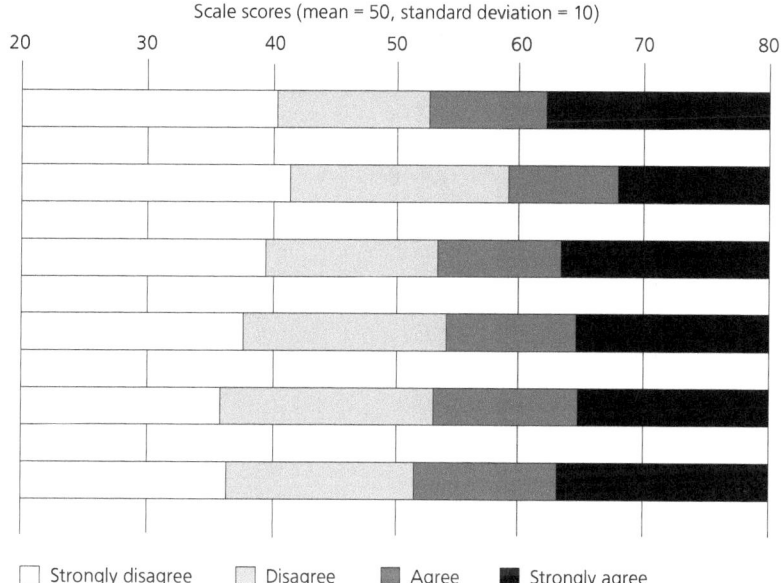

Scale scores (mean = 50, standard deviation = 10)

My school does not have sufficient ICT equipment (e.g., computers).

My school does not have access to digital learning resources.

My school has limited connectivity (e.g., slow or unstable speed) to the internet.

The computer equipment in our school is out of date.

There is not sufficient provision for me to develop expertise in ICT.

There is not sufficient technical support to maintain ICT resources.

☐ Strongly disagree ☐ Disagree ▨ Agree ■ Strongly agree

International Item Frequencies (row percentages)

Statement	Strongly disagree	Disagree	Agree	Strongly agree	Sum
My school does not have sufficient ICT equipment (e.g., computers).	19	38	29	14	100
My school does not have access to digital learning resources.	24	54	17	5	100
My school has limited connectivity (e.g., slow or unstable speed) to the internet.	18	42	28	12	100
The computer equipment in our school is out of date.	15	47	28	10	100
There is not sufficient provision for me to develop expertise in ICT.	13	48	31	9	100
There is not sufficient technical support to maintain ICT resources.	13	43	34	11	100

Note:
Average percentages for 12 equally weighted participating countries that met sample participation requirements. Because results are rounded to the nearest whole number, some totals may appear inconsistent.

Figure E.12: Item-by-score map for teachers' positive views on using ICT in teaching and learning

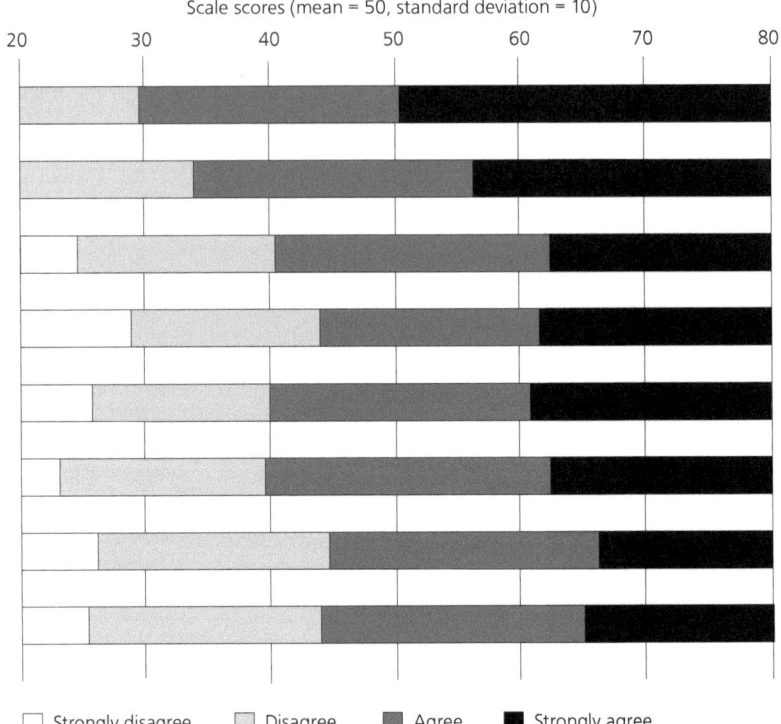

To what extent do you agree or disagree with the following statements about using ICT in teaching and learning at school?

International Item Frequencies (row percentages)

	Strongly disagree	Disagree	Agree	Strongly agree	Sum
Enables students to access better sources of information	0	4	50	46	100
Helps students to consolidate and process information more effectively	0	9	62	29	100
Helps students learn to collaborate with other students	2	21	63	15	100
Enables students to communicate more effectively with others	3	28	52	17	100
Helps students develop greater interest in learning	2	20	61	18	100
Helps students work at a level appropriate to their learning needs	1	19	65	15	100
Helps students develop skills in planning and self-regulation of their work	2	32	56	10	100
Improves academic performance of students	2	30	57	11	100

Note:
Average percentages for 12 equally weighted participating countries that met sample participation requirements. Because results are rounded to the nearest whole number, some totals may appear inconsistent.

Figure E.13: Item-by-score map for teachers' negative views on using ICT in teaching and learning

To what extent do you agree or disagree with the following statements about using ICT in teaching and learning at school?

□ Strongly disagree ▧ Disagree ▨ Agree ■ Strongly agree

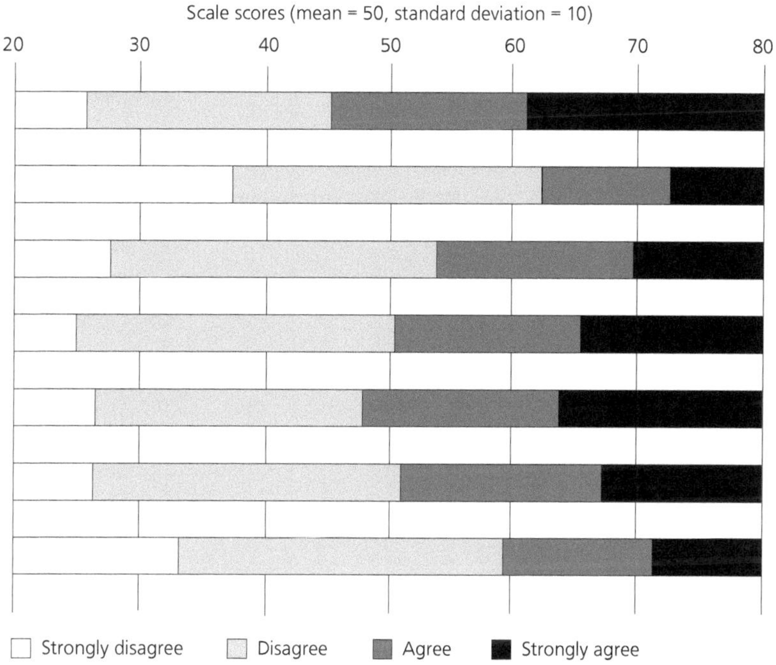

International Item Frequencies (row percentages)

	Strongly disagree	Disagree	Agree	Strongly agree	Sum
Results in poorer writing skills among students	3	30	47	20	100
Only introduces organizational problems for schools	18	65	14	3	100
Impedes concept formation better done with real objects than computer images	6	55	34	6	100
Only encourages copying material from published internet sources	4	47	39	11	100
Limits the amount of personal communication among students	4	38	44	14	100
Results in poorer calculation and estimation skills among students	5	47	39	9	100
Only distracts students from learning	11	65	20	4	100

Note:
Average percentages for 12 equally weighted participating countries that met sample participation requirements. Because results are rounded to the nearest whole number, some totals may appear inconsistent.

Figure E.14: Item-by-score map for teachers' ICT self-efficacy

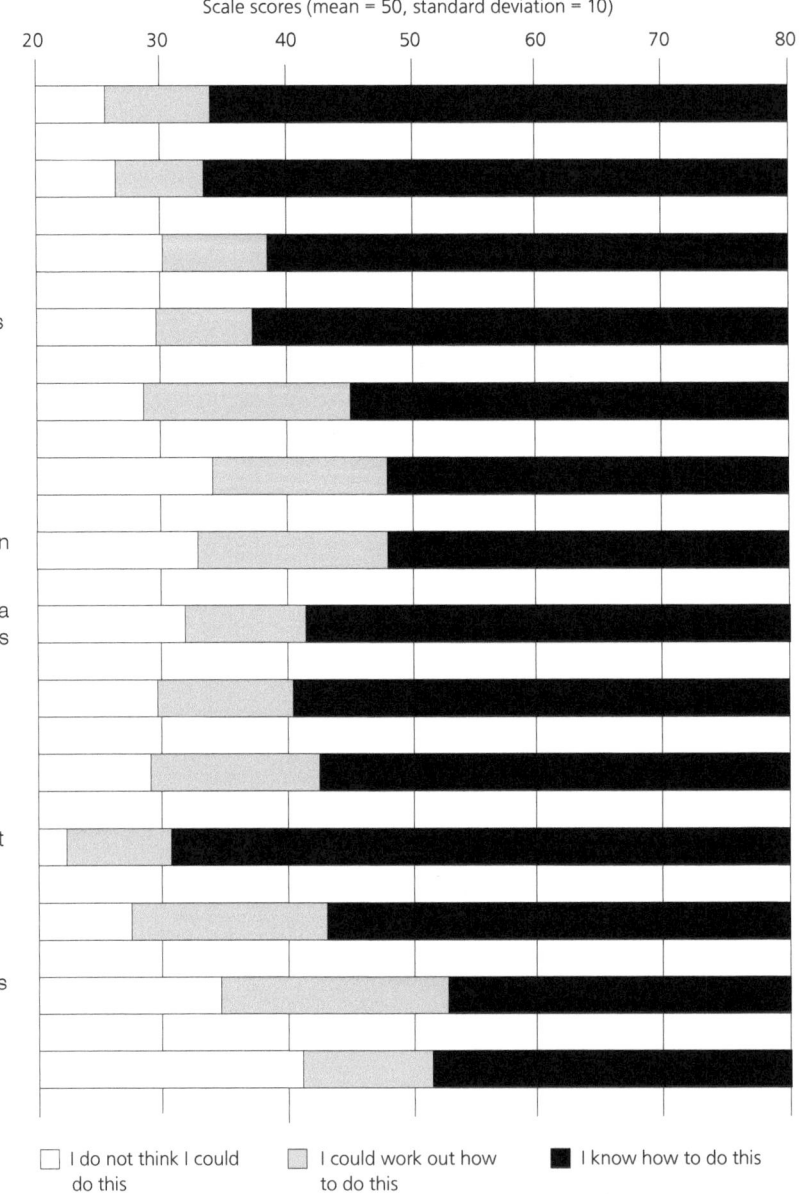

How well can you do these tasks on a computer by yourself?

Scale scores (mean = 50, standard deviation = 10)

☐ I do not think I could do this   ☐ I could work out how to do this   ■ I know how to do this

Figure E.14: Item-by-score map for teachers' ICT self-efficacy (contd.)

International Item Frequencies (row percentages)

				Sum
Producing a letter using a wordprocessing program	3	9	89	100
Emailing a file as an attachment	3	8	89	100
Storing your digital photos on a computer	5	13	82	100
Filing digital documents in folders and subfolders	5	11	84	100
Monitoring students' progress	5	30	65	100
Using a spreadsheet program (e.g., [Lotus 1 2 3 ®, Microsoft Excel ®]) for keeping records or analyzing data	10	31	59	100
Contributing to a discussion forum/user group on the internet (e.g., a wiki or blog)	9	33	58	100
Producing presentations (e.g., [PowerPoint® or a similar program]), with simple animation functions	7	18	76	100
Using the internet for online purchases and payments	5	18	77	100
Preparing lessons that involve the use of ICT by students	5	22	74	100
Finding useful teaching resources on the internet	2	6	92	100
Assessing student learning	4	25	71	100
Collaborating with others using shared resources such as [Google Docs®]	12	45	44	100
Installing software	22	31	47	100

Note:
Average percentages for 12 equally weighted participating countries that met sample participation requirements. Because results are rounded to the nearest whole number, some totals may appear inconsistent.

Figure E.15: Item-by-score map for teachers' use of specific ICT applications

How often did you use the following tools in your teaching of the reference class this school year?

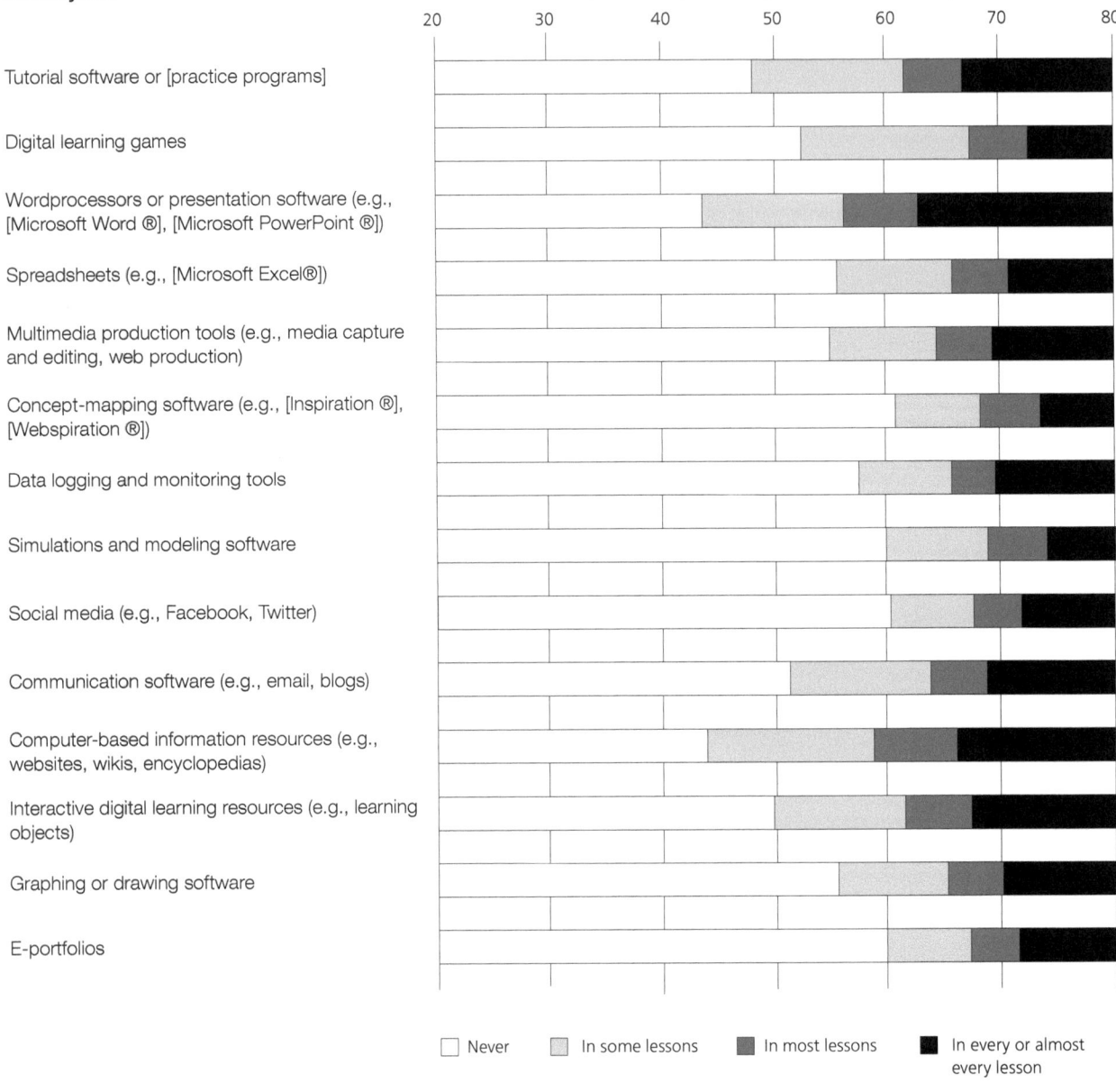

Figure E.15: Item-by-score map for teachers' use of specific ICT applications (contd.)

International Item Frequencies (row percentages)

				Sum
Tutorial software or [practice programs]	42	43	10	5	100
Digital learning games	58	37	4	1	100
Wordprocessors or presentation software (e.g., [Microsoft Word ®], [Microsoft PowerPoint ®])	31	38	19	11	100
Spreadsheets (e.g., [Microsoft Excel®])	64	30	5	2	100
Multimedia production tools (e.g., media capture and editing, web production)	64	27	6	2	100
Concept-mapping software (e.g., [Inspiration ®], [Webspiration ®])	81	16	3	1	100
Data logging and monitoring tools	72	22	4	2	100
Simulations and modeling software	80	17	2	1	100
Social media (e.g., Facebook, Twitter)	80	17	3	1	100
Communication software (e.g., email, blogs)	52	38	7	3	100
Computer-based information resources (e.g., websites, wikis, encyclopedias)	32	45	17	6	100
Interactive digital learning resources (e.g., learning objects)	47	38	11	4	100
Graphing or drawing software	65	28	5	2	100
E-portfolios	79	17	3	1	100

Note:
Average percentages for 12 equally weighted participating countries that met sample participation requirements. Because results are rounded to the nearest whole number, some totals may appear inconsistent.

APPENDIX F:

Effects of indicators of missing school and teacher data

Table F.1: Effects of indicators of missing school and teacher data

Country	Indicator Variables of Missing School and Teacher Data							
	School data				Teacher data			
	Model 1		Model 2		Model 1		Model 2	
Australia	-12.8	(10.5)	**-16.8**	(8.2)	12.2	(11.8)	2.8	(8.9)
Chile	25.3	(19.9)	8.8	(9.8)	25.3	(19.9)	8.8	(9.8)
Croatia	-8.5	(13.4)	-10.9	(9.5)	-8.5	(13.4)	-10.9	(9.5)
Czech Republic	0.2	(1.4)	0.3	(1.4)	0.2	(1.4)	0.3	(1.4)
Germany[t, tt]	-8.3	(19.5)	-14.2	(11.7)	2.9	(14.6)	1.9	(8.2)
Korea, Republic of	**7.3**	(2.7)	**5.4**	(2.1)	**7.3**	(2.7)	**5.4**	(2.1)
Lithuania	-15.5	(13.8)	-13.9	(14.3)	-15.5	(13.8)	-13.9	(14.3)
Norway (Grade 9)[1,tt]	7.6	(7.0)	4.5	(5.5)	**-18.3**	(7.8)	**-15.0**	(5.6)
Poland	7.9	(6.5)	-4.5	(5.8)	7.9	(6.5)	-4.5	(5.8)
Russian Federation[2]	18.9	(13.6)	15.7	(12.3)	4.7	(16.0)	3.2	(15.3)
Slovak Republic	**71.8**	(22.4)	**45.1**	(21.9)	**71.8**	(22.4)	**45.1**	(21.9)
Slovenia	6.4	(10.3)	7.7	(8.3)	13.7	(9.5)	4.5	(6.6)
Thailand[2]	8.7	(22.2)	10.9	(18.2)	-44.2	(30.3)	-40.9	(26.5)
Turkey	-26.6	(28.6)	-28.4	(26.5)	-26.6	(28.6)	-28.4	(26.5)
ICILS 2013 average	5.9	(4.2)	0.7	(3.5)	2.4	(4.4)	-3.0	(3.8)
Countries not meeting sample requirements								
Denmark[tt]	-4.1	(10.3)	-12.0	(8.7)	-2.7	(9.1)	-6.1	(6.7)
Hong Kong SAR[tt]	9.2	(16.3)	9.8	(16.0)	-33.2	(17.6)	-29.9	(17.9)
Benchmarking participants								
Newfoundland and Labrador, Canada	-7.1	(10.3)	-7.7	(9.8)	-24.4	(13.2)	-14.2	(12.2)
Ontario, Canada[tt]	-7.2	(6.6)	-9.2	(6.6)	-8.5	(7.2)	-3.5	(7.3)

Notes:

* Statistically significant ($p < 0.05$) coefficients in **bold**.

() Standard errors appear in parentheses. Because some results are rounded to the nearest whole number, some totals may appear inconsistent.

[t] Met guidelines for student survey sampling participation rates only after replacement schools were included.

[tt] Did not meet sampling participation rates for teacher survey.

[1] National Desired Population does not match International Desired Population.

[2] Country surveyed the same cohort of students but at the beginning of the next school year.

APPENDIX G:

Organizations and individuals involved in ICILS

International study center

The international study center is located at the Australian Council for Educational Research (ACER). Center staff at ACER were responsible for designing and implementing the study in close cooperation with the IEA Data Processing and Research Center (DPC) in Hamburg, Germany, and the IEA Secretariat in Amsterdam, the Netherlands.

Staff at ACER

Julian Fraillon, *research director*

John Ainley, *project coordinator*

Wolfram Schulz, *assessment coordinator*

Tim Friedman, *project researcher*

Daniel Duckworth, *test development*

Karin Hohlfeld, *test development*

Eveline Gebhardt, *data analyst*

Renee Chow, *data analyst*

Jorge Fallas, *data analyst*

Louise Wenn, *data analyst*

International Association for the Evaluation of Educational Achievement (IEA)

IEA provides overall support in coordinating ICILS. The IEA Secretariat in Amsterdam, the Netherlands, is responsible for membership, translation verification, and quality control monitoring. The IEA Data Processing and Research Center (DPC) in Hamburg, Germany, is mainly responsible for sampling procedures and processing ICILS data.

Staff at the IEA Secretariat

Dirk Hastedt, *executive director*

Paulína Koršňáková, *director of the IEA Secretariat*

David Ebbs, *research officer (translation verification)*

Alana Yu, *publications officer*

Roel Burgers, *financial manager*

Isabelle Gemin, *financial officer*

Staff at the IEA Data Processing and Research Center (DPC)

Heiko Sibberns, *director*

Ralph Carstens, *co-project manager, deputy unit head*

Michael Jung, *co-project manager*

Sabine Meinck, *research analyst (sampling)*

Robert Whitwell, *research analyst (sampling)*

Sabine Tieck, *research analyst (sampling)*

Diego Cortes, *research analyst (sampling)*

Duygu Savasci, *research analyst (sampling)*

Dirk Oehler, *research analyst*

Christine Busch, *research analyst*

Tim Daniel, *research analyst*

Sebastian Meyer, *research analyst*

Alena Becker, *research analyst*

Hannah Köhler, *research analyst*

Meng Xue, *head of software unit*

Limiao Duan, *programmer*

Devi Potham Rajendra Prasath, *programmer*

Christian Harries, *programmer*

Poornima Mamadapur, *software tester*

Bettina Wietzorek, *meeting and seminar coordinator*

SoNET Systems

SoNET Systems was responsible for developing the software systems underpinning the computer-based student assessment instruments. This work included development of the test and questionnaire items, the assessment delivery system, and the web-based translation, scoring, and data-management modules.

Staff at SoNET Systems

Mike Janic, *managing director*

Stephen Birchall, *general manager of software development*

Erhan Halil, *senior analyst programmer*

Rakshit Shingala, *analyst programmer*

Stephen Ainley, *quality assurance*

Ranil Weerasinghe, *quality assurance*

ICILS Project Advisory Committee (PAC)

PAC has, from the beginning of the project, advised the international study center and its partner institutions during regular meetings.

PAC members

John Ainley (chair), *ACER, Australia*

Ola Erstad, *University of Oslo, Norway*

Kathleen Scalise, *University of Oregon, United States*

Alfons ten Brummelhuis, *Kennisnet, the Netherlands*

ICILS sampling referee

Jean Dumais from Statistics Canada in Ottawa was the sampling referee for the study. He provided invaluable advice on all sampling-related aspects of the study.

National research coordinators

The national research coordinators (NRCs) played a crucial role in the study's development. They provided policy- and content-oriented advice on developing the instruments and were responsible for the implementation of ICILS in the participating countries.

Australia
Lisa De Bortoli
Australian Council for Educational Research (ACER)

Buenos Aires (Argentina)
Silvia Montoya
Assessment and Accountability, Ministry of Education

Canada
Mélanie Labrecque
Council of Ministers of Education (CMEC)

Chile
Gabriela Cares
Education Quality Assurance Agency

Croatia
Michelle Braš Roth
National Centre for External Evaluation of Education

Czech Republic
Josef Basl
Czech School Inspectorate

Denmark
Jeppe Bundsgaard
Department of Education, Aarhus University

Germany
Wilfried Bos
Institute for School Development Research, TU Dortmund University

Birgit Eickelmann
Institute for Educational Science, University of Paderborn

Hong Kong SAR
Nancy Law
Centre for Information Technology in Education, the University of Hong Kong

Korea, Republic of
Soojin Kim
Korea Institute for Curriculum and Evaluation

Lithuania
Eugenijus Kurilovas
Asta Buineviciute
Center of Information Technologies in Education

Netherlands
Martina Meelissen
Department of Research Methodology, Measurement and Data Analysis, University of Twente

Alfons ten Brummelhuis
Kennisnet

Norway
Inger Throndsen
Department of Teacher Education and School Research, University of Oslo

Geir Ottestad
Norwegian Center for ICT in Education

Poland
Kamil Sijko
The Educational Research Institute (IBE)

Russian Federation
Svetlana Avdeeva
National Training Foundation (NTF)

Slovak Republic
Andrea Galádová
National Institute for Certified Educational Measurements (NUCEM)

Slovenia
Eva Klemenčič
Barbara Brecko (field trial)
Center for Applied Epistemology, Educational Research Institute

Switzerland
Per Bergamin
Swiss Distance University of Applied Sciences

Thailand
Chaiwuti Lertwanasiriwan
Institute for the Promotion of Teaching Science and Technology (IPST)

Turkey
Gülçin Öz
Meral Alkan (field trial)
Ministry of National Education, General Directorate of Innovation and Educational Technologies

References

Ainley, J., Enger, L., & Searle, D. (2009). Students in a digital age: Implications for teaching and learning. In J. Voogt & G. Knezek (Eds.), *International handbook of information technology in primary and secondary education* (pp. 63–80). Heidelberg, Germany: Springer.

Ananiadou, K., & Claro, M. (2009). *21st century skills and competences for new millennium learners in OECD countries* (OECD Education Working Papers, No. 41). Paris, France: OECD Publishing.

Anderson, R., & Ainley, J. (2010). Technology and learning: Access in schools around the world. In B. McGaw, E. Baker, & P. Peterson (Eds.), *International encyclopaedia of education* (3rd ed., pp. 21–33). Amsterdam, the Netherlands: Elsevier.

Anderson, R., & Dexter, S. (2009). National policies and practices in ICT in education: United States of America. In T. Plomp, R. Anderson, N. Law, & A. Quale (Eds.), *Cross-national information and communication technology policies and practices in education* (2nd ed., pp. 697–715). Charlotte, NC: Information Age Publishing.

Anderson, R. E., & Plomp, T. (2010). National contexts. In N. Law, W. J. Pelgrum, & T. Plomp (Eds.), *Pedagogy and ICT use in schools around the world: Findings from the IEA SITES 2006 study* (pp. 38–66). Hong Kong SAR: CERC-Springer.

Aubusson, P., Burke, P., Schuck, S., & Kearney, M. (2014). Teachers choosing rich tasks: The moderating impact of technology on student learning, enjoyment and preparation. *Educational Researcher, 43*(5), 219–229.

Australian Curriculum, Assessment and Reporting Authority (ACARA). (2012). *National Assessment Program: ICT literacy Years 6 & 10 report 2011.* Sydney, NSW, Australia: Author. Available online at http://www.nap.edu.au/ verve/_resources/nap_ictl_2011_public_report_final.pdf

Bakia, M., Murphy, R., Anderson, K., & Trinidad, G. E. (2011). *International experiences with technology in education: Final report.* Washington, DC: U.S. Department of Education.

Bandura, A. (1993). Perceived self-efficacy in cognitive development and functioning. *Educational Psychologist, 28*(2), 117–148.

Bebell, D., Kay, R., Surh, K. A., Hernandez, D. A., Grimes, D., & Warschauer, M. (2010). One to one computing: A summary of the quantitative results from the Berkshire Wireless Learning Initiative. *Journal of Technology, Learning and Assessment, 9*(2), 5–57.

Bennett, S., Maton, K., & Kervin, L. (2008). The "digital natives" debate: A critical review of the evidence. *British Journal of Educational Technology, 39*(5), 775–786.

Binkley, M., Erstad, O., Herman, J., Raizen, S., Ripley, M., Miller-Ricci, M., & Rumble, M. (2012). Defining 21st century skills. In P. Griffin, B. McGaw, & E. Care (Eds.), *Assessment and teaching of 21st century skills* (pp. 17–66). Heidelberg, Germany: Springer.

Blurton, C. (1999). *New directions in ICT use in education.* Paris, France: UNESCO.

Bradley, R. H., & Corwyn, R. F. (2002). Socioeconomic status and child development. *Annual Review of Psychology, 53,* 371–399.

Branden, N. (1994). *The six pillars of self-esteem.* New York, NY: Bantam Books.

Buchmann, C. (2002). Measuring family background in international studies of education: Conceptual issues and methodological challenges. In A. Porter and A. Gamoran (Eds.), *Methodological advances in cross-national surveys of educational achievement* (pp. 150–197). Washington, DC: National Academy Press.

Burbules, N. (2007). E-lessons learned. *National Society for the Study of Education 2007 Yearbook, 106*(2), 207–216.

Charalambos, V., & Glass, G. (2007). Teacher professional development and ICT: Strategies and models. *National Society for the Study of Education 2007 Yearbook, 106*(2), 87–102.

Cohen, J., & Cohen, P. (1975). *Applied multiple regression/correlation analysis for the behavioral sciences.* Hillsdale, NJ: Lawrence Erlbaum Associates.

© International Association for the Evaluation of Educational Achievement (IEA) 2014
J. Fraillon et al., *Preparing for Life in a Digital Age*, DOI 10.1007/978-3-319-14222-7

Crook, C. (2008). Theories of formal and informal learning in the world of Web 2.0. In S. Livingstone (Ed.), *Theorising the benefits of new technology for youth: Controversies of learning and development* (pp. 30–34). Oxford, UK: Oxford University Press.

Cuban, L. (2001). *Oversold and underused: Computers in the classroom*. Cambridge, MA: Harvard University Press.

Dede, C. (2009). *Comparing frameworks for 21st century skills*. Cambridge, MA: Harvard Graduate School of Education: Author.

Dede, C., Ketelhut, D. J., Clarke, J., Nelson, B., & Bowman, C. (2005). *Students' motivation and learning of science in a multi-user virtual environment*. Paper presented at the 2009 annual meeting of the American Educational Research Association, Montréal, Québec, Canada.

Educational Testing Service (ETS). (2002). *Digital transformation: A framework for ICT literacy*. Princeton, NJ: Author. Retrieved from http://www.ets.org/Media/Tests/Information_and_Communication_Technology_Literacy/ictreport.pdf

Elley, W. B. (1992). *How in the world do students read?* The Hague, the Netherlands: International Association for the Evaluation of Educational Achievement (IEA).

Entwistle, D. R., & Astone, N. M. (1994). Some practical guidelines for measuring youth's race/ ethnicity and socioeconomic status. *Child Development, 65*, 1521–1540.

Ertmer, P. A. (1999). Addressing first- and second-order barriers to change: Strategies for technology integration. *Educational Technology Research and Development, 47*(4), 47–61.

Ertmer, P. A., Ottenbreit-Leftwich, A. T., Sadik, O., Sendurur, E., & Sendurur, P. (2012). Teacher beliefs and technology integration practices: A critical relationship. *Computers & Education, 59*(2), 423–435.

European Commission. (2006). *Recommendation 2006/962/EC of the European Parliament and of the Council of 18 December 2006 on key competences for lifelong learning* (Official Journal L 394 of 30.12.2006). Luxembourg Brussels: Author. Retrieved from http://eur-lex.europa.eu/ legal-content/EN/TXT/ PDF/?uri= CELEX:32006H0962&from=EN

European Commission. (2008). *Digital Literacy European Commission working paper and recommendations from Digital Literacy High-Level Expert Group*. Brussels, Belgium: Author. Retrieved from http://www.ifap.ru/library/book386.pdf

European Commission. (2009a). *Indicators of ICT in primary and secondary education (IIPSE)*. Brussels, Belgium: Author.

European Commission. (2009b). *Benchmarking Digital Europe 2011–2015: A conceptual framework*. Brussels, Belgium: Author.

European Commission. (2013). *Survey of schools: ICT in education. Benchmarking access, use and attitudes to technology in Europe's schools* (final report). Brussels, Belgium: Author. Retrieved from https://ec.europa.eu/digital-agenda/sites/digital-agenda/files/KK-31-13-401-EN-N.pdf

European Commission Joint Research Centre-IPTS on behalf of DG Education and Culture (2013). *DIGCOMP: A framework for developing and understanding digital competence in Europe*. Brussels, Belgium: Author. Retrieved from http://ftp.jrc.es/EURdoc/JRC83167.pdf

Eurydice. (2011). *Key data on learning and innovation through ICT at school in Europe 2011*. Brussels, Belgium: Author.

Ferrari, A. (2012). *Digital competence in practice: An analysis of frameworks*. Seville, Spain: Institute for Prospective Technological Studies, European Commission. Retrieved from http://www.ifap.ru/ library/book522.pdf

Fletcher, G., Schaffhauser, D., & Levin, D. (2012). *Out of print: Reimagining the K–12 textbook in a digital age*. Washington, DC: State Educational Technology Directors Association (SETDA).

Fraillon, J., Schulz, W., & Ainley, J. (2013). *International Computer and Information Literacy Study assessment framework*. Amsterdam, the Netherlands: International Association for the Evaluation of Educational Achievement (IEA). Retrieved from http://www.iea.nl/fileadmin/user_upload/ Publications/Electronic_versions/ICILS_2013_Framework.pdf

Fraillon, J., Schulz, W., Friedman, T., Ainley, J., & Gebhardt, E. (Eds.) (forthcoming). *International Computer and Information Literacy Study 2013 technical report*. Amsterdam, the Netherlands: International Association for the Evaluation of Educational Achievement (IEA).

Fredericks, J., Blumenfeld, P., & Paris, A. (2004). School engagement: Potential of the concept, state of the evidence. *Review of Educational Research, 74*(1), 59–96.

Ganzeboom, H. B. G., de Graaf, P. M., & Treiman, D. J. (1992). A standard international socioeconomic index of occupational status. *Social Science Research, 21*(1), 1–56.

Gottfried, A. (1985). Measures of socioeconomic status in child development research: Data and recommendations. *Merrill-Palmer Quarterly, 31*(1), 85–92.

Hauser, R. M. (1994). Measuring socioeconomic status in studies of child development. *Child Development, 65*, 1541–1545.

Institute of Education Sciences, National Center for Education Statistics. (2012). *National Assessment of Educational Progress (NAEP) technology and engineering literacy (TEL) assessment*. Washington, DC: Author. Retrieved from http://nces.ed.gov/nationsreportcard/tel/

International Labour Organization. (2007). *International Standard Classification of Occupations: ISCO-2008*. Geneva, Switzerland: International Labour Office.

International Society for Technology in Education (ISTE). (2007). *National educational technology standards for students* (2nd ed.). Eugene, OR: Author.

Jones, A. (2004). *A review of the research literature on barriers to the uptake of ICT by teachers*. Coventry, England: British Educational Communications and Technology Agency (BECTA).

Kao, G. (2004). Social capital and its relevance to minority and immigrant populations. *Sociology of Education, 77*, 172–183.

Kao, G., & Thompson, J. S. (2003). Racial and ethnic stratification in educational achievement and attainment. In K. S. Cook & J. Hagan (Eds.), *Annual Review of Sociology* (Vol. 29, pp. 417–442). Palo Alto, CA: Annual Reviews.

Korea Education and Research Information Service (KERIS). (2013). *2013 white paper on ICT in education Korea 2013: Summary*. Daegu, Korea: Author.

Koutropoulos, A. (2011). Digital natives: Ten years after. *MERLOT Journal of Online Learning and Teaching, 7*(4). Retrieved from http://jolt.merlot.org/vol7no4/koutropoulos_1211.htm

Kozma, R. (Ed.). (2003a). *Technology, innovation, and educational change: A global perspective*. Eugene, OR: International Society for Technology in Education (ISTE).

Kozma, R. (2003b). ICT and educational change: A global phenomenon. In R. Kozma (Ed.), *Technology, innovation, and education change: A global perspective: A report of the Second Information Technology in Education Study (SITES) Module 2* (pp. 1–18). Eugene, OR: International Society for Technology in Education (ISTE).

Kozma, R. (2008). Comparative analyses of policies for ICT in education. In J. Voogt & G. Knezek (Eds.), *International handbook of information technology in education* (pp. 1083–1096). Berlin, Germany: Springer Science.

Kozma, R., & McGhee, R. (2003). ICT and innovative classroom practices. In R. Kozma (Ed.), *Technology, innovation, and education change: A global perspective: A report of the Second Information Technology in Education Study (SITES) Module 2* (pp. 43–80). Eugene, OR: International Society for Technology in Education (ISTE).

Law, N., Pelgrum, W., & Plomp, T. (2008). *Pedagogy and ICT use in schools around the world: Findings from the IEA SITES 2006 study*. Hong Kong SAR: Comparative Education Research Centre/Springer, University of Hong Kong.

Lehmann, R. (1996). Reading literacy among immigrant students in the United States and former West Germany. In M. Binkley, K. Rust, & T. Williams (Eds.), *Reading literacy in an international perspective* (pp. 101–114). Washington DC: National Center for Education Statistics (NCES).

Li, Q., & Ma, X. (2010). A meta-analysis of the effects of computer technology on school students' mathematics learning. *Educational Psychology Review, 22*(3), 215–243.

Marsh, H., & Shavelson, R. (1985). Self-concept: Its multifaceted hierarchical nature. *Educational Psychologist, 20*(3), 107–123.

Martin, M. O., Mullis, I. V. S., Foy, P., & Stanco, G. M. (2012). *TIMSS 2011 international results in science*. Chestnut Hill, MA: TIMSS & PIRLS International Study Center, Boston College.

Martin, M. O., Mullis, I. V. S., Gonzalez, E., Smith, T., & Kelly, D. (1999). *School contexts for learning and instruction: IEA's Third International Mathematics and Science Study (TIMSS)*. Chestnut Hill, MA: TIMSS & PIRLS International Study Center, Boston College.

Ministerial Council on Education, Early Childhood Development and Youth Affairs (MCEECDYA). (2010). *National assessment program: ICT literacy Years 6 & 10 report 2008*. Carlton South, VIC, Australia: Curriculum Corporation. (ERIC Document ED534805) Available online at http://www.nap.edu.au/verve/_ resources/2008_nap_ictl_public_report.pdf

Ministerial Council on Education, Employment, Training and Youth Affairs (MCEETYA). (2007). *National assessment program: ICT literacy Years 6 and 10 report 2005*. Carlton South, VIC, Australia: Curriculum Corporation. Available online at http://www.nap.edu.au/verve/_resources/2005_ICTL_Public_Report_ file_main.pdf

Ministry of Education of the City of Buenos Aires. (2013). *El plan S@rmiento*. Buenos Aires, Argentina: Author. Retrieved from http://sarmientoba.buenosaires.gob.ar/?menu_id=34179 (in Spanish).

Ministry of Education of Uruguay. (2013). Plan Ceibal [website]. Retrieved from www.ceibal.org. uy (in Spanish).

Moos, D., & Azevedo, R. (2009). Learning with computer-based learning environments: A literature review of computer self-efficacy. *Review of Educational Research, 79*(2), 576–600.

Mueller, C. W., & Parcel, T. L. (1981). Measures of socioeconomic status: Alternatives and recommendations. *Child Development, 52*(1), 13–30.

Mueller, J., Wood, E., Willoughby, T., Ross, C., & Specht, J. (2008). Identifying discriminating variables between teachers who fully integrate computers and teachers with limited integration. *Computers & Education, 51*(4), 1523–1537.

Mullis, I. V. S., Martin, M. O., Foy, P., & Arora, A. (2012). *TIMSS 2011 international results in mathematics*. Chestnut Hill, MA: TIMSS & PIRLS International Study Center, Boston College.

Mullis, I. V. S., Martin, M. O., Foy, P., & Drucker, K. T. (2012). *PIRLS 2011 international results in reading*. Chestnut Hill, MA: TIMSS & PIRLS International Study Center, Boston College.

Mullis, I. V. S., Martin, M. O., Kennedy, A., & Foy P. (2007). *PIRLS 2006 international report: IEA's Progress in International Reading Literacy Study in primary schools in 40 countries*. Chestnut Hill, MA: TIMSS & PIRLS International Study Center, Boston College.

Muthén, L. K., & Muthén, B. O. (2012). *Mplus: Statistical analysis with latent variables. User's guide*. (Version 7). Los Angeles, CA: Muthén & Muthén.

Nasah, A., DaCosta, B., Kinsell, C., & Seok, S. (2010). The digital literacy debate: An investigation of digital propensity and information and communication technology. *Educational Technology Research and Development, 58*(5), 531–555.

Office of Educational Technology, US Department of Education. (2010). *Transforming American education: Learning powered by technology* (US National Education Technology Plan 2010). Washington, DC: Author. Available online at http://www.ed.gov/sites/default/files/netp2010.pdf

Organisation for Economic Co-operation and Development (OECD). (1999). *Classifying educational programmes: Manual for ISCED-97 implementation in OECD countries*. Paris, France: OECD Publications.

Organisation for Economic Co-operation and Development (OECD). (2005). *Are students ready for a technological world? What PISA studies tell us*. Paris, France: OECD Publishing.

Organisation for Economic Co-operation and Development (OECD). (2010). *Equally prepared for life? How 15-year-old boys and girls perform in school*. Paris, France: OECD Publishing.

Organisation for Economic Co-operation and Development (OECD). (2011). *PISA 2009 results: Students on line*. Paris, France: OECD Publishing.

Organisation for Economic Co-operation and Development (OECD). (2013). *PISA 2012 results: Vol. 2. Excellence through equity: Giving every student the chance to succeed*. Paris, France: OECD Publishing.

Organisation for Economic Co-operation and Development (OECD). (2014a). *OECD skills surveys: Main elements of the survey of adult skills (PIAAC)* [website]. Retrieved from: http://www.oecd.org/site/piaac/mainelementsofthesurveyofadultskills.htm

Organisation for Economic Co-operation and Development (OECD). (2014b). *TALIS 2013 results: An international perspective on teaching and learning*. Paris, France: OECD Publishing.

Pedersen, S. G., Malmberg, P., Christensen, A. J., Pedersen, M., Nipper, S., Græm, C. D., & Norrgård, J. (Eds.). (2006). *E-learning Nordic 2006: The impact of ICT on education*. Copenhagen, Denmark: Ramboll Management. Retrieved from http://www.oph.fi/download/47637_eLearning_Nordic_English.pdf

Pekrun, R., Goetz, T., Titz, W., & Perry, R. P. (2002). Academic emotions in students' self-regulated learning and achievement: A program of qualitative and quantitative research. *Educational Psychologist, 37*(2), 91–105.

Pelgrum, W. J., & Anderson, R. E. (Eds.). (2001). *ICT and the emerging paradigm for life-long learning: An IEA educational assessment of infrastructure, goals, and practices in twenty-six countries* (2nd ed.). Amsterdam, the Netherlands: International Association for the Evaluation of Educational Achievement (IEA). Retrieved from http://www.iea.nl/fileadmin/user_upload/Publications/Electronic_versions/SITES-M1_ICT_Emerging_Paradigm.pdf

Pelgrum, W. J., & Doornekamp, B. D. (2009). *Indicators on ICT in primary and secondary education* (IIPSE: EACEA-2007-3278/001-001). Brussels, Belgium: European Commission Directorate General Education and Culture.

Pelgrum, W. J., & Plomp, T. (1991). *The use of computers in education worldwide: Results from the IEA "Computers in Education" survey in 19 educational systems*. Oxford, UK: Pergamon Press.

Pelgrum, W. J., Reinen, I. A. M. J., & Plomp, T. (Eds.). (1993). *Schools, teachers, students and computers: A cross-national perspective* (IEA-COMPED Study, Stage 2). Enschede, the Netherlands: University of Twente. Retrieved from http://files.eric.ed.gov/fulltext/

Plomp, T., Anderson, R. E., Law, N., & Quale, A. (Eds.). (2009). *Cross national policies and practices on information and communication technology in education* (2nd ed.). Greenwich, CT: Information Age Publishing.

Prensky, M. (2001). Digital natives, digital immigrants: Part 1. *On the Horizon, 9*(5), 1–6.

Qualifications and Curriculum Authority. (2007). *About information and communication technology: Assessment guidance*. London, UK: Author. Retrieved from http://web.archive.org/web/20040815054520/http://www.qca.org.uk/7889.html

Rasch, G. (1960). *Probabilistic models for some intelligence and attainment tests*. Copenhagen, Denmark: Nielsen & Lydiche.

Raudenbush, S. W., & Bryk, A. S. (2002). *Hierarchical linear models: Applications and data analysis methods*. Newbury Park, CA: Sage Publications.

Román, M., & Murrillo, J. (2013). Estimación del efecto escolar para la competencia digital. Aporte del liceo en el desarrollo de las habilidades TIC en estudiantes de secundaria en Chile [Investigation into the effect of school on digital competency: The contribution of the lyceum to the development of ICT in Chilean high school students]. In CEPPE, *Desarrollo de habilidades digitales para el siglo XXI en Chile: ¿Qué dice el SIMCE TIC?* [Developing digital skills for the twenty-first century in Chile: What does ICT SIMCE say?] (pp. 141–176). Santiago, Chile: LOM Ediciones.

Saha, L. J. (1997). Introduction: The centrality of the family in educational processes. In L. J. Saha (Ed.), *International encyclopedia of the sociology of education* (pp. 587–588). Oxford/New York/Tokyo: Elsevier.

San Martín, E., Claro, M., Cabello, T., & Preiss, D. (2013). Habilidades TICs para el aprendizaje y su relación con el conocimiento escolar en lenguaje y matemáticas [ICT skills for learning and their relationship to school knowledge in language and mathematics]. In CEPPE, *Desarrollo de habilidades digitales para el siglo XXI en Chile: ¿Qué dice el SIMCE TIC?* [Developing digital skills for the twenty-first century in Chile: What does ICT SIMCE say?] (pp. 229–248). Santiago, Chile: LOM Ediciones.

Sauers, N. J., & McLeod, S. (2012). *What does the research say about school one-to-one computing initiatives?* Lexington KY: University of Kentucky.

Scheerens, J. (1990). School effectiveness and the development of process indicators of school functioning. *School Effectiveness and School Improvement, 1*(1), 61–80.

Scheerens, J., & Bosker, R. J. (1997). *The foundations of educational effectiveness*. Oxford, UK: Pergamon.

Schulz, W. (2006). *Measuring the socioeconomic background of students and its effect on achievement in PISA 2000 and PISA 2003*. Paper presented at the annual meeting of the American Educational Research Association, San Francisco, CA, April 7–11, 2006.

Schulz, W. (2009). Questionnaire construct validation in the International Civic and Citizenship Education Study. *IERI Monograph Series: Issues and Methodologies in Large-Scale Assessments*, Vol. 2, 113–135.

Schulz, W., Fraillon, J., Ainley, J., Losito, B., & Kerr, D. (2008). *International Civic and Citizenship Education Study assessment framework*. Amsterdam, the Netherlands: International Association for the Evaluation of Educational Achievement (IEA).

Selwyn, N. (2009). The digital native: Myth and reality. *Aslib Proceedings: New Information Perspectives, 61*(4), 364–379.

Severin, E., & Capota, C. (2011). *Modelos uno a uno en América Latina y el Caribe. Notas técnicas* [One to one models in Latin America and the Caribbean: Technical notes]. Washington, DC: Banco Interamericano de Desarrollo. Retrieved from http://idbdocs.iadb.org/wsdocs/getdocument.aspx?docnum=35838865

Severin, E., Santiago, A., Ibarrarán, P., Thompson, J., & Cueto, S. (2011). *Evaluación del programa "Una laptop por niño" en Perú: resultados y perspectivas. Aporte n°13, diciembre* [Evaluation of "One laptop per child" in Peru: Results and perspectives. Contribution No. 13, December]. Washington, DC: Banco Interamericano de Desarrollo. Retrieved from http://idbdocs.iadb.org/wsdocs/getdocument.aspx?docnum=36750488

Sirin, S. R. (2005). Socioeconomic status and academic achievement: A meta-analytic review of research. *Review of Educational Research, 75*(3), 417–453.

Stanat, P., & Christensen, G. (2006). *Where immigrant students succeed: A comparative review of performance and engagement in PISA 2003*. Paris, France: OECD Publications.

Sturman, L., & Sizmur, J. (2011). *International comparison of computing in schools*. Slough, UK: National Foundation for Educational Research (NFER).

Tamin, R., Bernard, R., Borokhovski, E., Abrami, P., & Schmid, R. (2011). What forty years of research says about the impact of technology on learning: A second-order meta-analysis and validation study. *Review of Educational Research, 81*(1), 4–28.

Thomson, S., & De Bortoli, L. (2007). *PISA 2003: ICT use and familiarity at school and home* (ACER Research Monograph No. 62). Melbourne, VIC, Australia: Australian Council for Educational Research (ACER).

Tobias, S., Fletcher, J., Yun Dai, D., & Wind, A. (2011). Review of research on computer games. In S. Tobias & J. Fletcher (Eds.), *Computer games and instruction* (pp. 101–126). Greenwich, CT: Information Age Publishing.

Travers, K. J., Garden, R. A., & Rosier, M. (1989). Introduction to the study. In D. F. Robitaille & R. A. Garden (Eds.), *The IEA Study of Mathematics II: Contexts and outcomes of school mathematics curricula*. Oxford, UK: Pergamon Press.

Travers, K. J., & Westbury, I. (1989). *The IEA Study of Mathematics I: Analysis of mathematics curricula*. Oxford, UK: Pergamon Press.

U.S. Department of Education, Office of Educational Technology. (2011). *International experiences with educational technology: Final report*. Washington, DC: Author.

United Nations Development Programme (UNDP). (2009). *Indicators: Human development report 2009*. New York, NY: Author. Retrieved from http://hdrstats.undp.org/en/indicators

United Nations Development Programme (UNDP). (2010). *Indicators: Human development report 2010*. New York, NY: Author. Retrieved from http://hdrstats.undp.org/en/indicators

United Nations Educational, Scientific and Cultural Organization (UNESCO). (2006). *ISCED 1997: International standard classification of education* (rev. ed.). Paris, France: UNESCO-UIS.

United Nations Educational, Scientific and Cultural Organization (UNESCO). (2013). *ICT in education policy, infrastructure, and ODA status in selected ASEAN countries*. Bangkok, Thailand: Author.

Valentine, J. C., DuBois, D. L., & Cooper, H. (2004). The relation between self-beliefs and academic achievement: A meta-analytic review. *Educational Psychologist, 39*(2), 111–133.

van den Beemt, A. (2010). *Interactive media practices of young people: Origins, motives, background and patterns*. Oesterwijk, the Netherlands: Uitgeverij BOXPress. Retrieved from http://igitur-archive.library.uu.nl/dissertations/2010-1118-200300/beemt.pdf

van Dijk, J. (2006). Digital divide research, achievements and shortcomings. *Poetics, 34*(4–5), pp. 221–235. doi:http://dx.doi.org/10.1016/j.poetic.2006.05.004

Vereecken, C., & Vandegehuchte, A. (2003). Measurement of parental occupation: Agreement between parents and their children. *Archives of Public Health, 61*, 141–149.

von Davier, M., Gonzalez, E., & Mislevy, R. (2009). What are plausible values and why are they useful? *IERI Monograph Series: Issues and Methodologies in Large-Scale Assessments*, Vol. 2, 9–36.

Warschauer, M., & Matuchniak, T. (2010). New technology and digital worlds: Analyzing evidence of equity in access, use, and outcomes. *Review of Research in Education, 34*(1), 179–225.

WestEd. (2010). *Technology and engineering literacy framework for the 2014 National Assessment of Educational Progress pre-publication edition*. Retrieved from http://www.edgateway.net/cs/naepsci/download/lib/249/ prepub_naep_tel_ framework.pdf?x-r=pcfile_d

Woessmann, L. (2004). *How equal are educational opportunities? Family background and student achievement in Europe and the United States* (IZA Discussion Paper 1284). Bonn, Germany: Institute for the Study of Labor (IZA).